ecpr PRESS

Growing into Politics

Contexts and Timing of Political Socialisation

Edited by
Simone Abendschön

ecpr PRESS

First published by the ECPR Press in 2013

Paperback edition first published by the ECPR Press in 2014

The ECPR Press is the publishing imprint of the European Consortium for Political Research (ECPR), a scholarly association, which supports and encourages the training, research and cross-national cooperation of political scientists in institutions throughout Europe and beyond.

ECPR Press
University of Essex
Wivenhoe Park
Colchester
CO4 3SQ
UK

Typeset by Anvi

Printed and bound by Lightning Source

British Library Cataloguing in Publication Data

A catalogue record for this book is available from the British Library

Hardback ISBN: 978-1-907301-42-1

Paperback ISBN: 978-1-910259-38-2

www.ecpr.eu/ecprpress

Europeanisation and Party Politics
ISBN: 9781907301223
Edited by Erol Külahci

Great Expectations, Slow Transformations: Incremental Change in Post-Crisis Regulation
ISBN: 9781907301544
Edited by Manuela Moschella and Eleni Tsingou

Interactive Policy Making, Metagovernance and Democracy
ISBN: 9781907301131
Edited by Jacob Torfing and Peter Triantafillou

Perceptions of Europe
ISBN: 9781907301155
Edited by Daniel Gaxie, Jay Rowell and Nicolas Hubé

Personal Representation: The Neglected Dimension of Electoral Systems
ISBN: 9781907301162
Edited by Josep Colomer

Political Participation in France and Germany
ISBN: 9781907301315
Oscar Gabriel, Silke Keil, and Eric Kerrouche

Political Trust: Why Context Matters
ISBN: 9781907301230
Edited by Sonja Zmerli and Marc Hooghe

Practices of Interparliamentary Coordination in International Politics: The European Union and Beyond
ISBN: 9781907301308
Edited by Ben Crum and John Erik Fossum

Contents

List of Figures and Tables

Figures

Tables

Contributors

SIMONE ABENDSCHÖN is Assistant Professor and researcher in the Department of Social Sciences at Goethe University Frankfurt. Her main research interests encompass political socialisation, civic education, value orientations, political and social participation and social inequality. She has published in several edited volumes and international journals such as *Political Psychology*.

ALEXANDRE BLANC is a Doctor of Political Science at Sciences-Po Aix, France. He is interested in European comparative studies, history of political thought and the study of national constructions. He has analysed school teaching in various European countries in order to understand the national values transmitted to pupils.

NICOLETTA CAVAZZA is Associate Professor in Social Psychology at the Communication and Economics Department of the University of Modena and Reggio Emilia (Italy). Her current main research interests include attitude change, political psychology, persuasive communication and social aspects of eating. She is author of books in the field of communication and persuasion and she has co-authored articles published in international journals such as *European Journal of Political Research* and *European Journal of Social Psychology*.

PIERGIORGIO CORBETTA is Research Director at Istituto Cattaneo of Bologna. His main research interests include political participation, electoral behaviour, political culture and values. In these fields he has published several books and articles in international journals.

BERNARD FOURNIER is a researcher at the Department of Political Science at the Vrije Universiteit Brussel and guest professor at the Haute école de la province de Liège. He has published numerous articles on youth and politics and is the co-convenor of the Standing Group on Citizenship at the ECPR.

CAROL GALAIS is currently a postdoctoral fellow at the Canadian Research Chair in Electoral Studies, in the Political Science Department, Université de Montréal. Her research interests focus on political socialisation, civic duty, political engagement attitudes and local political participation.

GEMA GARCÌA-ALBACETE is a postdoctoral fellow at the Department of Political Science and International Relations, University Autonoma of Madrid. Her research interests focus on political participation and the development of political attitudes. She has published in several edited volumes and in international journals such as *Acta Politica* and *American Behavioral Scientist*.

LENA HAUG is a PhD candidate at the University of Mannheim. Her current research interests are the intensity and the development of political interest and democratic orientations in primary school children.

RUXANDRA PAUL is a PhD candidate in the Department of Government at Harvard University. Her research interests include migration and immigration, European Union politics, state-building, citizenship, democratisation, development, Central and Eastern Europe, communism and post-communism, civil society, transitional justice, cyberpolitics and new media. Paul is an affiliate of the Minda de Gunzburg Center for European Studies and a research associate at the Center for Geographical Analysis at Harvard. She was a Harvard Academy Fellow (2011–2012) and a Chateaubriand Fellow of the French Government (2009–2010).

ELLEN QUINTELIER is a postdoctoral researcher of the Flanders Research Foundation at KU Leuven (Belgium). Her research interest lies in political behaviour, political sociology and comparative politics. More specifically, she focuses on patterns of inequality in political participation, the effect of political socialisation agents and personality on political participation. Previously, she has published in *European Union Politics*, *Political Research Quarterly* and *Nonprofit and Voluntary Sector Quarterly*.

STEVE SCHWARZER is Research Director for Methods and Statistics at TNS Opinion in Brussels, an international coordination centre specialised in conducting multi-country research projects. He studied political science, philosophy and literature and received his doctoral degree in social sciences in 2010. Specialised in the field of survey methodology and public opinion research, he also has a research focus on topics such as political socialisation, political engagement as well as civic education of youth.

DARIO TUORTO is Assistant Professor in the Department of Education Sciences at the University of Bologna. His main research interests concern turnout, party activism, youth political and social involvement, family change and transitions to adulthood.

EVA ZEGLOVITS is Assistant Professor at the University of Vienna, Department of Methods in the Social Sciences, and part of the team working on the Austrian National Election Study AUTNES. Her main research interests encompass electoral behaviour, political participation and political socialisation.

Chapter One

Introduction: Political Socialisation in a Changing World

Simone Abendschön

'Who learns what from whom under what circumstances with what effects?' Almost half a century ago, Greenstein (1965: 13), borrowing from Lasswell, put this crucial question at the heart of political socialisation research. The question is far from being fully answered – on the contrary, it faces new challenges in light of recent political and social changes. This volume shows that this question is still an important and valid one today, and sheds light on its key aspects.

The concept of political socialisation, first used explicitly by Hyman in 1959, describes the process of how individuals find their place within a political community by acquiring knowledge, skills and attitudes with respect to the political system. Possible explanations for how and when people learn and form these political orientations and whether these orientations change over the course of their lives, date back to the heyday of (US) political socialisation research in the 1960s. The roots of adult civic and political attitudes and involvement are considered a product or 'a distillation of a person's lifetime experiences, including childhood socialization' (Zaller 1992: 23). This renders the discussion of political socialisation and political learning in democracies one of the oldest debates in the study of political behaviour and public opinion.

Political socialisation is significantly shaped by the parameters of the society in which it is embedded. Contemporary conceptualisations of political socialisation therefore have to take into account the fact that political learning nowadays occurs under different circumstances and faces dissimilar challenges as compared to a few decades ago, when the field of political socialisation was considered by some as the new research 'growth stock' (Greenstein 1970). Rapidly changing conditions facing children growing up have left their imprint on the current political involvement and orientations of today's youngest citizens. Three developments illustrate this vividly. First, mediatisation processes over the past few decades have altered the face of political communication and democracy. As a consequence, for example, political parties play an ever-diminishing role as agents of a general political socialisation; this might also have an impact on party identification as an indicator of political learning. What are the new contexts and influences replacing the role traditionally played by political parties? Second, empirical findings that stress a decline in political interest and involvement in adolescents today (e.g. Henn and Weinstein 2006; Sloam 2007) have brought the topic of political learning and civic education to the forefront of debates again. Third, at the macro level of politics and society, geopolitical transformations such as European integration, economic and political migration, and the democratic transformation of former totalitarian regimes are just some of the main developments that are likely to shape political socialisation processes on the individual level as well (Sapiro 2004). They challenge traditional political identities and create a socialisation context in which new generations are said to develop multiple political identities or multiple levels of identities rather than a single national one (Renshon 2003; Sapiro 2004; Jennings 2007).

These developments necessitate a fresh look at the study of political socialisation. In the following pages, I discuss current questions and trends in the field along the lines of the interrogatives of Greenstein's question.

Political socialisation does not stop once citizens have reached voting age; rather, it should be understood as a lifelong process (e.g. Niemi and Sobieszek 1977). Therefore the 'Who' part of Greenstein's question is not restricted to children and youth, although the formation of political attitudes and behaviour in adulthood is mainly researched under the label of political behaviour research, whereas the study of political socialisation focuses on the processes related to growing up. While the 1960s saw a boom in research on young children (Greenstein 1965; Hess and Torney 1967; Easton and Dennis 1969), the concurrent theoretical and methodological critiques removed children from the agenda of socialisation research. As a consequence, political learning is nowadays almost exclusively studied with youth, but only rarely with younger children. Both recent societal changes with regard to the understanding of children and politics, as well as empirical findings from educational studies and developmental psychology, suggest the relevance of and the need for further research on political socialisation processes in childhood. Moreover, the aforementioned geopolitical changes raise the question of how political socialisation works in the case of first and second generation migrant populations who have to adapt to new political settings (Lin 2005).

The question 'What is learned?' refers to the content of political socialisation processes. Here, first of all, we must ask what characterises or constitutes the 'political' in political learning. Broader approaches to the 'political' can be distinguished from approaches that conceptually try to narrow the contents of political socialisation. Whereas Hyman defines the subject matter as the 'social patterns corresponding to his [the learner's] societal positions' (Hyman 1959: 25) and Greenstein would include 'formal and informal, deliberate and unplanned [...] [and] also nominally nonpolitical learning that affects political behavior' (Greenstein 1968: 551), others maintain that the learning processes should be restricted to more core 'political' aspects such as explicit knowledge and orientations with regard to the political system (e.g. Almond and Verba 1963). Such restrictions can be useful for analytical purposes and specific research questions. However, we have to take into account the fact that there are politically relevant socialisation processes that are not explicitly political in nature but that can be assumed to constitute antecedents of political identity, such as social and moral learning (e.g. Flanagan and Gallay 1995: 38). Moreover, scholars continue to disagree over the nature of the content of political socialisation although they all have normative expectations regarding the outcomes of socialisation. Political culture research emphasises the learning of 'the knowledge, values and attitudes that contribute to support of the political system' (Gimpel *et al.* 2003: 13). This can be criticised as a rather affirmative perspective of political socialisation, one which contrasts with critical theory's emphasis on a critical engagement with politics (Claußen 1984). Against this background, civic education stresses the need for competent citizens who both support democratic principles and are ready to critically engage in political matters (e.g. Print and Lange 2013).

One of the most important and widely accepted explanations of how political socialisation works involves learning via social interaction, mediated by different agents and institutions in society. Greenstein's query 'from whom?' therefore refers to agents responsible for political socialisation. The scholarly literature has tended to focus on family and parents, school, peers, media and voluntary associations as institutions that provide information on processes and concepts of politics, attitudes, norms, and abilities. In particular, the relevance of the family, once the classic and main socialisation milieu for political learning, has been widely discussed (e.g. Butler and Stokes 1969; Jennings and Niemi 1974). Some recent studies have noted the persistence of parental influence, despite changes in political context and family life (e.g. Jennings *et al.* 2009). By contrast, others have questioned the central role of the family and focused on supposedly 'novel' contexts, such as the role of the neighbourhood or social media. However, comprehensive accounts of the impact of different political socialisation institutions are lacking. This is partly due to the fact that the study of socialisation agents has been dispersed into different disciplinary subfields of the social sciences and the latter tend to focus exclusively on a single institution, e.g. political communication research analyses the role of media, while civic education research is interested in contributions of education. What is more, general socialisation research has tended to focus on the concept of self-socialisation, and in doing so, has assigned greater weight to the individual's developmental processes. This is accompanied by criticisms of a rather deterministic understanding of the influences of socialisation agents. Some have therefore substituted the term 'agent' with the term 'context' to allow for the interactivity between the subject and socialisation institutions (Abendschön 2010; Grusec and Hastings 2007). This discussion should also be considered in political socialisation research. We also have to take into account that political socialisation does not occur in a vacuum, that socialisation contexts overlap, interact and work simultaneously. It is therefore difficult to establish which socialisation context is responsible for which outcomes.

Related to the question of the sources of political socialisation is the question of when contexts or agents are effective or are most powerful. This indicates the dependence of the efficacy of socialisation contexts on age and personal circumstances. The question of the role time plays in an individual's political biography, however, has not yet been satisfactorily answered (Sears and Levy 2003). Two connected hypotheses, primacy and the structuring principle, have long dominated research since the 1960s. They assume a priority, if not persistence, of attitudes and competencies developed early in life in adult political behaviour. Even though there is scarce empirical evidence to date concerning these two principles (e.g. Searing *et al.* 1973) and it therefore remains unclear 'whether early childhood factors have lasting relevance or whether these factors tend to be overwhelmed by more proximate events' (Alford *et al.* 2005: 153), these assumptions have been widely used as a reference point for the study of political behaviour. On the one hand, this suggests a need for complex longitudinal research designs, and on the other hand, we can ask, if the question of persistence should not be examined in a more differentiated way. Political socialisation research does not require 'invariant permanence of dispositions from childhood' (Cook 1985: 1081).

The question, 'From whom?' is further related to the question 'Under what circumstances?' The latter refers to the conditions and mechanisms of socialisation processes: how does political learning within different socialisation contexts work? Political socialisation research has emphasised the role of value transmission via social learning and social interaction. There is, however, only sparse research in the field dealing with the mechanisms of political learning. Borrowing from developmental psychology, processes of social construction and co-construction (e.g. Youniss 1983; Valsiner 1988) could be highlighted and should be examined. Additionally, the question of circumstances also points to the relevance of social and demographic factors such as gender, ethnicity and socio-economic status; these shape socialisation settings and can easily enforce or impede political learning.

'With what effects?' refers to the outcomes of political socialisation that are generally thought to be both attitudinal and behavioural in nature. Political socialisation research has mostly studied orientations such as political support, political interest and so forth. The question of whether certain political behaviours may be attributed to processes of political learning is even more complicated to study because norms and orientations only provide directions and guidelines for political action and behaviour. So the effect of socialisation on behaviour is even more difficult to establish than the effect of socialisation on attitudes. Again, complex research designs are needed to study the behavioural aspects as well.

The availability of new individual level data and recent findings in the field are bringing all of these questions to the forefront again, reopening classic debates regarding the subjects, timing, key agents and the content of political socialisation. The present volume brings together new relevant research in this regard.

Structure of the book

This book presents a dialogue about the crucial link between political socialisation, individual political involvement and democracy. It addresses primarily political socialisation processes in childhood and adolescence and offers both conceptual and empirical contributions to recently emerging developments regarding political identity formation. The volume's chapters contribute to several important discussions in the study of political socialisation, thereby integrating new approaches in order to discuss the timing of the acquisition of political orientations; the role of socialisation contexts and actors; and the mechanisms involved in these socialisation processes.

One main focus of the volume looks at agents and contexts of political socialisation. The articles examine classic socialisation institutions such as family and school and 'new' ones such as migration contexts, social media and political discourse. The need to re-examine the political relevance of the period of childhood and to support this research with new data is another focus of the book. Older political socialisation studies emphasised the indispensability of young children's political views for political support and macro-level system stability in democracies (e.g. Easton and Dennis 1969). After the prime of the field in the 1960s and 1970s, political socialisation research 'lost its children' (Conover and Searing 1994: 24) due to methodological and theoretical shortcomings. Together with new empirical findings, the ongoing paradigm change in childhood research and the emerging civic education views on children suggest that important political socialisation processes do take place in childhood. However, we have hardly any up-to-date evidence about the beginnings of these processes in childhood. How do children think about politics and democracy and what do their politically relevant value orientations look like? It is argued here that the relevance of studying young children derives from their status as present rather than future citizens. A third perspective presents new frontiers in political socialisation research in several respects. It introduces new or neglected methods in the field and deals with novel challenges of socialisation.

Piergiorgio Corbetta, Dario Tuorto and Nicoletta Cavazza commence this volume with a study of parental socialisation influences over time. In 1975 a team of social scientists directed by Samuel Barnes and Max Kaase examined political attitudes in eight Western nations, including Italy. Among those subjects were a subsample of adolescents (aged 16–20) whose parents were already part of the general sample. This dataset of parent-child pairs has never before been analysed. The authors have recently replicated the research using a questionnaire which largely reproduces the same questions asked in 1975 in order to study what has changed in the intergenerational transmission of political attitudes in Italy thirty-five years after the first survey. They compare the datasets on various political dimensions between the family and the child. How do changes in family life and parenting styles in the intervening period affect political socialisation?

In Chapter Three, Simone Abendschön looks at parental influences on the value orientations of children. The chapter argues that recent societal changes highlight the necessity of re-examining the youngest citizens' political involvement. Such a re-examination also implies, however, bringing parents back into the discussion as a major socialisation institution for politically relevant socialisation processes, since the family represents the prime socialisation context in childhood. The chapter examines family socialisation by focusing on direct value transmission on the one hand and the influence of socio-structural family characteristics on the other hand. The analyses draw on the unique data of a German study that include questions posed to children and their parents at the beginning and at the end of the children's first school year.

After the important context of family has been dealt with, the following articles pick up on the topic of political socialisation through civic education in school.

The school can impact political socialisation processes in a variety of ways, not only via direct knowledge transfer but also through factors such as classroom and school climate as well as teaching styles. The classic setting, however, is represented by civics courses, which are intended to influence pupils' views on political participation more systematically through teaching on the democratic system and related norms and values (Galston 2004, Nie *et al.* 1996, Niemi and Junn 1998). The role of civic education, however, has been especially disputed in the past. Some researchers deny school and its civics courses any influence at all, while others deliver a more complex picture in this regard (e.g. Niemi and Junn 1998). The three chapters, consisting of two case studies and one cross-national approach, shed light on different aspects of the role of school education in the political learning of pupils.

In Chapter Four Eva Zeglovits and Steve Schwarzer examine how 16- and 17-year-old Austrian first-time voters perceive the role of their schools in preparing them for the election. Zeglovits and Schwarzer ask if civic instructions have an impact on the voting behaviour of first-time voters in Austria. The authors investigate two interesting innovations in Austria. First, civic and citizenship education was introduced as a subject only at the beginning of the 2008 winter term, in combination with history and social studies for all types of schools and grades. Until then, civics was a horizontal teaching domain (taught in all subjects). The reform was directly related to the government's decision to lower the voting age to sixteen – the second innovation. The chapter presents an analysis of the school's influence from the perspective of the first-time voters themselves. How do they perceive the contribution of their schools in preparing them for their first elections?

How civic education can foster pupils' political interest is the topic Gema Garcìa-Albacete addresses in Chapter Five. She explores the role played by civic education in schools in the development of students' political interest from a cross-country comparative perspective. In addition to the examination of the relationship between civic education and levels of political interest across schools, the study also explores the effectiveness of the diverse forms of civic education teaching for promoting concern for public affairs. Furthermore it tests a key finding of earlier studies on civic knowledge and political engagement, namely that the success of civic education in increasing the levels of political interest depends on students' backgrounds. Finally, it proposes that civic education has a greater potential for increasing the political interest of those students who have not yet acquired such interest at home. The International Civic and Citizenship Education Study conducted in 2009 offers a unique opportunity to explore the role of schools in the development of political interest. Results indicate that civic education does matter for the development of politically interested citizens. Therefore, the efforts of diverse institutions are valuable but the success of civic education depends on interactions between the type of civic education preferred by the school on the one hand and the characteristics of the students on the other. Overall, results point to the importance of studying the diverse socialisation agents from an interrelated perspective.

A long neglected perspective of political socialisation via education is analysed in Chapter Six. Alexandre Blanc studies the role of school textbooks in selected countries for political learning about the EU. Ongoing European integration should leave its imprint on school education and on the pupils. The chapter shows the different images of the EU presented to the students in different countries or regions of the EU and tries to find some reasons for the representations that still emphasise national perspectives.

Following the chapters that deal with the two 'biggest' socialisation contexts, Ellen Quintelier shows in Chapter Seven that it is possible with the help of sophisticated research designs and the use of panel data to assess and compare the power of different socialisation institutions. Quintelier argues that although there is a lot of debate over which political socialisation institution is the most important for political participation, most current research fails to compare the significance of different agents. Quintelier's chapter fills this gap by jointly comparing the impact of five different political socialisation agents on political participation: parents, school, peers, media and voluntary associations. The analyses are not limited to one specific age group, but compare the effects of these agents at ages sixteen, eighteen and twenty-one, using the Belgian Political Panel Study. This allows us to discern not only the most important agents of political socialisation, but also the age at which political socialisation agents have the most prominent effects.

Whereas the first seven chapters deal with classic topics of political socialisation research, the remaining four examine new perspectives, in terms of either topics or methods. Hence, the last thematic section can also serve as a kind of outlook on the future of political socialisation research. In Chapter Eight Carol Galais' comparative study examines the socialisation effects of digital media on personal autonomy values. We tend to believe that digital media can change the way people perceive the world and themselves, and that this has consequences for political participation and culture. However, Galais contends that these effects are significantly conditioned by contextual features: the potential consequences of internet use for changing values are enhanced under certain economic and political circumstances. A comparative analysis of forty countries allows us to draw two main conclusions. First, the effect of digital media use seems to play a role in personal autonomy in some contexts but not in others. Second, the relationship between digital media and personal autonomy is stronger when socio-economic development and democratic quality are high, acting as a reinforcing factor in interaction with democratic institutional settings.

In Chapter Nine Ruxandra Paul sheds light on the political socialisation of migrants who wander from Eastern European countries to richer EU countries for work without formally immigrating to the latter countries. Her chapter develops a theoretical and conceptual frame for analysing such political socialisation processes. She argues that temporary intra-EU migrants from post-communist Eastern Europe undergo a second political socialisation at their workplaces abroad. Basically, European integration does not work only on institutions and legislative frameworks from the top down, but also from the bottom up, by exposing migrants to new environments, ideas and political realities. Paul conducted in-depth interviews with transnational migrants in four countries of origin and four destinations and finds significant changes in the way migrants relate to the state and in their views of the nation, identity and diversity.

The last two chapters are innovative in terms of methods. In Chapter Ten, Bernard Fournier is interested in the role that political discourse can play as a source of political socialisation and in the impact of political discourse on attitude formation and change. This is examined in an experiment that invited young people to discuss the question of lowering the voting age to sixteen. This issue, which is rarely discussed by the public at large in Belgium, seems an ideal topic for an experimental debate, in which the confrontation of ideas may change opinions and reveal – or even modify – young people's global attitudes towards political interest and participation. A non-random sample of nearly two hundred 16- to 22-year-old young people in French-speaking Belgium was selected to discuss the possibility of lowering the voting age to sixteen, as well as political interest and political participation, during one day with four experts. Based on Shawn Rosenberg's approach to political socialisation, Fournier analyses the discussions of the young people in the focus groups and teases out real patterns of political reasoning in the discourses. The results open interesting research paths for the further study of political socialisation.

The last chapter of the book, Chapter Eleven, returns to children's political socialisation. Lena Haug argues that recognising childhood as a period of early political socialisation implies potential methodological problems. Common methods in socialisation research cannot easily be adapted to research on children without significant revision. As a consequence, new methods of data collection must be found that should be suitable for children and must comply with scientific standards. Haug argues that the use of children's drawings as a child-typical, age-appropriate and language-independent data collection method could open up new possibilities for political socialisation research. With a study that includes 230 children aged between four and ten years, Haug illustrates how children's political interest can be researched using children's drawings and demonstrates the opportunities, difficulties and limitations of political socialisation research based on children's drawings.

References

Abendschön, S. (2010) *Die Anfänge demokratischer Bürgerschaft. Sozialisation von politischen und demokratischen Werten im jungen Kindesalter,* Baden-Baden: Nomos.

Alford, J., Funk, C. and Hibbing, J. (2005) 'Are political orientations genetically transmitted?', *American Political Science Review,* 99: 153–167.

Almond, G. A. and Verba, S. (1963) *The Civic Culture: Political attitudes and democracy in five nations,* Princeton: Princeton University Press.

Butler, D. and Stokes, D. (1969) *Political Change in Britain: Forces shaping electoral choice,* London: Macmillan.

Claußen, B. (1984) *Politische Bildung und kritische Theorie. Fachdidaktisch-methodische Konzeptionen emanzipatorischer Sozialwissenschaft,* Opladen: Leske + Budrich.

Conover, P. and Searing, D. (1994) 'Democracy, citizenship and the study of political socialization', in I. Budge and D. McKay (eds), *Developing Democracy,* London: Sage: 24–55.

Cook, T. E. (1985) 'The bear market in political socialization and the costs of misunderstood psychological theories', *The American Political Science Review,* 79(4): 1079–1093.

Easton, D. and Dennis, J. (1969) *Children in the Political System: Origins of political legitimacy,* New York: McGraw-Hill.

Flanagan, C. and Gallay, L. S. (1995) 'Reframing the meaning of "political" in research with adolescents', *Perspectives on Political Science,* 24(1): 34–42.

Galston, W. A. (2004) 'Civic education and political participation', *PSonline,* 37: 263–266.

Gimpel, J. G., Lay, J. C. and Schuknecht, J. E. (2003) *Cultivating Democracy: Civic environments and political socialization in America,* Washington D.C.: Brookings Institution Press.

Greenstein, F. I. (1965) *Children and Politics,* New Haven: Yale University Press.

— (1968) 'Political Socialization', in D. L. Sills (ed.) *International Encyclopedia of the Social Sciences,* New York: Macmillan: 551–555.

— (1970) 'A note on the ambiguity of "Political Socialization": Definitions, criticisms, and strategies of inquiry', *The Journal of Politics,* 32(4): 969–978.

Grusec, J. E. and Hastings, P. D. (eds) (2007) *Handbook of Socialization: Theory and research,* New York and London: The Guilford Press.

Henn, M. and Weinstein, M. (2006) 'Young people and political (in)activism: Why don't young people vote?', *Policy & Politics,* 34(3): 517–534.

Hess, R. D. and Torney, J. V. (1967) *The Development of Political Attitudes in Children,* Chicago: Aldine.

Hyman, H. (1959) *Political Socialization,* Glencoe, Illinois: Free Press.

Jennings, M. K. (2007) 'Political socialization', in R. J. Dalton and H.-D. Klingemann (eds), *The Oxford Handbook of Political Behaviour,* Oxford: Oxford University Press: 29–44.

Jennings, M. K. and Niemi, R. (1974) *The Political Character of Adolescence,* Princeton: University Press.

Jennings, M. K., Stoker, L. and Bowers, J. (2009) 'Politics across Generations: Family transmission re-examined', *Journal of Politics*, 71 (3), 782–799.

Lin, A. C. (2005) 'Networks, gender, and the use of state authority: Evidence from a study of Arab immigrants in Detroit' in A. S. Zuckerman (ed.), *The Social Logic of Politics,* Philadelphia: Temple University Press: 171–184.

Nie, N., Junn, J. and Stehlik-Barry, K. (1996) *Education and Democratic Citizenship in America,* Chicago: University of Chicago Press.

Niemi, R. G. and Junn, J. (1998) *Civic Education: What makes students learn?* New Haven: Yale University Press.

Niemi, R. G. and Sobieszek, B. (1977) 'Political socialization', *Annual Review of Sociology*, 3: 209–233.

Print, M. and Lange, D. (eds) (2013) *Civic Education and Competences for Engaging Citizens in Democracies,* Rotterdam, Boston, Taipei: Sense Publishers.

Renshon, S. A. (2003) 'Political socialization in a divided society and dangerous world', in M. Hawkesworth and M. Kogan (eds) *Encyclopedia of Government and Politics*, vol. 1, second edition, London: Routledge: 427–456.

Sapiro, V. (2004) 'Not your parents' political socialization: Introduction for a new generation', *Annual Reviews,* 7(1): 1–23.

Searing, D., Schwartz, J. and Lind, A. (1973) 'The Structuring Principle: Political socialization and belief systems', *American Political Science Review*, 67(2): 415–432.

Sears, D. O. and Levy, S. (2003) 'Childhood and adult political development', in D. O. Sears, L. Huddy and R. Jervis (eds), *The Oxford Handbook of Political Psychology,* New York: Teachers College Press: 69–97.

Sloam, J. (2007) 'Rebooting democracy: Youth participation in politics in the UK', *Parliamentary Affairs*, 60(4): 548–567.

Valsiner, J. (ed.) (1988) *Child Development within Culturally Structured Environments Volume 2: Social co-construction and environmental guidance of development,* Norwood: Ablex.

Youniss, J. (1983) 'Social construction of adolescence by adolescents and parents', *New Directions for Child and Adolescent Development,* 22: 93–109.

Zaller, J. R. (1992) *The Nature and Origin of Mass Opinion,* Cambridge: Cambridge University Press.

Chapter Two

Parents and Children in the Political Socialisation Process: Changes in Italy Over Thirty-Five Years

Piergiorgio Corbetta, Dario Tuorto, Nicoletta Cavazza

The intergenerational transmission of political traits within the family, in particular from parents to children, has been widely discussed in the political literature of the 1950s and 1960s, and several recent studies have also demonstrated the persistence of such a linkage (Quintelier *et al.* 2007; McDevitt and Chaffe 2002; Plutzer 2002). The present paper aims to compare the levels of similarity/dissimilarity between parents and children on the key dimension of left-right self-placement in two different periods. Our recent survey (2010) on a representative sample of parent-child dyads replicated the research conducted in Italy in 1975 by Samuel Barnes and Max Kaase on a sample of adolescents (aged 16 to 20) and their parents. Results show the emergence of important discontinuities over time. The general level of parent-child left-right (L-R) dissimilarity has remained stable, but its direction has reversed. In 1975, diverging orientations were mainly rooted in dyads of right-wing parents and left-wing children, while today they prevail where children are right-wing and less interested in politics. Moreover, unlike the 1970s, similarity on the left-right dimension is no longer related to other similarities in attitudes and political orientation, as the two political-ideological labels seem to have lost any specific political content.

Family as an agency of socialisation

To study social change is a complex task because transformations at a societal level occur very slowly. The only way to detect and capture them empirically is by repeating the same survey over a large time span, but this condition is rarely met. In the case presented in this chapter we decided to address this difficulty by replicating one of the first empirical research studies conducted on the political attitudes of Italian voters. The topic of this chapter is the political socialisation of adolescents within the family and its transformation over the last thirty-five years.

Since the 1950s, research on behaviours, attitudes, and the political values of parents and (their) children has been widely discussed in political and sociological literature and has focussed on the idea that the family is a stable and solid base for the development of adolescent political identity (Hyman 1959; Lane 1959; Easton and Dennis 1969). Studies of parent-child dyads have generally tried to find domains in which transmission would be particularly efficacious, and where the effects would be durable over time. The most important empirical study that tackles these questions is undoubtedly the Youth-Parent Socialisation Panel Study, carried out by the University of Michigan's Survey Research Center under the direction of Kent Jennings and Richard Niemi. The project started in 1965 and the first wave included 1,700 interviews with student-parent pairs. Subsequent surveys conducted in 1973, 1982 and 1997 produced a panel of almost 1,000 individuals included in each of the four waves, a very impressive result given the large time span (Jennings and Niemi 1974; Percheron and Jennings 1981; Jennings *et al.* 1999). The main finding of their study was that, despite transformations in the general political environment and in the context of family life, parents continued to play a decisive role in the political education of their offspring throughout the three decades. In particular, the study reported that transmission rates tended to vary according to the type of political trait, being higher in case of electoral behaviour and party preference. Annick Percheron, in a large research study of 900 parent-child pairs in France, reached a similar conclusion using left-right (L-R) self-placement instead of party identification (Percheron and Jennings 1981). Returning to Jennings and Niemi (1974), the authors also found that, when compared with party preference, the level of similarity inside the family was clearly weaker for other political traits such as trust, allegiance to political regime, individual position on single political issues and social-group evaluations. In the scholars' opinion, more salient, long-lasting, and affect-laden constructs (such as partisanship) can be expected to produce more successful transmission (Jennings and Niemi 1974).

In order to explain how the transmission of political orientations within the family generally works, scholars have referred to two main processes. The first of these, based on a functionalist approach, is the social learning process. At the heart of social learning theory (Bandura 1976) is the idea that people learn behaviours and attitudes suited to their circumstances through observation and the imitation of others' behaviours, particularly of those figures assumed to function as role models (i.e. the modelling process). This observational learning model assumes an asymmetric relationship between a subject without abilities and knowledge and influential people who are already socialised in specific social contexts. The learning process is thought to remain active over the entire lifespan, though having a particularly crucial impact during adolescence when the individual experiments with the need to be part of new significant life contexts. In political terms, the theory conceptualises the adolescent as a *tabula rasa*, on which political marks (such as their parents' orientations and political values) can be made and continually reinforced through direct teaching and imitation (Hess and Torney 1967; Percheron and Jennings 1981: 421). An effective process of political socialisation guarantees, in this sense, the continuity of political preferences from one generation to the next, and it guarantees the stability of the party system.

The second mechanism of transmission is based on the idea that parent-child similarity in political attitudes is not just the product of a successful socialisation or of psychosocial influences; it has more to do with the intergenerational transmission of structural factors such as class, race and religion. In other words, the family provides children with a social identity and a location within the social structure, which affects their political orientation (Glass *et al.* 1986).

Although two different approaches have been referred to, the two perspectives are not mutually exclusive. In fact, the effects of social learning and social position can be integrated. Both approaches suggest the possibility that learning is enhanced by 'transmission belts' (Schönpflug 2001); in other words, individual, familiar and contextual factors can all facilitate or impede the transmission of political (and non-political) traits between parents and children. In this vein, many studies have analysed the role played by the gender combination of dyads (father-mother, son-daughter, etc.), age, social class and territorial dimension.

As regards gender, according to social learning theory, individuals should tend to assume and use as models those figures perceived to be particularly competent (in the case of politics, the father is traditionally assumed to have such a role), or similar to themselves (children are thought to imitate the same-sex parent). In fact, studies on political socialisation have found a more intense transmission from father to son (Acock and Bengston 1978) and within same-sex dyads (Niemi *et al.* 1978; Portney *et al.* 2009) than in mixed-sex and mother-child dyads.

As far as age is concerned, studies have shown that the intensity of relational involvement between parents and children changes over the life-course. The theory of psychosocial development (Erikson 1968) holds that, after a preadolescent stage when familial linkages are particularly strong and influential, adolescent children (12- to 18- year-olds) face the task of elaborating their identity as individuals separate from their family of origin. The transition to young adulthood produces a different dynamic. On the one hand, multiple interactions in new contexts (at a familial or professional level) become more intense; on the other hand, children face adult experiences similar to those of their parents, and thus may tend to converge in their opinions. The direct effect of transmission due to extended exposure to the role model weakens, while influences deriving from the household's social class increase (Glass *et al.* 1986: 687–96).

The impact of social status is more controversial. Traditionally, scholars have maintained that growing up in families of higher socio-economic status facilitates the transmission of political values because families with more resources encourage actions which increase the level of political knowledge (reading newspapers, discussion of politics, etc.) more so than families with less resources (Milbrath 1965; Verba and Nie 1972). However, an intense political socialisation could also take place in families of lower status depending on the interplay between familial characteristics and local context. Seminal studies conducted by Butler and Stokes (1969) on the transmission of party identification within English working-class neighbourhoods have produced interesting findings in this vein. In the case of Italy, the presence of strong political subcultures in large parts of the country (i.e. the socialist/communist 'red belt' regions of central Italy or the Catholic culture in the north-eastern regions) have facilitated the reproduction of political orientations through the mutual reinforcement of familial transmission and social influences.

Other factors at a familial level could influence the intensity of transmission. In particular, the degree of politicisation in the home environment could play an important role. Following social learning theory, children are more likely to adopt their parents' political beliefs and attitudes if the political climate within the family is active and if discussions involving requests for and exchange of political information (between father and mother, and parents and children) are frequent. Parent-child transmission rates for any given political attribute should be influenced by the clarity and the consistency of the cues that parents provide and by the stability and coherence of the responses they furnish over the whole period of socialisation (Jennings *et al.* 1999). It has also been claimed that the level of family politicisation produces an effect on party identification and political trust or cynicism but not on the transmission of other values (Jennings and Niemi 1968). As regards the general family climate, an intense identification between parents and children in terms of positive relationships, frequent communication and a high level of agreement, is expected to act positively on the socialisation of political orientations.

Hypotheses and research design

Our research aims to study how the level of political similarity between parents and children has changed in Italy in the last few decades, focussing on a specific and meaningful dimension: self-placement on the left-right (L-R) continuum. The decision to use L-R position as a dependent variable in the analyses derives from the importance that young people and also adults attach to this dimension when they have to face a very complex political context such as the Italian one (Caniglia 2001, 2007; Cavazza and Corbetta 2008; Corbetta *et al.* 2009). Moreover, research on political socialisation has shown how parental influence on their children is stronger in the L-R orientation than in other dimensions.

The research hypotheses are based on the assumption that diverging dynamics over time have acted on the family and influenced its role as an agent of political socialisation. In the last few decades in Italy – and also in other countries – the process of generational reproduction of political orientation, seriously weakened by the protest movements in the 1960s and 1970s, has been subject to important transformations. As discussed in the literature (Klingemann and Fuchs 1995; Pharr and Putnam 2000), growing instability in electoral preferences, the crisis of traditional political parties and widespread voter disaffection with politics have complicated the transmission of party identification and specifically, of political identity from parents to children. These factors were particularly evident in the Italian context. One of their effects was the weakening of the two political subcultures (socialist/communist and Catholic) that have dominated the public scene since the Second World War. Moreover, a specific discontinuity has been introduced into Italian politics by the transition to a new political asset (the so-called 'Second Republic') based on a bipolar system with new parties. Given all this, a sharp intensification of political divergence between parents and children is the expected result. Our first hypothesis asserts that the parent-child legacy should be weaker today than it was thirty-five years ago. Indeed, recent research conducted on a sample of Italian adolescents and their parents indirectly supports this argument, showing that the closeness between parent-child values and priorities is not very high and that intergenerational differences are evident particularly for those values which relate to the dimension of 'openness to change/ conservatism' (Barni *et al.* 2011).

However, during the last two or three decades a model of the so-called 'long family' (Scabini 1995) has dominated Italian culture and society. Nowadays, fathers and mothers play a crucial role in their children's identity formation process beyond the age of majority. Several processes form the basis of this dynamic. Delay in the transition to adulthood, particularly in terms of leaving home, and the growing instability in economic and familial conditions of the younger generation (increasing unemployment, low-income profiles, marital disruptions) have, as a consequence, resulted in the prolongation of parental responsibilities (Cavalli and Galland 1996). Furthermore, the authoritarian model of education which characterised the family environment in the past has declined in favour of more egalitarian relationships (de Jong Gierveld *et al.* 1991). As a result of these processes, even if sources of political information and influence are many, it is not surprising that young Italians indicate their father or mother as the first and the most important figure for their political socialisation (Bettin Lattes 2001; Garelli *et al.* 2006). Our second hypothesis is based on this assumption. We expect a stronger parental legacy than has been expressed in the past on the political dimension as well. Even if politics is less relevant today for both generations, this lack of salience is balanced by a higher concordance and higher rates of transmission.

Our research is based on a comparison between two similar datasets of parent-child dyads collected in different periods. A team of sociologists and political scientists, directed by Samuel Barnes and Max Kaase, conducted an ambitious research study on political attitudes in eight Western nations, including Italy, thirty-five years ago. That investigation was extended to a subsample of adolescents (aged 16–20) whose parents were part of the general sample. The Italian dataset has never been analysed before. During 2010 our team replicated this research using a questionnaire, which largely reproduced the questions asked in 1975, in order to study what has changed in the intergenerational transmission of political attitudes in Italy over the three or four decades since the first survey.[1]

The parent-child sample in 1975 was composed of 227 dyads; in 2010 the total number of pairs interviewed was extended to 411 dyads. In constructing the sample, parent and child gender was taken into account by selecting the same number of pairs for every possible combination. The comparison between the two datasets, collected thirty-five years apart following similar procedures, represented an unrivalled opportunity for research. However, there were two important limitations. In order to make the datasets comparable, most of the questions asked in 1975

---

1. In 1975 the survey was based on face-to-face interviews, while in 2010 we conducted telephone interviews, using Computer-Assisted Telephone Interviewing (CATI) with stratified sampling.

were included in the 2010 interviews. Unfortunately, the original questionnaire was influenced by the peculiar climate of the period. This means, for example, that items about international politics (e.g. the Cold War), were excluded and, *vice versa*, some important contemporary issues (e.g. attitudes towards immigration or regionalism) were not present in the original questionnaire but added to the revised one. The second limitation has to do with the characteristics of the sample: in 1975 the sample included only children aged 16–20.

In Italy, 1975 was a time of political and social turmoil. The effects of social mobilisation in the late 1960s (the 1968 movement, the *Autunno caldo operaio* [literally, *Hot Autumn of the Workers*] in 1969) extended to political institutions, with the Communist Party (PCI) attaining its highest level of support and equalling the electoral result of the dominant Christian Democratic Party (DC). In 1974, the approval of divorce laws following a referendum introduced a wave of secularism in a still conservative culture. During this period, the presence of the younger generation made its mark through two particular political events: lowering of the voting age to eighteen and increased popular support for the women's movement.

By 2010 very different circumstances dominated and the framework of opportunities for the younger generation seemed to have radically changed into an expression of a sort of generalised marginality (Livi Bacci 2010; Buzzi *et al.* 2007; Censis 2010; Diamanti 2011). The younger generation is increasingly becoming a minority in demographic terms, facing the prospect of life in a precarious job market (despite high levels of education), reduced social mobility, under-representation in the groups leading official political debate and the redistribution of welfare resources. Moreover, a large majority of young adults in Italy still live with their parents.[2]

In the following analysis, the crucial dependent variable is the relationship between L-R self-placement of parents and children. First, we illustrate how the level of intergenerational L-R dissimilarity has changed as a function of parents' and children's social characteristics. In the following steps we articulate a number of specific research questions: whether L-R dissimilarity is related to parents' and children's political positions and to their political involvement; whether other shared political factors are associated with L-R self-placement; and whether L-R dissimilarity is influenced by family climate. While it is true that semantic changes regarding the L-R dimension might have occurred over the thirty-five years since 1975, the analysis is based on a long-term comparison. Moreover, recent research (Corbetta *et al.* 2009) shows that in Italy the central concerns associated with the political left and right did not change radically. In any case, changes in meanings of 'left' and 'right' ultimately influenced the 'absolute' position of parents and children on the L-R axis, but not their 'relative' position. Indeed if meanings have

---

2. A comparative European survey reported that the percentage of young Italian people (18–34) still in the parental home was 73 per cent for men and 60 per cent for women, the highest percentages in Europe, where the mean percentage is 42 per cent and 31 per cent (European Foundation for the Improvement of Living and Working Conditions, 2010).

changed, this occurred for both parents and children so that the change should not have affected the differences between them.

Starting with a simple bivariate analysis, the study develops a set of multivariate regressions, where parent-child L-R dissimilarity is always the dependent variable. Socio-demographic variables are included as control variables and, in separate regression models, political orientations, parents' and children's political involvement, parent-child dissimilarity on other political dimensions and family climate are introduced as predictors.

Parent-child L-R dissimilarity and the effect of socio-demographic characteristics

As noted above, the key variable in the analysis is self-placement on the L-R political-ideological scale. Taking the L-R self-placement of both parents and children in 1975 and 2010, we calculated a parent-child absolute political difference score, obtaining for each dyad an index of L-R dissimilarity which indicates how many points on the scale lie between parents and their children, regardless of their individual positions on the scale,[3] or the direction of the difference. Low values obtained on this scale indicate greater similarity (identical if the value is zero), while higher values indicate greater difference. The comparison of values in the two surveys allows an assessment to be made of how this difference has changed over time.

A first indication comes from the means and frequency distribution for 1975 and 2010. Table 2.1 reveals two salient pieces of information: *(1)* the average difference between parents and children on the L-R dimension has not changed over time,[4] and *(2)* the difference seems to be broadly modest.[5]

The same result is obtained when classifying the L-R dissimilarity scores into three categories. The incidence of *strong dissimilarity* (a difference of greater than 3) is very low (around 10 per cent) and is similar in 1975 and 2010. However, there has been a decline in the *no dissimilarity* category (a difference of 0–1) in 2010, balanced by an increase in the *moderate dissimilarity* category (a difference of

---

3.   For example, if a parent and child are both on position 3, or both on position 5, the L-R dissimilarity index is computed as 0; if the parent is on position 2 and the child on position 4, or *vice versa*, or if the parent is on position 5 and the child on position 3, the index has value of 2 and so on.

4.   ANOVA F-test statistic was non-significant ($p = 0.84$).

5.   As reported above, in our analysis we have taken into account only cases in which both the parents and the children agreed to place themselves on the L-R dimension, and excluded all the dyads where either parent or child (or both) did not answer the question. These cases represent around one third of the total number of dyads in 1975 and 2010. This is a considerable number, but the numbers as well as the internal configurations of the dyads (the proportion of dyads with one or two non-classified persons) are substantially similar in the two surveys. Because it is impossible to investigate the reason(s) for their refusal to answer, we decided to exclude all these cases from the analyses, preferring a limited sample dimension to the risk of mistakenly considering unknown situations as political similarity (parents and children who refuse to indicate their position) or difference (only one of them placed on the scale).

Table 2.1: Parent-child L-R dissimilarity, 1975 and 2010 (Percentages)

	1975	2010
Mean	1.64	1.67
Standard deviation	1.68	1.53
No dissimilarity (Difference of 0–1)	60.7	53.5
Moderate dissimilarity (Difference of 2–3)	28.6	34.6
Strong dissimilarity (Difference greater than 3)	10.7	11.9
N	150	292

2–3). The overall picture describes minimal discrepancy between the positions of parents and children and substantial stability across time. A possible interpretation of these first general findings is that the family may still act as an effective agency for political socialisation and its effectiveness does not appear to have changed over time.[6] None of the two hypotheses we originally introduced are fully supported by the data; that is, neither the hypothesis of a minor socializing impact of family as a result of the crisis of political identities, nor the assumption that there would be greater political homogeneity between generations due to the diffusion of the 'long family' model.

Previous studies have, however, suggested that the level of similarity may vary according to specific individual, family and contextual characteristics. For this reason, we have conducted a preliminary exploration of the relations between the parent-child index of L-R dissimilarity and socio-demographic variables such as: *(a)* the gender of parents and children; *(b)* the age of the children; *(c)* their social class; *(d)* education as a measure of the cultural capital of the family; and *(e)* the city size and the zone of residence.[7]

---

6.   In order to evaluate the net effect of parental influence independently of the more general contextual effects (culture or political climate that parents and children could share) we followed the procedure implemented by Birch (1980) and used in other studies on parent-child similarities (i.e., Guidetti and Cavazza 2008). This procedure is based on the construction of 'random' dyads of adults and young people not bound by ties of kinship. We assumed the given dimension concerning children (in our case, L-R dissimilarity) as a dependent variable of a hierarchical regression, in which a 'random' parent effect was added in the first step (in order to operationalize the contextual effect), before the introduction of the 'real' parent. The introduction of a random adult did not produce a result which was statistically significant and for this reason it has been excluded from the presentation of the results.

7.   The classification used for social class is: upper class (entrepreneurs, managers, professionals); clericals (white collar workers, teachers, technicians); petit bourgeoisie (shopkeepers, craftsmen, self-employed with fewer than fourteen employees); and working class (blue collar workers). In the case of non-employed people we have referred to the head of the family, while retired people are computed with regard to their last job. This classification uses Goldthorpe's scheme (1980) and has been applied in Italy by Cobalti and Schizzerotto (1994). The variable *education* reflects the combination of fathers' and mothers' attributes, categorised into three levels (low, medium, high). The *zone of residence* differentiates three geopolitical areas. The 'red belt' includes regions of central Italy such as Emilia-Romagna, Toscana, Umbria, Marche. This classification is taken

The results are reported in Table 2.2.[8] Gender did not significantly influence L-R dissimilarity in 1975, while it had an impact in 2010, with sons being politically further from their fathers and mothers than daughters. When parental gender is considered, L-R dissimilarity appears higher in the case of dyads including mothers, but only in 2010. Regarding age, we expected that younger children would have higher L-R similarity, because children who are growing up should be more prone to acquiring autonomous positions. This hypothesis is true for the 1975 dataset, but in 2010 the direction of difference is reversed, with younger children being more dissimilar than the older ones. The effect of social class on the results is, in general, not remarkable (the differences in 2010 are significant only at the $p<0.2$ level). Level of education manifests an influence in 2010 only, in the sense that families with parents of lower education are more politically heterogeneous. Finally, looking at the territorial variables, L-R dissimilarity is undoubtedly higher in small cities, although this trend was only statistically significant in 1975. A comparison between the two time periods, although not tested for statistical significance, indicates an increase in L-R dissimilarity in the 'red belt' regions; among the working class and petit bourgeoisie; and in families with low levels of education. However, the modest correlation between socio-demographic dimensions and the dependent variable suggests that other factors should be taken into account.

The impact of political orientation and involvement on L-R dissimilarity

Our analysis has highlighted minimal changes in parent-child L-R dissimilarity between 1975 and 2010 (despite a thirty-five year gap and a new socio-political context), but it has also revealed a fairly weak relationship between L-R dissimilarity and the socio-demographic variables so far considered. Therefore, in order to better specify the context in which political orientations are produced and shared in the two periods, we must explore those dimensions which are more contiguous to politics. First, L-R dissimilarity could be related to parents' or children's actual position on the L-R dimension. The youth protest of early 1975 was, above all, a rebellion of revolutionary children against traditional and politically conservative families. For this reason, the political divergence in 1975 is more likely to have concerned right wing parents *vis-à-vis* their left wing children. But the same cannot be assumed for 2010.

A second variable that could influence L-R dissimilarity is parents' and, above all, children's political involvement. Assuming the theoretical perspective of the

---

from previous classical studies on the territorial background of voting in Italy (Galli, 1968).

8. In the tables we report the respective means for the dissimilarity index and the level of significance of the coefficients. Given the low number of cases in the samples (N = 150 in 1975 and N = 292 in 2010) the upper limit for the significance interval has been extended from the conventional value of $p<0.05$ to $p<0.20$, as reported in the tables. In the comparison of the results it should be noted that the significance of the coefficients is strongly influenced by sample size and also by the different magnitude of the samples in the two surveys.

Table 2.2: L-R dissimilarity scores compared across socio-demographic variables (means)

		1975	2010
Overall		1.64	1.67
Parent's gender	Father	1.70	1.54
	Mother	1.60	1.80
	p	ns	^
Child's gender	Male	1.65	1.89
	Female	1.63	1.44
	p	ns	~
Child's age	16–18	1.46	1.96
	19–20	1.89	1.33
	p	^	**
Social class	Working class	1.62	1.82
	Petit bourgeoisie	1.74	2.21†
	Clerical	1.63	1.53
	Upper class	1.67†	1.61
	p	ns	^
Family level of education	Low	1.51	2.08
	Medium	1.82	1.64
	High	1.60	1.39
	p	ns	*
Geopolitical zone	Northern regions	1.61	1.66
	'Red belt' regions	1.38	1.71
	Southern regions	1.81	1.65
	p	ns	ns
City size	Less than 5,000 inhabitants	2.56†	1.83
	5,000–30,000 inhabitants	1.31	1.75
	30,000–100,000 inhabitants	1.41†	1.74
	More than 100,000 inhabitants	1.55	1.33
	p	**	ns

Notes: ^p<0.2; ~p < 0.1; *p < 0.05; **p < 0.01; ns=not significant; † N<30. Given the low number of cases in the samples (N = 150 in 1975 and N = 292 in 2010) the upper limit for the significance interval (P) has been extended from the conventional value of 0.05 to 0.20

Table 2.3: Regression models of parent-child L-R dissimilarity with ideological position and political involvement variables, 1975 and 2010

Variables[a]		1975 (N=147)		2010 (N=292)	
		R^2	Standardised Beta	R^2	Standardised Beta
Socio-demographic		0.03		0.06	
L-R self-placement[b]	Parent	0.12	0.33**	0.06	-0.02
	Child	0.09	-0.27‾	0.08	0.14*
Political involvement[c]	Parent	0.03	-0.05	0.06	-0.05
	Child	0.04	0.13	0.07	-0.13*

Notes: ^p<0.2; ‾p < 0.1; *p < 0.05; **p < 0.01 (significance levels of Beta values correspond to the significance of the change in R^2 for the variable concerned, over and above the socio-demographic variables); a. all analyses include socio-demographic variables plus the one other variable listed; b. higher scores indicate leaning to the right; c. higher scores indicate greater involvement.

'critical citizen' (Inglehart 1990; Dalton 1996), we can hypothesise that political awareness leads children to express autonomous positions which are opposed to their parents' more than is the case for apathetic children who could passively acquire their parents' orientation simply because of their detachment from politics. In this case, the effect of children's political involvement on L-R dissimilarity should be noticeable, both in 1975 (more divergence if children are politically interested) and in 2010 (more similarity if children are apathetic).

In order to test these hypotheses, we ran five regression models for each year. In the first model, only socio-demographic variables were been included.[9] The next four analyses all included the socio-demographic variables plus one other variable (these were parents' position on the L-R axis, children's position on the L-R axis, parents' political involvement[10] and children's political involvement,[11] as shown in Table 2.3.

The results are partially in line with our hypotheses but are also partially unexpected. With regard to parents' and children's political positions the following can be said:

---

9. These variables are: gender (of parent and child), social class, level of education (a conjoint measure for father and mother), city size and zone of origin.

10. Parents' and children's political orientations are computed using L-R self placement. It is not usual to find in a regression, as an independent variable, the same dimension (L-R collocation) used to produce the dependent variable (parent-child L-R dissimilarity index). The operation would be confounded if L-R dissimilarity were the algebraic difference between the parent and child position. But in our case we calculate the absolute difference which is not related to the two separate scores reported by the parent and the child (demonstration is available if required).

11. Variables of political involvement combined in the index are: *(a)* interest in politics; *(b)* frequency of political discussion.

- In 1975, the variance accounted for (indicated by R^2) increases significantly when parents' or children's L-R self-placement are included in the model. As expected, dissimilarity is relatively higher when a parent is right wing and/or a child is left wing.
- In 2010, the variance accounted for (indicated by R^2) reaches statistical significance only when children's L-R positions are included. In this case, the relation of this variable to L-R dissimilarity is the opposite of 1975, with dissimilarity being relatively higher when the child is right wing.

The second dimension – political involvement – seems not to be relevant in relation to parents (parents' interest in politics does not significantly increase the variance in L-R dissimilarity accounted for), whilst children's involvement exerts an influence in 2010 only, although in an unexpected direction. Higher dissimilarity appears not to occur when children are more involved in politics, but when they are apathetic: in fact, the Beta coefficient in Table 2.3 (-0.13) indicates a negative correlation between the two variables.

These results show that in the period between 1975 and 2010, the impact of examined variables on L-R dissimilarity changed in direction and significance. In 1975, the individual L-R positions of parent and child (included as two distinct covariates in the model) exerted a strong influence on L-R dissimilarity: political divergence was concentrated in families with right wing parents and left wing children. In 2010, intra-family political divergence is much less influenced by the specific political orientations of parents and the residual influence of the child's orientation goes in the opposite direction: L-R dissimilarity is higher when the child is leaning to the right. Moreover, in 2010 the most politically heterogeneous families are those with politically apathetic children, while in 1975 the generational political conflict tended to be higher when children were politically involved.

The political content of L-R dissimilarity

Thus far we have explored the two mechanisms through which parent-child L-R dissimilarity was mediated in 1975 and 2010; namely, through left wing protests by children of the 1975 cohort and political apathy in today's children, separating them from their parents' ideals. However, our data reveal some crucial evidence: between 1975 and 2010 the overall degree of political difference between children and parents remains stable and weak.

Should we conclude that the family was and is an efficient political socialisation agency? This is true if the similarity in L-R self-placement is rooted in similarity of attitudes towards concrete political content, like political parties and salient issues such as social inequality, welfare, forms of political protest, authoritarianism, democracy and so on. Otherwise, the similarity in L-R self-placement is due to an empty formula that children have been exposed to and have learned uncritically.

In order to address this problem empirically, we measured parent-child similarity with reference to certain political opinions and computed this both for 1975 and 2010 on the following four indices:

- Expectations of the future
- Importance attributed to national socio-political issues
- Attitudes toward forms of protest
- Preferred party

'Expectations of the future'[12] has the weakest political meaning of the four indices considered. The second index compares the importance children and parents attach to five relevant social problems.[13] Low scores indicate agreement (i.e. children and parents, independent of their own individual position on the problem, think that it has the same importance), and high scores indicate disagreement about the importance of the issues. The third index was computed in the same way and concerned the degree of similarity between children and parents in terms of their approval of different forms of political protest.[14] Finally, we computed parent-child similarity in their preferred political party for the fourth index.[15]

Following the same procedure detailed in the previous section, four separate regression analyses on parent-child L-R dissimilarity were performed: each regression included the socio-demographic variables plus one of the four political opinion indices listed above. We also conducted a fifth analysis including all the political opinion variables entered simultaneously. Table 2.4 reports the results.[16] For interpretative purposes, we focus on the statistical significance of the standardised Beta values which correspond to the significance of the change in R^2 for the variable concerned, over and above the socio-demographic variables. In particular, we observe that: *(a)* parent-child closeness with regard to expectations of the future does not correlate to closeness on the L-R dimension; *(b)* the same is true for similarity in the evaluation of the importance of social issues; *(c)* attitudes

---

12. The question states, 'I'd like to ask you something about you and your family situation. Think about the material side of your life, the things you can buy and do. On a scale of 0 to 10 (where 0 means maximum satisfaction and 10 maximum dissatisfaction) where would you put yourself today? Where do you expect you might put yourself in five years' time?'

13. The interviewees gave their views on the importance (on a scale of 1–4) of the following problems: jobs for all, good education, adequate medical care, fighting pollution and fighting criminality.

14. Protest actions included in the index were: signing a petition, engaging in peaceful demonstration, taking part in violent actions or riots, painting slogans on the walls, occupying buildings or factories and blocking traffic.

15. Both for 1975 and 2010 we categorised all the parties by eight labels or political areas; then they were ordered along a left-right sequence by four Italian political scientists blind to our hypotheses. Parent-child distance was calculated as the difference between the preferred party position expressed by the parents and the same information expressed by their children.

16. Because of missing data (particularly in the case of preferred political party), models have different sample sizes (as reported in Table 2.4). This potentially influences the value of the R^2 coefficient and, as a consequence, the comparison of the same model over time. We have preferred to adopt this procedure, instead of producing models with the same number of cases, in order to maximise the dimension of samples. In any case, further controls confirmed that the final results do not change, regardless of the procedure adopted.

Table 2.4: Regression models of parent-child L-R dissimilarity with political opinion variables, 1975 and 2010

Variables[a]	1975			2010		
	R^2	Standardised Beta	N	R^2	Standardised Beta	N
Expectations	0.04	-0.08	131	0.07	0.05	265
Dissimilarity on social problems	0.04	-0.07	146	0.06	-0.04	292
Dissimilarity on political protest	0.12	0.30**	142	0.07	0.10⁻	292
Dissimilarity on preferred party	0.32	0.51**	102	0.18	0.21**	152
All political opinion variables[b]	0.37		89	0.19		145
Dissimilarity on political protest		0.19⁻				
Dissimilarity on preferred party		0.46**			0.16*	

Notes: ^p<0.2; ⁻p < 0.1; *p < 0.05; **p < 0.01 (significance levels of Beta values correspond to the significance of the change in R^2 for the variable concerned, over and above the socio-demographic variables); a. all analyses include socio-demographic variables plus the one other variable listed; b. only significant Beta values in this model listed (other Beta values non-significant).

toward forms of protest affect the dependent variable, but only in 1975; and, *(d)* in the same way, similarity in preferred political party is correlated to similarity in L-R self-placement in 1975, but this relationship is weaker in 2010.

If we add the four political opinion variables into the regression simultaneously (along with socio-demographics), their influence on L-R dissimilarity appears statistically significant in 1975 but not in 2010.

To summarise, thirty-five years ago, parent-child political similarity on the L-R axis was related to their closeness in attitudes toward political questions like their preferred political party or attitudes toward accepting or refusing forms of protest. This relationship has almost completely disappeared in 2010.

We must acknowledge that our analysis has a limitation: political transformations which have occurred in the last thirty-five years have also changed the agenda and the relevance of certain political questions (a clear example is the salience of the Cold War in the past and of immigration today), as well as the social sensibilities and points of reference for political debate. Therefore, the lack of significant relationships in 2010 may be due to the fact that the variables concerning political opinions – which were necessarily based on the original 1975 questionnaire – are simply less relevant today. The same may be said for 1975: questions

Table 2.5: Regression models of parent-child L-R dissimilarity with period-specific variables, 1975 and 2010

	Variables[a]	R^2	Standardised Beta	N
1975	Feeling thermometer	0.17	0.38**	144
	Law and order	0.04	0.14	139
	All political opinion and period-specific variables[b]	0.45		86
	Dissimilarity on political protest		0.18~	
	Dissimilarity on preferred party		0.41**	
	Feeling thermometer		0.25~	
2010	Values	0.06	0.01	292
	Authoritarianism/conventionalism	0.06	0.07	291
	Civicness	0.06	0.02	292
	All political opinion and period-specific variables[b]	0.19		145
	Dissimilarity on preferred party		0.17*	

Notes: ^p<0.2; ~p < 0.1; *p < 0.05; **p < 0.01 (significance levels of Beta values correspond to the significance of the change in R^2 for the variable concerned, over and above the socio-demographic variables); a. all analyses include socio-demographic variables plus the one other variable listed; b. only significant Beta values in this model listed (other Beta values non-significant).

about pertinent issues at that time (such as the student movement, feminist claims, trade union struggles, etc.) were not included in the 2010 questionnaire.

In order to overcome this problem, we computed further indices based on items specific to the different time periods. The following two indices were computed for 1975: a *feeling thermometer* (including feelings about trade unions, big industry, the police, student protests, the feminist movement and revolutionary groups), and an index of orientation to *law and order*.[17] The following three indices were computed for 2010: *value endorsement, conventionalism/authoritarianism*, and sense of *civicness*.[18] Table 2.5 illustrates the results of the regression models

---

17. In the *feeling thermometer* the interviewees indicated on a scale of 0–100 how favourable/unfavourable they felt towards the named groups. The battery of items on *law and order* asked about the level of approval/disapproval (on a scale of 1–6) of various kinds of action that the government and authorities could take: police using force against demonstrators, courts giving severe sentences to protestors who disregard the police, government passing a law to forbid all public demonstrations and government using troops to break strikes.

18. The battery of items on *value endorsement* asked (on a scale of 1–4) questions about the importance of: being rich and having expensive things, giving the same opportunities in life to everyone, having success, being ambitious and occupying a position of command. The battery of items on *authoritarianism/conventionalism* asked for the level of approval or disapproval (on a scale of 1–4) on five issues: today Italy needs a stronger leader, firms should have more freedom to hire

performed, adding these new indices to the socio-demographic variables, using only the new indices specific to the year.

At this point, if we combine the latter analysis with the former we get a sufficiently clear and coherent empirical picture. In 2010 the closeness of children and parents on L-R self-placement seems to be empty of political content (no shared expectations for the future, evaluation of social issues, attitudes towards protest). The analysis from which this conclusion derives included as many as twenty-four questions, all designed to capture strong political meaning (e.g. opinions on the freedom of companies to fire workers, attitudes towards immigrants, attitudes towards the rights of unmarried couples, etc.). The same was not true thirty-five years ago, where, we have found, various indices of parent-child political proximity were correlated with their similarity on the L-R dimension. There was a strong correlation in terms of preferred political parties and also in attitudes towards political voice and towards groups with political significance like trade unions, big industry, and so on. In statistical terms, the coefficient for the model including socio-demographics and all four indices of political opinion was $R^2=0.37$ in 1975 and a lower $R^2=0.19$ in 2010 (*see* Table 2.4). When we add the new period-specific variables (*see* Table 2.5), the R^2 values reaches 0.45 in 1975, but remains at 0.19 in 2010.

Family climate

The question that follows is how to explain that today's parents and their children place themselves closely together on the L-R axis but are at the same time dissimilar with respect to all of the descriptors of political opinion we included in our analyses.

To answer this question, we explored the role of family climate including the transformations observed in the time period considered. Indeed, the relatively stable levels of political similarity may be accompanied by change in political opinions. In 1975, parents' and children's placement on the L-R axis derived from shared positions on several other political opinions; while today, the similarity in self-placement could be induced simply by a positive family climate, resulting from parental relationships that are stronger and more harmonious than in the past. Empirical evidence of this evolution in the Italian family has been observed (Sciolla 2005). In recent studies we can read about the 'pacified family' (Garelli *et al.* 2006), the 'tuning' between parent and children, the 'high level of satisfaction that young people express in respect to their life in the family' (Facchini 2002: 183), the 'new family climate characterised by a low level of conflict, even when children are adolescents' (Sartori 2007: 114; *see also* Scabini and Cigoli 2000; Cesareo 2005). However, these are interpretations drawn from data about the

---

and fire, immigrants are a threat to our culture and identity, unmarried couples should be assured of the same rights by law and homosexuals should be assured of the same rights by law. The battery on *civicness* evaluated the gravity (on a scale of 1–4) of the following behaviours: not paying for tickets on the bus, not paying taxes and buying something while aware that it has been stolen'.

Table 2.6: Indices of family climate, 1975 and 2010 (means)

	1975	2010	p
Talk with parents	0.57	0.69	**
Agree with parents	0.63	0.72	**
Wish to live the same life as his/her parents	0.21	0.36	**

Notes: **p < 0.01; variable ranges are all 0–1

Table 2.7: Regression model of parent-child L-R dissimilarity with family climate, 1975 and 2010

Variables[a]	1975			2010		
	R^2	Standardised Beta	N	R^2	Standardised Beta	N
Family climate[b]	0.28	-0.24¯	140	0.07	-0.11¯	292

Notes: ^p<0.2; ¯p < 0.1; *p < 0.05; **p < 0.01 (significance levels of Beta values correspond to the significance of the change in R^2 for the variable concerned, over and above the socio-demographic variables); a. all analyses include socio-demographic variables plus the one other variable listed; b. values of Cronbach Alpha for 'family climate index' are 0.77 for 1975 and 0.69 for 2010.

current situation; they cannot really claim to be about social change since they do not compare the present with a past social situation. Our study allows for such a comparison: the 1975 questionnaire included some questions posed to children on the quality of communication exchange and perception of agreement in the family when discussing school, work and politics. These questions were replicated in 2010. We combined the answers into an index of communication and agreement with parents about school, work and politics. We also considered children's desire to lead a life that is similar to or different from that of their parents as an indicator of their tendency to project themselves onto their parents and their propensity to adopt their parents as role models.[19]

Table 2.6 provides the mean values for these indices. It clearly shows that between 1975 and 2010 family climate has significantly improved. Mean scores for all three items increased significantly between 1975 and 2010. Furthermore,

19. In this case the questions are: 'How often do you talk with your father about public affairs or politics? About study or work?'; 'How much do you usually agree/disagree with your father about politics? About study or work?' The same questions were replicated for the mother. We also included this question: 'Looking ahead, how much do you want your own life to be like that of your parents?' All the questions on frequency of talk were used to compute an index of *dialogue*, whilst questions on agreement/disagreement have produced an index of *accordance*. The two indices and the question about the 'same life of the parents' were standardised on a 0–1 scale.

the questions on family climate are those for which we observed the greatest changes between the two data gathering exercises.

We expected to observe a positive relationship, particularly in 2010, between family communication and political similarity, because harmony in everyday life should also extend to values and political attitudes. In other words, we reasoned that political agreement should be a reflection of a broader family agreement (this could be characterised as 'I feel politically close to my father – even if I do not fully understand what that means.').

Applying again the method previously used, we ran a regression analysis in which a family climate variable (combining *Talk with parents* and *Agree with parents*) was added along with the socio-demographic variables. We observed a significant relationship between family climate and L-R dissimilarity in 1975 (the negative Beta value indicate that increased family harmony is associated with decreased L-R dissimilarity), but this same relationship is weaker and does not reach statistical significance in the 2010 model, so whether it is present or absent, the level of dialogue and agreement between parents and children does not influence either similarity or difference in L-R self-placement.

This finding is hard to explain. Other studies have shown that children's political concern and their propensity to participate in politics develops primarily in families that are able to set a coherent example in this direction, by giving importance to politics and being available to discuss matters of public interest with their children (Garelli *et al.* 2006: 178–181). On the contrary, in our case, not only is the dyadic self-placement similarity not associated with shared political opinions, but apparently it seems not to require a transmission vehicle such as family climate.

Conclusion

Our research project about family political socialisation and the changes that have taken place in Italy between 1975 and 2010 started from two competing hypotheses. The first one predicted a decrease in parent-child political similarity due to a more general process of the weakening of political identities. In this context one would expect that the crisis of ideologies, the disappearance (in Italy) of the traditional parties, the increasing instability of electoral preference, citizens' disaffection with politics, the weakening of various different collective identities (i.e. class, territory, religion) in favour of personal ones, would also weaken the sense of political belonging amongst the adult generation and, as a consequence, their ability to transmit it to their children.

The second hypothesis predicted, on the contrary, a possible change in the opposing direction due to the progressive manifestation of a 'long family' model. Between 1975 and 2010 the significant increase in the age at which young people leave the family home (both for cultural and economic reasons), the disappearance of intra-family protest typical of 1968 and the years thereafter, the greater immaturity of today's adolescents in comparison to adolescents thirty-five years ago, should correspond to a greater dependence of children on parents and, consequently, a greater homogeneity in family political views in comparison with those of 1975.

Actually, our findings did not clearly support any of these hypotheses. The family seems to work efficiently as a political socialisation agency both in the past and in the present, since political differences between parents and children appear to be limited and substantially unchanged. However, our analyses have highlighted two major changes in the time period under consideration. The first such change was revealed when parents' and children's political orientation and concerns were included in the model. In the past, the dyadic dissimilarity was generated by the protests of offspring identifying with a political and engaged left, and the conflict was located in families with right wing parents. Today, the same dissimilarity seems to be the result of children's tendency to place themselves politically to the right of their parents, along with their political apathy. Therefore, a similar quantitative dissimilarity derives from two opposing dynamics.

The second major change concerns the dissimilarity of political content. In 1975 shared political self-placement in the family was substantiated by political content, in that parent-child closeness meant also the sharing of political world-views and evaluations. Today, this content sharing is no longer evident and the similarity of political self-placement has been emptied. It probably remains as a sort of decision shortcut that helps young people reduce the complexity of their political choices. The absence of any influence exercised by family climate, as we have seen above, suggests that political self-placement similarity involves such a level of sharing superficial enough so that it does not have to be supported by a good level of intra-family communication.

In summary, if the dynamics of family socialisation in the political field seem plausibly interpretable in 1975, every possible interpretative hypothesis seems far less convincing today. The development of further lines of research is needed to clarify and solve the (almost apparent) contradictions we observed.

References

Acock, A. C. and Bengston, V. L. (1978) 'On the relative influence of mothers and fathers: A covariance analysis of political and religious socialization', *Journal of Marriage and Family*, 40: 519–530.

Bandura, A. (1976) *Social Learning Theory*, Englewood Cliffs: Prentice Hall.

Barnes, S. H. and Kaase, M. *et al.* (1979) *Political Action: Mass Participation in Five Western Democracies*, London and Beverly Hills: Sage.

Barni, D., Ranieri, S. and Rosnati, R. (2011) 'Similarità dei valori nello scambio intergenerazionale tra genitori e figli adolescenti', *Psicologia Sociale*, 6: 171–193.

Bettin Lattes, G. (ed.) (2001) *La politica acerba*, Soneria Mannelli: Rubbettino.

Birch, L. L. (1980) 'The relationship between children's food preferences and those of their parents', *Journal of Nutrition Education*, 12: 14–18.

Butler, D. and Stokes, D. (1969) *Political Change in Britain: Forces shaping electoral choice,* London: Macmillan.

Buzzi, C., Cavalli, A. and De Lillo, A. (2007) *Rapporto giovani: sesta indagine dell Istituto IARD sulla condizione giovanile in Italia*, Bologna: Il Mulino.

Caniglia, E. (2001) 'Percorsi generazionali nelle rappresentazioni di destra e sinistra', in G. Bettin Lattes (ed.) *La politica acerba*, Soneria Mannelli: Rubbettino: 327–355.

— (2007) 'La destra e la sinistra, Identità e significati', in M. Bontempi and R. Pocaterra (eds) *I figli del disincanto*, Genova: Bruno Mondadori: 124–146.

Cavalli, A. and Galland, O. (eds) (1996) *Senza fretta di crescere. L'ingresso difficile nella vita adulta,* Napoli: Liguori Editore.

Cavazza, N. and Corbetta, P. (2008) 'Destra e sinistra. Vale ancora la pena di parlarne?', *Il Mulino*, 1: 84–93.

Censis (2010) *44° Rapporto sulla situazione sociale del paese 2010*, Milano: Franco Angeli.

Cesareo, V. (2005) *Ricomporre la vita. Gli adulti giovani in Italia*, Roma: Carocci.

Cobalti, A. and Schizzerotto, A. (1994) *La mobilità sociale in Italia*, Bologna: Il Mulino.

Corbetta, P., Cavazza, N. and Roccato, M. (2009) 'Between ideology and social representations: Four theses plus (a new) one on the relevance and the meaning of the political left and right', *European Journal of Political Research*, 48: 622–641.

Dalton, R. J. (1996) *Citizen Politics: Public opinion and political parties in advanced industrial democracies*, New York: Chatham House /Seven Bridges Press.

de Jong Gierveld J., Liefbroer A. C. and Beenink, E. (1991) 'The effect of parental resources on patterns of leaving home among young adults in the Netherlands', *European Sociological Review*, 7: 55–71.

Diamanti, I. (2011) 'La sindrome della giovinezza', *Repubblica*, 17 January 2011.

Easton, D. and Dennis, J. (1969) *Children in the Political System: Origins of political legitimacy,* New York: McGraw-Hill.

Erikson, E. (1968) *Identity: Youth and crisis*, New York: Norton.

European Foundation for the Improvement of Living and Working Conditions (2010) *Second European Quality of Life Survey*, Dublin. Online. Available: http://www.eurofound.europa.eu/publications/htmlfiles/ef09108.htm (accessed 3 April 2012).

Facchini, C. (2002) 'La permanenza dei giovani nella famiglia di origine' in C. Buzzi, A. Cavalli and A. De Lillo (eds) *Giovani del nuovo secolo. Quinto rapporto IARD sulla condizione giovanile in Italia*, Bologna: Il Mulino.

Galli, G. (1968) *Il comportamento elettorale in Italia*, Bologna: Il Mulino.

Garelli, F., Palmonari, A. and Sciolla, L. (2006) *La socializzazione flessibile*, Bologna: Il Mulino.

Glass, J., Bengtson, V. L. and Chorn, D. C. (1986) 'Attitude similarity in three-generation families: socialization, status inheritance, or reciprocal influence', *American Sociological Review*, 51(5): 685–698.

Goldthorpe, J. H. (1980) *Social Mobility and Class Structure in Modern Britain*, Oxford: Clarendon Press.

Guidetti, M. and Cavazza, N. (2008) 'Structure of the relationship between parents' and children's food preferences and aversions: An explorative research', *Appetite*, 50: 83–90.

Hess, R. D. and Torney, J. V. (1967) *The Development of Political Attitudes in Children*, Chicago: Aldine Publishing Company

Hyman, H. H. (1959) *Political Socialization: A study in the psychology of political behaviour*, Glencoe Illinois: Free Press.

Inglehart, R. (1990) *Cultural Shift in Advanced Democracies*, Princeton: Princeton University Press.

Jennings, M. K. and Niemi, R.G. (1968) 'The transmission of political values from parent to child', *American Political Science Review*, 62: 169–184.

——   (1974) *The Political Character of Adolescence: The influence of family and school*, Princeton: Princeton University Press.

Jennings, M. K., Stoker, L. and Bowers, J. (1999) 'Politics across generations: Family transmission re-examined', paper presented at Political Science Association Convention, Atlanta, September 1999.

Klingemann, H.-D. and Fuchs, D. (1995) *Citizens and the State*, Oxford: Oxford Press.

Lane, R. E. (1959) *Political Life: Why people get involved in politics*, Glencoe Illinois: Free Press.

Livi Bacci, M. (2010) *Avanti giovani, alla riscossa: come uscire dalla crisi giovanile in Italia*, Bologna: Il Mulino.

McDevitt, M. and Chaffee, S. (2002) 'From top-down to trickle-up influence: Revisiting assumptions about the family in political socialization', *Political Communication*, 19(3): 281–301.

Milbrath, L. W. (1965) *Political Participation: how and why do people get involved in politics?* Chicago: Rand McNally.

Niemi, R. G., Ross, R. D. and Alexander, J. (1978) 'The similarity of political values of parents and college-age youth', *Public Opinion Quarterly*, 42: 503–520.

Percheron, A. and Jennings, M. K. (1981) 'Political continuity in French families', *Comparative Politics*, 13(4): 421–436.

Pharr, S. J. and Putnam, R. D. (eds) (2000) *Disaffected Democracies: What's troubling the trilateral countries?* Princeton: Princeton University Press.

Plutzer, E. (2002) 'Becoming a habitual voter: Inertia, resources, and growth in young adulthood', *American Political Science Review*, 96(1): 41–56.

Portney, K. E., Eichenberg, R. C. and Niemi, R. G (2009). 'Gender differences in political and civic engagement among young people', paper presented at Annual meeting of the American Political Science Association, Toronto, Canada, September 2009.

Quintelier, E., Hooghe, M. and Badescu, G. (2007) 'Parental influence on adolescents' political participation', paper presented at the International Conference on Political Socialization, Orebro, Sweden.

Sartori, F. (2007) 'La vita con la famiglia di origine', in C. Buzzi, A. Cavalli, and A. De Lillo (eds), *Sesta indagine dell'Istituto IARD sulla condizione giovanile in Italia*, Bologna: Il Mulino.

Scabini, E. (1995) *Psicologia della famiglia*, Torino: Bollati Boringhieri.

Scabini, E. and Cigoli, V. (2000) *Il familiare. Legami, simboli e tradizioni*, Milano: Cortina editore.

Schönpflug, U. (2001) 'Intergenerational transmission of values: The role of transmission belts', *Journal of Cross-Cultural Psychology*, 32: 174–185.

Sciolla, L. (2005) 'La lunga tregua fra le generazioni', *Il Mulino*, 6: 1032–1042.

Verba, S. and Nie, N. H. (1972) *Participation in America: Political democracy and social equality*, New York: Harper & Row.

Chapter Three

Children's Political Socialisation within the Family: Value Transmission and Social Milieu Factors

Simone Abendschön

Introduction

The development of value orientations constitutes an important part of political socialisation processes related to the formation of other orientations such as political support, attitudes, and competence (e.g. Pye 1968). Values themselves can be defined with Kluckhohn (1967: 395) as 'conceptions [...] of the desirable which influence the selection from available modes, means, and ends of action'. Moreover, these notions of what is desirable represent a moral discourse – meaning that they reflect what 'ought' to be done. This 'sense of oughtness' (Hechter and Opp 2001: xiii) is delivered by culturally shared rules and norms that are regarded as a central and necessary resource for the success of social life. Values and norms therefore link the micro with the macro level of a democratic system. On the micro level – via the personality of individual citizens – they are part of the individual value system and serve as a guideline for political and social behaviour. On the macro level common values integrate citizens and contribute to political involvement, legitimacy and operability of democracy. In terms of the persistence of the democratic system, there is a perceived need to pass down the existing values and norms from one generation to the next. Socialisation processes play a crucial role here.

Explicit political and democratic value orientations are said to be the terminus of longer developmental sequences of so-called 'pre-political' attitudes and dispositions like moral autonomy and pro-social orientations (*see* Hopf and Hopf 1997: 8; Flanagan and Gallay 1995). It has been suggested that the more basic, fundamental and general political orientations, such as values, are acquired early in life (Sears 1983; Jennings 1990). Even if primacy and structuring principles have been heavily disputed (Searing *et al.* 1973; 1976), we can nevertheless assume that normative socialisation processes start early in the course of an individual's life.

As has been mentioned in the introduction to this volume, children's political orientations have not been studied since the heyday of political socialisation research in the 1960s and 1970s. Among other reasons, such as methodological problems, early studies came under criticism because they implied that the family had an omnipotent role in these processes. As research into early political socialisation was abandoned, the family seemed to shrink in significance. Yet the family and several of its characteristics can still be considered the primary socialisation context, exerting a major influence on children's orientations especially at a young age. Above all, parents have an important place in their children's lives and are crucial role models in the latter's normative socialisation via value transmission (e.g. Dalhouse and Frideres 1996). Parents are also the source of the socio-economic background in which children grow up.

Despite the plausibility of early political socialisation processes, the socialisation of politically relevant value orientations in early childhood has not been examined for several decades. Social changes and a recent paradigm change in childhood research, however, demand a new perspective on children's political socialisation processes.

This chapter will examine the value socialisation processes of young children within the family. What aspects of parental orientations and social milieu are especially effective in this regard? How does this parental influence 'react' to the appearance of a new socialisation context – the school – when the child enters primary school? Due to the scarcity of research on young children, the following analyses inevitably have an explorative character and are but an initial foray into politically relevant value socialisation in early childhood.

The analyses draw on data of the unique German study, *'Demokratie leben lernen'* ('Learning to Live Democracy'), which questioned children and their parents at the beginning and the end of the children's first school year. After a brief overview of the study, its data, and basic descriptive results, the following paragraph discusses how parental value transmission on the one hand and social milieu characteristics on the other can influence children's value socialisation. The chapter then examines empirically how value socialisation is influenced by parental value transmission and socio-economic background. This also allows for a comparison of the effects of two socialisation pathways. The chapter concludes with a discussion of the findings and future research perspectives.

The 'Learning to Live Democracy' study

The German study 'Learning to Live Democracy' (LLD)[1] wants to close the research gap with regard to political orientations of young children in Germany and to improve the theoretical and empirical knowledge of political socialisation in early childhood. Starting from the basic assumption that crucial impulses for the development of democratic personalities are already effective at a young age, the study seeks to obtain information on the political and social orientations of young children, and on the influence of the two main socialisation contexts at a

1. The study was initiated in 1999 at the Mannheim Centre for European Social Research by Jan W. van Deth, who has directed the project since its inception. From 2004 to 2007, the German Science Foundation (DFG) has fully financed this study (Grants DE 630/11–1 and 11–2). This support is gratefully acknowledged here. For more information on the study *see*: http://www. mzes.uni-mannheim.de/d7/en/projects/learning-to-live-democracy-lld (accessed 15 May 2013).

young age, family and school. The beginning of school life is an important event in early childhood. It is the child's first encounter with an institutionalised life which, unlike nursery school or kindergarten, is compulsory in Germany. Thus, a research design with two survey waves – the first at the very beginning of the children's education, immediately after they are enrolled in school; the second, at the end of the first school year – was set up. More than 800 young children at the beginning and at the end of their first school year 2004/05 were invited to respond to a standardised children's questionnaire on their political knowledge, attitudes and social orientations as well as their recreational activities such as media use, etc.[2] The two waves of the study enable researchers not only to follow the development of children's orientations but also to separate school and family influences. Besides this core of the study, both parents (of the children involved) were asked to fill out a questionnaire in order to assess their influence on their child's socialisation.[3] They were questioned on their political and social orientations as well as democratic and political value orientations, family life, socio-economic background, parenting practices and on the perceived personality traits of the child.

Children's politically relevant value orientations

Altogether, seventeen items of the children's questionnaire captured children's 'conceptions of the desirable' with regards to democracy and society; and their attitudes toward politically and socially 'adequate' behaviour (*see* Appendix Table 3.A.5 for an extract from the questionnaire). Children were asked about their stances on rules and norms; gender equality; and the characteristics of the good citizen (for a detailed presentation of the items *see* Abendschön 2007; 2010). These orientations represent politically relevant values for the political socialisation process.

The descriptive analysis of these items (not shown here but presented in detail in Abendschön 2007; 2010) present a first indication that 6- to 7-year-old respondents were obviously capable of answering an adequate questionnaire.[4] It presents

---

2.   The development of a standardised questionnaire suitable for young children who are not yet able to read and write presented a methodological challenge. To find out how children of this age group think and talk about affairs of social and political life, a pilot phase was necessary in which qualitative interviews with children of the corresponding age group were conducted. Based on these findings an initial children's questionnaire was designed and pretested with first-graders (for information about the methods and findings of this pilot phase *see* Berton and Schäfer 2005; Rathke 2007; van Deth *et al.* 2007, 2011). The questionnaire consists only of symbols and pictures. Instead of 'Yes', 'No' or 'Don't Know' you will find 'Smileys' with happy and sad faces and question marks.

3.   The children were given two questionnaires for their parents: one for each parent or foster parent. If we take the unique child as a basis, we can account for 345 of the interviewed children with at least one parental questionnaire completed. *See* Appendix Table 3.A.1 which describes the relevant empirical data collection with the respective case numbers and response rates.

4.   This conclusion can partly be derived in light of the relative low number of missing and invalid values. If the children had not understood the questions, we would expect more missing and invalid values.

an initial impression of their social understanding and normative endorsement. Support for rewarding socially desirable citizenship qualities such as helpfulness, work and law-abidingness was very high in both waves. Religious practice, and popularity and wealth, on the other hand, were seen as considerably less acceptable, especially in the second survey. The majority of the children (in both waves) were, moreover, very supportive of keeping promises and of following rules and norms in school and in social life. On gender equality, we find a more differentiated picture. The children clearly assigned some daily chores to one gender. There is an observable overall trend towards a more emancipated view on all the gender role items in the second as compared to the first wave of the survey. The children were now more supportive of both men and women taking responsibility for these tasks. A principal component analysis revealed a latent structure underlying fourteen of these items in both waves (*see* in detail Abendschön 2007).[5] Table 3.1 shows this structure.[6] The fact that a relatively clear picture could be detected serves as a further indicator that young children's orientations can be studied empirically in a meaningful way.[7] Four value orientations can be identified. Helping others, working hard, and always obeying the law constitute the first democratic factor, the *Civic Virtues* dimension, and represent the more official or civic education version of good citizenship. The second factor deals with the support of abstract as well as more concrete attitudes towards social *Rules and Norms*, and represents the second democratic value orientation. Being popular and wealthy distinctly belongs to a further dimension, which deals more with private and acquisitive orientations and is accordingly labelled *Prestige*. The fourth factor, *Gender Equality*, consists of the five items concerning attitudes towards gender roles. Children who favour gender emancipation by supporting both sexes working also demonstrate consistent attitudes toward child care, cleaning and cooking, driving the car, and repairing things.

---

5. Since values are suitable to establish consistency between attitudes and are assumed to represent 'the ultimate underpinnings of attitudes' (Feldman 2003: 479), the empirical relevance of the hypothetical construct values can be constituted when a coherent structure among attitudes is found: 'A set of patterned, or constrained attitudes we will call a value orientation' (van Deth and Scarbrough 1995: 22).

6. *See* Appendix Table 3.A.2 for the final model. Since the data of the second wave confirms more or less the structure that shows at the beginning of the first school year (although with slight differences), the latter is used as a structural basis for the following analyses to ensure the comparability between the value orientations. Consider also that there are now only fourteen items left, the items 'reward churchgoing', 'equal opportunities', and 'keeping promises with acquaintances' are left out because they do not contribute to a clear dimensional structure.

7. The reliability of the dimensions, measured with Cronbach's Alpha seems to be rather moderate (with values around 0.5). This, however, is not astonishing in light of the relatively few number of items per component. Moreover, since we deal with an analysis of a rather explorative children's survey, these values seem acceptable (*see* for a discussion of an 'adequate' Cronbach's alpha, *see* Pedhazur and Pedhazur Schmelkin 1991: 109–10).

Table 3.1: Structure of children's value orientations at beginning and end of the first school year

Civic Virtues	Prestige	Rules and Norms	Gender Equality
Reward Helpfulness	Reward Popularity	Report Rule Breach	Use Tools
Reward Hard Work	Reward Being Wealthy	Importance Rules in General	Work
Reward Law Abiding Behaviour		Importance Personal Rule Adherence	Take Care of Children
		Keep Promises with Friends	Household Chores
			Drive the Car

Next, to assess the children's level of support on the single value orientations, additive indices ranging from 0 to 1 for the dimensions are built.[8] Table 3.2 displays the mean scores on the two value dimensions for both interview waves as well as the difference score.

Table 3.2: Cross-sectional mean scores for the four value orientations at beginning and end of first school year

	Mean (SD) W1	Mean (SD) W2	Difference	Skewness (W1 / W2)	N (W1 / W2)
Civic Virtues	0.80 (0.29)	0.78 (0.29)	-0.02	-1.35 / -1.16	726 / 719
Prestige	0.47 (0.40)	0.30 (0.35)	-0.17***	-0.12 / -0.73	713 / 713
Rules and Norms	0.88 (0.16)	0.88 (0.16)	0.00	-1.12 / -1.56	629 / 701
Gender Equality	0.48 (0.29)	0.55 (0.28)	0.07***	0.06 / -1.32	628 / 701

Notes: ***$p < 0.001$ (two-sided t-tests); W1 = Wave 1; W2 = Wave 2.

The dimension of *Rules and Norms* leads in both interview waves – rules in schools as well as social norms like keeping promises are supported very strongly by the young respondents. This is followed by the dimension of *Civic Virtues*. *Prestige* and *Gender Equality* have the lowest level of support in both waves.

Whereas children who have just started school are rather supportive of qualities that ensure social esteem or prestige such as popularity and wealth, after one year of

8.   This has been done by adding values of the individual items that form one factor and calculating their average. The highest possible support for an orientation is indicated by 1; 0 stands for the lowest or no support. The highly positive and statistically significant correlations between the respective sum and factor scores (Pearson's r > 0.9) show that obviously both measures represent almost identical information.

school most of them have clearly formed the opinion that those two characteristics do not automatically make a good citizen. The mean scores of the children who took part in both waves of the survey changed significantly ($p<0.001$) for both the dimensions of *Gender Equality* as well as *Prestige* – the children obviously become more supportive of gender emancipation and less supportive of orientations toward material acquisition. In terms of *Gender Equality*, the respondents develop a more emancipated attitude during their first school year. The scores for *Prestige* show the greatest difference: at the end of first year, respondents recognise even more clearly that popularity and wealth do not qualify as prerequisites for good citizenship. The mean scores of other two dimensions remain almost the same. Those children who already had high scores at the beginning of their school life showed nearly the same high compliance to these norms in the second wave.

Socialisation of value orientations within the family: social milieu versus attitudinal pathway

The foundations of a political and democratic value system in the individual is already formed in childhood through socialisation processes. Political and democratic values are 'constructed, refined, and reconstructed in the course of growing up' (Flanagan and Gallay 1995: 36). Whereas early political socialisation studies focused almost exclusively on the family, the research interest in the family soon diminished and other socialisation contexts came to the fore.

The family can arguably still be regarded as a crucial actor in value socialisation process since it constitutes the primary socialisation context until the child enters school. It is commonly accepted as the so-called 'prime' socialisation institution (cf. Jennings 2007). It is in this environment, during a child's early social experiences and interactions, where he/she is first confronted with norms and rules on the one hand and socio-economic characteristics on the other (*see* for a summary of seminal studies in this regard the chapter by Corbetta *et al.* in this volume). Therefore this setting is also expected to exert a major influence on children's development and their levels of support for political and democratic values.

Family and parents effect value socialisation through different mechanisms (*see also* Corbetta *et al.* in this volume). We may make an analytical distinction between a social milieu pathway on the one hand and an attitudinal pathway on the other (Dalton 1982: 140).[9]

Social milieu pathway

The social milieu pathway exerts an influence on children's political value orientations via shared socio-economic characteristics such as social class and ethnicity. The socialisation of politically relevant values is related to the introduction

---

9.   It is plausible that the two pathways also interact with each other.

to values and norms that are specific to a social group or class (Jennings and Niemi 1974: 5). Children inherit these characteristics from their parents by being placed in a specific social milieu (cf. Dalton 1982: 140; Glass *et al.* 1986). This social milieu will result then, according to the hypothesis, in similar political (value) orientations as well. We can therefore expect to find influences from general determinants that accompany the major socialisation institution of the family. These include not only socio-economic and ethnic background, but also gender as another main socio-structural factor. As Sugarman (2007: 4) points out:

> [C]hildren like adults not only formulate their ideas according to their age, but also according to their status in the world. If a child is female, poor and of color living in an urban area, her view of the world differs from that of a white, wealthy male born in a rural Southern home.

In Germany, children from a non-native and low social status background suffer in terms of educational achievement and social integration (e.g. Gill 2005). Youth studies also detected disadvantages in political socialisation for lower status groups (Oesterreich 2002: 207; Verba *et al.* 2003). We can assume on these grounds that political socialisation processes are already influenced at an early age by these socio-structural factors. The same can be expected of gender. Empirical findings on adult normative and social orientations find that women and girls are – due to gender-specific socialisation influences – generally considered more socially and morally competent than men and boys, and demonstrate their interests in politics differently (e.g. Kulke 1998; Nunner-Winkler 2001). Girls and boys are raised to like different topics, to be more or less empathetic and caring. It can therefore be argued that men and women speak normatively 'in a different voice' (Gilligan 1982).

We expect therefore that children who experience social deprivation or come from an ethnic minority have different value priorities than their more privileged and/or German classmates. We also assume differences between male and female children.

Attitudinal pathway

The attitudinal pathway assumes direct value transmission from parents to the child, which works via social learning mechanisms such as imitation, identification and reinforcement processes. Analyses of parents and their children (who were mostly more than sixteen years old) found the attitudinal pathway especially relevant for party identification, political ideology and more general political orientations (Percheron and Jennings 1981; Jennings and Niemi 1974). It is supposed to already be in place in early childhood, but it has never been studied in that age group. Parents are regarded as especially important in value transmission processes (e.g. Geißler 1996; Hyman 1959), even if other family members such as siblings and grandparents or non-family acquaintances such as teachers can be assumed to transmit orientations as well. According to social learning theory, parents function as role models with whom children identify and whose values and norms they therefore adopt. At the same time, parents actively try to transmit values and norms that they consider important to their children (e.g. Hess and Torney 1967).

There is no general consensus on the value transmission thesis in political socialisation research. Some recent value transmission studies on older adolescents and their parents (e.g. Boehnke 2004) find only moderate correlations between parents' and their offspring's value orientations.[10] According to Jennings (2007: 38), however, the attitudinal transmission pathway generally proves to be more robust than social milieu models, which consider only socio-economic family characteristics (e.g. Glass *et al.* 1986; Jennings 1984). Kroh's study (2007) examining the transmission of (post-) materialistic orientations confirms this claim. The intergenerational value transmission from parents to children proved to be a stronger influence than the socio-economic household situation.

Studies of children's normative and moral development find that younger children especially identify with parents' normative orientations. Bott (2008: 58; 64–5) shows that the children in his study regard their parents as central authority figures when it comes to questions of norms and values. Parents' remarks are observed, imitated and internalised, even when this is not the parents' express intention. These findings suggest that we would find significant positive correlations between the values that children and parents support so that we expect to find a transmission effect in the value orientations in question.

It could also be shown empirically that the strength or intensity of value transmission processes depends on the degree of congruence between maternal and paternal value orientations. Congruent orientations mean that consistent and homogenous cues exert influences on the child, thus facilitating value transmission (Cavalli-Sforza and Feldman 1981; Jennings and Niemi 1968; Knafo and Schwartz 2003: 596).[11] This can be easily explained from a social learning perspective: when parents support the same values, children deal with similar role models that reinforce each other's influence. With regard to politically relevant value orientations, we can assume a positive transmission effect when both parents show a consistently high level of support for the respective orientation. But even where the value orientations of mothers and fathers are similar, this consistency can have different consequences in the transmission process (Jennings and Niemi 1974), because gender matters as well. Researchers concur that maternal orientations are more relevant than paternal ones (Jennings and Langton 1969; Rieker 2007: 35), mostly because childcare is – even in this day and age – still practically the woman's domain, and mothers still spend more time with children

---

10. There even seems to exist a reverse effect: successful value internalisation can be observed especially for values which are rejected rather than those which are endorsed by the parents (Boehnke 2004: 120–1). This reverse identification process, however, could be caused by the specific 'youth' situation where rebellious attitudes are quite normal.

11. Many studies find that couples over time become more similar with regard to their political value orientations (e.g. Boehnke 2004: 113). Regarding the homogeneity of political orientations in marriages *see also* Niemi (1974), Stoker and Jennings (2005) and Zuckerman *et al.* (2005).

than fathers.[12] With regard to parent-specific influences, we therefore expect that the level of maternal support should exert stronger influence on the child than the paternal one.[13] There is no empirical evidence with regard to the question of whether daughters or sons are better 'cue receivers' (Rieker 2007: 35). Direct gender effects (transmission from father to son or mother to daughter) that are stronger than general parental transmission effects have, however, been found in some studies (Boehnke 2004: 118; Wittebrood 1995: 188). The respective value influence of each parent should therefore be analysed separately for a detailed picture of value transmission processes. Therefore, we will examine if we can observe gender-specific value transmission: are girls' levels of normative support (for a particular value orientation) more strongly correlated with the maternal or the paternal level? Is there a stronger correlation between boys and fathers than between girls and fathers?

In terms of parental interaction we hypothesise that the more consistent both parents' support for a particular value orientation, the higher will be the positive correlation between parents' and children's levels of support. More specifically: if both parents show a congruent high level of support for that value, the child should also show a likewise high level of support.

As was argued before, the start of school represents an important biographical event in the lives of young children. It cannot be expected, however, that family factors will no longer exert their influence once the child begins to attend classes regularly. Therefore transmission effects should occur at both interview time points. We should not, however, be surprised if the relationship is stronger at the beginning of the first school year. As has been noticed by other studies before, direct value transmission might also work better for some orientations than for others - the 'content' of the value orientations might matter in this regard (*see also* Jennings and Niemi 1968: 142–48; Grolnick *et al.* 1997: 143).

---

12. This is especially true for Germany. Bertram (2006: 2) states in this regard that until the child's sixth birthday his/her upbringing mainly remains in the hand of parents, meaning, more concretely, in the hand of mothers. The LLD sample does not differ from this societal reality. A substantial number of the parents questioned (about 57 per cent) state that they share the responsibility of childcare. Nevertheless, 41 per cent of mothers declare that they are mainly responsible (compared to two per cent of fathers).

13. To specify this expectation or to adapt it to the situations where fathers are mainly responsible for the education of the child it could also be formulated that the support level of the person who spends more time with the child should be more influential than that of the person who spends less time with the child. This would reduce the sample substantially, however (*see* discussion in footnote 19), so that this expectation will not be analysed here.

Analyses and empirical findings

Attitudinal or social milieu pathway – analytic strategy

Correlation analyses are generally used to study value transmission and will be computed here as a first step in the analysis of the hypotheses on attitudinal pathways. To test our expectations of value transmission, we cannot simply use the mean between maternal and paternal scores, because we then lose information about the parental value environment; moreover, we also want to analyse gender specific transmission. Differently structured data has to be used: both complete parental information (N=545) and the data including both parents' answers (triadic data, N=200) will be considered. Next, maternal and paternal information will be used separately (N=324 for mothers, N=221 for fathers) to analyse potential gender-specific relationships. Since we expect positive correlations between parents and children in their levels of support for particular values, we will apply only one-sided significance testing.[14]

Hypotheses on the consistency and congruence of parental values and on the social milieu pathway will be analysed using multivariate regression modelling. As may be expected from Table 3.2, the value orientations *Civic Virtues* and *Rules and Norms* are skewed very much to the left and show only little variance. This means that they are not suitable for linear regression modelling because we cannot expect residuals to be normally distributed. Therefore, these two dependent variables have been dichotomised[15] for multivariate analysis and logistic regression analysis is used.[16]

The data permits the inclusion of socio-economic and ethnic background, gender, and age in the analyses. To examine the combined influence of both parents' support for a given value orientation and to account for the simultaneous influences of both parents, multivariate models will integrate both parents' value orientations and their consistency. Furthermore these regression analyses can also control for socio-structural determinants – in other words, the social milieu pathway.

Correlation analyses

Do we find evidence for ongoing value transmission at all? To analyse this expectation, Table 3.3 shows the correlation coefficients between parents and their children.[17]

---

14. *See* for the operationalisation of parental value orientations and socio-demographic variables Appendix Table 3.A.4.

15. Z-standardisation did not solve the problem. Therefore a median split with the sample was performed, meaning in this case that all children who reached a value of 1 were assigned a 1 (i.e. 'support'), the rest of the children were given 0 ('no support').

16. Appendix Table 3.A.3 shows frequencies for the dichotomised variables and the respective samples.

17. We consider here all parents and their children, we do not take into account the relationship between the respective parents here which means that we can use N=545 for this analysis.

Table 3.3: Correlations between parents' and children's values (Pearson's r)

	Civic Virtues	Prestige	Rules and Norms	Gender Equality
Wave 1	0.01	0.04	-0.03	0.20***
N	518	501	464	458
Wave 2	0.09**	0.11***	0.04	0.07*
N	503	492	485	477

*p < 0.1; **p < 0.05; ***p < 0.01 (one-sided)

Table 3.4: Correlations between mothers'/fathers' and children's values (Pearson's r)

	Civic Virtues		Prestige		Rules and Norms		Gender Equality	
	Mothers	Fathers	Mothers	Fathers	Mothers	Fathers	Mothers	Fathers
Wave 1	0.02	-0.02	0.03	0.04	-0.06	-0.02	0.18***	0.24***
N	307	212	295	207	279	187	275	184
Wave 2	0.13**	0.01	0.10**	0.11*	0.05	-0.02	0.08*	0.07
N	299	205	290	204	290	196	285	193

*p < 0.1; **p < 0.05; ***p < 0.01 (one-sided)

Table 3.3 illustrates a partial confirmation of our hypothesis. Statistically significant correlation coefficients can be found especially for *Gender Equality* – both in Wave 1 and in Wave 2. The correlation at the end of the first school year is more than three times higher than at the beginning of the first school year. *Civic Virtues* and *Prestige* only show significant coefficients at the end of the first school year.[18] We do not find any correlations for *Rules and Norms* and therefore cannot observe value transmission processes.

Are mothers indeed the primary transmitters of values in the family, as has been assumed? Table 3.4 shows the correlation coefficients between mothers and children as well as between fathers and children, and allows us to analyse whether mothers or fathers show stronger (transmission) relations with their child.

Again, the assumption can only be partially confirmed and only at the end of the first school year. Maternal transmission proves to be statistically significant for *Civic Virtues* and *Gender Equality*. While the correlation coefficients for *Prestige* are also significant at the end of the first school year, they do not differ between

---

18. Altogether the value of the correlation coefficients indicates only weak relations – it should be kept in mind, however, that value orientations had to be measured differently. The expectations also do not try to make a statement about size. Statistical significance of the coefficient is more important than size.

mothers and fathers. For *Rules and Norms* there are no significant correlations at all. At the start of school we even find a correlation against expectation: paternal support for *Gender Equality* correlates more strongly to the child's (than maternal support). The strength of this relationship however diminishes over the course of the first school year by two thirds, and by the end of the first school year, is no longer statistically significant. On the other hand, the maternal effect remains statistically significant, even if it has also diminished. All in all, the assumption that mothers would exert a stronger transmission influence on their offspring than their male partners can neither be confirmed for both waves nor for all of the four value orientations. The expected effect can only be found for *Civic Virtues* and *Gender Equality* at the end of the first school year. Before entering school, young children seem to be more influenced by their fathers than by their mothers when it comes to *Gender Equality*.[19]

To check for the suspected gender specific transmission effects, we can examine the correlations between mothers and daughters and fathers and sons. Table 3.5 displays these correlation coefficients for both waves.

First, it is notable that, except for *Prestige* and *Gender Equality*, significant coefficients can only be found at the end of the first school year. Furthermore the findings do not indicate gender-specific effects, or if they do, then these are noticeable only to a small extent. With regard to *Gender Equality,* fathers in fact exhibit a stronger tie with sons than with daughters; this difference, however, is not very pronounced. At the end of the first school year, there is, however, a statistically significant negative relationship in the levels of support for certain values between fathers and sons. Since fathers' support remained constant for both years (parents were only questioned once between the two children's waves), this finding suggests that the change is due to change in sons' value orientations. Fathers' and daughters' support for *Gender Equality* correlate in a positive and consistent way at both points in time. On the other hand, the correlations between mothers and sons are also slightly higher than the correlations between mothers and daughters.

We find opposite- rather than same-sex correlations for *Rules and Norms*, *Civic Virtues* and *Prestige* at the end of the first school year. At the end of the first school year, while there are correlations between fathers and sons in the dimension of *Civic Virtues*, the correlation between sons and mothers is slightly higher. The father-daughter relationship is negative in this regard. In the dimension of *Rules and Norms,* mothers exhibit a rather strong correlation with sons, while mothers

19. To test the expectation mentioned in footnote 13, namely, that the parent who spends most time with the child should demonstrate a level of support for a given value that is closer to the child's (as compared to the other parent), parental information from both parents is needed. This decreases the cases we could consider to 200. For these we only find one father who claimed primary responsibility for the child, in contrast to eighty mothers claiming primary responsibility; 108 cases declared shared responsibility; eleven parental pairs disagreed on their responsibilities. The remaining n for this analysis amounts to eighty-one cases. Since the findings of this separate analysis, with a few exceptions, resemble the one above, we will, due to the low case numbers, not go into detail here.

Table 3.5: Correlations between mothers' and daughters'/fathers' and sons' values (Pearson's r)

		Civic Virtues		Prestige		Rules and Norms		Gender Equality	
		Mothers	Fathers	Mothers	Fathers	Mothers	Fathers	Mothers	Fathers
Wave 1	Boys	0.01	-0.02	0.10*	0.03	-0.05	0.02	0.18**	0.24**
N		149	102	144	101	139	94	135	92
	Girls	0.00	-0.01	-0.05	0.03	-0.03	0.06	0.15**	0.21**
N		158	110	151	106	140	93	140	92
Wave 2	Boys	0.15**	0.14*	0.18**	0.02	0.23***	0.04	-0.02	-0.14*
N		143	99	137	98	137	93	133	91
	Girls	0.01	-0.14*	0.06	0.14**	-0.09*	0.00	0.13*	0.20**
N		156	106	153	105	153	103	152	102

*p < 0.10; **p < 0.05; ***p < 0.01 (one-sided)

and daughters are negatively correlated. In the dimension of *Prestige*, mothers correlate positively with their sons, while the support of fathers correlates with the support of daughters. We can conclude that there is hardly any evidence for gender-specific value transmission in early childhood.

Following the bivariate analyses of value transmission from parents to children, we assessed the influence of parental value consistency. It has been assumed that if parental value orientations are consistent, there should be a stronger transmission effect than if they are not. Table 3.6 displays the respective correlation coefficients between mothers, fathers and their children, in cases of both consistent and inconsistent parental value support.[20]

A first glance shows that there are hardly any significant correlations between the respective parental groups and their children. There are a few exceptions: if both the father and mother support *Gender Equality* in a consistent way, then there is a significant positive correlation of both parents with the child. The correlations are also stronger when the partner exhibits the same level of support for a particular value orientation.

The correlation coefficients for parents who do not agree show that paternal support is more strongly correlated (compared to maternal support) with the child's on *Gender Equality*. This means that on the one hand where *Gender Equality* orientations of the parents are consistent, influence is exerted via mothers and fathers, but if there is no agreement, the father proves to be the stronger transmitter. These relations, however, are only valid at the beginning of the first school year. This finding is the only confirmation of the consistency expectation. At the end of the first school year, however, we find that for *Civic Virtues*, *Prestige*, and *Rules and Norms*, where parental support is inconsistent, mothers' levels (of support) still correlate positively with those of the child. For the other pairs we don't find any statistically significant correlations, regardless of whether parents agree on a value. On the basis of the bivariate analyses of the 200 parents and their children we have to conclude that parental value consistency hardly plays a role in value transmission. The hypotheses of value transmission between parents and young children could only be confirmed to some extent, with the findings partially pointing in the opposite direction. The stronger relationship that was expected between mothers and children could be found only at the end of the school year, in the dimensions of *Civic Virtues* and *Gender Equality*. The gender-specific effects were hardly discernible; there was even a cross-gender effect. What could be confirmed, however, was the assumption that there is value transmission within families and that value transmission works better for some value orientations than others. We found the strongest correlations in the dimension of *Gender Equality*. At the beginning of the school year, this orientation is especially dependent on the parental influence; most interestingly, the paternal orientations play a more important role here than the maternal ones.

---

20. Parental consistency is measured rather strictly: both parents must exhibit the same level of value support.

Table 3.6: Correlations in values between consistent and inconsistent mothers/fathers and their children (Pearson's r)

| | Civic Virtues | | | | Prestige | | | | Rules and Norms | | | | Gender Equality | | | |
| | Consistent | | Inconsistent | | Consistent | | Inconsistent | | Consistent | | Inconsistent | | Consistent | | Inconsistent | |
	Mothers	Fathers	Mothers	Fathers	Mothers	Fathers	Mothers	Fathers	Mothers	Fathers	Mothers	Fathers	Mothers	Fathers	Mothers	Fathers
Wave 1	-0.06	-0.06	-0.07	0.01	-0.05	-0.05	0.03	0.03	0.0	0.0	-0.06	0.10	0.26**	0.26**	0.20**	0.26***
N	58		133		66		118		52		119		44		123	
Wave 2	-0.02	-0.02	0.21***	0.02	-0.14	-0.14	0.26***	0.20**	0.13	0.13	0.15*	0.01	0.05	0.05	0.09	0.00
N	58		128		65		117		58		121		48		127	

*p < 0.1; **p < 0.05; ***p < 0.01 (one-sided)

Table 3.7: Influences of standard socio-structural determinants

	Civic virtues		Rules and norms		Prestige		Gender equality	
Model 1: Social structure	**W1**	**W2**	**W1**	**W2**	**W1**	**W2**	**W1**	**W2**
Female gender[a]		1.85***		1.56*			0.14**	0.16***
Low SES[b]		1.56*			0.16**	0.14**	-0.14**	
High SES[b]	1.79**			0.55*	-0.10*	-0.10*		
Turkish migration background[d]				0.33***	0.11*		-0.11*	-0.20***
Other migration background[d]					0.14**			
Oldest age[c]				0.58*				-0.12*
Youngest age[c]								
(Pseudo) R$^{2/}$ Pseudo	4.2	4.7	1.2	8.3	10.2	7.6	7.0	9.3
Adjusted R^2					7.7	4.2	5.1	7.1
N	314	303	283	294	308	300	283	294

Notes: *p < 0.1; **p < 0.05; ***p < 0.01; a. Reference category: male; b. Reference category: middle SES; c. Reference category: middle age group; d. Reference category: no migration background. Reported are significant Exp(B) coefficients of logistic regression models for *Civic virtues* and *Rules and norms* and significant standardised OLS regression coefficients for *Prestige* and *Civic equality*. W1 = Wave 1; W2 = Wave 2.

Social milieu model

The social milieu pathway attributes to socio-economic characteristics an important role in the political socialisation processes of adolescents. Can we already detect an influence of these social structural aspects of family background on the value orientations of children? Table 3.7 shows the significant regression coefficients.

The standard model shows that the gender of the child, as can be seen from the results, is indeed significant: being a girl increases the probability of the child's support for *Civic Virtues* and *Rules and Norms* at the end of the first school year. It also increases the level of support for *Gender Equality* at both points in time. No differences between boys and girls can be found for *Prestige*. These findings regarding gender differences in value orientations seem – at least partially – to confirm the expectation that girls and boys do have different value priorities.

Compared to the middle category, both a high status and a low status socio-economic family background (SES) turn out to be influential on all four value orientations of children. Children with low SES show significantly stronger support for *Prestige* and less support for *Gender Equality* than classmates from comparatively more socio-economically privileged families. Interestingly enough, the former also have a higher tendency to support *Civic Virtues* at the end of the first school year. Pupils with high family SES, on the contrary, score significantly lower on *Prestige* in both survey waves. Compared to the middle SES group they also are more likely to support *Civic Virtues* at the start of their school career.

A family background of migration also contributed in a more or less predictable way: children with a Turkish heritage were less likely than their compatriots to support *Gender Equality* both at the beginning and at the end of their first year of school. Compared to classmates with a native German background, children with a family background of migration, Turkish or otherwise, are more likely to support value orientations concerned with *Prestige*. This effect, however, can be seen only at the beginning of the first school year. At the end of the first school year the probability of their support for *Rules and Norms* decreases.

Age hardly has any effect on the value orientations of children examined here. The only exceptions can be found at the end of the first school year: older children favour *Gender Equality* and *Rules and Norms* less than their younger classmates. This finding indicates that the substantially older children in the first grade support normative value orientations less than their peers. All in all, these results support a social milieu pathway of value socialisation.

Value transmission and social milieu: multivariate analysis

The analyses conducted so far demonstrate bivariate relationships between the levels of support for different values in parents and their children. Our final analysis examines parental value transmission in a multivariate way. Three different analytical steps will be pursued to shed further light on the role of parental value consistency, which has not been tested thus far.

The first regression model simply inserts maternal and paternal value orientations as independent variables. In a second block the social milieu model is added. As can be seen in Tables 3.8 and 3.9, the regression models mostly confirm the relationships that have already been shown in the correlation analyses – even when controlling for the socio-structural determinants. Keeping the value orientation of the other parent constant, we find that maternal support for *Civic Virtues* and *Rules and Norms* augments the probability that the child will support the two value orientations. This, however, occurs only at the end of the first school year and, where *Rules and Norms* are concerned, only in the expanded model that takes social structure into account. At the beginning of the school year we cannot find significant value transmission effects, with the exception of *Gender Equality*. Even if we control for maternal level and the socio-structural characteristics, we find again that it is the father's support for *Gender Equality* that is more efficacious: the more supportive the father, the more supportive the child. With regard to the social milieu factors, we can see that most (but not all) of the effects discovered in the last paragraph are still effective, even when controlling for parents' value orientations.

The next analytical step tests consistency expectations. In order to do so we add a consistency measure to the support level of one parent in the regression model. Tables 3.10 and 3.11 display the significant coefficients.[21]

---

21. The regression models can only be estimated if one parent's support level is left out of the equation (because of the integration of the consistency measure). The maternal level is chosen here.

Table 3.8: *Influence of parental value orientations on the child's level of Civic Virtues and Rules and Norms*

	Civic Virtues				Rules and Norms			
	W1	Exp. W1	W2	Exp. W2	W1	Exp. W1	W2	Exp. W2
Value orientation mother			2.13**	2.29**				1.73*
Value orientation father								
Female gender				1.97**				
Low SES				2.48*				
High SES								0.50*
Turkish migration background						0.29*		0.17***
Other migration background								
Oldest age								0.46*
Youngest age								
Pseudo R^2	0.9	7.9	3.4	9.8	0.0	4.4	1.2	12.7
N	189	189	184	184	169	169	177	177

Notes: *$p < 0.1$; **$p < 0.05$; ***$p < 0.01$; reported are significant Exp(B) coefficients of logistic regression models; W1 = Wave 1; W2 = Wave 2; Exp. = expanded model; reference categories as in Table 3.7.

Table 3.9: Influence of parental value orientation on the child's level of Prestige and Gender Equality

	Prestige				Gender Equality			
	W1	Exp. W1	W2	Exp. W2	W1	Exp. W1	W2	Exp. W2
Value orientation mother								
Value orientation father						0.18*		
Female gender				0.14*	0.23**	0.19**		0.20**
Low SES		0.28***						
High SES		-0.12*						
Turkish migration background								-0.18**
Other migration background		0.16**						
Oldest age		-0.15*						
Youngest age								
R²	0.0	15.8	1.5	7.5	7.7	11.5	0.7	9.1
Adjusted R²	0.0	11.5	0.4	2.8	6.6	6.5	0.0	4.1
N	175	175	175	175	154	154	154	154

Notes: *p < 0.1; **p < 0.05; ***p < 0.01; reported are significant standardised OLS regression coefficients; W1 = Wave 1; W2 = Wave 2; Exp. = expanded model; reference categories as in Table 3.7.

Table 3.10. Influence of maternal value support and paternal consistency on the child's level of Civic Virtues and Rules and Norms

	Civic Virtues				Rules and Norms			
	W1	Exp. W1	W2	Exp. W2	W1	Exp. W1	W2	Exp. W2
Value orientation mother			1.96**	2.13**				1.70*
Consistency measure (dummy)					0.56*	0.54*		
Female gender				2.01**				
Low SES				2.54**				
High SES								0.51*
Turkish migration background						0.32*		0.17***
Other migration background								
Oldest age								0.44*
Youngest age								
Pseudo R²	1.1	7.2	3.5	10.1	2.3	6.5	0.0	13.0
N	189	189	184	184	169	169	177	177

Notes: *p < 0.1; **p < 0.05; ***p < 0.01; reported are significant Exp(B) coefficients of logistic regression models; W1 = Wave 1; W2 = Wave 2; Exp. = expanded model; reference categories as in Table 3.7

Table 3.11: Influence of maternal value support and paternal consistency of the child's level on Prestige and Gender Equality

	Prestige				Gender Equality			
	W1	Exp. W1	W2	Exp. W2	W1	Exp. W1	W2	Exp. W2
Value orientation mother	0.14*		0.12*		0.20***			
Consistency measure (dummy)			0.13*	0.12*	0.12*			
Female gender						0.20**		0.19**
Low SES		0.25***						
High SES		-0.12*						
Turkish migration background								-0.17**
Other Migration background		0.14*						
Oldest age		-0.14*						
Youngest Age								
R^2	2.0	16.0	2.9	8.9	5.7	10.5	0.5	7.9
Adjusted R^2	1.0	11.7	1.8	4.1	4.5	5.4	0.0	2.9
N	181	181	181	181	170	170	170	170

Notes: *p < 0.1; **p < 0.05; ***p < 0.01; reported are significant standardised OLS regression coefficients; W1 = Wave 1; W2 = Wave 2; Exp. = expanded model; reference categories as in Table 3.7

The regression analyses also present ambivalent findings on the effects of consistent support in both parents for a particular value orientation. We find that parental value consistency exerts an independent influence especially at the beginning of the school year. Consistency has positive effects on *Prestige* and *Gender Equality*. For *Gender Equality* we additionally find that maternal support exercises an independent effect. This means that both the maternal support of values and parental consistency are independent influences. These effects disappear, however, as soon as we integrate the social milieu factors into the model.

When both parents demonstrate consistent levels of support for *Rules and Norms*, there is a negative effect on the probability that their child will likewise support such value orientations; this runs counter to our expectations. Maternal effects on *Civic Virtues* are unvarying – mothers obviously transmit the value independent of their partner. The greater the mother's support for *Civic Virtues*, the greater the child's.

Summing up, we can confirm the consistency expectation for *Prestige* and *Gender Equality*. Regarding *Civic Virtues* there is no significant positive consistency effect, for *Rules and Norms* we even find that when both parents demonstrate consistently strong support for such value orientations, there is a negative impact on the child's support of such values. Again we also find expected significant influences of the socio-structural variables.

A last analytical step must be taken to evaluate our final hypothesis that value transmission should be especially effective when parental support is not only consistent but also consistently strong. The consistency analyses so far showed that consistent levels of support for values have a significant influence, independent of the precise degree of support. This cannot give us information about the strength of parental support to help us to evaluate the assumption. Therefore, we computed a multiplicative interaction effect between maternal and paternal level and integrated it into the regression model.[22]

As can be seen in Tables 3.12 and 3.13, the interaction effects only exhibit statistically significant influences for *Rules and Norms* and *Prestige*. The greater the common parental support for *Prestige*, the greater the child's support on that value orientation. With regard to *Rules and Norms*, the multiplicative term exerts a negative influence on the probability of the child's support. This finding could point at an early counter-movement of children to parental norm acceptance. For *Civic Virtues* we can detect a significant effect of the maternal influence at the end of the first school year. With regard to *Gender Equality*, it can be seen that holding both maternal and multiplicative influence constant, the father's degree of support proves to be influential on the child's support. This crucial role of the male parent regarding *Gender Equality* has been found throughout all of the analyses. The more supportive the fathers are of *Gender Equality*, the more supportive their children.

---

22. This approach first led to problems of multicollinearity. To solve these problems, the independent variables – the respective levels of parental support – were centred: VOcentred = VO – MeanVO. The interaction variable has then been calculated by multiplying the two centred variables: INT(VOM, VOF) = VOM, centred x VOF centred. (VOM=Value orientation mother; VOF=Value orientation father).

Table 3.12: *Influence of parental value orientations (and their interaction) on the child's level of Civic Virtues and Rules and Norms*

	Civic Virtues				Rules and Norms			
	W1	Exp. W1	W2	Exp. W2	W1	Exp. W1	W2	Exp. W2
Interaction term					0.42**	0.45*		
Value orientation mother			2.14**	2.28**				1.80*
Value orientation father								
Female Gender				2.01**				
Low SES				2.63**				
High SES								0.51*
Turkish migration background						0.35*		0.16***
Other migration background		0.55*						
Oldest age								0.46*
Youngest age								
Pseudo R²	1.0	8.2	4.3	11.0	3.9	7.3	1.6	13.3
N	189	189	184	184	169	169	177	177

Notes: *p < 0.1; **p < 0.05; ***p < 0.01; reported are significant Exp(B) coefficients of logistic regression models; W1 = Wave 1; W2 = Wave 2; Exp. = expanded model; reference categories as in Table 3.7

Table 3.13: *Influence of parental value orientations (and their interaction) on the child's level of Prestige and Gender Equality*

	Prestige				Gender Equality			
	W1	Exp. W1	W2	Exp. W2	W1	Exp. W1	W2	Exp. W2
Interaction term	0.18**							
Value orientation mother								
Value orientation father					0.21**	0.17*		
Female Gender				0.14*		0.14*		0.17**
Low SES		0.14*						
High SES								
Turkish migration background		0.16*						-0.21**
Other migration background		0.16**						
Oldest age								
Youngest age								
R²	3.0	11.6	1.9	7.1	6.8	10.3	0.8	9.6
Adjusted R²	1.3	6.5	0.2	1.7	5.0	4.6	0	4.1
N	207	207	207	207	184	184	184	184

Notes: *p < 0.1; **p < 0.05; ***p < 0.01; reported are significant standardised OLS regression coefficients; W1 = Wave 1; W2 = Wave 2; Exp. = expanded model; reference categories as in Table 3.7

Summary and discussion

Values and norms play a crucial role in democracy. This chapter argued that young children's value orientations are an important piece of the jigsaw in the story of democratic citizenship. The relevance of studying young children's value orientations are seen in two ways. Firstly, it can be assumed that value orientations are already formed early in life. This is confirmed by the fact that by six to eight years of age, children's notions of what is desirable already display a latent structure. Secondly, both the experience of childhood as well as our understanding of the idea of childhood has changed over the course of the last few decades and recent efforts to integrate children into the democratic process show that they should be regarded as present rather than future citizens.

In recent years, political socialisation research has neglected family influences, and focused instead on socialisation contexts such as peers and media as important influences on value internalisation processes. Nevertheless, it can be assumed that the family still plays a special role in children's normative development. Two analytically distinct mechanisms with regard to the family's role in the child's development of politically relevant value orientations have been identified: an attitudinal pathway that assumes value transmission from parents to child and a social milieu pathway that works via shared socio-structural characteristics. These two pathways were applied to analyses of young children's value socialisation. We found evidence that there are indeed value transmission processes from parents to children, but the expectations in this regard – based mainly on previous research with older adolescents and their parents – could only be partially confirmed. Moreover, the size of the correlation effects is rather moderate. These findings imply that direct value transmission via imitation and identification is not the whole story of children's value socialisation within the family context.

We also found that the social milieu pathway and therefore the 'usual suspects' from social science research can account for some of the variance in the children's value orientations – this holds for both survey waves. Gender, socio-economic environment and ethnic origin proved to be especially influential. The female gender is related to support for *Civic Virtues, Rules and Norms* and *Gender Equality* – as plausible as these clear findings are for the dimension of *Gender Equality*, it is surprising that at the tender ages of six and seven, most girls are already strongly in favour of *Gender Equality*, even though most of them are surely not affected directly by unequal household burdens. Being of Turkish origin proves to be a major impediment to support for *Gender Equality*; this factor negatively influences not only on the scores on the different waves of the survey but also the development of this orientation over the course of the school year.

All in all, the findings with regard to parental value transmission in early childhood are rather differentiated. We can conclude that for some value orientations, value transmission works better within the family. We found evidence of value transmission processes in early childhood; however, the effects are not as pronounced as we expected. This implies that there are additional factors influencing young children's support for values. The social milieu pathway is quite effective in this regard, even if we found that it does not apply equally to all orientations. Attitudinal and social milieu pathways also do not appear to be competing with each other. Value transmission influences mostly remain effective when controlled for the socio-structural factors and *vice versa*.

We did not find systematic differences between the results of the first and second waves. Some models even imply that parental and family factors are more effective at the end of the first school year than at the beginning. This could indicate that school also has a positive impact on the family's socialisation effectiveness. The fact that not all of the detected effects are visible at both points in time may be due to the new socialisation input of school, which sets the course for the children's recognition and/or re-evaluation of their parents' value orientations. The start of school is an important biographical event for young children; it signals a broadening of their worlds and minds in a new socialisation environment. Future analyses will have to take into account what aspects of school life leave an imprint on young children's value systems and how these influences interact with family life. For the moment we can conclude that family influences, such as the socio-economic situation of the family, the social integration of the child and parental value orientations still have considerable influence even after children begin school.

One could perhaps argue that young children's value systems are not yet fully formed or settled and that more clear-cut correlations can only be found later in life. Nevertheless, the child's value system seems to be refined enough to react to social-structural characteristics. Further analyses should definitely include other potential family factors such as family interaction and parenting styles and focus on alternative mechanisms such as interaction and co-construction (e.g. Youniss 1980). More attention should also be paid to the child's own personality and other individual characteristics that might 'filter' external socialisation influences.

This chapter also attempted to show that children's value socialisation can be studied in a meaningful way. There are, of course, also measurement issues to consider. The data of the LLD study provides a good starting point for up-to-date analyses of children's political socialisation processes within the contexts of family and school. The study is, however, only an initial explorative enterprise in revitalising political socialisation research on young children that should be followed up by further research.

Appendix

Table 3.A.1: Sample Sizes and Response Rates of the LLD study

		Target Population	Realised	Response Rate (%)
Children	Wave 1	833	736	88.4
	Wave 2	851	725	85.2
	Panel		634	
Parents		1597	545	34.1
Parental information per child		781	345	44.1

Table 3.A.2: Structure of children's value orientations at the beginning and end of the first school year (Final solution: wave 1: N_{min} 601, wave 2: N_{min} 681)

	Wave 1				Wave 2			
	Civic Virtues	Prestige	Rules and Norms	Gender Equality	Civic Virtues	Prestige	Rules and Norms	Gender Equality
Reward helpfulness	0.58				0.60			
Reward hard work	0.53				(0.30)			
Reward law-abiding behaviour	0.52				0.61			
Reward religious practice[a]						0.46		
Reward popularity		0.60				0.42		
Reward being wealthy		0.67				0.70		
Report rule breach			0.41					
Importance rules in general			0.59				0.62	

(Cont'd.)

Table 3.A.2. (Cont'd.)

	Wave 1				Wave 2			
	Civic Virtues	Prestige	Rules and Norms	Gender Equality	Civic Virtues	Prestige	Rules and Norms	Gender Equality
Importance personal rule adherence			0.58				0.64	
Keep promises with friends			0.36				0.41	
Equality of sexes: use tools				(0.39)				(0.38)
Equality of sexes: work				0.39				0.44
Equality of sexes: take care of children				0.51				0.45
Equality of sexes: household chores				0.53				0.50
Equality of sexes: drive car				0.40				0.45
Percentage of variance explained (%) Σ=46.9 (W1) Σ=47.7 (W2)	13.2	12.0	10.0	11.7	13.1	12.7	10.0	11.9
Cronbach's Alpha	0.54	0.49	0.52	0.58	0.50	0.41	0.64	0.56

Notes: a. only included in the second wave; Principal Component Analysis (Varimaxrotation), missing pair-wise data excluded, factor loadings under 0.4 not displayed (with the exception of *Equality of sexes: Use Tools* in first and second wave *Keep promises with friends* and *Equality of sexes: work* in the first wave *Reward work* n the second wave).

Table 3.A.3: Distribution of the dichotomised value orientations Civic Virtues and Rules and Norms (absolute numbers and per cent)

	Civic Virtues				Rules and Norms			
	W1 **(n)**	**W1** **(%)**	**W2** **(n)**	**W2** **(%)**	**W1** **(n)**	**W1** **(%)**	**W2** **(n)**	**W2** **(%)**
No support	279	37.9	310	42.8	299	40.6	316	43.6
Support	447	60.7	409	56.8	330	44.8	385	53.1
Missing	10	1.4	6	0.8	107	14.5	24	3.3
Total	736	100	725	100	736	100	725	100

Notes: W1 = Wave 1; W2 = Wave 2

Table 3.A.4: Operationalisation

Variable	Description / Question	Operationalisation[23] (Reference Categories in *Italics*)	
	Social structure		
Gender	Dummy variable	1= Female, *0= Male*	
Age	Youngest group: born May 1998- December 1998	1= Young, 0= Other	
	Middle Group: born November 1997- April 1998	*1= Middle,* 0= Other	
	Oldest Group: born January 1996- October 1997	1= Old, 0= Other	
Migration background	Two subgroups plus an additional 'other' group. Taking into account the country of origin of the parents and their nationality.	*1= German,* 0= Other 1= Turkish, 0= Other	
SES family[24]	SES is constructed by taking into account the below characteristics. A PCA is performed and the factor scores are used to multiply as the weight of the below variables. As a last step, the parents are divided into three equally strong groups.	1 = Low *2 = Middle* 3 = High	low
Education	1: CSE and less		
	2: Secondary schools and equivalent		
	3: A-Levels/ University entrance diploma		

(Cont'd.)

---

23. In cases where several variables form an index, an average value was constructed by adding all values (same scale did apply) and dividing by the number of variables. We consistently used the approach to tolerate one or two missing values (depending on the number of variables).

24. If two parents have answered this question inconsistently, the maximum between the two has been considered.

Table 3.A.4: (Cont'd.)

Variable	Description / Question	Operationalisation (Reference Categories in Italics)
Professional status	0: Long-term unemployed; unskilled workers; retirees; housewife; househusband	
	1: Workers	
	2: Workers with staff responsibility, skilled workers; employees or self-employed without university qualification	
	3: Employees or self-employed with university qualification; skilled workers with staff responsibility; self-employed with staff responsibility but without university qualification	
	4: Employees with staff responsibility, self-employed with staff responsibility and university qualification	
Household income per person	1: up to 360 € per month	
	2: from 361 to 750 € per month	
	3: more than 750 € per month	
Children's value orientations		
Civic Virtues	The Civic Virtues variable is constructed by summarising 'Reward Helpfulness', 'Reward Hard Work' and 'Reward Law Abiding Behaviour'. The sum of these three variables is then divided by the number of valid values in these variables to normalise the index to a scale between 0 and 1.	Index with range of values: 0–1
Prestige	The Prestige variable is constructed by summarising 'Reward Popularity' and 'Reward Being Wealthy'. The sum of these two variables is then divided by 2 to normalise the index to a scale between 0 and 1.	Index with range of values: 0–1
Rules and Norms	The Rules and Norms variable is constructed by summarising 'Report Rule Breach', 'Importance Rules in General', 'Importance Personal Rule Adherence' and 'Keep Promises with Friends'. The sum of these four variables is then divided by the number of valid values in these variables to normalise the index to a scale between 0 and 1.	Index with range of values: 0–1
Gender Equality	The Gender Equality variable is constructed by summarising 'Use Tools equally', 'Work equally', 'Take Care of Children equally', 'Household	Index with range of values: 0–1

(Cont'd.)

Table 3.A.4: (Cont'd.)

Variable	Description / Question	Operationalisation (Reference Categories in Italics)
	Chores equally' and 'Drive the Car equally'. The sum of these five variables is then divided by the number of valid values in these variables to normalise the index to a scale between 0 and 1.	
	Parents' value orientations[25]	
Norm acceptance (Rules and Norms)	Evaluation of: 'cheating on taxes, theft in a store, avoiding a fare on public transport'. 1: Very bad 2: Fairly bad 3: Not so bad 4: Not bad at all	Index with range of values: 1–4
	'In your opinion, what are the characteristics of a good citizen'?	
Civic Virtues	Show solidarity with the needy; voting; political activity; autonomous opinion formation... 1: Important 2: Fairly important 3: Not so important 4: Unimportant	Index with range of values: 1–4
Prestige	...Religion; hard work; popularity; wealth? 1: Important 2: Fairly important 3: Not so important 4: Unimportant	Index with range of values: 1–4
Gender Equality	Evaluation of the following statements: 'Girls should learn about household chores; boys should primarily be taught to assume responsibility; girls should not learn traditional 'male' professions; girls and boys should not be raised the same way; it is especially important for boys to receive a good education; girls should learn a 'female' profession' 1: I fully agree 2: I rather agree 3: I rather don't agree 4: I don't agree at all	Index with range of values: 1–4

---

25. The indices are all constructed on the basis of a PCA.

Table 3.A.5: Used items (extract from the interviewer's questionnaire; item names in brackets; children's questionnaires were without text, the images were coloured)

2 🏆 ('Cup-Question')

Imagine, the 'boss' of Germany, or some other important person, comes to your city and would reward adults who are especially good citizens. We will now show you different images and tell you what they mean. Think about who should be rewarded/given a prize to and who not. Should a reward/prize be given to…?

		Yes	No
	Someone Going to Church (or to Mosque) Frequently? [Reward religious practice]	☺	☹
	Someone Helping Others? [Reward helping others]	☺	☹
	Someone working very hard? [Reward hard work]	☺	☹
	Someone everybody likes? [Reward popularity]	☺	☹

	Someone always obeying the rules? [Reward law abiding behaviour]	☺	☹
	Someone with a lot of money? [Reward being wealthy]	☺	☹

20 📻 ('Radio-Question')

There are many different people in the world. For example, there are tall and small ones, people with light or dark skin, people from different countries. What do you think, should all people be free to do the same? (e.g. should all be allowed to go to school or to go to the movies?) [Equality of rights]

☺	☹	?
Yes	No	Don't Know

35a ✉ ('Letter-Question')

Thinking about rules in school, for example to raise your hand in order to say something or to work quietly – What do you think: How important is it that such rules exist? [Importance Rules in General]

☺	😐	☹	?
Important	Not That Important	Unimportant	Don't Know

35b 🕯 ('Candle-Question')

And how important is it that you yourself obey these rules? [Importance personal rule adherence]

☺	😐	☹	?
Important	Not That Important	Unimportant	Don't Know

36a 👓 ('Sunglasses-Question')
Thinking about a promise, given to a friend - how important do you think is keeping a promise given to a friend? [Keep promises with friends]

☺   😐   ☹   ❓
Important   Not That Important   Unimportant   Don't Know

36b ❤ ('Heart-Question')
And how important do you think is keeping a promise given to someone you barely know? [Keep promises in general]

☺   😐   ☹   ❓
Important   Not That Important   Unimportant   Don't Know

34 ✿ ('Flower-Question')

We asked you before who is doing different things at your home. Now we will show you once again the images you have already seen; but this time our question is different, please pay attention. If it was up to you: should these things rather be done by **women**, by **men**, or rather by **both**?

		Women	Men	Both	Don't Know
	Use Tools [Equality of sexes: use tools]	○	○	○	?
	Go to Work [Equality of sexes: work]	○	○	○	?
	Take Care of Children [Equality of sexes: take care of children]	○	○	○	?
	Do the Chores [Equality of sexes: household chores]	○	○	○	?
	Drive the Car [Equality of sexes: drive the car]	○	○	○	?

Source: LLD Study (translated from German into English).

References

Abendschön, S. (2007) 'Demokratische Werte und Normen', in J. W. van Deth, S. Abendschön, J. Rathke and M. Vollmar, *Kinder und Politik. Politische Einstellungen von jungen Kindern im ersten Grundschuljahr*, Wiesbaden: VS Verlag, pp. 161–203.

— (2010) 'The beginning of democratic citizenship: Value orientations of young children', *Politics, Culture and Socialisation*, 1(1): 59–82.

Berton, M. and Schäfer, J. (2005) *Politische Orientierungen von Grundschulkindern. Ergebnisse von Tiefeninterviews und Pretests mit 6- bis 7- jährigen Kindern*, Mannheim: Mannheimer Zentrum für Europäische Sozialforschung, Working Paper 86.

Bertram, H. (2006) *Zur Lage des Kindes in Deutschland: Politik für Kinder als Zukunftsgestaltung*, Innocenti Working Paper 2006–02. Florence: UNICEF Innocenti Research Centre.

Boehnke, K. (2004) 'Werden unsere Kinder wie wir? in D. Hoffmann and H. Merkens (eds) *Jugendsoziologische Sozialisationstheorie. Impulse für die Jugendforschung*, Weinheim: Juventa: 109–126.

Bott, K. (2008) *Kriminalitätsvorstellungen in der Kindheit. Eine explorative, kriminalsoziologische Studie*, Wiesbaden: VS Verlag.

Cavalli-Sforza, L. L. and Feldman, M. W. (1981) *Cultural Transmission and Evolution: A quantitative approach*, Princeton: Princeton University Press.

Dalhouse, M. and Frideres, J. S. (1996) 'Intergenerational congruency: The role of the family in political attitudes of youth', *Journal of Family Issues*, 17(2): 227–248.

Dalton, R. J. (1982) 'The pathways of parental socialisation', *American Politics Quarterly*, 10(2): 139–157.

Feldman, S. (2003) 'Values, ideology, and the structure of political attitudes', in D. O. Sears, L. Huddy and R. Jervis (eds) *Oxford Handbook of Political Psychology*, Oxford: Oxford University Press: 477–510.

Flanagan, C. and Gallay, L. S. (1995) 'Reframing the meaning of 'political' in research with adolescents', *Perspectives on Political Science*, 24(1): 34–42.

Geißler, R. (1996) 'Politische Sozialisation in der Familie' in B. Claußen and R. Geißler (eds) *Die Politisierung des Menschen. Instanzen der politischen Sozialisation. Ein Handbuch*, Opladen: Leske + Budrich: 51–70.

Gill, B. (2005) *Schule in der Wissensgesellschaft. Ein soziologisches Studienbuch für Lehrerinnen und Lehrer,* Wiesbaden: VS Verlag.

Gilligan, C. (1982) *In a Different Voice: Psychological theory and women's development*, Cambridge, London: Harvard University Press.

Glass, J., Bengtson, V. L. and Chorn, D. C. (1986) 'Attitude similarity in three-generation families: socialisation, status inheritance, or reciprocal influence', *American Sociological Review*, 51(5): 685–698.

Grolnick, W., Deci, E. L. and Ryan, R. M. (1997) 'Internalization within the family: The self-determination theory perspective', in J. E. Grusec and L. Kuczynski (eds) *Parenting and Children's Internalization of Values. A handbook of contemporary theory*, New York: John Wiley and Sons: 135–161.

Hechter, M. and Opp, K.-D. (2001) 'Introduction', in M. Hechter and K.-D. Opp (eds) *Social Norms*, New York: Russel Sage Foundation: xi–xx.

Hess, R. D. and Torney, J. V. (1967) *The Development of Political Attitudes in Children*, Chicago: Aldine Publishing Company.

Hopf, C. and Hopf, W. (1997) *Familie, Persönlichkeit, Politik: Eine Einführung in die politische Sozialisation*, Weinheim, München: Juventa Verlag.

Hyman, H. H. (1959) *Political Socialisation: A study in the psychology of political behavior*, Glencoe Illinois: Free Press.

Jennings, M. K. (1984) 'The Intergenerational Transfer of Political Ideologies in Eight Western Nations', *European Journal of Political Research*, 12(3): 261–276.

— (1990) 'The crystallisation of orientations', in M. K. Jennings and J. W. van Deth (eds) *Continuities in Political Action: A longitudinal study of political orientations in three Western democracies*, Berlin, New York: Walter de Gruyter: 313–348.

— (2007) 'Political socialisation', in R. J. Dalton and H.-D. Klingemann (eds) *The Oxford Handbook of Political Behaviour*, Oxford: Oxford University Press: 29–44.

Jennings, M. K. and Langton, K. P. (1969) 'Mothers versus fathers: The formation of political orientations among young Americans', *The Journal of Politics*, 31(2): 329–358.

Jennings, M. K. and Niemi, R. G. (1968) 'The transmission of political values from parent to child', *American Political Science Review*, 62 (1): 169–184.

— (1974) *The Political Character of Adolescence: The influence of families and schools*, Princeton: Princeton University Press.

Kluckhohn, C. (1967) 'Values and value-orientations in the theory of action: An exploration in definition and classification', in T. Parsons and E. A. Shils (eds) *Toward a General Theory of Action*, Cambridge: Harvard University Press: 388–433.

Knafo, A. and Schwartz, S. H. (2003) 'Parenting and adolescents' accuracy in perceiving parental values', *Child Development*, 74(2): 595–611.

Kroh, M. (2007) 'A sibling study of value preferences: 20-year panel data on postmaterialism', paper presented at the Annual Meeting of the Midwest Political Science Association, Chicago, Illinois, USA, April 2007.

Kulke, C. (1998) 'Politische Sozialisation und Geschlechterdifferenz', in K. Hurrelmann and D. Ulich (eds) *Handbuch der Sozialisationsforschung*, Weinheim, Basel: Beltz Verlag: 595–613.

Niemi, R. G. (1974) 'Political learning', in R. G. Niemi (ed.) *The Politics of Future Citizens*, San Francisco, London: Jossey-Bass: 1–6.

Nunner-Winkler, G. (2001) 'Geschlecht und Gesellschaft', in H. Joas (ed.) *Lehrbuch der Soziologie*, Frankfurt am Main: Campus Verlag: 265–288.

Oesterreich, D. (2002) *Politische Bildung von 14-Jährigen in Deutschland. Studien aus dem Projekt Civic Education*, Opladen: Leske + Budrich.

Pedhazur, E. J. and Pedhazur Schmelkin, L. (1991) *Multiple Regression in Behavioral Research: Explanation and prediction,* New York: Holt, Rinehart, & Winston.

Percheron, A. and Jennings, M. K. (1981) 'Political continuity in French families', *Comparative Politics*, 13(4): 421–436.

Pye, L. W. (1968) 'Political Culture', in D. L. Sills (ed.) *International Encyclopedia of the Social Sciences, Volume 12*, New York: MacMillan: 218–224.

Rathke, J. (2007) 'Welche Fragen zum richtigen Zeitpunkt? Entwicklung eines standardisierten Kinderfragebogens', in J. W. van Deth, S. Abendschön, J. Rathke and M. Vollmar (eds) *Kinder und Politik. Politische Einstellungen von Kindern im ersten Grundschuljahr*, Wiesbaden: VS Verlag: 29–82.

Rieker, P. (2007) 'Fremdenfeindlichkeit und Sozialisation in Kindheit und Jugend', *Aus Politik und Zeitgeschichte*, 37: 31–38.

Searing, D. D., Schwartz, J. J. and Lind, A. E. (1973) 'The structuring principle: political socialisation and belief systems', *American Political Science Review*, 67(2): 415–435.

Searing, D. D., Wright, G. and Rabinowitz, G. (1976) 'The primacy principle: Attitude change and political socialisation', *British Journal of Political Science*, 6(1): 83–113.

Sears, D. O. (1983) 'The persistence of early political predispositions: The roles of attitude object and life stage', *Review of Personality and Social Psychology*, 4: 79–116.

Stoker, L. and Jennings, M. K. (2005) 'Political similarity and influence between husbands and wives', in A. S. Zuckerman (ed.) *The Social Logic of Politics: Personal networks as contexts for political behavior*, Philadelphia: Temple University Press: 51–74.

Sugarman, S. (2007) *If Kids could Vote*, Lanham: Lexington Books.

van Deth, J. W. and Scarbrough, E. (1995) 'The concept of values', in J. W. van Deth and E. Scarbrough (eds) *The Impact of Values*, New York: Oxford University Press: 21–47.

van Deth, J. W., Abendschön, S., Rathke, J. and Vollmar, M. (2007) *Kinder und Politik. Politische Einstellungen von jungen Kindern im ersten Grundschuljahr*, Wiesbaden: VS Verlag.

van Deth, J. W., Abendschön, S. and Vollmar, M. (2011) 'Children and politics: An empirical reassessment of early political socialisation', *Political Psychology*, 32(1): 147–74.

Verba, S., Burns, N. and Schlozman, K. L. (2003) 'Unequal at the starting line: Creating participatory inequalities across generations and among groups', *The American Sociologist*, 34(1–2): 45–69.

Wittebrood, K. (1995) *Politieke socialisatie in Nederland. Een onderzoek naar de verwerving en ontwikkeling van politieke houdingen van havo- en vwoleerlingen*, Amsterdam: Thesis Publishers.

Youniss, J. (1980) *Parents and Peers in Social Development: A Sullivan-Piaget perspective*, Chicago: University of Chicago Press.

Zuckerman, A. S., Fitzgerald, J. and Dasovic, J. (2005) 'Do Couples Support the Same Political Party? "Sometimes": Evidence from British and German Household Surveys', in A. S. Zuckerman (ed.) *The Social Logic of Politics: Personal networks as contexts for political behavior*, Philadelphia: Temple University Press: 75–94.

Chapter Four

The Role of Schools in Preparing 16- and 17-year-old Austrian First-Time Voters for the Election

Steve Schwarzer and Eva Zeglovits

No doubt school is an important agent of political socialisation. Nevertheless, with respect to political participation in societies, the explanatory power of schooling is limited, as students, due to their age, are usually not eligible to vote or to become a candidate for elections. Voting is the only form of participation which is not open to high school students in most countries (Zukin *et al.* 2006). This changed when Austria lowered the voting age to sixteen in 2007.

This reform not only opened formal political participation to students, it also enabled researchers to review and analyse one specific direct impact of schools on political socialisation. In the scientific discussion on lowering the voting age, Franklin (2004) promotes a voting age as low as fifteen years as he assumed that this might have a positive impact on people's political involvement. His main argument is that first-time voters can then be prepared for their first election in school. He further expects that where this is accompanied by school activities and projects, the first election would be a 'good experience', allowing young voters to be prepared and hence to make an informed choice. In fact, public authorities in Austria accompanied the electoral reform with a bundle of measures including a change in school curricula to strengthen civic education; and awareness-raising campaigns and projects that reached a large proportion of young people via schools. Political elites gave schools a key role in implementing the reform and in preparing young people for their newly-achieved right to vote. This makes Austria an interesting case for the evaluation of whether Franklin's conjecture holds true, that is, if schools do contribute to preparing young voters for their first elections.

In this chapter we want to evaluate this assumption from the perspective of students. We will provide an in-depth understanding of how students recognised the role of schools in preparing them for their first formal political participation.

School as an agent of political socialisation – a short review

Individuals are not born as adults. The concept of political socialisation describes how individuals find their place in the political community and how they develop their individual norms and attitudes towards political objects, actors, symbols and processes. Political socialisation can be defined as a learning process through which the individual learns political attitudes and behaviours from generation to generation, influenced by political socialisation agents.

While some authors claim that political attitudes are already formed in the preadolescent years (Hyman 1959), others agree with the observation of Almond and Verba (1963) that the sources of political attitudes are many and can be found from early childhood to adolescence into adulthood. Any activity that puts young people in touch with a political or societal activity accompanied by an adult is likely to be part of the socialisation process (McIntosh and Youniss, 2010); this is why parents and schools are so important.

Bearing in mind the compulsory education system, school is an institution which has the power to socialise (Delli Carpini and Keeter 1996; Torney-Purta 2002a; Verba et al. 1995). Young people meet and interact with their peers in schools; in addition they interact with teachers. Early research suggested that school had little or no effect on students' political knowledge and political behaviour, a conclusion based largely on the research of Langton and Jennings (1968) in the 1960s. This result was not questioned until Niemi and Junn (1998) published their analysis of the civics exam included in the 1988 National Assessment of Educational Progress (NAEP). Contradicting Langton and Jennings, they claim that the civic curriculum has 'an impact of a size and resilience that makes it a significant part of political learning' (ibid.: 145) and conclude that taking civics courses has a significant impact on adolescents' levels of political knowledge.

But how can civic education be characterised? The theoretical discussion shows two models of civic education in schools: the traditional model of direct citizenship education and the indirect model, which is more related to processes of participation and decision making instead of teaching (Solomon et al. 2001; Torney-Purta 2002b). The direct model is related to Durkheim, who states that the same hierarchical orders operate in school as in society. Therefore, adolescents are prepared for society by going to school (Durkheim 1961). Following the direct citizenship model, schools are responsible for the transfer of knowledge.

In contrast, the indirect model can be traced back to the political philosophers Dewey (1966) and Kohlberg (1958). They believe that school is the institution where the youngest come in contact with the norms and value system of a community and that these norms should be part of everyday school life and of all the processes within a school. They place importance on the daily life and political and social culture of a school, especially the interaction of teachers and students as observable in their daily interaction and the school climate. Unlike in the case of didactic teaching, students learn about the rules, ideas and institutions of the political and societal system through participating in discussions. But, following the indirect model, political awareness is not only a question of teaching civic education. It is also about providing the experience of and strengthening self-efficacy through participating in decision-making processes. Flanagan et al. describe the function of schools as providing a place where one can learn to deal with a community: 'Schools are like mini polities where children can explore what it means to be a member of a community beyond their families' (Flanagan et al. 1998: 462). School democracy has the potential to be a field of practice for young people, because there they can have their first experiences of collective decision-making processes or even elections. School is the place where adolescents learn about the norms and values of a society (Henkenborg 2005). This again is associated with a deeper understanding of political processes or higher levels of political efficacy (Torney-Purta 2002a). Teachers have important roles as they are in a position to influence knowledge, attitudes and behaviour (Torney-Purta 2002a). The influence of peers is usually also seen within the context of schools (Campbell 1980; Yates and Youniss 1998) as classmates are most likely to form crucial parts of the peer group.

Recently both the direct and the indirect model of civic education have been used to explain how socialisation works in school by transferring civic knowledge in the form of civic education, and through the practising of politics in interaction with other students and teachers (Galston 2001; Galston 2004; Kirlin 2003; Lauglo and Øia 2008; Saha 2000; Tonge *et al.* 2012). If this is so, school could be seen as an institution that plays an important role in augmenting (Zukin *et al.* 2006) or even altering the primary socialisation of young people within families (Scherr 2008). Nevertheless, we still have 'a limited understanding of how schools do, or do not, foster political engagement among their adolescent students' (Campbell 2008: 438). In particular, little is known about the impact of school on preparing young people for participating in elections.

We next have to ask, what does it mean in particular to be prepared for an election? Public debate concentrated on the political interest, political knowledge and political participation of young people (or their possible lack of it). So what are the indicators that show whether young people are 'ready' to vote for the first time? In quantitative approaches, Hoskins and Mascherini defined indicators for active citizenship for adults (Hoskins and Mascherini 2008) including democratic values and various political activities. Torney-Purta *et al.* (2008) focus on adolescents and define indicators of 'preparation for civic life' that include indicators of knowledge and skills in the interpretation of political communication; democratic values and attitudes; trust in institutions; political efficacy; participation in school and organisations; and expected civic participation. As discussed above, several of these concepts are known to be affected by schools. In the particular case of being prepared for participating in an election, Franklin (2004) additionally takes into account how far young voters feel prepared for their first election, as he holds that the quality of the experience matters. Learning the essence of politics, learning to understand that the fundamentals of politics are present in everyday life – in school, in the family and within peer networks – makes students aware of the importance of political behaviour. Furthermore, the quality of experience also refers to the context that is required in order to support students and young individuals to develop their understanding of politics – engagement and decision making in schools needs to have a real perspective. Students need to feel that their engagement and their voice matters.

As mentioned above, Franklin (2004) presumes that, if the voting age were lowered to fifteen, the importance of schools would become even greater, as schools would be the place where young newly-eligible voters were prepared for their first election in 'a civic class project'.

This is where Austria comes into the picture. Due to the fact that Austria has lowered the voting age to sixteen, we can use these findings to examine whether and how young people *felt* prepared for their first election and what role schools played in the process of preparation.

Students are the objects of research on civic and citizenship education studies. They usually do not appear as subjects, meaning their perspective on civic education and political experiences is more or less absent from the debate. We argue that focusing on students' perceptions of how schools can prepare them for their role as citizens and voters will deepen our understanding of political socialisation processes in schools. Hence we examine how newly-enfranchised 16- and 17-year-olds in Austria experienced their first election. We want to answer the questions: did students feel prepared enough, and, more importantly, how did they perceive the role of schools within these processes?

The context: federal elections in Austria and regional elections in Vienna

Austria is the first of the EU member states, and one of the first countries in the world, to have a voting age of sixteen for all general elections, including European parliamentary elections. Austria lowered the voting age step by step, with some regions (*Länder*) leading the way when they lowered the voting age for regional and local elections in the first years of the twenty-first century. The city of Vienna followed this trend and lowered the voting age to sixteen in 2005.

In 2007 an electoral reform at national level set the voting age at sixteen years for all nationwide elections, including federal elections, presidential elections and elections for the European Parliament, as well as all forms of plebiscites (Hofer *et al.* 2008).

The electoral law reforms – regional and federal – were both accompanied by a package of measures. In the Viennese election campaign of 2005, when 16- and 17-year-olds were eligible to vote for the first time in Vienna, a range of projects for the youngest voters were launched by the city and its school authorities, including mock elections in schools and discussions with politicians. Information and awareness-raising campaigns accompanied these efforts with some degree of success (Karlhofer 2007). In 2008, activities accompanying the election included an awareness-raising campaign and some changes to the way in which civic and citizenship education were embedded in school curricula (BMUKK 2011). In Austria, civic and citizenship education was introduced as a subject only at the beginning of the winter term 2008, in combination with history and social studies in the eighth grade in all types of schools. Until then, civics was a horizontal teaching domain (taught in all subjects and at all school levels – from primary school up to general secondary education). Interestingly, this horizontal teaching domain was not replaced or affected by the reform of civic and citizenship education. Although the change in the curricula came into force only some weeks before the first general election and concerned younger pupils rather than the newly-enfranchised voters, it added to the impression that schools were assigned a key role in preparing first-time voters. The Austrian national assembly launched a project called 'democracy workshop' ('*DemokratieWerkstatt*') in October 2007, which has been inviting school classes to the Austrian Parliament ever since to participate in workshops and experience what happens in parliament. More than 41,000 adolescents attended the 'democracy workshop' between October 2007 and December 2011 (Austrian Parliament 2011: 72). Democracy workshops in Austria follow a similar approach to the democracy workshops in Scandinavian countries, where the aim is not only to take a tour of Parliament and learn what goes on there, but to experience and get involved in the decision-making process, e.g. through role-playing (Milner 2009). Although some of the projects took place outside of schools, the majority of activities were delivered in some way via schools. It might have even escaped the students' notice that certain activities within a school were part of these measures and campaigns (e.g. a discussion in school with local politicians might have been organised by teachers acting on the suggestions of public authorities).

Speculation regarding the turnout and electoral choices of newly-enfranchised voters was intense in the weeks preceding the election in 2008 (Lengauer and Vorhofer 2010). This is why we consider the lowering of the voting age as more than simply an electoral reform. Rather, it is a publicly-discussed event accompanied by selective measures.

Furthermore, there are several preliminary quantitative findings on young voters after Austria lowered the voting age, which suggest for example that interest in politics has increased since 2004; that the impact of schools on political interest has also increased (Zeglovits and Zandonella forthcoming); that turnout among 16- and 17-year-olds is high (Zeglovits 2011); and that the quality of voting choice is also high (Wagner *et al.* 2012). Earlier analysis had shown that, in Austria, knowledge and school activities had an impact on two forms of political participation: participating in a legal demonstration and trying to persuade someone to vote for a specific party or candidate in 2004 (before the voting age was lowered). It had also shown that interest in politics was positively correlated with various school activities, e.g. discussing the elections with a teacher (Schwarzer and Zeglovits 2009).

These preliminary results indicate that Dewey's (1966) indirect model of civic education is applicable: when projects and activities were carried out in schools they had an impact on young voters. What remains unexplored is how young voters link civic education and activities in schools with their experience of voting for the first time.

Data and method

To answer our research question of how young Austrians experienced their first elections and whether they perceived that schools did make a contribution, we will first present some quantitative data that illustrate *(a)* how many of the newly enfranchised voters are enrolled in the educational system and can in fact be influenced by schools; and *(b)* how many students report school activities preceding the elections. We use the survey results to help frame the qualitative findings. More importantly, we will use in-depth interviews to analyse how students experienced the preparations their schools made for their first elections.

By employing a qualitative approach, we follow recommendations which suggest that qualitative methods might capture a more accurate picture when investigating how young people experience politics (O'Toole et al. 2003; Henn et al. 2002). The top-down approach, typical of quantitative methods, may capture only some aspects of the relevant experiences. As we do not aim to measure attitudes but to examine experiences and perceptions, the qualitative approach allows us to address all kinds of experiences and perceptions without needing to define them beforehand.

The data we use to illustrate the Austrian case are two post-election studies conducted among the youngest eligible voters. This approach has some major limitations: the findings are limited to young people's view of things shortly after the elections. The second important limitation is, of course, the fact that we are not able to validate these findings against other elections, as the only data available relate to the first elections held after the voting age was reduced to sixteen. One study was carried out after the first regional election in Vienna after the lowering of the voting age in 2005 (Ogris et al. 2005), the other after the first federal election with a general voting age of sixteen in 2008 (Schwarzer et al. 2009). Both studies included a survey and in-depth interviews[1] with 16- and 17-year-olds (eleven interviews in 2005 and twelve interviews in 2008). The 2008 study also included two focus groups[2] with young voters aged sixteen to eighteen, one group with nine and one with ten participants. The interviews and focus groups were audio-taped and transcribed. We will refer to interviewees in the post-federal elections group as FED#; to the interviewees in the post-Viennese elections group as VIE#; and to focus groups participants of 2008 as FOC#.

We analysed the qualitative data in two ways following the distinction between the direct and indirect models of civic education. First, we focused on whether interviewees perceived schools as transferring knowledge or information when they discussed their experiences of the elections and their preparation. This accords with the direct model of civic education and will be easily identified by students. In a second step, we examined whether students reported more experiences of being prepared in schools, experiences that reflect the indirect model of civic education. Students will most likely not explicitly recognise these experiences as preparations for the elections. Nevertheless, the latter will complete the picture on the role played by schools in preparing first-time voters for the elections.

As our research question focuses on the impact of schools, we limited our analysis to people aged sixteen or seventeen attending a school or vocational college.

---

1. The interviews were carried out in the weeks after the elections and analysed for the project report by Dr. Ulrike Kozeluh. We used transcripts for this analysis.

2. The focus groups were carried out in Vienna, about a month after the federal elections and analysed for the project report by Dr. Flooh Perlot, Institut für Strategieanalysen. We used transcripts for this analysis.

Table 4.1: Students enrolled in schools by age (numbers)

Age at time of survey[a]	Enrolled in school		Apprentices enrolled in vocational education		Total attending school		Residents	
	Vienna	Austria	Vienna	Austria	Vienna	Austria	Vienna[b]	Austria
16	11,730	58,517	5,287	33,452	17,017	91,969	16,558	100,606
17	10,627	51,821	5,533	36,823	16,160	88,644	16,403	100,687

Notes: a. Vienna: age on 1 September 2006; Austria: age on 1 September 2008; b. the city of Vienna has more students/apprentices than inhabitants due to 'education commuters' who attend school in Vienna but live outside. Nevertheless, the data suggest that the great majority of 16- and 17-year-olds appear to be enrolled in a school.
Source: Statistik Austria.

What happened in Austrian schools?

Before examining the impact of schools, we must first establish how many 16- and 17-year-olds are enrolled in a school and therefore have the chance to be prepared for the elections in schools. Table 4.1 compares student numbers with the total numbers in the cohorts that cover the newly-enfranchised voters in the regional elections of 2005[3] and the federal elections of 2008. It is immediately apparent that a large proportion of 16- and 17-year-old inhabitants attend a school. Austria has a dual system for apprenticeships, in that apprentices are enrolled in vocational colleges which they attend alongside working at their placement. This holds true for the regional election in Vienna as well as the federal election.

Although the tables do not tell us exactly how many eligible voters are enrolled in a school, as they include people who are not Austrian nationals and people do not necessarily have to attend a school in the region where they live, it nevertheless suggests that about 90 per cent of 16- and 17-year-old Austrians were enrolled in a school in 2008 (when the federal election took place) and probably an even higher percentage in Vienna in 2006. Thus, restricting the sample to people attending a school does not significantly limit the generalisability of the data.

Having established the proportion of 16- and 17-year-olds covered by our analysis, we will now briefly describe their perceptions of the measures accompanying the first elections. Table 4.2 shows that very a high proportion of students reported some kind of election-related activities in schools.

Apprentices attending vocational colleges experienced significantly fewer activities than other students. This holds true for both the 2005 Viennese regional elections and the federal elections in 2008. Ninety-one per cent of students and 76 per cent of apprentices enrolled in colleges reported at least one activity in school preceding the regional elections in Vienna in 2005; and nearly all students and

---

3.   No data are available for 2005, so we used the 2006 data as a reasonable proxy.

Table 4.2: Reported activities in schools preceding federal and regional elections (Austria, 2008 and Vienna, 2006)

% reporting each activity	Austria, 2008		Vienna, 2005	
	Students	**Apprentices**	**Students**	**Apprentices**
Did school call attention to the elections	91	73	79	65
Did school inform you about the lowering of the voting age	89	81	76	64
Did school host a project related to the elections	--	--	26	16
Did school carry out mock elections	--	--	33	27
Did school host a discussion with politicians	29	15	23	13
Did you talk to a teacher about elections	76	27	63	46
Did a teacher summon you to participate in the election?	41	17	29	18
Any of these activities	98	87	91	76
N	525	142	507	111

Sources: post-election surveys, 16- and 17-year-old eligible voters, data weighted according to demographic structure (age, gender, region).

87 per cent of apprentices did so throughout Austria before the federal elections of 2008. Of course, schools addressed students in a wide variety of forms. Most commonly, students reported that schools called attention to the elections or informed them of the lowered voting age. In addition, many students reported that they had talked to their teachers about the elections. School-based projects, mock elections or discussions with politicians, which are mentioned in Franklin's (2004) approach, did not constitute a majority of the activities reported; nevertheless a large proportion of students did report these kinds of activities.

Most young Austrian (and Viennese) voters were apparently targeted by schools in some way, but *(a)* in many cases this seems to have involved less intensive activities, such as simply informing students of the lowering of the voting age; and *(b)* in the case of the more intensive activities, such as discussing the election with a teacher, there is a wide gap between high school students and apprentices attending a vocational college. This gap is even wider in the 2008 federal elections than in the 2005 Viennese elections.

Experiencing the first election at age sixteen or seventeen

What does it mean when young voters report in a survey that they have talked to teachers, or that their school informed them about the elections?

Interviewees were asked about their information-seeking behaviour, about political orientations (e.g. how they politically comprehend left and right), how they made their voting choices, how they experienced casting their ballot and how they feel today about the elections. There were no explicit questions about school. Nevertheless, the topic of school came up in many contexts during the interviews. Generally speaking, respondents in the interviews after the federal elections mentioned school more often than the persons interviewed after the regional elections in Vienna 2005, which is consistent with the higher numbers of school activities reported in the survey (Table 4.2).

It should be noted that young eligible voters in Austria expressed a feeling of obligation to become informed before casting their ballot and simultaneously assigned the responsibility for providing this information to schools, which perfectly fits the direct model of citizenship education. When interviewees were asked how they would like to be informed in the future,[4] schools, families and media were mentioned.

Well, at school [...], then newspapers, of course. And I will talk about it with my family again. (FED2)

Well, not from the internet again, but of course more material. [...] Yes, school, I do hope so [...]. In any case, I would like to get some information packs in fact, something written, that you can read. (FED5)

Well, I need some general information, because I don't know a lot [...]. I think it's best if you talk about it in school. (FED6)

In one of the focus groups, this idea of schools being responsible for getting young voters informed did come up and was not contradicted by any of the participants.

FOC1: There could be more civic education in school, particularly in the lower grades, that prepares you.

FOC8: And more clarification on everything.

FOC6: So that you start to get interested earlier in the topic [of politics], when it starts earlier in school.

FOC2: We have 'civic education and law' in school, but we went to vote before this subject started. We talked about that at the beginning of the [academic] year and many said that they did not vote because they did not have enough information. (...)

FOC8: True, because if you don't come across it in your family or in school,

---

4. This question was only asked in the in-depth interviews after the 2008 federal elections.

where else? What 16-year-old watches the [news on TV] every day and gets informed all by himself? We also have this class (...) and we dealt with the federal elections in much detail, and this is why it became interesting for us.

When students discussed the period before the election, the school was explicitly thought of as an information provider, reflecting the model of direct civic education in most of the interviews. Respondents reported that they received information regarding the elections at school:

We discussed the elections in, I think, three different classes, including geography, we had presentations on the different parties. (FED12)

We got a lot from our teachers, a lot of information. (FED8)

Everybody got these information packs, including our family. Then we discussed it in school, in civic education. We discussed [...] party manifestos [...], the polling stations, with the ballot box, etc., everything, how it is done. (VIE5)

Receiving information at school is regarded as matter of course. Some respondents even complained that the school had failed to provide them with information. In these cases, the school did not meet respondents' needs, and again, the school was assigned the role of information provider. One explicitly blamed a teacher for not informing them properly, when recalling the casting of her ballot:

No, I didn't know precisely, that you go there [the polling station], that you sign up, with an identification card. [...] Yes, we do have politics, but we have such a confused teacher, who does not know his stuff. (FED9)

We did discuss things in school, but actually my mum told me what happens at the election. (VIE4)

However, school was not only perceived as a place where information is provided, but also as a place where you can discuss political matters, either in class with teachers or informally in between classes with peers, pointing to the importance of respondents' social integration in school for political behaviour (Settle *et al.* 2011).

In my class, two people are in the FPOE[5], something to do with youth, the youth wing [...]. Yes, they are involved in that, and I talked to them as well. (FED8)

In school, we talk sometimes [...], during breaks, of our own accord, not in front of a teacher (...). We don't always agree, everybody says different things. (FED6)

Before the elections, it was the thing we talked about most in our free time. Because some [classmates] had become campaign workers. One for each party, one for the Greens, one for the Blacks, one for the Reds [...] and one for the Blues. (VIE2)

---

5.   FPOE= Austrian Freedom Party, a populist radical right wing party.

One respondent explicitly reported that discussions in school made him cast his ballot; otherwise he would have been a non-voter:

First, I thought about not voting, because [...] I am simply not interested and I thought, well, I don't know much anyway. [...] Yes, but then we talked a lot in school about it, and we did a lot [...]. Yes, and then everybody said, it's stupid not to vote, that every vote counts. (FED6)

The same young man also stated that he changed his mind about his party choice because of discussions in school. He had obviously relied on the result of online voting advice provided by *wahlkabine.at*,[6] but came to understand the advice and the questions used by the decision-making tool better after discussing them in school:

Then we talked in school, we analysed the questions and then I changed my mind, because I had interpreted some of the questions wrongly. (FED6)

In addition, there is also evidence that schools triggered political information-seeking behaviour. When asked about reading newspapers or online newspapers, most people reported that they read the newspapers that were available at home or the free newspapers found on public transport in Austria. They only bought a newspaper or did online research in newspaper archives if required for school:

I will buy 'Der Standard'[7] again tomorrow, basically because I need it for school. (FED9)

Online? Only for research. (FED2)

Reflecting Franklin's (2004) idea of schools preparing students for their first election and thus making the first election a good experience, students report several activities, such as mock elections.

Several respondents described casting a ballot as not especially challenging, because they had held a mock election in school:

Yes, we had some mock elections in school (...) where we got a ballot paper that looked just like the real one. That made it easier. (FED7)

We have the same teacher in history and psychology and she carried out mock elections in class before the regional elections and discussed things with us. (VIE9)

We held mock elections in class. (VIE5)

One interviewee mentioned that a politics-related project conducted in school raised his awareness of political issues, which again supports what Franklin (2004) holds, that projects in school have an impact:

---

6.   *wahlkabine.at* is an online voting advice application which 'serves as a quick guideline through party opinions and helps to compare your political views with those of the parties in full anonymity' (*see* www.wahlkabine.at).

7.   One of the leading newspapers in Austria.

Basically, you become more aware of politics, you spot the little things, like when there is [a notice] in a side-column in the newspaper that another bank went broke in America, or that a bill was carried, you basically question what is said more. (FED1)

When reflecting on their experience of the first election, interviewees emphasised two main differences: being more informed and having a greater sense of political efficacy.

The most frequent comment about their first election was that they felt obliged to inform themselves, and this changed their information-seeking behaviour. They made an effort to become informed in order to be able to make a choice. Interviewees also said that they are now better informed and more aware of political issues.

I definitely have more knowledge now. (FED6)

Not that I carried on reading newspapers all the time, but before I didn't really follow [politics] – I mean, I knew roughly which parties there were, but now, not till now, I know much better. (FED11)

Well, not until I paid attention to [politics], which started six months ago [...] that's when I noticed how interesting and exciting it can be, and since then I've carried on observing it. (FED10)

Well, I thought that you really should get informed and not, for example, just vote for the same party just because you have been voting for this party for twenty years, but you should really decide what most appeals to you. (FED7)

I probably became more aware of what things are associated with right wing parties and the people that have this kind of ideology [...]. And I tried to check whether the problems they always denounce really exist. That has affected me. (FED1)

Second, we find young people expressing a sense that they can influence change and that their interests are taken into account. This can be interpreted as political self-efficacy, which is one of the indicators of preparedness for civic life (Torney-Purta *et al.* 2008).

It was nice in a way to see that what you think [...] counts, even if it is only a tiny, tiny fraction, but it counts, and I appreciate that. (FED9)

... that I can take part in decision making, that I can raise my voice [...] And [my voice] counts, ultimately. (VIE6)

This leads us to conclude that young people in Austria came out of this first voting experience with a positive feeling, which relates back to Franklin's quality of experience.

Conclusion

To sum up, we can demonstrate that for 16- and 17-year-old eligible voters in Austria, school is indeed perceived as an important agent of political socialisation, including preparation for participation in an election. To regard voting as the only form of political participation that is not possible for high school students and that cannot therefore be affected by schools (Zukin *et al.* 2006), no longer applies in the Austrian case.

First, schools in Austria have the potential to reach a large proportion of enfranchised young people. Although compulsory school attendance ends before young people are enfranchised, most of them continue to attend school or vocational college.

Second, large proportions of 16- and 17-year-old newly-enfranchised voters reported activities in schools that were related to the elections. Franklin's (2004) surmise that schools might play a key role in preparing young people for their first election by means of different projects holds true for both the elections that were examined here. But schools did not target all students equally. For both elections, we observe a remarkable gap between high schools and vocational colleges. In high schools, a larger proportion of young people reported school activities. We thus observe a bias in political activities, i.e., that most political education programmes do not reflect the fact that a considerable number of students are enrolled in vocational colleges.

Third, our findings indicate that schools played a role in preparing young people for an election in many ways: according to the direct model of civic education, schools were successfully circulating information and imparting knowledge. Here, schools fulfilled the youth's expectations of what it means to be prepared: namely the ability to make an informed choice. 16- and 17-year-old Austrians report that they made some effort to become informed and thus prepared and that school played a crucial role in providing this information, alongside families, newspapers and television. Schools are assigned a prominent role in this information-gathering process. On the one hand, the interviews show that schools and teachers did in fact provide young people with information that enabled them to make an informed choice. On the other hand, young people actively assign this role to schools – they want schools to provide objective information on elections, the choices they have, how the system works, the fact that their participation is important and worthwhile. The results hold true for both the 2008 federal elections and the 2005 regional elections, but in 2008 the impact of school seems to have been even more visible or perceptible to young people. As explained by the indirect model, schools provided opportunities to discuss and reflect on opinions, to practice politics. Interestingly enough, young people do not explicitly ask for opportunities for discussion in schools as they seem to reduce the school's role to providing information. Nevertheless, they repeatedly talked about informal discussions among classmates and formal discussions within classes. They themselves emphasise the fact that political discussions are an essential part of civic education, even if they do not explicitly realise what it is precisely that civic education entails. Nevertheless, school is the institution in which the youngest are introduced to the norms and value systems of a community and are taught that these norms should be part of their everyday life in school and permeate all the processes within a school. They attribute importance to the daily life and the political and social culture of a school, especially the interaction of teachers and students as expressed in the school's customs and climate. Students learn about the rules, ideas and institutions of the political and societal system through participating in discussions, rather than through explicit teaching. They learn that democratically organised processes deal with different individual interests and that democracy can cope with these kinds of different positions within arguments. Arguments and discussions are part of the political sphere and could be an emotional barrier to participation in politics.

Schools in Austria helped young people to some extent to become informed, to reflect on their opinions among peers. All the different measures which took place in schools raised awareness of political issues and stimulated a sense of political efficacy.

Of course, these findings are limited. Most importantly, we can never be sure about causalities in an empirical setting like this. In addition, the first elections in Austria might be exposed to a Hawthorne effect: we cannot necessarily project schools' key role onto future elections, when voting at sixteen is no longer new and when efforts to prepare 16- and 17-year-olds might decline.

Nevertheless, we find evidence strong enough to support Franklin's conjecture that schools might add something to make one's first election a positive experience. Further research needs to address the link between civic education programmes and political participation. So far, we do not know enough about what really triggers political participation in general and the participation in elections of first-timers in particular. In order to shed light on this particular aspect, research needs to deploy more quantitative and qualitative parent-child projects.

References

Almond, G. A. and Verba, S. (1963) *The Civic Culture: Political attitudes and democracy in five nations*, Princeton: Princeton University Press.

Austrian Parliament (2011) *Jahresbericht 2011 Nationalrat*, Wien.

BMUKK [Federal Ministry of Education, Arts and Culture] (2011) *Entscheidend bist du!* Online. Available: http://www.bmukk.gv.at/schulen/ebd/archiv/index.xml (accessed 9 September 2011).

Campbell, B. A. (1980) 'A theoretical approach to peer influence in adolescent socialization', *American Journal of Political Science*, 24: 324–344.

Campbell, D. E. (2008) 'Voice in the classroom: How an open classroom climate fosters political engagement among adolescents', *Political Behavior*, 30: 437–454.

Delli Carpini, M. X. and Keeter, S. (1996) *What Americans Know about Politics and Why it Matters*, Yale: University Press.

Dewey, J. (1966) *Democracy and Education*, New York: Free Press.

Durkheim, E. (1961) *Moral Education*, New York: Free Press.

Flanagan, C. A., Bowes, J. M., Jonsson, B., Csapo, B. and Sheblanova, E. (1998) 'Ties that bind: Correlates of adolescents' civic commitments in seven countries', *Journal of Social Issues*, 54: 457–475.

Franklin, M. N. (2004) *Voter Turnout and the Dynamics of Electoral Competition in Established Democracies since 1945*, Cambridge: Cambridge University Press.

Galston, W. A. (2001) 'Political knowledge, political engagement and civic education', *Annual Review of Political Science*, 4: 217–234.

—   (2004) 'Civic education and political participation', *Political Science and Politics*, 37 (2): 263–266.

Henkenborg, P. (2005) 'Politische Bildung als Schulprinzip: Demokratie-Lernen im Schulalltag', in W. Sander (ed.) *Handbuch Politische Bildung*, Schwalbach am Taunus: Wochenschau Verlag.

Henn, M., Weinstein, M. and Wring, D. (2002) 'A generation apart? Youth and political participation in Britain', *British Journal of Politics and International Relations*, 4: 167–192.

Hofer, V., Ladner, K. and Reichmann, G. (2008) 'Herabsetzung des Wahlalters auf 16 Jahre – Fortschritt oder Irrweg', *Journal für Rechtspolitik*, 16: 27–32.

Hoskins, B. and Mascherini, M. (2008) 'Measuring active citizenship through the development of a composite indicator', *Social Indicators Research*, 90: 459–488.

Hyman, H. H. (1959) *Political Socialization*, Glencoe, Illinois: Free Press.

Karlhofer, F. (2007) 'Wählen mit 16: Erwartungen und Perspektiven', *Informationen zur Politischen Bildung*, 27: 37–42.

Kirlin, M. (2003) *The Role of Civic Skills in Fostering Civic Engagement*, CIRCLE Working Paper. Online. Available: http://www.civicyouth.org/PopUps/WorkingPapers/WP06Kirlin.pdf (accessed 28 May 2013).

Kohlberg, L. (1958) *The Development of Modes of Moral Thinking and Choice in the Years Ten to Sixteen*, Chicago: University of Chicago.

Langton, K. and Jennings, M. K. (1968) 'Political socialization and the high school civics curriculum in the United States', *American Political Science Review*, 62: 862–867.

Lauglo, J. and Øia, T. (2008) 'Education and civic engagement among Norwegian youth', *Policy Futures in Education*, 6: 203–223.

Lengauer, G. and Vorhofer, H. (2010) *Wahlkampf am und abseits des journalistischen Boulevards: Redaktionelle Politikvermittlung im Nationalratswahlkampf 2008.* In F. Plasser (ed.) *Politik in der Medienarena. Praxis politischer kommunikation in Österreich,* Wien: facultas.wuv: 145–192.

McIntosh, H. and Youniss, J. (2010) 'Toward a political theory of political socialization of youth', in L. R. Sherrod, J. V. Torney-Purta and C. A. Flanagan (eds) *Handbook of Research on Civic Engagement in Youth*, Hoboken, New Jersey: Wiley.

Milner, H. (2009) 'Youth electoral participation in Canada and Scandinavia', in J. Youniss and P. Levine (eds) *Engaging Young People in Civic Life,* Nashville and Vanderbildt: University Press.

Niemi, R. G. and Junn, J. (1998) *Civic Education: What makes students learn?* New Haven: Yale University Press.

Ogris, G., Kozeluh, U., Kromer, I., Nitsch, S., Reichmann, A., and Zuba, R. (2005) *Wählen heißt erwachsen werden! Analyse des Wahlverhaltes 16- bis 18-jähriger Jugendlicher bei den Wiener Landtagswahlen 2005.* Online. Available: http://www.sora.at/fileadmin/downloads/projekte/2005_nachwahlanalyse-wien_gesamtbericht.pdf (accessed 28 May 2013).

O'Toole, T., Lister, M., Marsh, D., Jones, S. and McDonagh, A. (2003) 'Tuning out or left out? Participation and non-participation among young people', *Contemporary Politics*, 9: 45–61.

Saha, L. J. (2000) 'Political activism and civic education among Australian secondary school students', *Australian Journal of Education*, 44: 155–174.

Scherr, A. (2008) 'Sozialisation, Person, Individuum', in H. Korte and B. Schäfers (eds) *Einführung in die Hauptbegriffe der Soziologie*, Wiesbaden: VS Verlag für Sozialwissenschaft.

Schwarzer, S., Zandonella, M., Zeglovits, E., Perlot, F. and Kozeluh, U. (2009) *Wählen mit 16' Eine Post Election Study zur Nationalratswahl 2008. Befragung-Fokusgruppen-Tiefeninterviews.* Wien: SORA/ISA.

Schwarzer, S. and Zeglovits, E. (2009) 'Wissensvermittlung, Politische Erfahrungen und Politisches Bewusstsein als Aspekte Politischer Bildung sowie deren Bedeutung für Politische Partizipation', *Österreichische Zeitschrift für Politikwissenschaft*, 3: 325–340.

Settle, J. E., Bond, R. and Levitt, J. (2011) 'The social origins of adult political behavior', *American Politics Research*, 39: 239–263.

Solomon, D., Watson, M. S. and Battistich, V. A. (2001) 'Teaching and schooling effects on moral/prosocial development', in V. Richardson (ed.) *Handbook of research on teaching*, Washington DC: American Educational Research.

Tonge, J., Mycock, A. and Jeffery, B. (2012) 'Does Citizenship Education Make Young People Better-Engaged Citizens?' *Political Studies,* 60(3): 578–602.

Torney-Purta, J. V. (2002a) 'The school's role in developing civic engagement: A study of adolescents in twenty-eight countries', *Applied Development Science*, 6: 203–212.

— (2002b) 'What adolescents know about citizenship and democracy', *Educational Leadership*, 59: 45–50.

Torney-Purta, J. V., Barber, C., Wilkenfeld, B. and Homana, G. (2008) 'Profiles of civic life skills among adolescents: Indicators for researchers, policymakers, and the public', *Child Indicators Research*, 1: 86–106.

Verba, S., Schlozman, K. L. and Brady, H. E. (1995) *Voice and Equality: Civic voluntarism in American politics*, Cambridge: Harvard University Press.

Wagner, M., Johann, D. and Kritzinger, S. (2012) 'Voting at 16: Turnout and the quality of vote choice', *Electoral Studies*, 31: 372–383.

Yates, M. and Youniss, J. (1998) 'Community service and political identity development in adolescence', *Journal of Social Issues*, 54: 495–512.

Zeglovits, E. (2011) 'Votes at 16 – turnout rates among 16- and 17-year-old Austrians', paper presented at the ÖGPW 'Tag der Politikwissenschaft' conference, Salzburg, December 2011.

Zeglovits, E. and Zandonella, M. (forthcoming) 'Political interest of adolescents before and after lowering the voting age: the case of Austria', *Journal of Youth Studies*.

Zukin, C., Keeter, S., Andolina, M., Jenkins, K. and Delli Carpini, M. X. (2006) *A New Engagement? Political participation, civic life, and the changing American citizen*, New York: Oxford University Press.

Chapter Five

Promoting Political Interest in Schools: The Role of Civic Education

Gema M. Garcìa-Albacete

In the last decade there has been an increasing concern about young people's political involvement. Several trends have been identified in Western countries among young people that justify such concern: declining turnout rates (*see* for instance Wattenberg 2003; Blais *et al.* 2004; Franklin 2004); increased apathy towards institutional politics (*see* Henn *et al.* 2002; Henn and Weinstein 2006; Sloam 2007); higher levels of distrust and lack of support for democratic institutions (Dalton 2004); reduced interest in public affairs (Rubenson *et al.* 2004); and a reduced willingness to participate in collective efforts (Putnam 2000).[1]

Concerns regarding these trends have resulted in several institutional initiatives designed to promote young people's engagement with politics. Among them, the EU has been influential in its commitment to promote active citizenship and its recommendation that member states include civic education in schools. The EU's emphasis on citizenship education started in 1997 with the discussion of the values and abilities that are necessary for individuals to become active citizens (for a review of recent European and international civic education initiatives *see* Martín 2006). This first stage culminated in the European Council's declaring 2005 as the 'European Year of Citizenship through Education' in order to draw attention to the crucial role education plays in developing active citizenship, democratic culture and social cohesion.[2] Subsequent programmes undertaken by the European Commission, such as the 'Europe for Citizens' programme running from 2007 to 2013, have also emphasised the role of education and are directed at promoting active citizen participation.

But what makes citizens active? Political behaviour research has discussed profusely the individual determinants that explain why citizens participate in politics (*see* for example Kaase and Barnes 1979; Inglehart 1990; Jennings and van Deth 1990; Brady, Verba and Schlozman 1995; Norris 2002). Among them, political interest has been shown to be a strong predictor of political participation even when controlling for time, country and various socio-demographic variables (for instance Lane 1959: 144; Milbrath 1965: 40; van Deth 1990; Verba *et al.* 1995:

---

1. For a review of the broader debate regarding young people's political participation in Europe *see* Garcia-Albacete (2011).

2. *See also* the Recommendation (2012) of the Committee of Ministers to member states on education for democratic citizenship (adopted by the Council of Europe Committee of Ministers on the 16 October 2002).

334). Political interest is understood here as the 'degree to which politics arouses a citizen's curiosity' (van Deth 1990: 278). Other things being equal, citizens participate politically when they have an interest in public affairs. Therefore, political interest is a key prerequisite for an active citizenry (Van Deth 1990: 276; Martín 2004: 3; van Deth and Elff 2004: 478). A recent comparative study of young people and generational differences in participation across countries in Europe corroborates the classical assumption that interest is a prerequisite for participation: young people participate differently to adults, but, as with former cohorts, they only participate when they are interested in politics (García-Albacete 2011).

Recent research has shown that political interest develops early in life and grows only marginally afterwards (Prior 2010). We also know that young adults' level of political interest is significantly influenced by their family (Neundorf *et al.* 2013). However, there is less evidence concerning the role that other contexts in which children are embedded influence their future curiosity for political affairs. Together with the family, the school is traditionally considered an agent of socialisation (Beck 1977). If we are investing in citizenship education in schools to promote active participation and we believe that political interest is a key antecedent of political involvement, then we are assuming that schools can be effective in promoting political interest. Furthermore, we would expect schools to play a particularly relevant role in engaging those citizens who have not acquired political interest at home and who are therefore more open to external political influences (Jennings *et al.* 2009: 796; Neundorf *et al.* 2013). For these reasons, this chapter concentrates on exploring the role that schools play in developing students' interest in politics by addressing three interrelated questions: do schools promote political interest? What type of education is more effective for this purpose? And, if civic education indeed influences political interest, is it equally capable of promoting curiosity about political issues among students with different backgrounds?[3]

To answer these questions the chapter briefly discusses the origins and the development of political interest and what we expect to find regarding how the form and content of civic education in schools might promote political interest. It then presents the International Civic and Citizenship Education Study used for the analyses and the instruments used for the empirical evaluation. The expectations are then tested using multilevel regression models that allow us to include both schools' and students' characteristics. The concluding section summarises the results and proposes further venues for research to better comprehend how to best promote political interest in schools.

---

3. Several studies have examined similar questions but have concentrated on political participation. Particularly interesting is the recent work by Quintelier and Hooghe (2013) and Dassonneville *et al.* (2012) analysing the effect of civic education on students' intentions to participate politically. However, studying students' participation is difficult at such an early stage. Students have not yet had the opportunities to confront the political system, they might not have the necessary resources to participate and can only provide information regarding their willingness to participate, which does not necessarily imply real participation. Furthermore, we could expect that attitudes such as political interest and behaviour have differing developmental paths and react to distinct influences. For these reasons, this chapter concentrates on the development of a basic orientation such as political interest that strongly correlates with political engagement.

Political interest and civic education

Political socialisation research suggests that general political orientations are acquired early in life (Sears 1983; Jennings 1990; van Deth *et al.* 2011). Those basic orientations will persist throughout the lifespan (Kinder and Sears 1985) and shape the cognitive template used to structure future experiences (Ryder 1965: 848). Without disregarding lifelong learning processes, political attitudes that crystallise during early adulthood are considered to remain largely stable throughout the lifespan. Disentangling the mechanisms that shape those basic orientations is, however, a tremendous task. Children's attitudes are formed while embedded in several institutions including the family, school, peers, the media and so on. Interactions between these institutions are difficult to disentangle. An additional challenge is that citizens' attitudes might also be subject to future change depending on life experiences.[4]

Within political science, a special emphasis has been placed on the role of the family in influencing children's or young adults' political attitudes. The most extensive and robust evidence comes from examining the intergenerational transmission of party identification, ideology and political participation (for instance Campbell *et al.* [1960]1980; Jennings and Niemi 1974; Percheron and Jennings 1981). When it comes to political interest, recent research has revisited earlier studies by exploiting the benefits of large longitudinal datasets that follow the same individuals over a long period of time and that allow comparison of parent-child pairs. Prior's study offers a picture of early acquisition of political interest with little change after young adulthood (2010). Further empirical evaluations of this claim point to the determining influence of the family in the acquisition of political interest during young adulthood (Neundorf *et al.* 2013). But, as suggested by Jennings *et al.* (2009), those individuals whose families were not that interested in politics – and thus did not acquire political interest at home – are more sensitive to external influences and have more potential to develop political interest elsewhere (Neundorf *et al.* 2013). We can thus expect that for those students who did not acquire political interest at home, the school may have a better chance of raising young adults' interest in politics.

The impact of schools on students' political orientations has been widely discussed since the 1960s. However, early socialisation studies reached contradictory conclusions regarding schools' role in promoting political orientations. While some suggested that schools had little effect on young people's political development (Hyman 1959; Langton and Jennings 1968), others concluded that they played the greatest part in building conceptions and beliefs about the political world (Hess and Torney 1967: 217). Some decades later, studies

---

4. As summarised in Kinder and Sears' review (1985), the 'persistence hypothesis' is only one of the four that have been proposed regarding the potential for change in dispositions across age or life stages. However, their overview of empirical findings suggests that the more plausible hypothesis is a view that combines the 'persistence' and 'impressionable years' hypotheses with the possibility of small but still noticeable levels of change.

confirmed the impact of schools on political attitudes, knowledge and engagement. Nie *et al.* (1996) concluded that taking civics courses does have a significant impact on adolescents' levels of political knowledge and democratic attitudes; and provides students with a more critical perspective towards the media. One of their findings was that civic education does not replace the influence of the family, but complements it. Similar results have been found in Great Britain in the evaluation of the effects of civics courses introduced in 1999 (Whiteley 2005, 2012).

As stated by Campbell (2008) the next step is to examine what type of civic or social science courses foster political engagement. In their review, Geboers *et al.* (2012) identified four main forms in which citizenship education is provided in schools: in the school curriculum, in the out-of-school curriculum (which includes activities such as organised government visits or service learning programs), in the pedagogical climate and in extra-curricular activities. The three modes that take place in the school have been found to influence students' democratic attitudes and political engagement positively. In addition to the findings already reviewed on the positive effect of civics courses (Nie *et al.* 1996), the literature points to the positive effects of an open classroom climate – in which students feel free to discuss political and social issues – on students' levels of political knowledge and engagement (Quintelier and Hooghe 2013; Nie *et al.* 1996; Torney-Purta 2002; Campbell 2008; Quintelier 2010; Schulz *et al.* 2011). Extra-curricular activities such as community service (which combines formal instruction with a related service in the community) also have a positive effect on civic knowledge and willingness to participate in politics (Gibson and Levine 2003; Campbell 2008), although some students might perceive such activities as separate from formal politics (Galston 2004). Furthermore, Dassonneville *et al.* (2012) conclude in their study of Belgian late-adolescents that there is no reason to privilege specific forms of civic education, since each form relates to different attitudes and behaviours.

As reviewed by Shani (2009), numerous studies have concentrated on the effect of civics courses or extra-curricular activities on political knowledge or behaviour and less often on political attitudes such as trust or political efficacy. In her comprehensive study of the origins of political interest, Shani (2009) finds that civics courses have a modest but positive effect on individuals' political interest, although the 'enjoyment of social studies' has a larger and more persistent influence. Contrary to these findings, Dassonneville *et al.* (2012: 6) conclude that when it comes to political interest, classroom instruction (formal education) has a stronger effect than an open classroom climate (Dassonneville *et al.* 2012: 6). The reason why both studies differ in their conclusions might be that they use different measures to address aspects of civic education. Nevertheless, overall, we can expect that the ability of civic education to raise levels of interest will depend on the contents and types of civic education citizens receive in school.

Furthermore, available evidence points towards a differentiated effect depending on students' background, although its direction remains unclear. As suggested above, civic education could be particularly relevant for those students with less politicised families and who have therefore not yet acquired political interest. Scholars have suggested the possibility that an open classroom climate increases inequalities since those who are initially more advantaged profit more from it (Shani 2009). According to Shani (2009), the explanation would be that high status children feel more comfortable in an open classroom climate and are more willing to participate in class, therefore receiving more attention and feedback from teachers and peers. Other scholars have made the opposite claim: Campbell (2008) finds that exposure to an open classroom climate can partially compensate for the disadvantages of young people with low socio-economic status. Gainous and Martens' results also suggest that civic education influences only those students who come from less privileged backgrounds (2012). Consequently, we can expect that civic education will have a differentiated effect on political interest according to students' socio-economic background.

The International Civic and Citizenship Education study

While classical political socialisation studies have focused mainly on the USA, renewed interest in political socialisation places emphasis in the need for comparative studies (Sapiro 2004); the same is true for civic education studies (Quintelier and Hooghe 2013). The International Association for the Evaluation of Educational Achievement (IEA) has studied young people's civic knowledge in lower secondary schools in a wide range of countries. To date, three studies have been conducted. The first IEA civic education study was conducted in 1971 in nine countries and found differences in civic knowledge achievement; in democratic attitudes; and in the influence of the family and classroom on students' attitudes across countries (*see* Torney *et al.* 1975). A second study started in the early 1990s with qualitative case studies that examined the context of civic education (Torney-Purta *et al.* 1999) and served as the basis for a second quantitative phase in which nationally representative samples in twenty-eight countries were tested on their civic knowledge and skills (Torney-Purta *et al.* 2001). The second study provided evidence, among others things, that 14-year-old students in most countries had an understanding of democratic values and institutions but were sceptical about traditional forms of political engagement and that both home environment and educational resources had a substantial impact on civic knowledge.[5] The third IEA study, the 'International Civic and Citizenship Education Study 2009' (ICCS), is the basis for the empirical exploration of the effect of civic education on students' levels of political interest presented in this chapter. The empirical outcome of this project is still being explored, however several reports are already available (*see* for instance the international report by Schulz *et al.* 2010 and an examination of the results by Schulz *et al.* 2011).

Although the main aim of the ICCS is to examine the levels and the development of civic knowledge, it provides an impressive amount of information on the subject of students' attitudes and behaviours and also information regarding the context in

---

5. For detailed information about IEA's civic education studies, reports and publications visit the IEA website. Online. Available: http://www.iea.nl/completed_studies.html

which learning and the acquisition of democratic attitudes take place. In addition to the civic knowledge test, it makes use of several tools: a student questionnaire; a teachers' questionnaire containing questions about the school context; a school questionnaire completed by head teachers about the school's characteristics and community context; and information about the civic and citizenship education policies in the national context. To answer the research questions about civic education and political interest, this chapter uses data from these sources, specifically the student questionnaires and the school questionnaires.

Average levels of political interest and types of civic education in schools

Political interest is measured by the student questionnaire. Students were asked about their level of interest in several areas: community issues, social issues, the environment, Europe, their country, other countries and international politics. In what follows, a conservative measure of political interest is used, calculated as the mean value of political interest in local, national and international issues. The resulting index has values from 0 ('not interested at all') to 3 ('very interested').

Regarding the type of civic education practiced in each school, the ICCS provides three different types of information. First, head teachers were asked how civic and citizenship education is taught in the school at the target grade. Head teachers were presented with six items and were asked to tick 'Yes' or 'No' as appropriate. The items were: *(a)* it is taught as a separate subject by teachers of civic and citizenship related subjects; *(b)* it is taught by teachers of subjects related to human and social sciences; *(c)* it is integrated into all subjects taught at school; *(d)* it is an extra-curricular activity; *(e)* it is considered the outcome of school experience as a whole; and *(f)* it is not considered part of the school curriculum. Answers are not mutually exclusive. To explore the possibilities of constructing an indicator containing the possible types of civic education, dimensionality was tested using factor analysis but no clear solution emerged.[6] This is not a surprise since the question permitted multiple choices and had no limit on number of responses. For this reason, the solution proposed here was to retain each individual indicator providing information on distinct styles of civic education inclusion in schools.

Secondly, as noted above, scholars have long stressed the relevance not only of the inclusion of civic education *per se*, but also of classroom dynamics.

---

6. Factor analysis offered a two-factor solution with the following characteristics. The first factor includes the middle positions (from b to e above) and the second factor includes civic education as a separate subject or no civic education in the school. A non-parametric item-level analysis (Mokken Scale Analysis) was also unsuccessful in providing a meaningful scale. Only one scale could be constructed with a low scalability coefficient, excluding half of the items. Furthermore, it should be noted that half of the dataset contained missing values for the item 'taught as a separate subject'. In order to not to lose the data those missing values were recoded as 0, implying no civic education being taught in the school.

Specifically, an open classroom climate has been found to have a positive effect on the development of democratic attitudes and willingness to engage politically. The ICCS contains measures about this. Students were asked about their perception of openness with respect to classroom discussions of political and social issues. In this case the analyses rely on the scale provided by the ICCS organisation. The scale was tested by the ICCS team using Rasch modelling to produce a cross-national equivalent scale.[7]

Finally, head teachers were also asked about the key aims of civic and citizenship education at school. This question provides information about the actual contents of civic education independently of the form it takes in each school. Among a list of ten possible answers,[8] head teachers were asked to indicate what they considered to be the three most important aims. An indicator measuring the emphasis placed by the school on active engagement within civic education was built by adding the number of aims selected that directly refer to politics and active engagement (i.e. promoting knowledge of social, political and civic institutions; promoting students' participation in the local community and in the school; and preparing students for future political engagement).[9] With this information, a scale (with values from 0 to 2) was constructed. The value 0 indicates that none of the participatory aims are included in the main three goals of the school regarding civic education; the value 1 indicates that one of the three most important aims refers to active engagement; 2 refers to schools where two or three participatory aims are included among the most important.[10]

---

7. The original question read as follows: 'When discussing political and social issues during regular lessons, how often do the following things happen? *(a)* Students are able to disagree openly with their teachers; *(b)* Teachers encourage students to make up their own minds; *(c)* Teachers encourage students to express their opinions; *(d)* Students bring up current political events for discussion in class; *(e)* Students express opinions in class even when their opinions are different from most of the other students; *(f)* Teachers encourage students to discuss the issues with people having different opinions; *(g)* Teachers present several sides of the issues when explaining them in class.' The response options for each item were from 1 'never' to 4 'often'.

8. The list includes: *(a)* promoting knowledge of social, political and civic institutions; *(b)* promoting respect for and safeguarding of the environment; *(c)* promoting the capacity to defend one's point of view; *(d)* developing students' skills and competencies in conflict resolution; *(e)* promoting knowledge of citizens' rights and responsibilities; *(f)* promoting students' participation in the local community; *(g)* promoting students' critical and independent thinking; *(h)* promoting students' participation in school life; *(i)* supporting the development of effective strategies for the fight against racism and xenophobia; *(j)* preparing students for future political engagement.

9. Other items included in the original question but not in the scale are: *(b)* promoting respect for and safeguarding of the environment; *(c)* promoting the capacity to defend one's point of view; *(d)* developing students' skills and competencies in conflict resolution; *(e)* promoting knowledge of citizens' rights and responsibilities; *(g)* promoting students' critical and independent thinking; *(i)* supporting the development of effective strategies for the fight against racism and xenophobia.

10. The emphasis on participatory aims in a school also indicates engagement with 'norms of citizenship'. Norms of citizenship are important for political participation because people will engage in politics in accordance with how they think a good citizen should behave. A citizen who thinks voting or getting involved in politics is a civic duty will be more likely to turn out to vote. Norms of citizenship also provide reasons why people choose to be active or inactive in certain ways

Can we observe differences in political interest according to the type of civic education offered in schools? Since scarce attention has been paid to the relationship between type of civic education and political interest, I start with a descriptive approach. Let us have a look at the levels of political interest across type and content of civic education in the member states of the EU.[11] Our expectation is that the inclusion of civics courses in schools will foster higher levels of students' political interest. Furthermore, we also expect a positive relationship between an open classroom climate and the inclusion of active political engagement aims in the school. Figure 5.1 shows the average level of students' political interest according to whether the school includes citizenship education as a separate subject, as an extra-curricular activity, integrated into all subjects, taught by teachers of related subjects (such as social sciences) or not part of the school curriculum. The bivariate analysis only shows the expected relationship for the inclusion of civic education in extra-curricular activities. The average level of students' political interest is significantly higher in schools where civic education is included in the form of extra-curricular activities.[12] Unexpectedly, the average level of students' political interest is significantly lower in schools where civic education is included as a separate subject compared to schools that do not provide civic education at all. There are no other significant differences between types of civic education delivery.

In order to examine the relationship between an open-discussion classroom climate and political interest without imposing a functional form on the data, a locally weighted smoothing scatter plot (LOWESS) is presented in Figure 5.2. This shows that political interest increases as student perception of an open climate increases, confirming the expected relationship. Furthermore, the correlation is statistically significant (Pearson's $r=0.17$, $p < .001$). We also observe the expected relationship between political interest and schools' aims to promote student engagement. In schools where at least one of the aims of civic education is to promote active student engagement with politics, student political interest is significantly higher (*see* Figure 5.3).

(Theiss-Morse 1993: 365; van Deth 2007: 403). In addition, the norms of those around us matter; an individual embedded in a social context that considers voting a duty will also be more likely to cast a vote (Pattie *et al* 2004: 143; Gerber and Rogers 2009).

11. Among the countries included in the dataset, only the twenty-two EU member countries are included in the analyses. This selection will facilitate the interpretation of the results. Including countries from other areas, particularly non-democratic or non-industrialised societies, would complicate the task. The countries included are Austria, Belgium, Bulgaria, Cyprus, Czech Republic, Denmark, England, Spain, Estonia, Finland, Greece, Ireland, Italy, Lithuania, Luxembourg, Latvia, Malta, the Netherlands, Poland, Slovak Republic, Slovenia, Sweden.

12. When interpreting these results we should keep in mind that types of civic education are not mutually exclusive. Therefore, the existence of extra-curricular activities does not imply that civic education is only delivered in the school in that form.

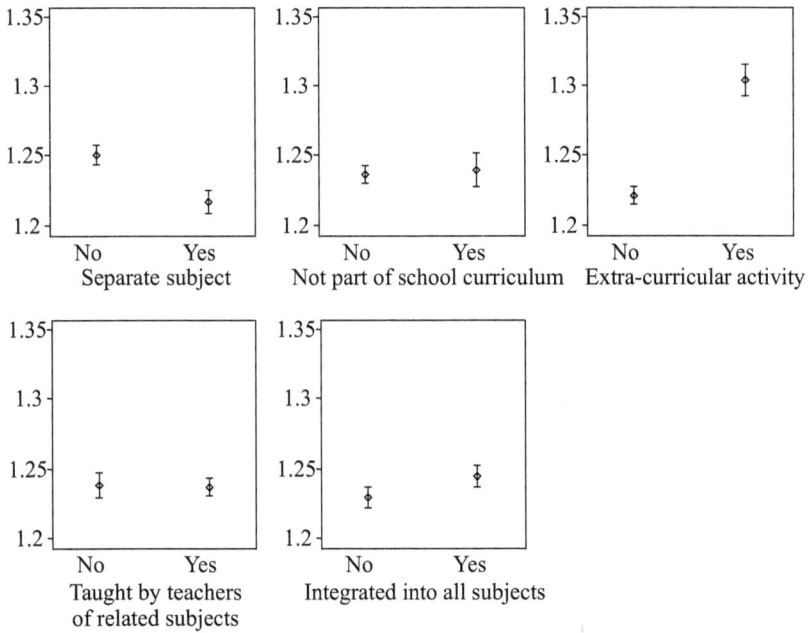

Figure 5.1: Students' political interest according to type of civic education taught in schools (means and 95% confidence intervals)

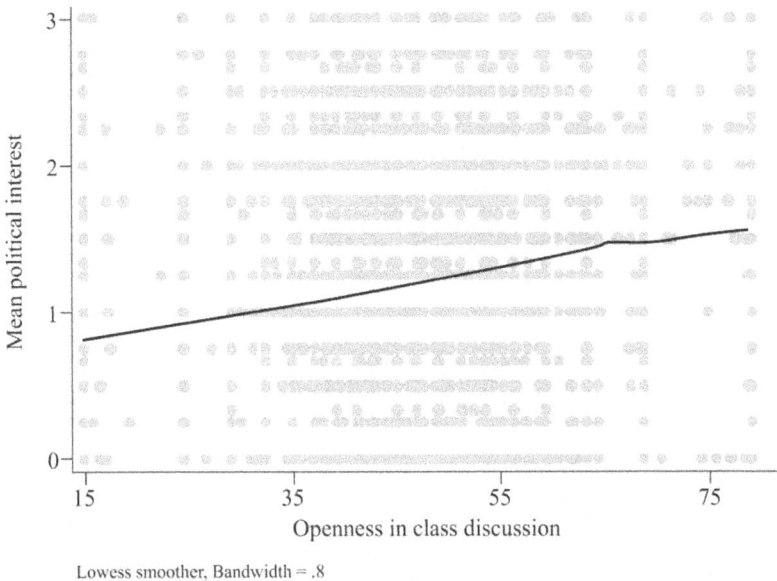

Lowess smoother, Bandwidth = .8

Figure 5.2: Relationship between students' political interest and perceived openness in class discussion (LOWESS plot)

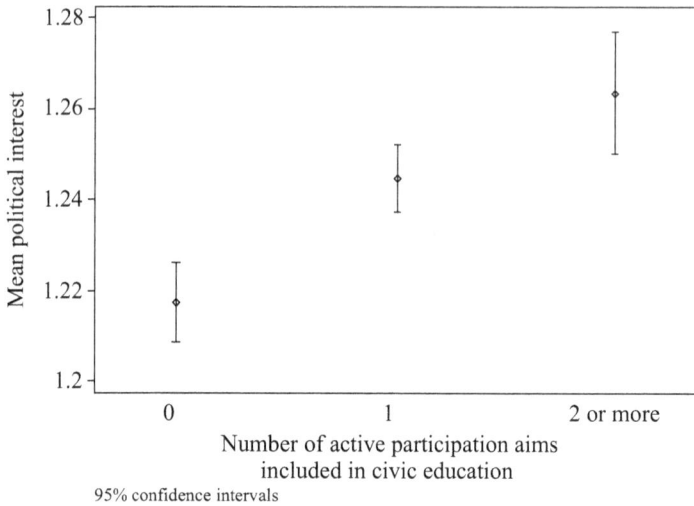

Figure 5.3: Students' political interest according to schools' political engagement aims (means and 95% confidence intervals)

The development of political interest in schools: multilevel models

The relationship between type and content of civic education and political interest could be mediated by a number of factors such as the socio-economic context of the family or the school. Furthermore, we expect an interaction between civic education and individual determinants of political interest, particularly the family. These hypotheses are now tested in a multivariate linear regression model that allows us to control for several individual and contextual factors. Since students are embedded in schools, the appropriate technique is multilevel analysis. The data has a hierarchical and nested structure since it is measured at different levels (that is, students and schools).[13]

The impact of civic education on political interest was controlled by the following two characteristics of the students: age and gender (0=male;

---

13. At the same time, schools are also nested within countries, which would require a three level model. However, for the sake of simplicity only two levels were included (schools and students). The reason for this decision is theoretical: the information regarding the aims and shape of civic education, the main independent variable, is available at the school level. Still, the fit to the data of a model in which students are nested in countries was also examined but showed that the variance in political interest is higher across schools than across countries. The variance partition coefficient (VPC) is higher at the school level (9.7 per cent) than at the country level (4.7 per cent). Furthermore a comparison of individual versus school level models draws highly significant tests: the Likelihood Ratio Chi-Square with one predictor is 2951.74 (p<0.000). Therefore, the school is expected to have an effect on students' level of political interest. Moreover, a three level model including schools nested within countries is not statistically better than the two-level model selected.

1=female).[14] The two following factors included in the analysis are expected to mediate the impact of the school on students' political interest: the student's socio-economic background and his or her parents' level of political interest. Since the ICCS did not ask students for their parents' or household's income, the highest level of education achieved by parents will be used as a proxy for students' socio-economic background. Parental education levels are provided by the ICCS using the 'International Standard Classification of Education' (ISCED). The scale's categories were reduced by pooling the three first categories together, in order to avoid having categories that would be too small for subsequent analysis.[15] Parents' political interest is measured by the frequency with which politics is discussed at the student's home. Following Gabriel and van Deth (1995: 396), political discussions can be understood as a behavioural manifestation of political interest. The exact wording of the question was the following: 'How often are you involved in each of the following activities outside of school? Talking with your parent(s) about political or social issues?' This question is coded on a scale from 1 (Never or hardly ever) to 4 (Daily or almost daily).

School characteristics are included next in the analysis since they might also have an effect on the overall levels of students' political interest. The school's socio-economic context is calculated as the mean score for the highest level of parental education. The second characteristic of the school is the head teacher's perception of social tension in the local community. This measure is provided by the ICCS team and is considered to be an indicator of social problems in the community that could have a negative effect on learning outcomes (*see* Schulz *et al.* 2011). Finally, whether the school was in a post-communist country or not is included in the analysis as an additional control variable.

Due to the complexity of the data, the multilevel regression analysis is performed by adding student and school characteristics in a series of steps and including fixed effects. Model 1 in Table 5.1 presents the empty model in which variance in students' political interest can be broken down into individual and school levels. It shows that most of the variation is at the individual level. However, the school also has an effect on levels of political interest, accounting for 9 per cent of the total variance. In Model 2, the individual student variables are added. The control variables age and gender show that political interest increases with age and that female students are comparatively less interested in politics than their male counterparts. As expected, the level of education achieved by parents has a positive effect on students' political interest. Furthermore, the strongest positive effect belongs to the frequency of political discussions with parents at home.

---

14. We can expect that female students are less interested in politics and that political interest will generally increase as they grow older. Although these differences are interesting *per se* they will not be further explored here in order to concentrate on finding general patterns and differences according to students' socio-economic backgrounds.

15. The scale was reduced by adding the lowest three levels of education: 'did not complete ISCED level 1', 'ISCED level 1 completed' and 'ISCED level 2' into one single category. The resulting scale has four categories: ISCED < 3, ISCED = 3, ISCED = 4 or 5b, and ISCED= 5a or 6.

Table 5.1: Multilevel models of political interest with fixed effects

	Model 1	Model 2	Model 3	Model 4
Female		-0.04***	-0.04***	-0.07***
		(0.01)	(0.01)	(0.01)
Age		0.03***	0.03***	0.02***
		(0.01)	(0.01)	(0.01)
Highest parental education level		0.01*	0.01**	0.01*
		(0.00)	(0.00)	(0.00)
Political discussion at home		0.29***	0.29***	0.28***
		(0.00)	(0.00)	(0.00)
School average parental education			-0.00**	-0.00***
			(0.00)	(0.00)
Social tensions community			0.00***	0.00***
			(0.00)	(0.00)
Post-communist countries			-0.02**	-0.02~
			(0.01)	(0.01)
Open discussion				0.01***
				(0.00)
Participatory aims included				0.02**
				(0.01)
Separate subject				-0.03***
				(0.01)
Extra-curricular activities				0.07***
				(0.01)
No part in the curriculum				-0.00
				(0.01)
Integrated in all subjects				0.01
				(0.01)
Intercept	1.240***	0.359***	0.351***	0.04
	(0.01)	(0.07)	(0.08)	(0.08)
N	61083	61083	61083	61033
Variance School	0.05	0.03	0.03	0.02
Variance Residual	0.46	0.39	0.39	0.38
ICC	0.09	0.06	0.06	0.06
AIC	128350	118105	118079	116990
BIC	128377	118168	118170	117135

Notes: ~ $p < 0.10$; * $p < 0.05$; ** $p < 0.01$; *** $p < 0.001$; Standard errors are in parentheses; ICC=Intraclass Correlation; AIC= Akaike Information Criterion; BIC= Bayesian Information Criterion;
Source: ICCS 2009.

These results corroborate former political socialisation studies regarding the strong influence of the family on children and young adults' political orientations (for example Jennings *et al.* 2009).

In Model 3, school variables are added to the analyses. Contrary to expectations, higher levels of school resources measured by the overall level of parent educational achievement have a negative effect on students' levels of political interest (*see* Table 5.1). Unexpected results are also found regarding the head teacher's perception of social tension in the local community, which has a significant positive effect. A variety of explanations could account for the unexpected results regarding the relationship between school characteristics and political interest. Differences with other studies might be due to the fact that models presented here include only selected variables, while former studies included all relevant school characteristics. For a more complete account *see* the work by Schulz *et al.* (2011) in which a comprehensive list of school characteristics is tested to explain students' civic knowledge. Furthermore, school characteristics might have different effects according to whether students already acquired political interest from their families. Students in schools with higher socio-economic status might have already developed political interest to a large extent at home, hence schools have a more limited effect. Other speculations could also be explored, such as the possibility that the existence of social tension in the community increases students' awareness of political issues. Although this question remains open, the examination conducted in this chapter concentrates on the effect of civic education.

Finally, Model 4 presents the results of adding type of civic education into the analysis. In line with former research about civic knowledge and political engagement, the analysis presented here shows that an open classroom climate and the existence of extra-curricular activities related to civic education have a statistically significant positive effect on students' political interest. In addition, the school having explicit aims to promote student political participation also increases the likelihood of students being interested in politics. Having no programme of civic education or having the programme integrated across all subjects does not have any impact on students' political interest. Finally, corroborating the descriptive data presented above, having civic education as a separate subject has a negative effect on the development of political interest in schools. Overall, adding type of civic education improves the model significantly, reducing the Intraclass correlation (ICC) by 4.9 per cent (*see* Table 5.1).[16]

The empirical examination presented so far supports the expectation that civic education in school has an effect on individual levels of student political interest. An open classroom climate in which students have the opportunity to discuss and give their opinion on social and political issues; the existence of civic education by means of extra-curricular activities; and schools' explicit aim of promoting students' political knowledge and future political participation all favour the development of political interest. However, as described above, we can expect the effects of civic

---

16. The Bayesian Deviance Information Criterion is also significantly reduced (*see* Table 5.1).

education to differ according to students' background; even if it is unclear for which group civic education has more or less impact – those with the highest or lowest socio-economic status.

Two different hypotheses are explored in relation to students' background. We anticipate that civic education in school has a greater potential to increase the political interest of those students who have not acquired it previously at home. Moreover, the question remains open regarding whether students from the highest or lowest socio-economic backgrounds benefit more from the inclusion of citizenship education courses and practices in schools. To examine the existence of differentiated effects according to students' socio-economic background a series of cross-level interaction effects were included in the models. For each type of civic education that had an overall positive effect, a new analysis was run to show the effect of parental education level and the frequency of political discussions with parents at home. One full model was computed for each interaction term. The mere inclusion of those interactions does not result in significant coefficients for the interaction terms. However, since the coefficient of a multiplicative term and its level of significance is not necessarily informative (Brambor *et al.* 2006), for each case the marginal effects were computed and the results visually inspected.[17]

The inclusion of interaction terms shows differences across students' backgrounds but also different patterns according to each civic education characteristic examined. Illustrating the impact of an open classroom climate according to parental education level, Figure 5.4 shows that openness in class discussions has a positive and statistically significant effect for all student groups. However, the contrast between groups shows that the effect is stronger (and the level of statistical significance higher) for those students whose parents have either the highest or the lowest level of education. The effect is still positive but lower on students' political interest for students whose parents are in the middle categories of education. Understanding parental education as a proxy for students' socio-economic background, the results imply that the classroom climate is more effective in fostering political interest for students at both extremes of the socio-economic spectrum.

A similar conclusion can be drawn regarding the effect on students' political interest of schools having explicit participatory aims. Figure 5.5 shows the marginal effects of schools having explicit participatory aims on political interest (broken down by parental education). Again, civic education seems more capable of promoting political interest in those students that come from the highest and lowest socio-economic backgrounds. This effect is even clearer than for classroom climate, since the increase in political interest as participatory aims are strengthened is positive but not statistically significant for students whose parents are in the middle categories of the education scale, while it is statistically significant for the highest and lowest categories ($p < 0.001$).

---

17. For the same reason and given that the strategy implies running six more models, the coefficients for the interaction terms are not shown. The computation of marginal effects for all tests and the contrast for each situation resulting from the combination of variables is available from the author.

When it comes to the marginal effect of extra-curricular activities, however, the effect is different than in the former two cases. According to the results of the interaction with parental education, extra-curricular activities in schools have a positive and statistically significant impact on all groups except for those whose parents have the lowest level of education. Although Figure 5.6 shows that the existence of extra-curricular activities results in a higher likelihood of political interest, subsequent significant tests show that the effect is only significant for those students whose parents have at least completed the third level of education in the ISCED scale (corresponding to upper secondary education).

Again, the effects of each type of education are different if we examine students' background according to their exposure to political discussions at home. The hypothesis put forward is that civic education will have a stronger effect on those students that spend less time discussing political issues with their parents. This effect can indeed be observed in terms of schools having explicit participatory aims. Where schools have more explicit aims to develop active political engagement, there is a statistically significant positive effect but only on those students who never (or hardly ever) spent time discussing political issues at home (*see* Figure 5.7). The hypothesis regarding the inclusion of extra-curricular activities in school is also supported empirically. Extra-curricular activities are positively correlated with political interest for those students that never (or hardly never) discuss political issues at home and for those that do it monthly, but have no statistically significant effect for students that discuss political issues more often with their parents.[18]

Finally, the effect of an open classroom climate differs and does not support the hypothesis. As showed in Figure 5.8, an open classroom discussion has a positive effect for all groups when the frequency of political discussions at home is examined. However, the effect is statistically significant only for those students in the middle categories – students that discuss politics at home monthly or weekly – but not for those that discuss politics with a higher or lower frequency. This effect is illustrated in the graph by the steeper lines belonging to the middle groups.

---

18. The figure is not shown here since it is very similar to Figure 5.7. It is available from the author on request.

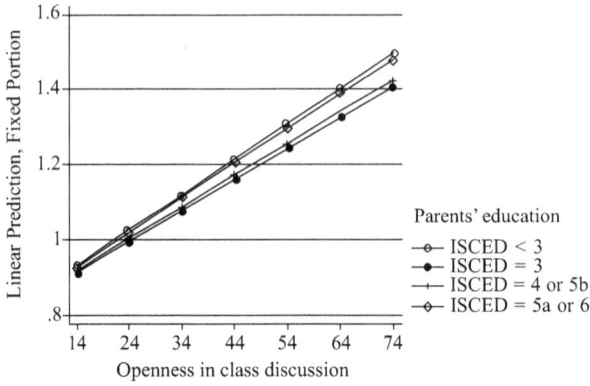

Figure 5.4: Marginal effects of openness in class discussion on political interest according to parental education

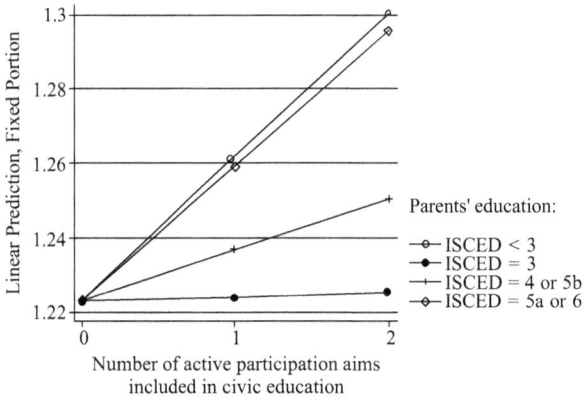

Figure 5.5: Marginal effects of schools having participatory aims on political interest according to parental education

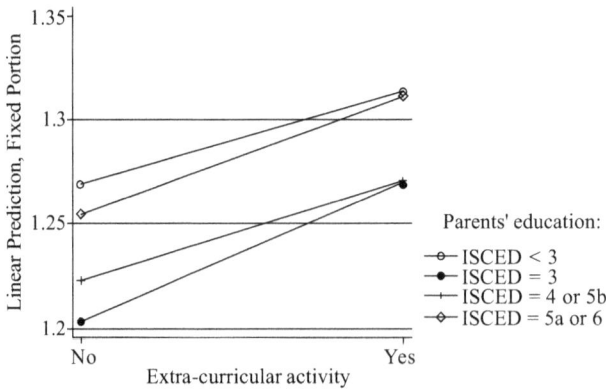

Figure 5.6: Marginal effects of extra-curricular activities in schools on political interest according to parental education

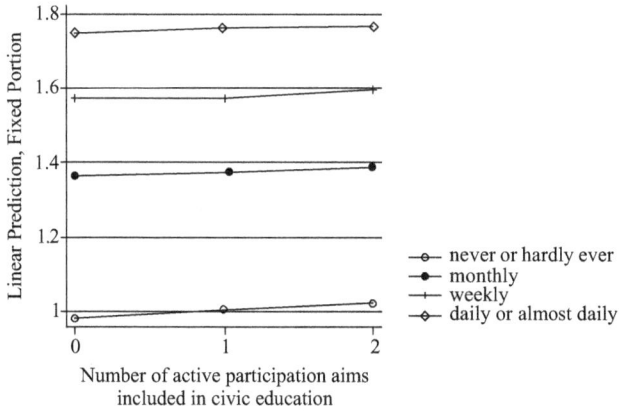

Figure 5.7: Marginal effects of schools having participatory aims on political interest according to frequency of political discussion at home

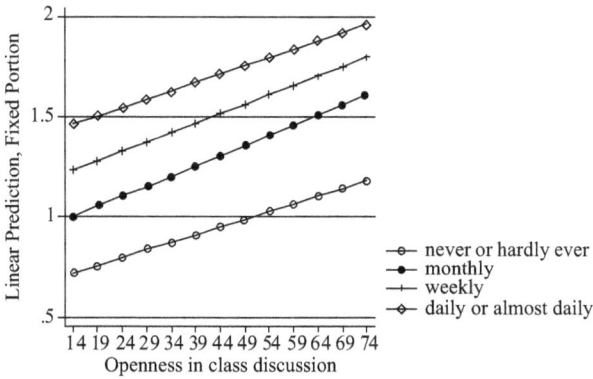

Figure 5.8: Marginal effects of openness in class discussion on political interest according to frequency of political discussion at home

Conclusion

Returning to the opening questions at the beginning of this chapter, we now have evidence that schools can indeed promote political interest. However, the type of civic education chosen can have positive or negative effects. The mere inclusion of civic education might not be enough to promote political interest. Moreover, the inclusion of a separate civic education subject can have a negative effect on students' levels of political interest in comparison to schools with other models or even in comparison to schools that do not include civic education in the curriculum at all. The most successful formula appears to be the inclusion of extra-curricular activities. Still, the type of information included in the analysis requires caution when interpreting the results since the measures used do not properly discriminate between the many possible combinations of types of civic education. For example, we could not examine the effect of including civic education both as a separate subject and as an integrated approach or in combination with other types of civic education.

In line with former studies, the results point to the very relevant role played not only by the formal inclusion of civic education in schools but also by the type of education provided. As previous studies have stressed, the existence of an open classroom climate is important for the development of civic knowledge, political engagement and, as shown here, political interest. The results also show convincingly that where schools have as explicit aims to promote active citizenship, there is a positive effect on students' levels of political interest, pointing to the importance of exploring further the other types of content incorporated into civic education courses.

Furthermore, we have seen that schools can be more or less successful in promoting political interest depending on students' backgrounds. However, effects differ depending on the type of civic education being considered and on whether we examine students' socio-economic background or the frequency with which they are exposed to political discussions at home. There has been an ongoing controversy about whether civic education results in higher inequality either because it encourages political interest among those already privileged in terms of socio-economic resources, or conversely, because it does so for students with greater economic disadvantage. The results shown here suggest a third alternative. An open classroom climate and schools having explicit aims to promote active citizenship promote political interest in the most advantaged and disadvantaged students, having in fact, a more limited effect in students coming from middling socio-economic backgrounds. However, extra-curricular activities are more likely to increase political interest in those students that are socio-economically advantaged, which could result in fostering existing inequalities.

The final proposition in this chapter was that, given the known importance of the family in transmitting political interest to young citizens, the impact of schools would be higher for those students who had not already developed political interest at home. Our results suggest that this is indeed the case where extra-curricular activities and schools having explicit participatory aims are concerned. Both these elements have a positive and stronger effect on those who are less exposed to politics at home. The dynamics of the school in terms of openness of classroom climate has an effect only on those who already discuss political issues at home but not very often.

Numerous debates have taken place recently about the most appropriate content for civic education, particularly in those countries in which new legislation has been passed to incorporate citizenship education into schools in the last few years, such as the UK or Spain. However, empirical evidence concerning which specific elements have the potential to foster active engagement and democratic attitudes remains limited and often contradictory. This chapter has explored this question by examining the impact of schools having explicit aims to promote political knowledge about social, political and civic institutions; promote students' participation in the school and the local community; and prepare students for political engagement.

The main conclusion that can be drawn is that civic education does matter for the development of politically interested citizens. Therefore, efforts being made in this respect are valuable. However, the type of civic education provided can interact with the characteristics of the students to make civic education more or less successful. Furthermore, counter-intuitive effects such as the negative influence of some types of civic education call for further analysis that takes into account more complex configurations of form and content of civic education courses and practices. The best formula for civic education will depend on students' development of political orientations at home and their socio-economic background. As suggested by Shani (2009), the finding that some types of civic education might imply increasing inequalities since high status students profit more from them does not mean that, for instance, schools should not include extra-curricular activities. Rather, schools should adapt the way civic education is taught in order that it reaches students from different backgrounds and that all students feel sufficiently able to benefit from the activities. A better grasp of the mechanisms by which civic education interacts with socio-economic background is desirable and points to the importance of studying the diverse socialisation agents from an interrelated perspective.

References

Beck, P. A. (1977) 'The role of agents in political socialisation', in S. A. Renshon (ed.) *Handbook of Political Socialisation: Theory and research*, New York: Free Press.

Blais, A., Gidengil, E., Nevitte, N. and Nadeau, R. (2004) 'Where does turnout decline come from?', *European Journal of Political Research*, 43(2): 221–236.

Brady, H. E., Verba, S., Schlozman, K. L. (1995) 'Beyond SES: A resource model of political participation', *American Political Science Review*, 89(2): 271–294.

Brambor, T., Clark, W. R. and Golder, M. (2006) 'Understanding interaction models: Improving empirical analyses', *Political Analysis*, 14(1): 36–82.

Campbell, A., Converse, P. E., Miller, W. E. and Stokes, D. E. ([1960]1980) *The American Voter*, Chicago: University of Chicago Press.

Campbell, D. E. (2008) 'Voice in the classroom: How an open classroom climate fosters political engagement among adolescents', *Political Behavior*, 30(4): 437–454.

Dalton, R. J. (2004) *Democratic Challenges, Democratic Choices: The erosion of political support in advanced industrial democracies*, Oxford: Oxford University Press.

Dassonneville, R., Quintelier, E., Hooghe, M. and Claes, E. (2012) 'The relation between civic education and political attitudes and behavior: A two-year panel study among Belgian late adolescents', *Applied Developmental Science*, 16(3): 140–150.

Franklin, M. N. (2004) *Voter Turnout and the Dynamics of Electoral Competition in Established Democracies since 1945*, Cambridge: Cambridge University Press.

Gabriel, O. W. and van Deth, J. W. (1995) 'Political interest', in J. W. van Deth and E. Scarbrough (eds), *The Impact of Values*, Oxford: Oxford University Press: 390–411.

Gainous, J. and Martens, A. M. (2012) 'The effectiveness of civic education: Are "good" teachers actually good for "all" students?', *American Politics Research*, 40(2): 232–266.

Galston, W. A. (2004) 'Civic education and political participation', *PS: Political Science & Politics*, 37(2): 263–266.

Garcìa-Albacete, G. M. (2011) *Continuity or Generational Change? A longitudinal study of young people's political participation in Western Europe*, unpublished thesis, University of Mannheim.

Geboers, E., Geijsel, F., Admiraal, W. and Dam, G. (2012) 'Review of the effects of citizenship education', *Educational Research Review*. Online. Available: http://www.sciencedirect.com/science/article/pii/S1747938X12000176 (accessed 23 December 2012).

Gerber, A. S. and Rogers, T. (2009) 'Descriptive social norms and motivation to vote: Everybody's voting and so should you', *Journal of Politics*, 71(1): 178–191.

Gibson, C. and Levine, P. (2003) *The Civic Mission of Schools*, Carnegie Corporation of New York and CIRCLE. Online. Available: http://www.civicyouth.org/ PopUps/CivicMissionofSchools.pdf (accessed 17 May 2013)

Henn, M. and Weinstein, M. (2006) 'Young people and political (in)activism: Why don't young people vote?', *Policy & Politics*, 34(3): 517–534.

Henn, M., Weinstein, M. and Wring, D. (2002) 'A generation apart? Youth political participation in Britain', *British Journal of Politics and International Relations*, 4(2): 167–192.

Hess, R. D. and Torney, J. V. (1967) *The Development of Political Attitudes in Children*, New Brunswick, New Jersey: Aldine Transaction.

Hyman, H. H. (1959) *Political socialisation*, Glencoe, Illinois: Free Press.

Inglehart, R. (1990) *Culture Shift in Advanced Industrial Society*, Princeton, New Jersey: Princeton University Press.

Jennings, M. K. (1990) 'The crystallization of orientations', in M. K. Jennings and J. W. van Deth (eds) *Continuities in Political Action: A longitudinal study of political orientations in three Western democracies*, Berlin and New York: De Gruyter: 313–348.

Jennings, M. K. and Niemi, R.G. (1974) *The Political Character of Adolescence: The influence of families and school*, Princeton, New Jersey: Princeton University Press.

Jennings, M. K., Stoker, L. and Bowers, J. (2009) 'Politics across generations: Family transmission reexamined', *Journal of Politics*, 71(3): 782–799.

Jennings, M. K. and van Deth, J. W. (1990) 'Conclusion: Some consequences for systems and governments', in M. K. Jennings and J. W. van Deth (eds) *Continuities in Political Action: A longitudinal study of political orientations in three Western democracies,* Berlin and New York: De Gruyter.

Kaase, M. and Barnes, S. H. (1979) 'The future of political protest in Western democracies', in S. H. Barnes and M. Kaase *et al.* (eds), *Political Action: Mass participation in five Western Democracies*, Beverly Hills, California: Sage: 523–537.

Kinder, D. R. and Sears, D. O. (1985) 'Public opinion and political action', in G. Lindzey and E. Aronson (eds), *The handbook of social psychology*, New York: Random House, 659–741.

Lane, R. E. (1959) *Political Life: Why people get involved in politics*, Glencoe, Illinois: Free Press.

Langton, K. P. and Jennings, M. K. (1968) 'Political socialisation and the High School civics curriculum in the United States', *The American Political Science Review*, 62(3): 852.

Martín, I. (2004) *Los orígenes y significados del interés por la política en dos nuevas democracias: España y Grecia,* unpublished thesis, Universidad Autónoma de Madrid.

—   (2006) *Una propuesta para la enseñanza de la ciudadanía democrática en España,* Estudios de Progreso, 22/2006. Madrid: Fundación alternativas.

Milbrath, L. W. (1965) *Political Participation: How and why do people get involved in politics?*, Chicago: Rand Mcnally College.

Neundorf, A., Smets, K. and Garcìa-Albacete, G. M. (2013) 'Homemade citizens: The development of political interest during adolescence and young adulthood', *Acta Politica,* 48(1): 92–116.

Nie, N. H., Junn, J. and Stehlik-Barry, K. (1996) *Education and Democratic Citizenship in America*, Chicago: University of Chicago Press.

Norris, P. (2002) *Democratic Phoenix: Reinventing political activism*, Cambridge: Cambridge University Press.

Pattie, C., Seyd, P. and Whiteley, P. (2004) *Citizenship in Britain: Values, participation and democracy*, Cambridge: Cambridge University Press.

Percheron, A. and Jennings, M. K. (1981) 'Political continuities in French families: A new perspective on an old controversy', *Comparative Politics*, 13(4): 421–436.

Prior, M. (2010) 'You've either got it or you don't? The stability of political interest over the life cycle', *Journal of Politics*, 72(3): 747–766.

Putnam, R. D. (2000) *Bowling Alone: The collapse and revival of American community*, New York: Simon & Schuster.

Quintelier, E. (2010) 'The effect of schools on political participation: a multilevel logistic analysis', *Research Papers in Education*, 25(2): 137–154.

Quintelier, E. and Hooghe, M. (2013) 'The Relationship between political participation intentions of adolescents and a participatory democratic climate at school in 35 countries', *Oxford Review of Education*.

Rubenson, D., Blais, A., Fournier, P., Gidengil, E. and Nevitte, N. (2004) 'Accounting for the age gap in turnout', *Acta Politica*, 39(4): 407–421.

Ryder, N. B. (1965) 'The cohort as a concept in the study of social change', *American Sociological Review*, 30(6): 843–861.

Sapiro, V. (2004) 'Not your parents' political socialisation: Introduction for a new generation', *Annual Review of Political Science*, 7: 1–23.

Schulz, W., Ainley, J., Fraillon, J., Kerr, D. and Losito, B. (2010) *Initial Findings from the IEA International Civic and Citizenship Education Study*, Amsterdam: IEA.

Schulz, W., Fraillon, J., Ainley, J. and van de Gaer, E. (2011) 'Multi-level analysis of factors explaining differences in civic knowledge', paper presented at the Annual Meetings of the American Educational Research Association, New Orleans, April 2011. Online. Available: http://iccs.acer.edu.au/uploads/File/ AERA2011/AERA_ICCS_MLA_CK%28NewOrleans2011%29. pdf (accessed 23 December 2012).

Sears (1983) 'The persistence of early political predispositions: The roles of attitude object and life stage', in L. Wheeler and P. Shaver (eds) *Review of Personality and Social Psychology*, Beverly Hills, California: Sage: 79–116.

Shani, D. (2009) *On the Origins of Political Interest*, unpublished thesis, Princeton University.

Sloam, J. (2007) 'Rebooting democracy: Youth participation in politics in the UK', *Parliamentary Affairs*, 60(4): 548–567.

Theiss-Morse, E. (1993) 'Conceptualizations of good citizenship', *Political Behavior*, 15(4): 355–380.

Torney, J. V., Oppenheim, A. N. and Farnen, R. F. (1975) *Civic Education in Ten Countries: An empirical study*, New York: Halsted Press.

Torney-Purta, J. V. (2002) 'The school's role in developing civic engagement: A study of adolescents in twenty-eight countries', *Applied Developmental Science*, 6(4): 203–212.

Torney-Purta, J. V., Lehmann, R., Oswald, H. and Schulz, W. (2001) *Citizenship and Education in Twenty-eight Countries: Civic knowledge and engagement at age fourteen*, Amsterdam: International Association for the Evaluation of Educational Achievement.

Torney-Purta, J. V., Schwille, J. and Amadeo, J. (1999) *Civic Education across Countries: Twenty-four national case studies from the IEA Civic Education Project*, Amsterdam: International Association for the Evaluation of Educational Achievement.

van Deth, J. W. (1990) 'Interest in politics', in M. K. Jennings and J. W. van Deth (eds), *Continuities in Political Action: A longitudinal study of political orientations in three Western democracies,* Berlin and New York: De Gruyter: 275–312.

—— (2007) 'Norms of citizenship', in R. J. Dalton and H.-D. Klingemann (eds) *The Oxford Handbook of Political Behaviour*, Oxford: Oxford University Press: 402–417.

van Deth, J. W., Abendschön, S. and Vollmar, M. (2011) 'Children and politics: An empirical reassessment of early political socialisation', *Political Psychology*, 32(1): 147–174.

van Deth, J. W. and Elff, M. (2004) 'Politicisation, economic development and political interest in Europe', *European Journal of Political Research*, 43(3): 477–508.

Verba, S., Schlozman, K. L. and Brady, H. E. (1995) *Voice and Equality: Civic voluntarism in American politics*, Cambridge: Harvard University Press.

Wattenberg, M. P. (2003) 'Electoral turnout: The new generational gap', *Journal of Elections, Public Opinion and Parties*, 13(1): 159–173.

Whiteley, P. (2005) *Citizenship Education Longitudinal Study: Second literature review. Citizenship education: The political science perspective*, RR631, London: Department for Education and Skills. Online. Available: http://dera.ioe.ac.uk/5607/1/RR631.pdf (accessed 23 December 2012).

—— (2012) 'Does citizenship education work? Evidence from a decade of citizenship education in secondary schools in England', *Parliamentary Affairs*. Online. Available: http://pa.oxfordjournals.org/content/early/2012/12/ 13/pa.gss083 (accessed 23 December 2012).

Chapter Six

Emergence of the European Union in Upper Secondary Education: A Comparative Analysis of French, English, German and Catalonian History Textbooks

Alexandre Blanc

School education is an important source of socialisation. The generalisation and development of a state school system was influential in the construction of national identities in Europe during the second half of the nineteenth century. This education has largely served national interests. The teaching implemented by states since the late decades of the nineteenth century was largely used to legitimise the state and the nation as standard social structures (Thiesse 1999; Weber 1976). This function is preserved to this day (Heidenheimer 1997).

While school education remains organised at a national level, there are more and more impulses to instil a European identification among pupils. With the new and increasing importance of the European Union (EU), it would seem logical that each of the member states attaches a greater importance to the description of this new reality in school teaching, in compliance with the European treaty now coming into force.[1] Though, the organisation of school is, in fact, far from being shared with actors organised at a European level (Frazier 1995): the state strictly handles this sector, sometimes together with infra-state level regions.

However, this reality should become balanced with new dynamics in play. Among these, globalisation and European integration are playing a key role in every European country and are driving a transition from a Europe divided into nations to a more integrated Europe. It is hard to imagine the future of the European construction but it is clear that this dynamic produces significant effects on the modern system of sovereign states and nations. The increasing importance of the EU in the everyday life of Europeans is more and more obvious, even if it induces both hope and fear. Even though the EU is not completely legitimised by the population, it transforms broader fields such as the economy, social policies, foreign affairs and law.

Indeed, European integration seems to announce a different way of conceiving the processes of socialisation. Traditional socialisation carried out by school

---

1. 'Union action shall be aimed at: developing the European dimension in education'. Article 165 §2 of the Consolidated Version of the Treaty on the Functioning of the European Union (OJ C115, 9.5.2008).

teaching largely stresses a state approach and officially serves national ambitions. This assertion remained valid when the targeted objectives of socialisation were to fulfil national ideals (Thiesse 1999; Hobsbawm 1990; Anderson 2006). The transition toward a more European perspective is supposed to lead to some evolutions (Bartolini 2005). How does school teaching, which inherits national traditions, attempt to introduce new realities that involve a change in direction of traditional political socialisation?

I propose to focus on the transition toward a more integrated Europe and to show how school teaching evolves in order to adapt to 'Europeanisation'. For this aim, I would like to show what images of the EU and its institutions are given to pupils and how these are taught as new realities in the cases of France, England, Germany (Baden-Württemberg) and Catalonia.[2] These cases all belong or correspond to strong or old states with a key position in Europe and a will to influence the whole of Europe (Davies 1997; Rokkan and Urwin 1983). They are interesting because they show different conceptions and patterns of nation (Hobsbawm 1990).[3] How does the transition from a largely national oriented socialisation to a new one that implicates the increasing introduction of the EU operate?

In each case, I focus on upper secondary school levels of general teaching, i.e. non-vocational teaching.[4] I limit the research to the subject of history, because it is taught in every case and is given a certain importance; this allows a comparison of its content. I examine geography only in the case of France because it is closely linked with history; both disciplines are taught within the same subject and by the same teacher. History is also very relevant because it offers the opportunity to introduce the details of the EU from an historical, social and political point of view. I base my empirical research on the reading and interpretation of textbooks for pupils. I consider these pedagogical documents relevant insofar as they contain the sum of knowledge a student should or can master at his/her level (Pingel 1999).

I briefly present the main characteristics of this empirical material and some comparative data that allows me to determine the significance of the cases. After these preliminary considerations, I highlight the increasing quantitative importance

---

2.   France is a centralised country: concerning teaching, official curricula are conceived by the central government and have to be adhered to throughout the country even for private schools. In the three other countries – the UK, Germany and Spain - official curricula are adapted for the regions that are largely autonomous regarding education. For these latter cases, we respectively focus on England, Baden-Württemberg and Catalonia.

3.   I chose cases with different characteristics. France is considered a centralised country. England is considered as a political centre within the UK. Catalonia is considered as a peripheral political entity within Spain (Rokkan and Urwin 1983). Baden-Württemberg is one of the biggest German *Länder* with a very important Ministry of Education.

4.   In France, this refers to the three years of *Lycée Général* (called *Seconde, Première* and *Terminale*; normally for 15- to 18-year-olds). In England, this refers to the two years of Sixth Form College (for 16- to 18-year-olds) that prepare students for A-Levels. In Baden-Württemberg, this refers to the two years of *Gymnasiale Oberstufe* (called *Klasse 12* and *Klasse 13*; for 16- to 18-year-olds). In Catalonia, this refers to the two years of *Batxillerat* (for 16- to 18-year-olds).

of content devoted to the EU. In this part of the study, I consider only the French and English cases. This binational comparison over a longer period allows us to estimate the increasing, though not linear, importance of the EU in two countries that show opposite dynamics in their participation in this institution. I point out the ways in which the EU is made significant and how more space might be devoted to it in a deeply nation-oriented history. I then stress the different qualitative visions of this institution in the different history textbooks of France, England, Catalonia and Baden-Württemberg.

Significance of history teaching at upper secondary level

The school is a powerful socialisation agent because it allows a broad population to absorb a homogenous knowledge and common references. From the end of the nineteenth century onwards, almost all European states have built an education system in order to provide common values that tend to legitimate themselves as nations. In France in 1922 the French sociologist Émile Durkheim underlined how necessary it was for the state to educate its population in order to create a community (Durkheim 2006). School teaching was built as the conveyor of knowledge by the state because of its potential for targeting a broad population. In this logic, the subject of history was very important because it directly allowed for a selection of a particular history from past events and enabled a presentation of the state's idealistic vision of itself. Nowadays in Europe, school teaching remains a socialisation agent that is mainly structured by the states or by infra-state organisations. They can manage or at least participate in the structure of the school system and propose curricula in order to regulate what to teach to pupils or even transmit specific values (Bauvois-Cauchepin 2002; Gellner 1989).

The aims of school education can vary significantly according to the objectives recognised by each society. School education may give priority to a universal knowledge that each pupil is supposed to master before leaving school. Another model gives the priority to practical knowledge for pupils and the purpose of school is to provide them training for the job they are to perform. Even if in reality each school system tries to realise both aims, a system will offer more possibilities for the attainment of one of them in accordance with historical choices, cultural values or as a response to specific needs (Waterkamp 2006). Roughly speaking, France and Catalonia may be considered bound by the ideal of universal knowledge, whereas the UK and Germany are more strongly bound by the ideal of practical knowledge.[5] Thus, general education at upper secondary level targets relatively

---

5. More precisely, in France, 54 per cent of pupils who obtained the *Baccalauréat* (the official examination at the end of upper secondary level) in 2007 were enrolled on the general degree (according to France's Education Ministry. Online. Available: http://www.education.gouv.fr/cid143/le-baccalaureat.html). Seventy-two per cent of upper secondary Spanish pupils were enrolled in 2007 on a general course (about the same figure for Catalonia). In 2002, 28 per cent of upper secondary British pupils and 37 per cent of upper secondary German pupils took general education courses according to Eurydice data.

more students in France and Catalonia than in the UK and Germany (Fialaire 1996; Vaniscotte 1996).

The subject of history is compulsory in France, Baden-Württemberg and Catalonia. For the latter, an introduction to the history of Spain is compulsory in the second year whereas the study of the contemporary world is optional in the first year.[6] On the other hand, English pupils preparing for A-levels must choose three or four subjects they want to learn: history is therefore optional at upper secondary level and only chosen by a few – only 6 per cent of the pupils.[7] There is evidently a huge difference in the number of pupils that learn history at this level among European countries.[8]

History teaching also depends on the education policies of the state and the delegation of competences among infra-state levels. In France, Germany and Catalonia, there is quite a precise curriculum about what to teach and how to teach it. In France, the curriculum is decided at state level, whereas in Germany, different curricula are adopted by each *Bundesland* (federal state). In the latter, the *Land* makes independent decisions about teaching and school organisation, although recent dynamics toward the homogenisation of education for the entire state can be observed. If in Germany the drive is toward a greater homogeneity, in Spain the opposite is true.

In Spain, the education sector depends on a compromise between the state and the *Comunidad Autónoma.* In the Catalonian case, this compromise is the object of intense debate, because of the will of Catalonia to see its autonomy guaranteed. In order to organise the sharing of competences, the elaboration of curricula is distributed among the Catalan *Departament d'Educació* and the centralised Spanish *Ministro de Educación y Ciencia.* Officially the Catalan *Departament d'Educació* can write 45 per cent of the curriculum, whereas the Spanish *Ministro de Educación y Ciencia* can decide on 55 per cent of its content. This precise distribution is hard to establish in practice; at the very least, we can say that the Catalan region does possess a remarkable amount of autonomy in decisions on teaching. Moreover, history, like all other topics, is taught in the Catalan language.

In the UK, each 'nation' independently administers education. In England, great freedom is given to teachers in the upper secondary level. However, pupils have to pass final exams. These exams are entirely designed by private examination boards which organise the exams and assess the pupils. For each subject, various boards are in competition; they are totally independent from the schools and the teachers have to choose one of them in order to assess all students. Examination boards

6.   In Catalonia, the upper secondary level is divided in two years. The first one is called *Batxillerat 1* and the second one is called *Batxillerat 2.*

7.   Statistics from the Department for Children, Schools and Family for the years 2008/9. Online. Available: http://www.education.gov.uk/researchandstatistics/statistics (accessed 10 October 2013).

8.   All the statistical references and information about the school system are found on the Eurydice website. Online. Available: http://eacea.ec.europa.eu/education/eurydice/index_en.php. (accessed 10 October 2013) The education ministries of each country also publish data on their official websites.

play a key role in this system because they determine the type of examination for a whole class of pupils. They determine the curriculum for the exam and types of exercises required. They strongly influence teachers' curricula.

Finally, we also have to take into account the patterns of history teaching. In France, Germany and Catalonia, this topic follows a chronological order: the more advanced the pupil, the more recent the period being studied. In England, teaching is thematic: teachers choose the topic they would like to teach, only taking into account the constraints of the examination board.

These different ways of organising history teaching should be kept in mind when carrying out a comparison. In each case, history teaching has different objectives. Institutional contexts and social debates largely explain the content of history teaching. Moreover, the pattern and organisation of this subject give information about possible further evolutions regarding the integration of new topics such as European integration.

Relevance of history textbooks for the analysis of school socialisation

Despite the importance of textbooks as common documents, there is little scholarly interest in them; this is especially marked in political socialisation research.[9] Some general studies on these documents have been published (Choppin 1992; Børre Johnsen 1993) yet few analyses of the content of textbooks with a comparative perspective have been undertaken (Baeyens 2001; Prats 2001; Schissler and Soysal 2005). The Council of Europe has recently launched a scholarly research project on European history textbooks (Pingel 2000; Stradling 2001) in order to estimate the importance of the national perspective and to push forward greater consideration of the European dimension.[10]

Although textbooks are supposed to be fairly easy to read insofar as they are normally published for young pupils, their interpretation is much more complicated. Indeed, textbooks largely exceed their pedagogical function: 'A textbook is neither just subject content, nor pedagogy, nor literature, nor information, nor morals nor politics. It is the freebooter [*sic*] of public information, operating in the gray zone between community and home, science and propaganda, special subject and general education, adult and child' (Børre Johnsen 1993). Beyond the pupils for whom the books are normally written, there is a larger population that has a stake in these textbooks. Many people who are involved in school

---

9. Very important studies about textbooks are carried out at the Georg-Eckert Institute that is located in Braunschweig, Germany. This institute gathers large numbers of history textbooks from various countries and researchers then examine them. This institute has been built on the idea that the misinterpretation of history in textbooks could be responsible for modern international conflict (Pingel 1999).

10. Indeed, the Council of Europe proposes an important programme that tries to promote the European dimension in the teaching of history with recommendations for each member state. Online. Available: http://www.coe.int/t/dg4/education/historyteaching/projects/europeandimension/Europeandimensionint ro_E N.asp?

education at different levels, e.g. teachers, pupils' parents, associations, religious actors, etc., all demand something different from textbooks. This is even more obvious where history textbooks are concerned because history has to deal with issues faced by the society in question (Choppin 1992). Moreover, textbooks can be considered as authoritative documents among pupils insofar as they present a knowledge that the latter should learn. Coupled with the capacity to define social issues and positions on these issues, there are many social and political actors interested in the steps involved in the conception of textbooks (Pingel 1999). First of all, there are the public institutions (centralised *Ministère de l'Éducation nationale* in France, or regional institutions elsewhere) that define the curricula. Textbooks are linked with public institutions since they must take into account the official curricula. In Baden-Württemberg, authorisation by the federal Ministry of Education (*Ministerium für Kultus, Jugend und Sport*) prior to the publication of textbooks is compulsory. The same is true of Catalonia, where an accreditation from the *Department d'Educació* of Catalonia is necessary prior to the publication of a textbook.[11] France does not have the same restrictive measures, but teachers' inspectors often participate unofficially as textbook authors (Blanc 2011; Choppin 1992). Nowadays, generally speaking, history textbook editors respect the terms of the official curricula, on which they depend.

We must also take into account various interest groups from a variety of fields. Economic, religious, political and cultural actors try to influence the content of textbooks (Børre Johnsen 1993). In the present case, we would note the incentives offered by the Council of Europe, which encourage a European dimension in the study of history (Pingel 1999). Meanwhile, textbook publishers compete for customers i.e. the teachers who impose the same book on the whole class (Choppin 1992). In England, textbooks need to respond to the requirements of university admission and above all to the demands of the private examination boards (Jones 2003; Singh 1995).[12] Textbook editors may integrate these factors with the official curricula while taking into account their own editorial choices. The authors of the textbooks are also selected by editors according to the latter's own criteria. The writers are often teachers of upper secondary level schools or universities. In France, they may also be school inspectors (Choppin 1992).

Although the primary stated objective of history textbooks is to respond to didactic goals, many political variables influence the conception of these documents. Each history textbook tends to propose a certain interpretation of historical events, which tends overall to be a national interpretation, since they are closely linked to official curricula organised on a national basis. Also, while it is true that textbooks are not the entirety of school teaching, in other words, they do not in themselves constitute what the pupils learn or know, these books are a relevant witness to what can be taught or even 'safely' taught in a classroom.

---

11. *See* information on the Eurydice website or on official websites of the educational institutions.

12. In the case of England, the examination system for A-Levels is private. The examination boards are in competition and they fix their own curricula and examination procedures.

Indeed, in history textbooks one tends to find that histories take on board the curricula and then integrate different social consensuses. Even if textbooks are not read by every pupil and differ from teacher to teacher, one can argue that at the very least they represent a marker or a basis of a history that is shared enough to be transmitted to a younger generation. If history textbooks are not a socialisation agent as such, they are a good witness of one mode of history that can be taught.

Data and Method

For each country, a comparable number of contemporary textbooks was selected. I considered only the educational levels at which pupils have to study the history of the second half of the twentieth century. In each case, I surveyed books with a significant number of editions, which were also published by major publishers, i.e., those most popular among teachers. For Baden-Württemberg, I selected three textbooks edited for the *13 Klasse* (Bahr *et al.* 2003; Dilger *et al.* 2002; Pfändtner and Weber 2002). For Catalonia, I selected three textbooks for the *Batxillerat 1* (Trepat *et al.* 1999; Quinquer Vilamitjana *et al.* 1999; Alarcia *et al.* 1998) and five for the *Batxillerat 2* (Prats and Trepat 2003; García Sebastián *et al.* 2001; Masip i Uset *et al.* 1999; Llorens *et al.* 1999; Casassas *et al.* 1999). For England, I selected from among major educational publishers seven textbooks that deal with the second part of the twentieth century (Smith 1999; Murphy 2000; Todd 2001; Petheram 2001; Roberts 2001; Aldred 2004; Rowe 2004). Finally, for France, I selected five history textbooks for the *Terminale* level (Brisson *et al.* 1989; Lambin 2008; Falaize *et al.* 2008; Bourel and Chevallier 2008; Marseille 2008), four geography textbooks for the *Terminale* level (Joyeux 2008; Mathieu 2004; Jalta *et al.* 2008; Ciattoni 2008), and four geography textbooks for the *Première* level (Joyeux 2003; Mathieu 2003; Ciattoni 2003; Jalta *et al.* 2003). Textbooks are from the most popular publishers, i.e. Hachette, Nathan, Magnard and Hatier. There are few significant differences between textbooks in each country, but there are huge differences between countries.[13] I also considered two French-German textbooks that were published in 2006 (Geiss and Le Quintrec 2006a; 2006b) because of the originality of the common initiative. However, I did not use their content in the analysis because these textbooks show more a juxtaposition of two visions than a mix of them.

In my comparative study of history textbooks, I focussed on the way the EU has emerged in a context where an emphasis on the national approach is pre-eminent. I selected the history textbooks available for general upper secondary level. Information about the EU is available in textbooks on other subjects such as

---

13. The process of textbook publishing limits any real innovations or originality. First, the constraints for the production of these documents do not allow independent editors to propose textbooks. Next, these books present few significant differences within countries because of the strong competition between major publishers, the demands of the official curricula and the rapid production of textbooks. However, there are real differences in textbooks, such as shape and content, in terms of the examples studied here.

social studies or political studies, but depending on the country, different treatment is given to this topic. However, I focussed only on history, because this subject is important and is taught in every case under consideration. It was easier to compare the content of the books of various countries. Only for France did I also consider geography textbooks, since both subjects are closely linked and are taught by the same teacher.

Once I selected the examples, I read the books and carried out a content analysis. I focussed mainly on the chapters that contained either special topics on, or simply evocations of the EU. The objective of my qualitative hermeneutic analysis was to understand the message transmitted by textbooks (Pingel 1999). To do so, I extracted the main ideas of the chapter, illustrated by the most representative quotes. The comparison was a necessary step to interpret and to distinguish between specific descriptions of the EU.

There were two steps in this analysis. The first was a quantitative approach carried out only for France and England to underline the increasing importance of the EU as an emerging object of historical study. Using a chronological perspective, I show that the EU as a topic was integrated very slowly and relatively late in history textbooks; its incorporation lagged far behind the beginning of the EU's actual construction. The second step focused on the textbooks currently used in France, England, Baden-Württemberg and Catalonia. Using a qualitative approach, I describe the ways the EU is evoked and demonstrate how different meanings are attached to this new institution in each geographical entity.

Introduction of the European Union as a topic in history lessons in France and England

The introduction of the EU into history teaching and textbooks was not obvious within the largely nation-oriented content. The topic emerged very progressively and differently in each case. In this chapter, I present two examples of the incorporation of the EU into textbooks. I selected the French and English cases because they represent different patterns.[14] The study of the EU is increasingly proposed as a teaching topic for upper secondary pupils. In parallel, EU treaties encourage the introduction of this topic into history teaching. This might take place in two ways: the EU could be described in terms of its institutions, historical evolution or political issues; additionally, the Council of Europe proposed the possibility of interpreting historical events from a European perspective in order to diminish the emphasis on the national dimension in traditional teaching. Indeed, the study of the EU has an increasing presence in history curricula and

---

14. The cases of Baden-Württemberg and Catalonia are put aside for the moment. Spain joined the European Economic Community (ancestor of the EU) in 1986 and so there is not a long enough time span over which to measure the evolution of the EU in textbooks. We can only say that no Catalonian history textbooks have more than ten pages on this topic. Generally, the topic occupies three to four pages. The Baden-Württemberg history textbooks show an increasing importance given to the EU, similar to French textbooks. However, the French sample was more complete allowing a full chronological observation.

consequently, in history textbooks. Even if the national dimension remains largely the norm in history, there are tendencies in curricula and in textbooks that give more weight to the presentation of events from a European point of view.

Various scholars admit (with hope or regret) that European integration calls for changes to traditional ways of teaching history to pupils (Rousselier 1993). This observation was the topic of a general meeting held in Blois, France on the 13th and 14th October 2000 (Rioux 2001). It was organised by the French Ministry of Education when France presided the rotating presidency of the European Council. This meeting gathered the representatives of each of the then fifteen EU member states: staff from education ministries, teachers and historians. Some propositions about how to teach students about Europe and the EU were put forward. The main criticism was of the nation-oriented teaching of history in schools: the construction of a national memory, the encouragement of national feeling, the teleological rebuilding of the national process. The meeting's aim was to find new practical ways of teaching history; 'Europeanisation' provided an opportunity to move on from old habits. However no precise recommendations emerged about teaching content about Europe or the EU.

From a chronological point of view, I describe the emergence of the EU as a new topic to be covered in history textbooks. In parallel, I note observations about the textbooks and official curricula, especially for France, because new textbook editions were generally printed after the implementation of a new curriculum.

The case of France

With regards to 'Europeanisation', general (non-vocational) history teaching in upper secondary schools in France shows increasing incorporation of the European dimension.[15] The year 1995 represented a transition for the *Seconde* and *Première* levels (Garcia and Leduc, 2003). Since then, a more thematic approach and a greater interest in a more European dimension have become more prominent including the study of Athenian democracy, the twelfth century, the Renaissance and the Industrial Revolution.[16] Following the implementation of the 1995 curriculum, certain dynamics have encouraged the understanding of Europe as a whole, not only as a mosaic of states. The Maastricht Treaty can be seen as one of the instigators of these developments.[17] Previously, while the whole of Europe

---

15. The French *Lycée* is composed of three levels: the first one is called *Seconde* (15-year-olds), the second one is called *Première* (16-year-olds) and the last one is called *Terminale* (17-year-olds).

16. Albeit in *Seconde*, from 1981 to 1986, history teaching gave the study of civilisations a prominent place.

17. Article 128 §1: 'The Community shall contribute to the flowering of the cultures of the Member States, while respecting their national and regional diversity and at the same time bringing the common cultural heritage to the fore'. Also, Article 128 §2: 'Action by the Community shall be aimed at encouraging cooperation between Member States and, if necessary, supporting and supplementing their action in the following areas: improvement of the knowledge and dissemination of the culture and history of the European peoples; conservation and safeguarding of cultural heritage of European significance.'

was taken into account (in teaching the Industrial Revolution and totalitarianism, for example), the study of these topics was largely divided into learning separate histories of each individual state.

The *Terminale* level (last year of upper secondary education) focuses on the period following the Second World War. Theoretically, it is at this level that the EU is supposed to be introduced. In examining a textbook published in 1989 (Brisson *et al.* 1989), we note that no more than eight pages concern the construction of Europe ('Chapter 4: the Occidental World: Western Europe Edification – 1946–57') and two other pages on this topic are integrated into a chapter on the geopolitical aspects of the Western world. In this chapter, a section called 'Europe looking for unity' is immediately followed by another: 'Unity should not occur at the expense of identity'. This manner of presentation highlights concerns about the old national cultures. The introduction of the European entity is very limited and this textbook gives preference to questions and doubts about the loss of national identities.

By comparison, the history textbooks based on the July 2002 curriculum that are currently in use at the *Terminale* level (Lambin 2008; Falaize *et al.* 2008; Bourel and Chevallier 2008; Marseille 2008) contain two entire chapters about the EU: one deals with the construction of Europe before 1989 and another with European integration after this date. This seems to mark progress where the study of the EU is concerned; however, ever since the implementation of the 2002 curriculum, the study of the EU has been reserved for pupils enrolled on either an economics course or a literature course, in other words, about 49 per cent of general upper secondary pupils.[18] For the science courses that the majority of pupils pursue, the EU is not studied at all.[19] However, for all courses, France devotes at least one third of the time to teaching the history of France. Hence, there is only one sense in which there has been progress and this only applies to half of the pupils. The national perspective remains the most important for all of them.

The EU is more prominent in the subject of geography. As mentioned previously, this is taught together with history as a single subject in France. The topic focuses on the 'Great Powers' at the *Terminale* level. In the October 1993 curriculum, the EU is not mentioned at all and is almost absent from textbooks. Approximately ten years later, after the introduction of the October 2002 curriculum, the economic structure of the EU is introduced in one textbook chapter for each edition. However, this chapter is relevant only to the pupils who are not enrolled on a science course. Therefore, at the *Terminale* level, there is currently no mention of the EU for more than half the pupils.

In geography at *Première* level, evolutions in history teaching are much more obvious. After the Second World War, the curriculum was devised so that studies

---

18. According to the data of French Ministry of Education in 2008. Online. Available: http://media. education.gouv.fr /file/2008/69/0/ NI_provisoire_BAC2008_31690.pdf

19. In France at upper secondary level, pupils choose between a scientific, an economic or a literature-based course of study. The teaching of history differs slightly between each course of study.

would focus on France and the French Union (colonies). Significantly, at the beginning of the 1980s, the study of the French colonies had been replaced by the study of Europe – which was in fact the European Economic Community (EEC). The historical context explains some of the evolutions in teaching: decolonisation was almost over and France shifted its focus toward the EEC. In parallel, European integration was in progress. It is quite telling that the study of the French colonies was replaced by the study of Europe. This is evidence of changes in French strategic policy around the 1980s. What is the situation nowadays? The October 2002 curriculum institutes the presentation of Europe in terms of its geography (including its geographical limits, cultures, etc.) and in terms of the introduction of the EU (its history, institutions, functioning, policy, enlargement and issues). This topic comprises about one third of the teaching time for the geography course at this level. In addition, the study of France continues to represent more than one third of the subject.

We can conclude that in history and geography courses taught in general upper secondary level in present day France, the European dimension is increasing, even if topics on the EU remain very limited. Only geography at the *Première* level provides an opportunity for all pupils to learn about this institution. In fact, the introduction of the EU as a topic of study is quite limited compared to its major impact on the everyday lives of Europeans. Instead, the endurance of nationhood is obvious: the topic of 'France' remains by far the most studied topic at upper secondary level. However, by comparison, it is still possible to assert that France remains one of the most advanced countries with respect to introducing the EU into the curriculum (Pingel 2000).[20] A look at English textbooks will confirm this assertion.

The case of England

In England, a teacher at upper secondary level can choose what topics to teach as long as it accords with the stipulations of the chosen examination board. In history, teachers generally choose a topic linked to English or at least to British history. European countries or issues with a European dimension are not usually included as topics. In fact, the most frequently chosen topics concern Great Britain during the dynasties of the Tudors and the Stuarts. Thus there is little emphasis on the EU at all. There is therefore, little likelihood that the few pupils who choose history at A-level will acquire information about the EU. Concerning the choice of textbook, teachers adopt the book considered to be the best for the chosen topics. In about thirty history textbooks published by Cambridge University Press, only two of them are about the twentieth century and could therefore include information on aspects of the EU (or its forerunners, the ECSC and the EEC). The first (Smith 1998) is entitled *British Imperialism 1750–1970*, and mentions the history of the EU very briefly. The second (Todd 2001) is entitled *Democracies and Dictatorships – Europe*

---

20. An overview of history textbooks in other European countries showed that German and French textbooks are those that give the greatest emphasis to the EU (Blanc 2011).

and the World, 1919–1989. In this book there is not a single mention of the EU. In about thirty history textbooks edited by Heinemann, one of the most well-known textbook editors, only two books discuss the EU. The first one (Aldred 2004) is entitled *British Imperial and Foreign Policy, 1846–1980.* It dedicates a whole chapter to the EEC but focuses on the difficulties the UK faces in conforming as a member state. The second book (Rowe 2004) is entitled *Britain 1929–98.* There is a chapter on the EU but the approach is also focused on the obstacles the UK faces as a member. These exemplar textbooks shed light on the character of history education in England which gives minimal importance to the EU.

We can conclude that the European dimension has progressed both in French and in English textbooks; the presence of the EU is increasing. However, nowadays, the study of the EU remains a minor topic. The evolution of the EU as a subject of historical study in school is very slow and is different for each country. For both France and England, the national focus remains very important.

The European Union in history textbooks

How is the EU presented in history textbooks currently in use in France, England, Catalonia and Baden-Württemberg in general upper secondary education?

In France, geography textbooks published for the *Première* level dedicate the greatest coverage to the EU. These books all use the same structure in presenting the EU. The first part presents Europe as a continent: more precisely, it describes the issue of geographical limits and the cultural identity of the continent. The second section uses the first as a basis upon which to describe the EU.

The chapters focusing on the EU in French geography textbooks for the *Première* level (Joyeux 2003; Mathieu 2003; Ciattoni 2003; Jalta *et al.* 2003) have been analysed. In terms of the number of pages dedicated to particular subjects, the enlargement of the EU appears as the most important issue. All editions present this topic with written text describing the issue along with practical exercises to complement the material. For instance, Joyeux (2003: 54) dedicates two pages to thoughts about the possibility of the future expansion of the EU under the heading 'The enlargement of Europe, how and how far?' EU enlargement is discussed over two pages, accompanied by documents on criteria and costs. The question of Turkey's membership is significant: should or will Turkey be integrated into the EU or not? Editors seem to deem this debate particularly relevant; three out of four editors stress the issue. Mathieu (2003: 58) even uses a double page spread with the heading: 'Turkey at the gates of Europe, pros and cons to EU integration'. In every textbook, the enlargement issue is linked mainly to questions about European identity.

Besides EU enlargement, the former make-up of the EU is another important topic. The history of the EU is introduced in different ways, by maps, chronology or through written text. Some editors stress ideals that could legitimise the make-up of the EU. For example, Ciattoni (2003: 46) emphasises the necessity for remaining independent while being caught in the middle of the two opposing blocs during the Cold War. The respect for democracy and liberal capitalism are the two principles that are promoted in this text in order to legitimise the establishment of the EU.[21] In parallel, Joyeux (2003: 48) emphasises the EU's role in peacekeeping.

Of lesser importance, the topic of EU institutions is presented in these textbooks. All of these books present this topic but in a variety of ways. In the case of Joyeux (2003: 50), a simple page of text is presented with the heading: 'How is the European Union functioning?'[22] In contrast, Mathieu (2003: 51) includes a synthetic diagram while Ciattoni (2003: 50) introduces a more critical description proposing reflections on the 'necessary reform of institutions'. Jalta *et al.* (2003: 58) emphasise the problems with the Union and even describe it in terms of an 'organisation far-removed from the citizen'. Where EU institutions are concerned, some textbooks (Ciattoni 2003; Joyeux 2003) present the institutional debate questioning the place of the state and introduce the contrast between a 'Europe of nations' and a federal Europe.

The concrete policies of the EU are mentioned less often but are still present. The Common Agricultural Policy (CAP) is the most frequent and obvious example. Mathieu (2003: 52) describes the policy critically, calling it 'an expensive success' and points to 'the deficiencies of other policies' as well.[23] The geography textbook of Jalta *et al.* (2003) contains the most precise description of concrete policies with a six-page highlighted presentation including various documents. The EU policy for students and universities, the CAP and the 'Natura 2000' programme are reviewed. Only one textbook (Ciattoni 2003) introduces a topic on the euro currency.

We should keep in mind that the current *Première* level curriculum for geography imposes a link between the EU as a topic and the description of Europe as a continent. As such, most textbooks present these topics together. Indeed the textbooks examined present the European continent as the basis for the establishment of the EU. Hence before discussing the EU, all the textbooks present a chapter on Europe that largely focuses on the nature of European identity. This material includes the issue of geographical boundaries of the continent as well as ideas about the demography of Europe. All textbooks reminisce about the existence of a European identity whose roots can purportedly be traced back to ancient times. Joyeux (2003: 24) defines Europe as a place that has been shaped since ancient times by the influences of Christianity, the Middle Ages, the Renaissance and the Enlightenment. Mathieu (2003: 14) gives this identity some specific characteristics:

> Europe is endowed with a strong identity and remains a reference for the world, not least because it is the cradle of certain principles on which contemporary civilisation are founded, such as democracy, human rights and economic liberalism.[24]

---

21. Original in French: '*Le respect de la démocratie et des règles du capitalisme libéral*'.

22. Original in French: '*Comment fonctionne l'Union européenne?*'

23. Original in French: '*politique agricole commune, un succès coûteux* [...], *les déficiences des autres politiques*'.

24. Textbook authors have stressed the words in bold. Original version in French: '*L'Europe est dotée*

A genuine European identity is described here. This is based on ancient historical origins, some perpetual provisions and peculiar characteristics. However all these textbooks highlight a paradox: even if European identity is said to be the result of an ancient culture, the most important feature of this culture is described in national terms. This quote from Mathieu (2003: 14) is relevant here:

> Europeans have shared a long and common history but Europe is not yet uniform. National cultures based on language, religion and political history of each state endure.[25]

Such an impression is reiterated in Joyeux (2003: 24):

> National culture is the product of history, customs and collective experiences and is characterised by the practice of language, religion and an attachment to a common past. This is the source of the existence of a political model: the nation-state. Nowadays, Europeans refer first of all to that national culture when they define themselves.[26]

These two quotes are particularly significant, for they highlight the main impression created by these textbooks: that national identity remains a priority. It seems that a genuine European identity is primarily a national one. The EU is introduced on this basis.

All of the observations pertaining to geography textbooks for the *Première* level are likewise valid for the history textbooks available at the *Terminale* level.[27] All these books contain two chapters about the EU: the first describes the period prior to 1989 and the second describes what happened after 1989. The topics on the EU are exactly the same as those seen in the geography textbooks at the *Première* level: enlargement, historical make-up, institutions and concrete policies. The main difference is in the way the EU topics are studied. The approach is more historical and more chronological. Also, these textbooks tend to highlight more often the original ideals of peace in the founding of the EU. Some textbooks present the key role played by the alliance between France and Germany in driving forward the union. Overall, these different aspects are more detailed in the history textbooks for the *Terminale* level but the overall meaning does not significantly change.

---

*d'une **forte identité** et reste une référence aux yeux du monde, ne serait-ce que parce qu'elle est le berceau de quelques principes qui ont fondé la civilisation actuelle, **comme la démocratie, les droits de l'homme et le libéralisme économique**'.*

25. Original version in French: '*Les Européens ont partagé une **longue histoire** commune, mais l'Europe n'est pas uniforme pour autant. **Les cultures nationales**, dont les fondements sont la langue, la religion et l'histoire politique de chaque Etat, restent vivaces*'.

26. Original version in French: '*La culture nationale est le produit de l'histoire, des habitudes, des pratiques collectives, et se caractérise par la pratique d'une langue, d'une religion, et par l'attachement à un passé commun. Elle est à la source de l'existence d'un modèle politique : l'Etat-nation. Aujourd'hui, c'est d'abord à cette culture nationale que les Européens font référence quand ils se définissent*'.

27. Note that the chapters on the EU at this level are only reserved for pupils that enrolled on economics or literary courses (less than half of pupils).

Geography textbooks available at the *Terminale* level introduce the EU as a great economic power (Joyeux 2008; Mathieu 2004). The EU is presented here as an important economic partner in global trade. However, all of the textbooks studied stress the weakness of this corporate actor and in doing so highlight some major disparities among member states. It is still considered above all as a union of states. For example, the following is seen in Joyeux (2008: 172):

> Do not confuse the EU with a state. For economic data, the EU is often compared with the United States. But only the association of states allows the EU to be compared with giants like the United States, Japan or even China. In the EU, only the five richest states are responsible for the most important economic achievements.[28]

We can conclude that in spite of a will to legitimise the EU, a strong persistence of the national dimension exists in the teaching of history and geography offered at the general upper secondary level in France. Europe as the ground of a European culture is introduced in textbooks but its direction appears to be dictated by a handful of strong nations. Emphasis on national heritage in history and geography teaching persists and discussion of the EU appears modest when compared to the national dimension. We may also note that the description of the EU seems to be cast in the same mould as that of the nation: a territory that shapes identity. The EU appears to be the extension of the nation according to the French model. Here, the EU is nothing more that the continuity of the nation and even serves to perpetuate a national point of view.

In Baden-Württemberg schools, the chronological approach is the traditional way of teaching history and the contemporaneous period is studied during the last year of upper secondary education. The history curriculum of Baden-Württemberg requires that pupils enrolled in *Klasse 13* study the period from the Second World War onward. As an approximate estimate of the importance of the EU in one of the textbooks (Bahr *et al.* 2003), only one of eighteen chapters covers this topic. Five chapters cover German history, four chapters are dedicated to other countries (France, the USSR, the USA and China), six chapters propose a European dimension (sometimes global) and two chapters deal with epistemology and method. The relative insignificance of the EU is also observable in the other Baden-Württemberg textbooks.

In the chapter on the EU, the textbooks highlight above all else the history of the organisation of Europe and the description of its institutions. The presentation of EU institutions is an important topic. Textbooks describe in great technical detail each element that ensures the continued functioning of the EU – the parliament,

---

28. Original version in French: '*Ne pas confondre : UE et Etat. Dans les données économiques, l'UE est souvent comparée aux Etats-Unis comme s'il s'agissait de la mise en relation de deux Etats. Seule leur association au sein de l'UE permet aux Etats européens de tenir la comparaison avec des géants comme les Etats-Unis, le Japon ou même la Chine. De même qu'au sein de l'UE, ce sont en réalité les 5 pays les plus riches qui assurent l'essentiel de ses performances économiques*'.

the council, the commission, etc. In this presentation, comparisons are often drawn between the functioning of the EU versus a federal state: 'The EU represents more than a confederation but has less competence than a state' (Bahr *et al.* 2003 178).[29]

The history of the EU's construction and its aims constitute a very important part of the chapter on this topic. The authors note that the European idea is quite old insofar as it dates back to the beginning of the twentieth century. However, in German textbooks, the European construction appears as an idea or as a will, whereas in French textbooks it is based on the existence of a European civilisation. German textbooks present the reasons that have motivated the construction of the EU, including security and the pursuit of peace. The textbooks argue that the construction of the EU is a direct consequence of the Second World War:

> The beginning of May 1945 was the end of the Second World War for Germany and for most other European states. Millions dead, millions crippled, millions of refugees; many destroyed cities, many broken bridges and desolation in the midst of a landscape in ruins [...]. Europe must reflect upon itself if it is not to become the ground for the hell of a Third World War (Dilger *et al.* 2002: 518).[30]

> The process of Western European integration after the Second World War was the affirmative response to a series of vital challenges with which the western states were confronted: the economic reconstruction of a Europe destroyed by war was not possible without an alliance of all the powers (Pfändtner and Weber 2002: 400).[31]

In Pfändtner and Weber (2002: 400), the EU is also seen as a necessity in the context of the Cold War:

> The fear of the hegemonic endeavours of Soviet military power also demanded appropriate measures in the interests of the West in a well-regulated collaboration with the Federal Republic of Germany, in order to stabilise the Western world. Moreover, many Europeans hoped that a united (Western) Europe could become a third force between the world powers and could prevent them from dangerous confrontation.[32]

---

29. Original version in German: '*Die EU [...] stellt mehr als einen Staatenbund dar, hat aber doch weniger Kompetenzen als ein Staat*'.

30. Original version in German: '*Anfang Mai 1945 endete für Deutschland und die meisten anderen europäischen Staaten der Zweite Weltkrieg. Millionen Tote, Millionen Krüppel, Millionen Flüchtlinge; viele Städte zerstört, viel Brücken gesprengt, Trostlosigkeit inmitten einer Trümmerlandschaft [...]. Europa musste sich neu besinnen, wenn es nicht im Inferno eines Dritten Weltkrieges zu Grunde gehen sollte*'.

31. Original version in German: '*Der Prozeß der westeuropäischen Integration nach dem Zweiten Weltkrieg war die positive Antwort auf eine Reihe existentieller Herausforderungen, denen sich die westlichen Staaten gegenübergestellt sahen: Der wirtschaftliche Wiederaufbau des vom Kriege zerstörten Europa war ohne eine Zusammenfassung aller Kräfte nicht möglich*'.

32. Original version in German: '*Die Furcht vor den hegemonialen Bestrebungen der sowjetischen Militärmacht verlangte ebenso nach geeigneten Maßnahmen wie das Interesse des Westens an einer geregelten Zusammenarbeit mit der Bundesrepublik zur Stärkung der westlichen Welt. Viele*

Besides security and peace, the other reasons that legitimise the construction of Europe – the cultural, economical and environmental justifications – receive less mention. There are some similarities among the member countries that could explain a will to form a union. The textbooks show the positive consequences of European integration, such as the free movement of people, goods and capital. Indeed, these textbooks are palpably optimistic about the construction of Europe.

In conclusion, the Baden-Württemberg history textbooks used at upper secondary level do not propose a parallel between Europe and the EU, unlike the French texts. On the contrary, the needs of this new institution are seen as an answer to the conflicts that had previously erupted across Europe. In the textbooks, the construction of the EU is described as a fairly positive process in which Germany is largely implicated. I argue that the EU is presented in these German textbooks as an institution that has helped Germany to legitimise itself as a state, and even as a newly-fashioned pacifist nation. This conclusion is supported by the comment: 'Ultimately, for the people of the Federal Republic of Germany, the European association offered the opportunity for a quick recovery from their international reputation and a new identity after a time of enforced nationalism' (Pfändtner and Weber 2002: 400).[33]

In Catalonian history textbooks, there is little mention of the EU. Upper secondary education is divided into two levels: the *Batxillerat 1* and the *Batxillerat 2*. The study of contemporary world history (not including Spain) from the beginning of the nineteenth century onwards is the main topic for the first year (*Batxillerat 1*). The history of Spain from the beginning of the nineteenth century (the newest editions begin from the prehistory) is the main topic for the second year (*Batxillerat 2*). The history course is only compulsory in the second year and is optional in the first year. This points to the meagre attention accorded to the EU; indeed, in the textbook that gives the greatest weight to this topic, it is covered in a section that barely amounts to ten pages (Alarcia *et al.* 1998). Other editions explicate this topic in less than three pages for both the first and second year courses. Thus, our interpretive reading of these textbooks reveals little interest in the EU. Coverage of the EU that is present stresses the history of the construction, the presentation of the institutions and the functioning of the EU. These aspects are presented in a very technical way.

The history textbooks for *Batxillerat 1* cover the nineteenth and the twentieth centuries, except where Spain itself is concerned. This is described as the history of the contemporary world. However, this subject is an option available only to pupils enrolled in a course of social studies. The subject combines a mix of

---

Europäer hofften außerdem, daß ein vereintes (West-) Europa sich als dritte Kraft zwischen den Weltmächten etablieren und deren gefährliche Konfrontation verhindern könnte'.

33. Original version in German: '*Für die Menschen in der Bundesrepublik schließlich bot der europäische Zusammenschluß die Chance zur alsbaldigen Wiedergewinnung internationaler Reputation und einer neuen Identität nach einer Zeit des übersteigerten Nationalismus'.*

European and global dimensions with a historical account of individual states. The EU is described in few pages with some technical data. The main focus is on the economy. The EU is largely seen as an economic actor pertinent to the context of globalisation.

The compulsory history teaching at *Batxillerat 2* level focuses only on Spain. In Catalonia, textbooks highlight the relationship between Spain and Catalonia. On some occasions in various editions, Catalonia even appears dissociated from the rest of Spain. Comparisons and parallels between these two territories are often evident. In this regard, this quote is particularly apt:

> The process begun with the accession of the Spanish state into the European Economic Community in 1986 and continued with the ensuing integration among European Union founding states which has had a major impact on the Catalan and Spanish economies in recent years [...]. Catalonia especially has not been a beneficiary of European Union assistance because of its specific situation in the economic context of Spain and Europe. Catalonia is a relatively rich region if we compare it to the Spanish state context, but it is below the European average. Therefore, it would need European assistance if we compare it with other regions of the continent; however it is not an object of preferential treatment within the overall assistance going to the Spanish state because in this context it is considered a rich region (Casassas *et al.* 1999: 321).[34]

In the history textbooks under study, there is no whole chapter dedicated to the EU. The topic is invariably included within a chapter on the future of Spain and Catalonia. Once more, the EU is largely evoked as an economic actor. The Catalonian textbooks show little interest in the EU. The most important part of the history presented in these texts concerns the parallels between Spain and Catalonia. Reading the information about the EU, it appears that Spain and Catalonia are studied as two separate entities each with the same administrative structures operating on coeval levels. In Llorens *et al.* (1999: 324), the section about the EU is entitled: 'Spain and Catalonia into the EU'. Thus, in introducing the topic of the EU, the heading establishes Catalonia as an independent territory. This position is also made clear in the written text:

> From this moment on [1 January 2002, when the euro was put into circulation], once borders and national currencies are abolished, language will be the most visible difference when we cross the borders of EU member states (García Sebastián *et al.* 2001: 329).[35]

---

34. Original version in Catalan: '*El procés iniciat amb l'adhesió de l'Estat espanyol a la Comunitat Econòmica Europea el 1986 i la posterior inclusió d'Espanya entre els països fundadors de la Unió Europea ha tingut una incidència fonamental en l'economia catalana i espanyola dels últims anys [...]. Catalunya no ha estat mai especialment beneficiada pels ajuts de la Unió Europea a causa de la seva situació especial dins el contet e l'economia espanyola i europea. Cataluny és una regió esconòmicament rica si tenim en compte el context de d'Estat espanyol, però se situa per sota de la mitjana europea. Per tant, necessitaria ajuts europeus per equiparar-se a les altres regions del continent i, en canvi, no és objecte d'un tracte preferent en els ajuts que rep l'Estat espanyol, perquè en aquest context se la consdidar una regió rica*'.

35. Original version in Catalan: '*Des d'aquest moment, abolides les fronteres i les monedes nacion- als, l'idioma serà la diferència més observable quan es travesin les fronteres dels països membres de la Unió Europea*'.

Although introduced with circumspection and presented primarily as an economic actor, the EU in the Catalonian textbooks enables, above all, the positioning of Catalonia on a par with other European member states. Thus the treatment of the EU as a concept in these texts reinforces the idea that Catalonia is a separate entity to Spain.

English history textbooks covering the contemporary period are in the minority. Among them, the EU occupies only a minor role. Indeed, there are very few pupils who have the opportunity to learn about this modern entity. Where the EU is discussed, however, the main topic is the chronology of the construction of the EU. The chronologies are relatively exhaustive and precise but above all they stress the difficulties the UK faces in its accession to this union as a member state. The reasons for the first two membership applications from the UK being rejected are addressed, as well as its eventual integration in 1973. Difficult relations between the UK and the EEC (and later the EU) are presented in detail. One of the history textbooks (Rowe 2004: 102) specifically examines the reasons for euro-scepticism: 'What were the reasons for the "Eurosceptic" backlash?'

Some textbooks weigh the pros and cons of the UK's membership of the EU. Petheram (2001: 330) presents these in a table with one row displaying the benefits of membership – largely commercial – and another the disadvantages – loss of sovereignty and an all too formal bind with Europe which restricts trading links with Commonwealth countries. In this textbook, pupils are asked: 'What were seen as the benefits and disadvantages of Britain joining the EEC?' (Rowe 2001: 328). Discussion of the EU seems to be limited to a list of pros and cons, from which only the positive elements can be adopted. For instance, one exercise (Rowe 2001: 325) asks: 'What is the difference between economic and political union? Does economic union encourage political union or can a separate function be maintained?' Ultimately, the UK's accession to the EU is presented largely as a marriage of convenience. This caricature is presented explicitly in a cartoon image of a woman representing Great Britain marrying a man representing Europe (Rowe 2001: 329).[36] In the church setting where the scene takes place, a spectator representing the Commonwealth is nervously opposed to this union.

In English history textbooks, the European entity is described in less enthusiastic tones than, for example, in German textbooks. Pros and cons are weighed. Questions about the benefits of the UK's integration into the EU are paramount. Europe is presented largely as a possibility rather than a necessity. Some textbooks (Rowe 2004; Collins 2000) briefly present the positive links between Britain and the EU. Rowe (2004: 103) recognises that Great Britain is becoming more and more European:

> Yet there is one present-day contradiction that is genuinely historical: whatever the future relationships between Britain and Europe, British life has never been more European than in the late 1990s. British generations brought up on mass tourism and accustomed to the influx of migrants and refugees (not to mention European football) are accustomed to drinking red wine and cafe latte, to eating pasta and driving German cars. The daily lives of British citizens reflect a

---

36. Cartoon drawing by D. Low, published on the 24 March 1948 in the *Evening Standard* newspaper.

thousand other European influences from tourism to furniture to supermarkets. Fifty years after opting out of the Treaty of Rome, Britain is undeniably 'of Europe'.

Murphy (2000: 388) approaches the topic in a similar fashion: 'How European were the British at the end of the twentieth century?' The answer includes similar elements of society, culture and economy:

> Every British citizen was a 'citizen of the union'. They carried European Union passports, and could travel and work freely throughout Europe. Many British people took holidays in Spain [...]. For young people and students, European holidays became commonplace, and initiatives such as InterRail train tickets possible because of increased co-operation between EU member states [...]. Food also was one area in which the British were becoming increasingly 'European'. The fact that Europeans could also travel and work here improved the quality and variety of restaurants enormously. Pizza and pasta from Italy was the more obvious example of European food becoming as common as British 'national' dishes, like fish and chips [...]. Football was another element of British society where European membership had a large, visible effect.

The elements used to define 'European' culture are relatively contemporaneous. We cannot find attempts to link European culture with ancient roots, as seen in the French textbooks. On the contrary, British culture is first and foremost national and elements of 'Europeanisation' are relatively recent and quite marginal - food, holidays, free movement into Europe and football. In the English textbooks, British specificity is strongly demonstrated; yet this is a recent dynamic that opens it to European tendencies.

The latter textbook also exposes the discontent of the British and the British press with the EU. Pupils are encouraged to reflect in the following exercise: 'Why was Europe so unpopular in Britain at the end of the twentieth century?' The answer provided is that: 'The battle for the hearts and minds of the people over Britain's future relations with Europe was [...] far from won' (Murphy *et al.* 2000: 390). Among the few English history textbooks that study the EU, expressions of doubt are commonplace. The authors are not particularly enthusiastic and prefer to present UK participation in the EU in terms of a checklist of pros and cons. The presentation of the EU focuses on the list of ways in which it can improve British national life.

Conclusion

This study shows the simultaneous progressive emergence of the EU as a new topic alongside an enduring model of traditional nation-oriented history teaching. It was found that the EU has an increasing presence in history textbooks in all four geographical entities studied. The EU is a new topic that is presented with varying degrees of importance, detail and enthusiasm in textbooks for general upper secondary history studies in France, England, Catalonia and Baden-Württemberg. The introduction of this new topic in textbooks seems first and foremost to serve national needs.

We can observe different visions of the EU in each country. While the EU has been accorded a greater presence over time in the texts, its description tends to marry with the view of the EU in the country or state where the text was published. National interpretation of history remains predominant. The EU has the potential to change established modes of socialisation, bringing a new perspective to traditional teaching; yet, in the history textbooks studied, the power and endurance of national perspectives are evident. Socialisation in school continues to serve national interests. We have seen that a change of perspective is difficult to achieve after such a long tradition of national socialisation. This analysis supports the idea of a 'social habitus' as defined by Elias (2001). The EU is used by the different nations to legitimise themselves in a changing world. The question remains whether this dynamic is the result of resistance grounded in the national socialisation or of an entity (the EU) still under construction, with a subsequently weak capacity for socialisation.

The focus in this study has been on history textbooks. However, we should bear in mind that pupils also receive information about the EU in other subjects and these may present the topic from other perspectives. Moreover, relevant as these documents are, increasing pride of place is given to new technologies such as video and the internet. These media are increasingly present in the classroom and children also have greater access to them after school. The importance of history textbooks therefore needs to be placed in context so that we may have a better understanding of their capacity to support a particular mode of socialisation.

Nevertheless, the study of history textbooks remains useful. It may be relevant to examine any modifications that arise in these books as a result of the current economic difficulties in Europe. This form of study could allow us to see the way in which history textbooks record contextual evolutions.

References

Alarcia, M.A., Manchó, R., Del Rosario Perez, M. and Terol, A. (1998) *Història del Món contemporani,* Barcelona: Claret.

Aldred, J. (2004) *British Imperial and Foreign Policy, 1846–1980,* Oxford: Heinemann.

Anderson, B. (2006) *Imagined Communities,* London: Verso.

Bahr F., Banzhaf, A. and Rumpf, L. (2003) *Horizonte II, Geschichte für die Oberstufe in Baden-Württemberg,* Braunschweig: Westermann.

Bartolini, S. (2005) *Restructuring Europe: Centre formation, system building, and political structuring between the nation state and the European Union,* Oxford: Oxford University Press.

Baeyens, H. (2001) 'L'éducation à l'unification européenne des années 1950 à 1998: Une contribution au débat sur la citoyenneté et l'identité', *Politique européenne,* 2001/3(4): 171–174.

Bauvois-Cauchepin, J. (2002) *Enseignement de l'histoire et mythologie nationale : Allemagne-France du début du XXe siècle aux années 1950,* Bern: Peter Lang.

Blanc, A. (2011) *Intégration européenne et évolution du concept de l'État, Réflexions à partir des manuels de l'enseignement scolaire de différents pays de l'Union européenne,* unpublished thesis, Université Aix-Marseille III.

Børre Johnsen, E. (1993) *Textbooks in the Kaleidoscope,* Oslo: Scandinavian University.

Bourel, G. and Chevallier, M. (eds) (2008) *Histoire,* Paris: Hatier.

Brisson, E., Dermenjian, G., Filippi-Codaccioni, A. and Knight-Baylac, M. (1989) *Histoire,* Paris: Bordas.

Casassas, J., Ghanime, A. and Santacana, C. (1999) *Història,* Barcelona: Grup Promotor.

Choppin, A. (1992) *Les manuels scolaires: histoire et actualité,* Paris: Hachette.

Ciattoni, A. (ed.) (2003) *Géographie,* Paris: Hatier.

—— (ed.) (2008) *L'espace mondial,* Paris: Hatier.

Davies, N. (1997) *Europe: a history,* London: Pimlico.

Dilger, A., Frevert, U., Günther-Arndt, H., Hofacker, H., Hoffman, D., Maneval, U. and Zwölfer, N. (2002) *Geschichte,* Berlin: Cornelsen.

Durkheim, É. (2006) *Éducation et sociologie,* Paris: Presses Universitaires de France.

Elias, N. (2001) *Society of Individuals,* New York: Continuum.

Falaize, B., Lauby, J.P. and Sirel, F. (2008) *Histoire, le monde contemporain de 1945 à nos jours,* Paris: Magnard.

Fialaire, J. (1996) *L'école en Europe,* Paris: La Documentation française.

Frazier, C. (1995) *L'éducation et la Communauté européenne,* Paris: CNRS Editions.

Garcia, P. and Leduc, J. (2003) *L'enseignement de l'histoire en France, de l'Ancien Régime à nos jours,* Paris: Armand Colin.

García Sebastián, M., Gatell Arimont, C., Palafox Gamir, J. and Risques Corbella, M. (2001) *Història,* Barcelona: Vicens Vives.

Geiss, P. and Le Quintrec, G. (2006a) *L'Europe et le monde depuis 1945*, Paris: Nathan/Klett.

—   (2006b) *Europa und die Welt seit 1945*, Leipzig: Nathan/Klett.

Gellner, E. (1989) *Nations et nationalisme*, Paris: Éditions Payot.

Heidenheimer, A. (1997) *Disparate Ladders: Why school and university policies differ in Germany, Japan and Switzerland*, New-Brunswick: Transaction Publishers.

Hobsbawm, E. (1990) *Nations and Nationalism since 1780: Programme, myth, reality*, Cambridge: Cambridge University Press.

Jalta, J., Joly, J. F. and Reineri, R. (eds) (2003) *L'Europe, la France*, Paris: Magnard.

Jalta, J., Joly, J. F. and Riquier, J.C. (eds) (2008) *L'espace mondial*, Paris: Magnard.

Jones, K. (2003) *Education in Britain-1944 to the Present*, Cambridge: Polity.

Joyeux, A. (ed.) (2003) *Géographie*, Paris: Hachette.

—   (ed.) (2008) *Géographie*, Paris: Hachette.

Lambin, J. M. (ed.) (2008) *Histoire*, Paris: Hachette.

Llorens, M., Ortega, R. and Roig, J. (1999) *Història*, Barcelona: Vicens Vives.

Marseille, J. (ed.) (2008) *Histoire, le monde l'Europe, la France de 1945 à nos jours*, Paris: Nathan.

Masip i Uset, M., Quninquer i Vilamitjana, D. and Casals i Mesguer, X. (eds) (1999) *Història*, Madrid: McGraw Hill.

Mathieu, J. L. (ed.) (2003) *L'Europe, la France*, Paris: Nathan.

—   (ed.) (2004) *Géographie*, Paris: Nathan.

Murphy, D., Staerck, G., Goodlad, G., Fowler, S. and Institute of Contemporary British History (eds) (2000) *Britain, 1914–2000*, London: Collins Educational.

Petheram, L. (2001) *Britain in the 20th Century*, Cheltenham: Nelson Thornes.

Pfändtner, B. and Weber, J. (2002) *Deutschland zwischen Diktatur und Demokratie. Weltpolitik im 20. Jahrhundert*, Bamberg: C.C. Buchners Verlag.

Pingel, F. (1999) *UNESCO Guidebook on Textbook Research and Textbook revision*, Hannover: Verlag Hahnsche Buchhandlung.

—   (2000) *La maison européenne: représentations de l'Europe du 20e siècle dans les manuels d'histoire*, Strasbourg: Éditions du Conseil de l'Europe.

Prats, J. (ed.) (2001) *Los jóvenes ante el reto europeo*, Barcelona: Fundación 'la Caixa'.

Prats, J. and Trepat, C. (2003) *Història*, Barcelona: Barcanova.

Quinquer Vilamitjana, D., Supeña Nualart, A., Gutierrez Martínez, J. and Casals i Meseguer, X. (1999) *Història del Món contemporani*, Madrid: McGraw Hill.

Rioux, J. P. (2001) 'Le séminaire européen de Blois', *Vingtième Siècle, Revue d'Histoire*, 71: 55–61.

Roberts, M. (2001) *Britain, 1846–1964*, Oxford: Oxford University Press.

Rokkan, S. and Urwin, D. (1983) *Economy, Territory, Identity, Politics of West European Peripheries*, London: Sage.

Rousselier, N. (1993) 'Pour une réécriture européenne de l'histoire de l'Europe', *Vingtième Siècle, Revue d'Histoire*, 38: 74–89.

Rowe, C. (ed.) (2004) *Britain, 1929–98*, Oxford: Heinemann.

Schissler, H. and Soysal, Y.N. (eds) (2005) *The Nation Europe and the World: Textbooks and curricula in transition*, New York: Berghahn Books.

Singh, J. (1995) *L'Enseignement secondaire en Angleterre*, Strasbourg: Éditions du Conseil de l'Europe.

Smith, S. C. (1999) *British Imperialism, 1750–1970*, Cambridge: Cambridge University Press.

Stradling, R. (2001) *Enseigner l'histoire de l'Europe du XXe siècle*, Strasbourg: Éditions du Conseil de l'Europe.

Thiesse, A. M. (1999) *La création des identités nationales*, Europe XVIII – XXe siècle, Paris: Seuil.

Todd, A. (2001) *Democracies and Dictatorships-Europe and the World, 1919–1989,* Cambridge: Cambridge University Press.

Trepat, C. A., Freixenet D. and Tatche E. (1999) *Història del Món contemporani*, Barcelona: Barcanova.

Vaniscotte, F. (1996) *Les écoles de l'Europe: Systèmes éducatifs et dimension européenne*, Paris: INRP.

Waterkamp, D. (2006) 'L'effet déterminant des procédés organisationnels sur les cultures de l'école', in D. Groux, J. Helmchen and E. Flitner (eds) *L'école comparée: Regards croisés franco-allemands,* Paris: L'Harmattan: 365–381.

Weber, E. (1976) *Peasants into Frenchmen: The modernization of rural France, 1870–1914,* Stanford: Stanford University Press.

Chapter Seven

The Effect of Political Socialisation Agents on Political Participation Between the Ages of Sixteen and Twenty-One

Ellen Quintelier

Introduction

Political socialisation is generally defined as 'the learning process through which the individual learns political attitudes and behaviour from generation to generation, influenced by political socialisation agents (Quintelier 2009: 20). In the literature, five important political socialisation agents have been identified: parents, school, peers, media and voluntary associations (Langton 1969: 5). Whereas political sociologists used to consider at least some political socialisation agents jointly, recent research in the field of political socialisation almost always focuses on just one at a time. Several reasons have been put forward for this such as disagreement about the age at which political socialisation is most effective; the lack of sufficient data and appropriate methods to model political socialisation processes; and the lack of a grand political socialisation theory (Claes and Quintelier 2010; Niemi and Hepburn 1995). Furthermore, research has been spread across different disciplines such as communication, sociology or psychology (McLeod and Shah 2009). So, although there is a lot of discussion about which political socialisation agent is the most important for political participation and at what age, most current research lacks any direct comparisons.

The present chapter aims to address this by comparing the impact of the five aforementioned political socialisation agents on political participation. Furthermore, using data from the Belgian Political Panel Study, we will follow the cohort longitudinally and compare the effects at three different points in time: when participants are aged sixteen, eighteen and twenty-one. By performing regression analyses at each time point, we will assess which agents of political socialisation appear to be most important and at what age political socialisation agents have the most prominent effects. The article closes with some suggestions for the kinds of strategies that are most appropriate for increasing political participation.

Five agents of political socialisation

As noted above, there are five important agents of political socialisation. Although all have proven to be relevant to political participation, there is debate over which is the most influential (Verba *et al.* 2005). While some authors argue that the family is the most important political socialisation agent (Hyman 1959; Langton 1969; Jennings *et al.* 2009), others argue that it is school (Hess and Torney 1967; Campbell 2008) or peers (Jennings and Niemi 1981). Yet no studies have addressed the relative impact of all five agents (Campbell 1980; Hyman 1959). Furthermore, it has been argued that social contexts overlap and that the effect and influence of any one of the political socialisation agents would depend on the variable of interest (McClurg 2006; Scheufele *et al.* 2006). Young people belong to different social contexts: they belong to a family, have different friends, belong to different voluntary associations and use similar types of media. Political participation does not happen in isolation, but through interaction between different people in different social contexts (Huckfeldt 1979). Research on the relationship between different agents of socialisation has always been limited:

> The comparative assessment of these forces [agencies] and the extent to which they operate in concert or disharmony has only been begun. There are still remarkably few published findings comparing different agency inputs with their ostensible socialisation outputs, or relating both to the properties of learner and teacher as intervening variables (Dennis 1968: 109).

More recent research makes a similar claim:

> It is clear to us that, for political socialisation research to thrive and address the important questions of civic education and engagement for young people, future research needs to integrate the effect of the full range of agents. Political scientists have long been interested in the impact of the family, the education system, the media, and political campaigns on the socialisation process. Future work needs to be undertaken regarding the implicit connections among these various agents (Dudley and Gitelson 2002: 180).

Therefore, the impact of one political socialisation agent should be assessed while controlling for the effects of other agents of political socialisation. Finally, as noted by Hyman, the influence of different socialisation agents changes over time: while parents are important at a young age, the importance of parents will gradually be replaced by other agents such as school, peers and the workplace (Alwin *et al.* 1992: 12; Beck 1977: 117; Hyman 1959; Jennings and Niemi 1981). The aim of this chapter is, therefore, to study the joint impact of these five socialisation agents on political participation together, and to compare these effects over time. We will focus on political participation because this outcome has been largely neglected by political sociologists thus far. Political socialisation research has long neglected political behaviour (Marsh 1971: 455). Tapper (1976: 62) explains this 'negligence' by the fact that most studies that focused on political participation used adult samples and voting as an indicator, while most political socialisation studies were based on studies of young children. Similarly, Hess and Torney (1967: 13–17) distinguish between four phases of political involvement. In the first phase, children start to identify particular objects in the political sphere and develop their own opinions on the latter. In the second phase, young people develop more elaborate opinions on political subjects, on norms of appropriate citizen behaviour and on the ways in which people can participate in society. In the third phase, children develop subjective involvement in politics in that they show positive or negative feelings toward political subjects. In the fourth phase, people begin to participate actively in political life. Although Hess and Torney argued that these phases are not necessarily experienced in this sequence, it is clear that they consider active participation to be the final step in political socialisation. Although the relationship between political socialisation and participation seems evident, there is not much evidence to support this: the political participation literature rarely focuses on young people or on the influence of political socialisation agents, while the political socialisation literature fails to take all agents of political socialisation and/or political participation into account. Therefore, we want to assess the impact of different political socialisation agents on political participation in a Belgian context.

Family

The first agent of political socialisation is the family. Overall, we expect parental socialisation to have quite a large effect on political participation, especially at a young age. Families are the main context in which early socialisation occurs and the most important place for learning about moral and social values (Grusec 2011: 244, 262). However, as Plutzer (2002) correctly points out, the influence of parents diminishes as children grow older. But, as most 21-year-olds still live with their parents, significant socialisation effects are still to be expected. In the literature two types of socialisation mechanism have been identified: direct and indirect socialisation. The intergenerational transmission of attitudes can be relatively direct; for example, adolescents may adopt the same party identification as their parents or participate in the same activities. Intergenerational transmission can also take place in a more indirect manner; specific patterns of decision making within the family and ways of interacting with the outside world will have an impact on someone's political attitudes (Jaros 1973).

Parents and families play an important role in the direct political socialisation of their children (Hyman 1959; Jennings *et al.* 2009). Parental impact has been demonstrated in relation to several attitudinal and behavioural outcomes such as party identification (Achen 2002; Niemi and Jennings 1991) and social participation (Chan and Elder 2001; Siongers 2007). Direct influence can occur as a result of parents providing information to their children, talking or discussing politics with their children or specific media use (McIntosh *et al.* 2007; Eveland and Scheufele 2000; McDevitt and Chaffee 2002).

Indirect influences within the family have also been documented in the literature. Children will be more likely to participate in civic and political life if their parents tend to participate in elections (Plutzer 2002; Martikainen *et al.* 2005), in electoral campaigns (Roker *et al.* 1999), in politics in general (Plutzer 2002; McFarland and Thomas 2006; Dawson and Prewitt 1969) or if they are actively engaged in voluntary activities (Chan and Elder 2001). We can refer to this as an indirect effect since it is evident that the behaviour of parents is not designed explicitly to influence the behaviour of their children. A more likely explanation is that parents function as a political or social role model for their children, who pick up the habit of playing an active social role (Hess and Torney 1967; Roker *et al.* 1999). Using semi-structured interviews, Quéniart (2008: 211–212) has demonstrated that in politicised families, the route to participation is easily accessible. Young people who are involved in politics most likely have family members who are also active in politics. As Chan and Elder (2001: 26) note, 'Through their own involvement, parents socialise children into a civic culture [...] and encourage participation in youth groups.' Therefore, the hypothesis is that parents have a direct and indirect influence on the political participation of their children.

Peers

We expect that peers will have a major impact on one other. Although peers never have the monopoly on political socialisation as parents do, they nonetheless influence one other quite intensely. First of all, peers are key players in the political socialisation of adolescents who help to shape young people's attitudes about politics (Torney-Purta 1995; Dawson and Prewitt 1969). Peers also interact on a relatively equal footing with one another and share a similar social status (Jaros 1973; McLeod *et al.* 1999). We will focus here on the effect of the size of the network, as well as the political diversity of intimate friends and classmates.

Granovetter (1973; 1983) in particular has emphasised the 'strength of weak ties'. He argues that casual acquaintances (weak ties) can provide people with information and resources beyond those that are available within their immediate circle of close friends and relatives (strong ties). This is because casual acquaintances often serve as bridges to social circles beyond our own, bringing us into contact with ideas and information that we might otherwise not encounter. The more tightly knit a network is, the less likely it is that any one person in the network will provide new and different information. Without such information, people are arguably less likely to participate (Teorell 2003; Delli Carpini and Keeter 1996; Eveland and Scheufele 2000). Political discussions with people who hold different viewpoints forces people to 'constantly rethink and refine their issue stances as a result of potentially being challenged in their opinions by non-likeminded others', which makes them more likely to participate (Scheufele *et al.* 2004: 316; Huckfeldt *et al.* 2004). Putnam (2000) and others have emphasised that it is not only the intensity with which people interact but also the composition of social networks that effect political outcomes. 'Bonding social capital' refers to 'ties to people who are like you in some important way', while 'bridging social capital' refers to 'ties to people who are unlike you in some important way' (Putnam 2007: 143). Putnam claims that 'bridging' interactions with people from different social backgrounds are more conducive to the acquisition of political information than 'bonding' interactions with people from similar backgrounds. There is some evidence to support the argument about the importance of bridging ties for political outcomes. For example, Rubenson (2005) demonstrated that people who had more diverse networks were more likely to vote, sign petitions, attend political meetings, take part in demonstrations or boycotts and be active in a political group.

School

A third agent of political socialisation that will be discussed, in addition to family and peers, is school. Non-political institutions such as schools can equip pupils and students with important resources required for political participation (Verba *et al.* 1995). Although it has been argued that schools can serve as an important agent of socialisation (Dewey 1913; Almond and Verba 1963), it is not always clear how schools can help increase the political participation of young people. Westheimer and Kahne (2004: 241), for instance, argue that in spite of a general agreement that civic and democratic education is necessary, there is no agreement on 'what democracy [requires] and [...] what kind of school curricula will best promote it'. Schools not only foster political participation directly through the formal curriculum, but also indirectly through the school climate, peers and teachers (Langton 1969). Similary, as Verba *et al.* (1995: 422–423) rightly conclude, 'there have been relatively few empirical inquiries as to why schooling fosters activity'. In what follows, I will consider three types of citizenship education capable of influencing the political participation of young people: formal civic education, active learning strategies and an open classroom climate (Dassonneville *et al.* 2012).

Formal civic education

The first type of citizenship education is formal civic education, which is aimed at the direct transmission of political knowledge. Past studies have yielded little evidence of the effect of formal civic education on different political attitudes (Hyman 1959). Langton (1969) and Jennings and Niemi (1968) found that civics classes had no influence on political participation and other political attitudes. For a whole generation, their results engendered negative feelings regarding the possibility of increasing political participation through the formal curriculum. The tide has only turned recently with Niemi and Junns' (1998) seminal study. By applying multivariate methods to an appropriate dataset (National Assessment of Educational Progress Civics Assessment 1988) to focus on the age at which civic education is most effective and the way civic education is taught, they find that civic education does have some impact. Since then, analysts have been more positive about the effects of a formal role for civic education in curricula (Gimpel *et al.* 2003). Civics courses should increase students' knowledge about political institutions and processes; critical thinking; personal and cognitive development; and thereby, political participation.

Active learning strategies

In addition to the formal civics curriculum, schools can also encourage students to participate in politics by creating a 'participatory school culture' and by providing active learning opportunities through which students engage in 'real life' activities and can reflect upon their actions (Torney-Purta 2002; Galston

2004). Such experience-based teaching strategies 'orient students towards norms of civic commitment' (Kahne *et al.* 2006: 402). Hence, they can be considered an essential part in the development of young people's citizenship (Mezenes 2003). Examples of active learning strategies include organising group projects, visiting government buildings and inviting government officials to school as well as creating opportunities for young people to have their say through student councils. In this regard, authors have stressed the importance of good quality teaching as well as the incorporation of active learning strategies into the curriculum.

Open classroom climate

A third way for schools to foster political participation, apart from formal civic education and active learning strategies, is through an open classroom climate allowing space for discussion about (controversial) issues. In this respect, the style of instruction is of particular interest (Campbell 2008). A more participative, interactive and less authoritarian school climate leads to more positive outcomes in terms of political attitudes (Jaros 1973; Gimpel *et al.* 2003; Torney-Purta *et al.* 2007). An open classroom climate facilitates discussion of controversial issues, allows pupils to have their say in school decisions and increases the participation of young people (Torney-Purta and Vermeer 2006).

Media: news, television and the internet

The fourth agent that will be discussed is the media. In the literature, the media is portrayed as a major transmitter of knowledge (Chaffee *et al.* 1977; Delli Carpini and Keeter 1996). Young people consider media sources (television, newspapers and the internet) the most important for providing political information (Pasek *et al.* 2006; Shah *et al.* 2001). Although it is commonly assumed that the media stimulates political participation and political attitudes, the causal relationship is not as straightforward as it seems. In the literature on social capital, we find mixed results: media can also serve as a cause of civic and political disengagement. Time spent accessing the media cannot be devoted to civic and political activities (Putnam 2000; Kraut *et al.* 1998).

Television

The impact of television on civic engagement is a topic of recurrent concern within the social sciences. During the 1990s, this debate was still conducted in very general terms, with the stereotypical image of a new generation of 'couch potatoes' being depicted in various publications. The main claim in this line of research is quite straightforward: due to the increasing amount of time spent watching television, less time is left for social commitment and for various forms of social interaction. This has also been called a time-replacement effect (Putnam 2000). More importantly, however, a number of authors have also argued that the effects of television should no longer be seen as a purely one-dimensional phenomenon (Moy *et al.* 2004). Prior (2007) has introduced a distinction between the entertainment and information functions of television, with the expectation that the entertainment function of television will be negatively associated with political knowledge and civic engagement, while the opposite will be true for the information function. Norris and other authors found that watching television news raises the level of political knowledge; civic and political participation; interest; social trust; and efficacy (Shah *et al.* 2001; Norris 2000). Newton (1999) drew a similar conclusion, stating that watching television news increased political knowledge, political interest and the feeling that democracy works. Prior (2007) found that following the news on television led to more political knowledge, more interest and higher levels of political participation (turnout), especially among the less educated.

Internet

In little more than a decade, new information and communication technologies have dramatically changed our lives and interaction patterns. This is especially the case for adolescents who are among the most avid users of mobile phones, messaging services (SMS, Twitter), virtual communities, network sites, file sharing and other new forms of interaction (Di Gennaro and Dutton 2006; Xenos and Foot 2008: 57).

The amount of time people spend online might indeed influence levels of political participation: the more time people spend surfing the internet, the more likely they are to access political websites, news sites or receive political emails. Thus, online activities forge connections between people that might actually increase levels of political participation (Gibson *et al.* 2000). Krueger (2002), for instance, has found that the internet has the potential to draw new people to offline political participation, or at least increase political awareness.

Besides the time spent on the internet, different patterns of internet use also have different effects (positive or negative) on levels of political engagement (Turkle 1995; Polat 2005), which therefore enables variation in political participation (Chaffee and Frank 1996; Pasek *et al.* 2006). We would expect the internet to have a similar effect to television on political participation. If adolescents use the internet for news gathering, it will spur their levels of political participation. Cyber-optimists argue that the internet is a promising tool that can stimulate political participation (Norris 2001). As young people are more likely to seek news sources online, we expect large effects among this group (Jung *et al.* 2001; Polat 2005). Young people are becoming more dependent on the internet for all purposes, but especially for news gathering (Turkle 1995; Gibson *et al.* 2005).

Voluntary associations

The fifth and final agent of political socialisation that will be considered is voluntary associations. Membership of voluntary organisations makes people more likely to participate in politics and *vice versa*. This finding was noted in the 1830s by Alexis de Tocqueville: 'Les associations civiles facilitent donc les associations politiques; mais, d'une part, l'association politique développe et perfectionne singulièrement l'association civile' (de Tocqueville 1835: 156). So, two centuries ago, the exchange between political and civic associations was already evident. Voluntary memberships are therefore important in creating a vision of society. Furthermore, voluntary engagement makes people more inclined to participate politically (Rosenstone and Hansen 2003). Voluntary membership broadens people's sphere of interests and concerns, especially among young people (Knoke 1986). Finally, people in associations are more visible, more influential and therefore more frequently asked to participate (Verba *et al.* 1995; Rosenstone and Hansen 2003). Marzana *et al.* (2012) found that among 19- to 29-year-olds, similar variables predict both engagement in voluntary groups and engagement in politics. Additionally, several studies have shown that people who were involved in youth organisations and extra-curricular activities are more likely to engage in politics later in life. For instance, using the Parent-Child Socialisation Panel datasets for 1965–1973, Beck and Jennings (1982) demonstrated that organisational involvement is one of the 'pathways to participation': engagement in high school activities leads to adult participation later in life. Youniss *et al.* (1997) also argue that students who participated in high school activities (such as government and community service projects) were more likely to vote and to join community organisations fifteen years later than were young people who did not participate in these activities. More recently, McFarland and Thomas (2006) show that voluntary participation at a young age stimulates political participation in adulthood. Those organisations that encourage community service, representation and speaking in public forums are especially prominent in generating a communal identity.

Data and Methods

In the present study, we used data from the Belgian Political Panel Survey (BPPS) 2006–2011, a three-wave panel study following a cohort of young people at ages sixteen, eighteen and twenty-one. In 2006, a survey was conducted among 6,330 16-year-olds from 112 schools in Belgium. A response analysis demonstrated that respondents were representative of the population in terms of language, school type, education stream, gender and region. The study focused on adolescents' social and political attitudes and contained questions about their background characteristics, political activities and political attitudes. To obtain a nationally representative sample, all schools included in the survey were selected through stratified sampling, based on location and type of school. In each school, a minimum of 50 students were selected, some from each education stream in that school (Hooghe *et al.* 2006).

In 2008, the respondents were surveyed again, aged eighteen. While most of the initial respondents were still at the same school, for those who had left or changed schools, alternative ways of tracing them were needed. Of the initial 112 schools, 109 participated in the 2008 survey, allowing 2,988 students to be re-interviewed. The remaining students were contacted through the post. In total, 4,235 pupils (67 per cent) from the original panel were re-surveyed. In 2011, respondents who had participated in the previous two surveys were asked to complete a third survey. Of the initial 6,330 respondents, 3,025 (48 per cent) completed the third survey by post or online. Analyses indicate that this panel is representative of the initial study population (Hooghe *et al.* 2011). In the following analysis, we use the panel data to compare the age at which different political socialisation agents matter the most and whether their effects differ over time. First, we conducted a regression analysis of the three age groups separately, followed by a regression analysis for the 18- and 21-year-olds in which we controlled for previous levels of political participation. As a cohort study, our findings may not be replicable in cross-sectional studies. However, we see it as an advantage that we can compare the effects of the same agents among a specific group at different ages: at each time point, respondents will be referring to the same parents, peers, schools, etc., which makes the regression analyses more comparable. Nevertheless, we cannot identify causal effects because we study each time-point separately[1], except in Table 7.3, where we control for prior engagement.

The dependent variable is political participation. A political participation scale was created consisting of nine items: being a member of a political party, wearing a badge, signing a petition, participating in a legal protest march, boycotting products, forwarding political e-mails, displaying a political message, attending a political meeting and contacting politicians. For each activity (except party membership), respondents were asked whether they participated often, once in a while or not at all. Items were summed so that the overall score took into account the number of activities individuals participated in as well as the frequency (Quintelier *et al.* 2012). In Appendix Table 7.A.1, descriptives for each variable are presented.

Analyses

Table 7.1 shows the results for the 16-year-olds and 18-year-olds. For the 18-year-olds, two regression analyses were carried out: one for school respondents only and one for all respondents (to the postal and school surveys). The differences between these subsamples are not large. In all age groups, girls are more active than boys, suggesting the effect of gender remains stable over time. Overall, the models explain similar amounts of variance in political participation: 24 per cent for 16-year-olds and 25 per cent for 18-year-olds (or 27 per cent when excluding postal respondents).

The first agent of political socialisation under consideration is the family. To examine this influence we included a measure of socio-economic status of the family, the number of books at home.[2] This indicator does influence political

---

1. More information on causal analyses using this dataset can be found online. Available: http://soc. kuleuven.be/web/home/11/95/eng (accessed 10 October 2013).

2. We decided not to include other socio-economic status measures because they are probably also correlated with the socio-economic status of the family and parental socialisation.

participation, more so at age eighteen. Direct socialisation through political discussion at home appears to be a significant influence on political participation, but only at age eighteen. At age sixteen, other factors prevail. While indirect socialisation by parental volunteering does not lead to more political participation among their children, having a politically active parent proves to be a powerful determinant of political participation. Overall, we find that, contrary to our expectations, parents become more important for political participation at age eighteen, rather than age sixteen. This is indicated by the magnitude of the effects, as well as the explained variance (8 compared to 10 per cent).

The second agent of political socialisation that will be discussed here are peers. The analyses indicate that the size of the network does not have any influence on political participation, whereas we hypothesised a positive correlation. What does appear to matter, at ages sixteen and eighteen, is whether one discusses politics with friends. What also matters, but to a lesser extent, is the diversity of the peer group. However, the diversity of close friends matters more at sixteen than at eighteen, whereas the effect of the diversity of classmates is larger at age eighteen than at sixteen. Overall, we find that the effect of peers is quite large at both ages (accounting for 13 and 15 per cent of the variance respectively).

A third agent of political socialisation is the school. The school has only a modest impact, with an explained variance of 6 to 7 per cent and most individual items having no significant effect. Being a member of the school council leads to more political participation, both at age sixteen and eighteen. However, it is possible that respondents with higher levels of political interest self-select to join school councils (Quintelier, 2013). Frequently talking about political issues in class is related to more political participation at age sixteen and eighteen (all respondents). None of the other school variables appear to have significant effects on political participation.

The fourth agent of political socialisation is the media. We find evidence to support Putnam's (2000) claim that people who watch more television are less likely to engage in politics. However, this effect only exists in the cross-sectional data, so although watching more television leads to less political participation in the short term, the gap between the two age groups is not increasing (Quintelier 2009: 178–184). The internet, on the other hand, has a positive effect on political participation: not only following the news online, but also just being online more regularly, leads to more political participation. Following the news generally has smaller effects than following online news among young people. The explained variance of media as an agent of socialisation is also rather low: 6 to 7 per cent.

The fifth agent of political socialisation is voluntary associations. It was not possible to explore the effects of specific associations and so we created a summed scale of all memberships (out of a list of fifteen). Being a member of one or more associations seems to have a significant effect on increasing political participation: this sole indicator leads to an explained variance of 10 and 8 per cent respectively. This is quite high, although as a variable this tells us little about what sort of organisations these are and what skills and knowledge young people develop within them (Verba *et al.* 1995; Quintelier 2008). In Appendix Table 7.A.1, descriptives of all variables are presented.

Table 7.1: Effects of political socialisation agents on political participation at ages sixteen and eighteen

Standardised β	Sixteen	Eighteen (school)	Eighteen (all)
Gender (female)	0.06**	0.06**	0.06***
Family (Explained variance)	*7.7*	*10.2*	*10.2*
Books	0.07***	0.08***	0.09***
Parent volunteers	0.03	-0.01	0.02
Discuss politics at home	0.02	0.08***	0.07***
Parents politically active	0.06**	0.09***	0.09***
Peers (Explained variance)	*13.5*	*15.4*	*13.1*
Number of friends	-0.03	-0.01	-0.05**
Discuss politics with friends	0.19***	0.19***	0.20***
Political diversity (close friends)	0.08***	0.01	0.06***
Political diversity (classmates)	0.07**	0.10***	
School (Explained variance)	*5.8*	*7.6*	*6.4*
Member of school council	0.07***	0.08***	0.07***
Open classroom climate	0.00	-0.05*	-0.03
Have their say	0.02	0.01	
Group projects	0.03	0.00	
Community service	-0.00	0.04	
Talk about political issues	0.06***	0.04	0.07***
Media (Explained variance)	*5.9*	*6.9*	*6.9*
Watch television	-0.08***	-0.07***	-0.06***
Surf the internet	0.06**	0.08***	0.08***
Follow news online	0.05**	0.12***	0.10***
Follow news	0.05**	0.01	0.02
Voluntary associations (Explained variance)	*9.6*	*7.6*	*8.0*
Member of associations	0.20***	0.19***	0.18***
Total explained variance	24.4	27.1	25.2
N	2,423	1,851	2,753

Notes: *p<0.05, **p<0.01, ***p<0.001; Political diversity (classmates), Have their say, Group projects, and Community service are missing for 18-year-old respondents (all) because these questions were not asked in the postal survey.

Source: BPPS 2006-2011.

Table 7.2: Effects of political socialisation agents on political participation at ages sixteen, eighteen and twenty-one

Standardised β			
	Sixteen	**Eighteen**	**Twenty-one**
Gender	0.06***	0.08***	0.09***
Peers (explained variance)	*13.5*	*13.1*	*16.2*
Number of friends	-0.03	-0.04*	-0.06***
Discuss politics with friends	0.22***	0.25***	0.29***
Political diversity (close friends)	0.12***	0.07***	0.07***
Media (explained variance)	*5.9*	*6.9*	*9.3*
Watch television	-0.09***	-0.08***	-0.12***
Surf internet	0.05**	0.08***	0.05**
Follow news online	0.06***	0.12***	0.11***
Follow news	0.08***	0.04*	0.02
Voluntary associations (explained variance)	*9.6*	*8.0*	*9.2*
Member of associations	0.24***	0.23***	0.24***
Total explained variance	21.0	22.0	26.0
N	2,738	2,862	2,844

Notes: *p<0.05, **p<0.01, ***p<0.001; Political diversity (classmates), Have their say, Group projects, and Community service are missing for 18-year-old respondents (all) because these questions were not asked in the postal survey.

Source: BPPS 2006-2011.

Next, regression analysis was carried out for the 21-year-olds (*see* Table 7.2). However, because not all of these respondents were still at school or living with their parents, we excluded certain variables from the analysis, including only the variables for peers, media and voluntary associations.

At age twenty-one, the effect of gender seems to remain in place in that girls appear to engage more in different political activities in all three age groups. Overall, the model for 21-year-olds accounts for 26 per cent of the variance in political participation which is slightly higher than the models for 16- and 18-year-olds. On the whole, the influence of peers, media and voluntary associations remains quite stable across the three time points.

Peers are important at age sixteen, eighteen and, more so at twenty-one. This increase can partly be explained by the increase in political discussion with friends. Number of friends at twenty-one remains inversely related to political participation: people with fewer friends are more likely to participate in politics. Discussing politics with friends appears to have more of an impact on political participation than having a politically diverse network.

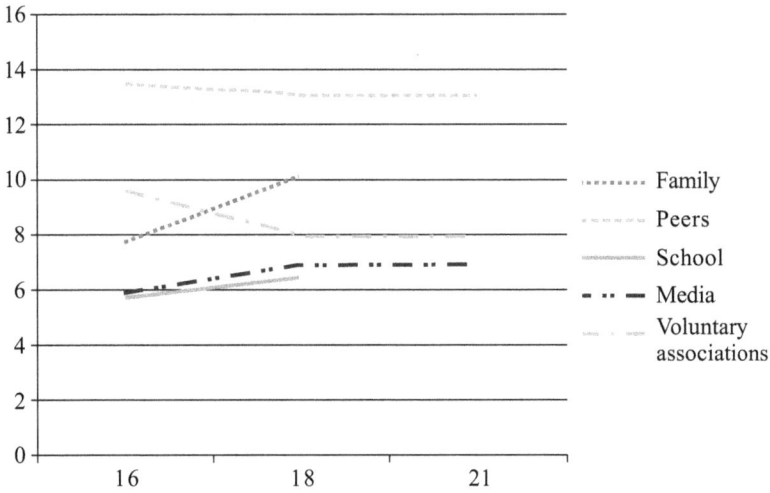

Figure 7.1: Effects of political socialisation agents on political participation at ages sixteen, eighteen and twenty-one (explained variance trends)

The influence of media increases slightly from 6 to 9 per cent as the young people get older. Watching television has a negative effect on political participation at all three time points. Surfing the internet is related to increased political participation, but following the news online has a larger effect. Following the news generally has a significant but modest effect at aged sixteen. This probably has to do with the fact that at age sixteen, only the most interested respondents would follow the news, whereas by eighteen this might be a more universal practice.

Finally, membership of voluntary associations has an impact on political participation at all three time points. Although respondents at twenty-one were given a slightly different (more extensive list) of associations for this measure, the overall impact of membership remains comparable. Even though most young people at twenty-one are in a transitional phase – they may be still studying, just started working or building a family, etc. – they still retain engagement in voluntary associations and thus develop new networks, cementing the habit of political participation (Plutzer 2002).

Figure 7.1 presents the explained variance trends for each socialisation agent. Although the comparison is limited because the data for 21-year-olds is incomplete, the results are nevertheless striking. Political socialisation mechanisms appear to be fairly stable across all three time points. Peers are the most important agents of political socialisation for all three age groups. Family and voluntary associations come next although parents become more important at eighteen while voluntary associations lose some influence. Media and school seem to be the least important agents of socialisation and their influence remains relatively stable over time.

Table 7.3: Effects of political socialisation agents on political participation at ages eighteen and twenty-one, controlling for prior levels of political participation

Standardised β	Eighteen	Twenty-one	Twenty-one
Gender (female)	0.05**	0.07***	0.07***
Peers			
Number of friends	-0.02	-0.04**	-0.02
Discuss politics with friends	0.19***	0.25***	0.21***
Political diversity close friends	0.05**	0.06***	0.05***
Media			
Watch television	-0.06***	-0.09***	-0.08***
Surf internet	0.06***	0.04**	0.03
Follow news online	0.08***	0.09***	0.08***
Follow news	0.03	0.02	0.03
Voluntary associations			
Member of associations	0.14***	0.19***	0.17***
Prior levels of participation			
Political participation aged 16	0.39***	0.27***	-
Political participation aged 18	-	-	0.37***
Total explained variance	35.0	32.0	37.0
N	2,770	2,755	2,798

Notes: *p<0.05, **p<0.01, ***p<0.001; Political diversity (classmates), Have their say, Group projects, and Community service are missing for 18-year old respondents (all) because these questions were not asked in the postal survey.

Source: BPPS 2006–2011.

Table 7.3 shows the results of the regression analyses after controlling for prior levels of political engagement. To predict the level of political participation at age eighteen, political participation at age sixteen was entered as a control variable; to predict political participation at age twenty-one, political participation at ages sixteen and eighteen were entered as control variables separately. Adding prior levels of political participation leads to the overall model accounting for 32 to 37 per cent of the variance. Political participation at age sixteen, therefore, exerts an influence on political participation five years later. Yet the effects of peers, media and voluntary associations remain important as well. Overall this means that prior political participation explains an additional 10 per cent of the variance in current political participation, but that political socialisation agents retain importance.

Conclusion

Political socialisation is a learning process and, according to our analyses, takes place quite early in life: by the age of sixteen, political socialisation agents exert a large and significant influence on political participation. More specifically, based on our analyses, we find that the different agents of political socialisation are equally effective at all ages. As far as we are aware, this is one of the first studies to compare the effects of different agents of political socialisation on political participation. Based on this study, we tried to assess the impact of different agents of socialisation and found that parents, peers and voluntary associations are the most important agents of socialisation (for all three age groups). School and media have only limited impact.

If we compare trends over time, we find that the impact of parents is slightly greater at age eighteen than at age sixteen. The key issue is having a political role model in the family; knowing someone who is politically active leads to more political participation. For peers, we find that they are most important at age twenty-one and, more specifically, through political discussion. Having diverse close friends matters at age sixteen but later in life the impact of a diverse network with acquaintances seemingly becomes more important. The most important predictor of political participation, however, is having frequent political discussions with friends. The effect of schools was only assessed at ages sixteen and eighteen. Their impact is quite limited but remains stable, even though most civic education efforts in Belgium are targeted at 17- and 18-year-olds. In the context of school, being a member of a school council and talking about political events have the strongest relationship with young people's political participation. Different forms of media also exercise a small but consistent influence on political participation, mostly when individuals follow the news online. A larger and more stable influence can be found from voluntary associations: the more associations people are members of, the more likely they are to engage in political participation.

Political socialisation is 'the learning process through which the individual learns political attitudes and behaviour from generation through generation, influenced by political socialisation agents'. The five political socialisation agents (parents, school, peers, media and voluntary associations) are all quite important for the political participation of young people. We find that political socialisation takes place at all ages from sixteen to twenty-one. Overall, we find that the effect of schools and media may be quite small relative to the expectations seen in political socialisation and civic education literature. Although Putnam (2000) hypothesised that television leads to lower levels of engagement, this is only true to a limited extent. More importantly, we found only modest effects for the Internet mobilisation hypothesis: although watching the news online leads to slightly more political participation, this effect is limited, possibly due to self-selection effects. Those who are more interested and likely to participate will be more likely to follow the news, but possibly thereby also experience more socialisation effects. The minimal effects of civic education on political participation are quite surprising, but can be explained quite easily. Because civic education is a cross-curricular subject in Belgium, it is quite difficult to measure the effect of civic education on political participation and other outcomes; the effects of different teachers, teaching methods and so on are all quite difficult to measure, and consequently, its political outcomes are difficult to assess.

Appendix

Table 7.A.1: Political Socialisation scale at ages sixteen, eighteen and twenty-one (means, standard deviations and missing values)

	16-Year-Olds			18-Year-Olds			21-Year-Olds		
	Mean	SD	Miss	Mean	SD	Miss	Mean	SD	Miss
Gender (1–2)	1.52	0.5	0						
Books (1–7)	4.09	1.6	83	4.19	1.58	20			
Parent volunteers (0–1)	0.19	0.4	74	0.18	0.38	30			
Discuss politics at home (1–4)	2.13	0.65	72	2.28	0.67	21			
Parents politically active (0–1)	0.26	0.44	106	0.31	0.46	25			
Number of friends (1–7)	4.08	1.58	15	3.63	1.33	14	3.67	1.30	20
Discuss politics with friends (1–4)	1.58	0.60	11	1.76	0.61	13	1.93	0.62	19
Political diversity close friends (1–7)	2.10	1.14	79	2.44	1.13	52	2.73	1.18	58
Political diversity class mates (1–7)	2.61	1.17	94	3.02	1.12	944	2.82	1.15	185
Member school council (0–1)	0.07	0.25	27	0.11	0.31	9			
Open classroom (1–4)	2.72	0.74	41	2.72	0.75	31			
Have their say (0–12)	1.65	1.60	147	1.64	1.52	990			
Group projects (1–4)	2.33	0.80	51	2.69	0.75	920			
Community service (0–1)	0.16	0.37	51	0.22	0.42	923			
Talk about political issues (0–18)	4.17	3.26	156	7.55	3.84	79			
Watch television (1–5)	3.24	0.89	16	3.03	0.88	10	2.84	0.93	33
Surf on the net (1–5)	3.08	1.09	14	3.04	0.99	9	3.29	0.96	18
Follow news online (1–5)	1.95	1.25	80	2.29	1.34	34	3.28	1.48	30
Follow news (1–5)	3.71	1.07	15	3.85	1.03	14	4.16	0.96	32
Member associations (0–13)	1.54	1.38	27	1.40	1.32	17	1.33	1.35	9

Notes: SD = standard deviation; Miss. = missing data

References

Achen, C. H. (2002) 'Parental socialization and rational party identification', *Political Behavior,* 24(2): 151–170.

Almond, G. A. and Verba, S. (1963) *The Civic Culture: Political attitudes and democracy in five nations,* Princeton: Princeton University Press.

Alwin, D. F., Cohen, R. L. and Newcomb, T. M. (1992) *Political Attitudes over the Life Span: The Bennington women after fifty years,* Madison: University of Wisconsin Press.

Beck, P. A. (1977) 'The role of agents in political socialization', in S. A. Renshon (ed.) *Handbook of Political Socialization,* New York: Free Press:115–142.

Beck, P. A. and Jennings, M. K. (1982) 'Pathways to participation', *American Political Science Review,* 76(1): 94–108.

Campbell, B.A. (1980) 'A theoretical approach to peer influence in adolescent socialization', *American Journal of Political Science,* 24(2): 324–344.

— (2008) 'Voice in the classroom: How an open classroom climate fosters political engagement among adolescents', *Political Behavior,* 30(4): 437–454.

Chaffee, S. H. and Frank, S. (1996) 'How Americans get political information: Print versus broadcast news', *Annals of the American Academy of Political and Social Science,* 54: 648–658.

Chaffee, S. H., Jackson-Beeck, M., Durall, J. and Wislon, D. (1977) 'Mass communication in political socialization', in S. A. Renshon (ed.) *Handbook of Political Socialization: Theory and research,* New York: Free Press: 223–258.

Chan, C. G. and Elder, G. H. (2001) 'Family influences on the social participation of youth: The effects of parental social involvement and farming', *Rural Sociology,* 66(1): 22–42.

Claes, E. and Quintelier, E. (2010) 'The current state of political socialization research: evidence from a panel study', paper presented at the ECPR Joint Sessions, Münster, March 2010.

Dassonneville, R., Quintelier, E., Hooghe, M. and Claes, E. (2012) 'The relation between civic education and political attitudes and behavior: A two-year panel study among Belgian late adolescents', *Applied Developmental Science,* 16(3): 140–150.

Dawson, R. E. and Prewitt, K. S. (1969) *Political Socialization: An analytic study,* Boston: Little Brown.

de Tocqueville, A. (1835) *De la Démocratie en Amérique, Tome Second,* Paris: Librairie de Médicis.

Delli Carpini, M. X. and Keeter, S. (1996) *What Americans Know about Politics and Why it Matters,* New Haven: Yale University Press.

Dennis, J. (1968) Major problems of political socialization research, *Midwest Journal of Political Science,* 12(1): 85–114.

Dewey, J. (1913) *The school and society,* Chicago: University of Chicago Press.

Di Gennaro, C. and Dutton, W. (2006) 'The Internet and the public: Online and offline political participation in the United Kingdom', *Parliamentary Affairs,* 59(2): 299–313.

Dudley, R. L. and Gitelson, A. R. (2002) 'Political literacy, civic education, and civic engagement: A return to political socialization', *Applied Developmental Science,* 6(4): 175–182.

Eveland, W. P. and Scheufele, D. A. (2000) 'Connecting news media use with gaps in knowledge and participation', *Political Communication,* 17(3): 215–237.

Galston, W. A. (2004) 'Civic education and Political Participation', *PSonline,* 37: 263–266.

Gibson, R., Lusoli, W. and Ward, S. (2005) 'Online participation in the UK: Testing a "contextualised" model of internet effects', *Policy Studies Association,* 7(4): 561–583.

Gibson, R. K., Howard, P. E. N. and Ward, S (2000) 'Social capital, Internet connectedness & political participation: A four-country study', Paper presented at the International Political Science Association, Quebec, Canada, August 2000.

Gimpel, J. G., Lay, C. J. and Schuknecht, J. E. (2003) *Cultivating democracy:. Civic Environments and Political Socialization in America,* Washington DC: Brookings Institution Press.

Granovetter, M. (1973) 'The strength of weak ties', *American Journal of Sociology,* 78(6): 1360–1380.

—— (1983) 'The strength of weak ties: A network theory revisited', *Sociological Theory,* 1: 201–233.

Grusec, J. E. (2011) 'Socialization processes in the family: Social and emotional development', *Annual Review of Psychology,* 62: 243–269.

Hess, R. D. and Torney J. V. (1967) *The Development of Political Attitudes in Children,* Chicago: Aldine.

Hooghe, M., Havermans, N., Quintelier, E. and Dassonneville, R. (2011) *Belgian Political Panel Survey (BPPS) 2006–2011, Technical Report,* Leuven: K.U. Leuven.

Hooghe, M., Quintelier, E., Claes, E. and Dejaeghere, Y. (2006) *Technisch rapport van het Jeugdonderzoek België. [Technical report of the Belgian Youth Survey],* Leuven: K.U. Leuven, Centrum voor Politicologie.

Huckfeldt, R. (1979) 'Political participation and the neighborhood social context', *American Journal of Political Science,* 23(3): 579–592.

Huckfeldt, R., Johnson, P. E. and Sprague, J. (2004) *Political Disagreement: The survival of diverse opinions within communication networks,* New York: Cambridge University Press.

Hyman, H. H. (1959) *Political Socialization,* Glencoe Illinois: Free Press.

Jaros, D. (1973) *Socialization to Politics: Basic concepts in political science,* Nairobi: Nelson.

Jennings, M. K. and Niemi, R. G. (1968) 'The transmission of political values from parent to child', *American Political Science Review,* 62(1): 169–184.

— (1981) *Generations and Politics: A panel study of young adults and their parents,* Princeton: Princeton University Press.

Jennings, M. K., Stoker, L. and Bowers, J. (2009) 'Politics across generations: Family transmission reexamined', *Journal of Politics,* 71(3): 782–799.

Jung, J. Y., Qiu, J. L. and Kim Y. C. (2001) 'Internet connectedness and inequality: beyond the divide', *Communication Research,* 28(4): 509–537.

Kahne, J., Chi, B. and Middaugh, E. (2006) 'Building social capital for civic and political engagement: The potential of high-school civic courses', *Canadian Journal of Education,* 29(2): 387–409.

Knoke, D. (1986) 'Associations and Interest Groups', *Annual Review of Sociology,* 12(1): 1–21.

Kraut, R., Patterson M., Lundmark V., Kiesler, S., Mukopadhyay, T. and Scherlis, W. (1998) 'Internet paradox: A social technology that reduces social involvement and psychological well-being?' *American Psychologist,* 53: 1017–1031.

Krueger, B. S. (2002) 'Assessing the potential of Internet political participation in the United States', *American Political Research,* 30(5): 476–598.

Langton, K. P. (1969) *Political Socialization,* New York: Oxford University Press.

Marsh, D. (1971) 'Political socialization: The implicit assumptions questioned', *British Journal of Political Science,* 1(4): 453–465.

Martikainen, P., Martikainen, T. and Wass, H. (2005) 'The effect of socioeconomic factors on voter turnout in Finland: A register-based study of 2.9 million voters', *European Journal of Political Research,* 44(5): 645–669.

Marzana, D., Marta, E. and Pozzi, M. (2012) 'Social action in young adults: Voluntary and political engagement', *Journal of Adolescence,* 35(3): 497–507.

McClurg, S. (2006) 'The electoral relevance of political talk: Examining disagreement and expertise effects in social networks on political participation', *American Journal of Political Science,* 50(3): 737–754.

McDevitt, M. and Chaffee, S. (2002) 'From top-down to trickle-up influence: Revisiting assumptions about the family in political socialization', *Political Communication,* 19(3): 281–301.

McFarland, D. A. and Thomas, R. J. (2006) 'Bowling young: How youth voluntary associations influence adult political participation', *American Sociological Review,* 71(3): 401–425.

McIntosh, H., Hart, D. and Youniss, J. (2007) 'The influence of family political discussion on youth civic development: Which parent qualities matter?', *PS: Political Science and Politics,* 40(3): 495–499.

McLeod, J. M., Scheufele, D.A., Moy, P., Horowitz, E. M., Holbert, R. L., Zhang, W., Zubric, S., and Zubric, J. (1999) 'Understanding deliberation: The effects of discussion networks on participation in a public forum', *Communication Research,* 26(6): 743–774.

McLeod, J. M. and Shah, D. V. (2009) 'Communication and political socialization: Challenges and opportunities for research', *Political Communication,* 26(1): 1–10.

Mezenes, I. (2003) 'Participation experiences and civic concepts, attitudes and engagement: Implications for citizenship education projects', *European Educational Research Journal,* 2(3): 430–445.

Moy, P., McCluskey, M., McCoy, K. and Spratt, M. A. (2004) 'Political correlates of local news-media use', *Journal of Communication,* 54(3): 532–546.

Newton, K. (1999) 'Mass media effects: "Mobilization or media malaise?"': *British Journal of Political Science,* 29(4): 577–599.

Niemi, R. G. and Hepburn, M. A. (1995) 'The rebirth of political socialization', *Perspectives on Political Science,* 24(1): 7–16.

Niemi, R. G. and Jennings, M. K. (1991) 'Issues and inheritance in the formation of party identification', *American Journal of Political Science,* 35(4): 970–988.

Niemi, R. G. and Junn, J. (1998) *Civic Education: What makes students learn?,* New Haven: Yale University Press.

Norris, P. (2000) *A Virtuous Circle: Political communications in postindustrial societies,* Cambridge: Cambridge University Press.

— (2001) *Digital Divide: Civic engagement, information poverty, and the Internet worldwide,* Cambridge: Cambridge University Press.

Pasek, J., Kenski, K., Romer, D. and Hall Jamieson, K. (2006) 'America's youth and community engagement: How use of mass media is related to civic activity and political awareness in 14- to 22-year-olds', *Communication Research,* 33(3): 115–135.

Plutzer, E. (2002) 'Becoming a habitual voter: Inertia, resources, and growth in young adulthood', *American Political Science Review,* 96(1): 41–56.

Polat, R. K. (2005) 'The Internet and political participation: Exploring the explanatory links', *European Journal of Communication,* 20(4): 435–459.

Prior, M. (2007) *Post-Broadcast Democracy: How media choice increases inequality in political involvement and polarizes elections,* Cambridge: Cambridge University Press.

Putnam, R. D. (2000) *Bowling Alone: The collapse and revival of American democracy,* New York: Simon & Schuster.

— (2007) 'E Pluribus Unum: Diversity and community in the twenty-first century. The 2006 Johan Skytte Prize Lecture', *Scandinavian Political Studies,* 30(2): 137–174.

Quéniart, A. (2008) 'The Form and Meaning of Young People's Involvement in Community and Political Work', *Youth & Society,* 40(2): 203–233.

Quintelier, E. (2008) 'Who is politically active: The athlete, the Scouts member or the environmental activist? Young people, voluntary engagement and political participation', *Acta Sociologica,* 51(4): 355–370.

— (2009) *Political Participation in Late Adolescence: Political socialization patterns in the Belgian Political Panel Survey,* PhD thesis, Leuven: K.U. Leuven.

Quintelier, E. (2013) 'Socialization or self-selection? Membership in deliberative associations and political attitudes', *Nonprofit and Voluntary Sector Quarterly*, 42(1): 174–192.

Quintelier, E., Stolle, D. and Harell, A. (2012) 'Politics in peer groups: Exploring the causal relationship between network diversity and political participation', *Political Research Quarterly,* 65(4): 867–884.

Roker, D., Player, K. and Coleman, J. (1999) 'Young people's voluntary and campaigning activities as sources of political education', *Oxford Review of Education,* 25(1/2): 185–198.

Rosenstone, S. J. and Hansen, J. M. (2003[1993]) *Mobilization, Participation, and Democracy in America,* New York: Longman.

Rubenson, D. (2005) 'Community heterogeneity and political participation in American cities', Paper presented at the Canadian Political Science Association in London, Ontario, June 2005.

Scheufele, D., Nisbet, M., Brossard, D. and Nisbet, E. (2004) 'Social structure and citizenship: Examining the impacts of social setting, network heterogeneity, and informational variables on political participation', *Political Communication,* 21: 315–338.

Scheufele, D. A., Hardy, B. W., Brossard, D., Waismel-Manor, I. S. and Nisbet, E. (2006) 'Democracy based on difference: Examining the links between structural heterogeneity of discussion networks, and democratic citizenship', *Journal of Communication,* 56(4): 728–753.

Shah, D. V., McLeod, J. M. and Yoon, S.-H. (2001) 'Communication, context, and community: An exploration of print, broadcast, and Internet influences', *Communication Research,* 28(4): 464–506.

Siongers, J. (2007) *Van generatie op generatie. Een cultuursociologische benadering van de gelijkenissen in houdingen en smaken tussen ouders en hun adolescente kinderen,* PhD thesis, Brussels: V.U. Brussel.

Tapper, T. (1976) *Political Education and Stability: Elite responses to political conflict,* London: John Wiley & Sons.

Teorell, J. (2003) 'Linking social capital to political participation: Voluntary associations and networks of recruitment in Sweden', *Scandinavian Political Studies,* 26(1): 49–66.

Torney-Purta, J. V. (1995) 'Psychological theory as a basis for political socialization research: Individuals' construction of knowledge', *Perspectives on Political Science,* 24(1): 23–33.

— (2002) 'The school's role in developing civic engagement: A study of adolescents in twenty-eight countries', *Applied Developmental Science,* 6(4): 203–212.

Torney-Purta, J. V., Barber, C. H. and Wilkenfeld, B. (2007) "Latino Adolescents" civic development in the United States: Research results from the IEA Civic Education Study', *Journal of Youth and Adolescence,* 36(2):111–125.

Torney-Purta, J. V. and Vermeer, S. L. (2006) *Developing Citizenship Competencies from Kindergarten through Grade 12: A background paper for policymakers and educators,* Denver: Education Commissions of the States.

Turkle, S. (1995) *Life on the Screen: Identity in the age of the Internet,* London: Weidenfeld.

Verba, S., Schlozman, K. L. and Brady, H. E. (1995) *Voice and Equality: Civic voluntarism in American politics,* Cambridge: Harvard University Press.

Verba, S., Schlozman, K. L. and Burns, N. (2005) *Family Ties: Understanding the intergenerational transmission of political participation,* Philadelphia: Temple University.

Westheimer, J. and Kahne, J. (2004) 'Educating the "good" citizen: Political choices and pedagogical goals', *PS: Political Science and Politics,* 37(2): 241–247.

Xenos, M. and Foot, K. (2008) 'Not your father's Internet: The generation gap in online politics', in L. W. Bennett (ed.) *Civic Life Online: How digital media can engage youth,* Cambridge: MIT Press: 51–70.

Youniss, J., McLellan, J. A. and Yates, M. (1997) 'What we know about engendering civic identity', *American Behavioral Scientist,* 40(5): 620–631.

Chapter Eight

The Socialisation Effects of Digital Media on Personal Autonomy Values

Carol Galais[1]

Introduction

The year 2011 proved to be one of political and social agitation. Both the so-called 'Arab Spring' and the Occupy movement evidence the increasingly important role played by digital media in citizens' political engagement and probably also in democratisation processes. Nevertheless, the literature on the role played by digital media in social and political change has yet to prove this link and needs to disentangle its causal mechanisms in order to avoid problems of endogeneity and selection bias (*see* for instance Anduiza *et al.* 2012). One plausible explanation for the link between digital media and political engagement is that internet use fosters a number of psychological orientations that pave the way for political participation, instilling a particular horizontal logic consonant with democratic and civic values (Yildiz 2002; Ward and Vedel 2006). The main argument behind this is that digital media are not only technologies that reduce costs of participation or facilitate mobilisation practices, but they also change the way citizens think, feel and behave in the public arena.

This chapter seeks to make a contribution to the current literature on the consequences of digital media by taking a comparative perspective. Its purpose is to assess the extent to which digital media use makes people more likely to value personal autonomy and to what extent this relationship is conditioned by contextual features. For this purpose, I first test whether internet use has the potential to facilitate cultural change, inspiring a value consistent with modernity and democracy, i.e. personal autonomy. This value is expected to have an effect on political engagement, attitudes towards democracy and political behaviour (Inglehart and Welzel 2005). This is a premise for most scholars who consider the internet to be a democratisation agent. Nevertheless, it is important to assess whether digital media possess a universal potential for facilitating cultural change or they are only able to reinforce some attitudes in specific contexts. If the latter is true and the internet only triggers personal autonomy – and, subsequently, other

---

1. I would like to thank Eva Anduiza for all her wise advice on this chapter. The funding that I received from her project POLAT also allowed me to present a first version of this work at the ECPR General Conference (Reykjavik 2011).

civic attitudes and political participation – under some circumstances, its potential as an agent of cultural change and democratisation would be very limited. Thus, I will test whether internet use is able to encourage political autonomy among its users regardless of a country's socio-economic development, democratic rights and the number of users.

The chapter is organised as follows. Firstly, the theoretical framework underpinning the relationship between digital media use and personal autonomy is presented, as well as the potential conditioning effects of contextual characteristics. Next, the research design and the dataset are introduced. Data are derived from the World Values Surveys, conducted between 2005 and 2008. Next, the research design and the dataset are introduced. First, the general hypothesis that the use of digital media can foster personal autonomy is tested, controlling for individual factors that may also affect these orientations. After verifying that there are indeed significant differences across countries regarding this relationship, these differences are further examined as to whether they can be explained with specific contextual variables related to the socio-economic and democratic context. Finally, I discuss the findings and present some considerations relevant to future research.

Theoretical framework: socialisation effects of digital media use on personal autonomy across countries

Digital media were welcomed by social activists as new mobilisation tools, since they provide more accessible information and different, alternative participation repertoires. However, they were also expected to change something deeper in the way people feel and think about the world, about politics and about themselves. Indeed, previous work has found that internet use has an effect on the set of political attitudes that precede political action, such as political interest (Xenos and Moy 2007; Prior 2007), knowledge, political efficacy or trust (Kenski and Stroud 2006; Tedesco 2007; Cantijoch *et al.* 2008; Pasek *et al.* 2009; Colombo *et al.* 2012). These works suggest that digital media may also affect political attitudes and beliefs through different mechanisms, including the expansion and diversification of personal networks; exposure to political stimuli and information; and increasing feelings of autonomy derived from continued use of the internet. This last element is particularly relevant for political participation. Indeed, personal autonomy is considered a pre-political value and, as such, it would precede all other attitudes related to civic engagement. Therefore, digital media would be able to generate the basis for a civic culture consonant with democracy. But what is personal autonomy and why would it be related to internet use?

Personal autonomy: relevance, definition and connection with the internet

Personal autonomy is a component of self-expression values (Inglehart and Welzel 2005), understood as 'an emancipative set of orientations that emphasise freedom of expression and equality of opportunities' (Welzel 2010: 153). Furthermore, Kohn (1976) and Foa (2007) state that personal autonomy values are reflected in the qualities parents value in their children such as understanding, curiosity, responsibility and self-control instead of obedience, good behaviour and tidiness. As conceived by those scholars, personal autonomy is a measure of the preferred values that parents choose to transmit to their children and thus involves not only individuals' preferences for a series of personal features, but also their leaning toward a particular parenting style that will result in a particular political socialisation. This can give us an indication as to why the internet may have the potential to cause not only attitudinal changes at the individual level, but cultural evolutions as a result of the transmission of the new values to the next generation

However, although studies on the effect of digital media use on personal autonomy are well known in the fields of education and pedagogy, it has mostly been ignored by scholars devoted to political behaviour. During the last decade, several psychologists and educationalists have highlighted the features that are distinctive to the so-called 'digital natives', the generation born after 1982 that is accustomed to the use of technology (the internet, software, hardware, consoles, audio devices and mobile phones) in their daily life, for leisure, working or studying (Prensky 2001; Visser n.d.) As a result, these 'digital natives' also value personal autonomy highly. They would have developed this value as a product of different factors.

First, the fact that digital media can be so specifically tailored to each individual means that adapting the internet to individuals' needs and likes (managing information; scheduling work and leisure; connecting with people etc.) becomes not only possible but also desirable (Wallis 2006). Additionally, the internet empowers individuals because it gives people much more control over what they do and how they do things online. As a result, younger generations are more prone to self-organising and providing services for themselves (Tapscott and Williams 2008). There may be other less positive consequences such as dependence on technology, as in the case of the 'I-kids' (Prensky 2008), increasing narcissism or a loss of respect for authority (Keen 2007). Nevertheless, higher levels of personal autonomy among internet users are to be expected.

The internet allows users to bypass traditional media gatekeepers and intermediaries of information control such as journalists or press agencies (Römmele 2003; Dutton 2005). In fact, blogging has been described as a force able to 'blow open holes in the gatekeepers' firewalls', thus ending journalism's reign of sovereignty (Rosen 2005). This may enhance a feeling of autonomy particularly with regard to traditional information sources.

Other authors have emphasised that digital media generate 'a culture of autonomy based on a technology of freedom' (Castells *et al.* 2004: 236). From this point of view, the internet triggers attitudinal changes not only among individuals, but also at the aggregate level. Two characteristics of the World Wide Web, and in particular of the so-called 'Web 2.0', are likely to be the main causes of this potential cultural change: interactivity and horizontality. Interactivity can be understood as 'the extent to which users can participate in modifying the form and content of a mediated environment in real time' (Steuer 1992: 84) making them more accessible, plural and participatory. Horizontality can be defined as the absence of explicit hierarchies and the acknowledgement of other users as a source of legitimacy and recognition. This feature of the internet has become increasingly important since the boom of social networks. Indeed, there is an emerging literature on the role of Facebook and other social networks in the channelling of political demands (Westling 2007; Park *et al.* 2009).

Since personal autonomy has been found to be related to altruism, social capital (Welzel 2010), internal political efficacy (Niemi *et al.* 1991: 1407) and political protest (Verba *et al.* 1995), it is reasonable to regard this value as a psychological basis for political engagement. Moreover, in non-democratic contexts, an increase in the aggregate levels of personal autonomy may subsequently trigger contestation and even democratisation, or at least set the foundation for a civic culture consonant with democracy. Yet, this would be the case only if the ability of the internet to trigger personal autonomy values works in any kind of institutional arrangement and, more specifically, in non-democratic regimes.

Heterogeneous effects: country context matters

Individualisation, empowerment, directness, horizontality and interactivity are features of digital media that are expected to enhance personal autonomy, which may in turn feed into the development of further civic attitudes and political participation. It is no wonder then, that many authors look at the internet as a potential agency for democratisation (Coleman *et al.* 1999; Hague and Loader 1999; Dahlgren 2000; Hoff *et al.* 2000).[2] Following their arguments, the introduction of new technologies in non-democratic countries such as Egypt (Abdulla 2005) or China (Lei 2011) should expand a series of civic attitudes that are consonant with democracy. Demands for democratisation and a civic culture that supports new institutions will follow as a result of digital media use. But is it really reasonable to expect so much from the new Information and Communication Technologies (ICTs)? In other words, is the internet really able to foster personal autonomy regardless of context?

However promising internet use may appear for personal autonomy, it remains to be seen to what extent this is actually happening and whether it happens everywhere regardless of contextual factors. Indeed, the potential effects of internet use on attitudes and/or values such as personal autonomy may not be evenly distributed across the globe. Effects of internet use are likely to be contingent on institutional, social and cultural settings. Just as other factors influencing political engagement, such as individual resources, vary across nations (Anduiza 2002; Gallego 2007), digital media use may have differential effects in different political and social contexts. Additionally, scholars concerned with the effects of digital media on politics would largely agree with the assumption that no mechanical

---

2. Scholars that emphasise the democratising effect of the internet highlight a series of mechanisms – pluralism, shaping group identities, building online communities, lowering the costs for political mobilisation participation, etc. – besides its effects on personal autonomy.

systematic effects can be attributed to technology, since it is not an agent in itself and must be understood as embedded in a specific context where it can enhance certain previously existing political and social processes (Castells *et al.* 2004). Therefore, it makes sense to ask under what contextual conditions digital media use is more likely to foster autonomy.

There is a lot less academic production in this respect. Previous research does not define a clear set of expectations from which to build hypotheses on the contextual conditionings of digital media use on attitudinal consequences and contradictory expectations are often found. However, we can distinguish two main broad sets of country-level variables that could condition the effect of digital media use on psychological orientations: the level of socio-economic development and the quality of democracy.

With regards to socio-economic development, I expect, as the theory of modernisation suggests, that only when the population's basic needs are covered will people look further for democratic, non-traditional values. The better the economic situation, the more civic the messages that citizens receive through socialisation agencies (Deutsch 1964; Inglehart 1977, 1990; Przeworski 1991; Lipset *et al.* 1993; Bell 1999), among which we can place digital media. This does not mean that digital media will necessarily have no effects for any kinds of relevant political outcomes in contexts of low development. Media can contribute to improving skills; increasing access to information and knowledge; and developing networks between people. All this may erode the elite's control and authority (D'Costa 2003; Tekwani 2003). However, the potential of digital media to enhance personal autonomy may still be higher in contexts of economic modernisation and post-industrialisation than in contexts with lower economic development.

An aspect of development that becomes especially relevant is the level of technological development. It seems reasonable to expect that a minimum number of digital media users are necessary for online communities to develop. In other words, personal autonomy will develop via digital media use when there is a sufficiently large number of people to interact with and to enforce the social norm that being active and independent is something desirable. Nevertheless, this 'critical mass' argument is not always supported by previous research. The internet may be considered the base for an egalitarian, non-traditional community of users, but only in its infancy when highly politically motivated citizens are the first and only to use the internet, and before it becomes professionalised and multitudinous (Margolis and Resnick 2000). Over time, leisure and commercial usage of the internet become more common while only politically active citizens continue to use it for political purposes. From this point of view, as the number of digital media users increases, the effects of this technology on attitudes should decrease and even become negative. So, there are no clear expectations regarding this contextual variable.

With regard to the level and quality of democracy, I expect that any positive impact on personal autonomy – a value consonant with modern, Western democracies – stemming from digital media use will be stronger in a consolidated, stable liberal democracy with relatively high levels of democratic quality. In the words of Inglehart: 'institutions do help shape their society's culture – along with many other factors' (1997: 206). In consolidated democracies, the values conveyed by media are more likely to be consonant with democratic qualities. The higher the democratic quality of the context, the more likely we are to find messages that reinforce personal autonomy when online.

Full democracies do not restrict users' rights and moves and thus users can share any kinds of opinions or impressions. In contrast, non-democratic regimes restrict the nature of the information that users can access; the software and protocols they may publish; foreign sites or even access to the internet itself (Abbott 2001; Harwit and Clark 2001; Lyon 2003; Penfold 2003; Yang 2003; Guillén and Suárez 2005). Under these circumstances, institutional incentives for personal autonomy are missing or even negative. Internet savvy, independent and critical users would find difficulties exercising their autonomy to bypass system restrictions and get in touch with other 'netizens'. Thus, I expect internet use to have a stronger impact on personal autonomy under conditions of full democracy.

This does not mean that digital media may not play a role in the liberalisation and democratisation of authoritarian regimes, as previous research has suggested (Ho *et al.* 2003; Kalathil and Boas 2003). As stated previously, at the systemic level, digital media are an alternative to censored traditional media that allow the bypassing of gatekeepers and the expression of dissent in non-democratic contexts (Ferdinand 2000; Abbott 2001; Zengh and Wu 2005; Howard 2010); but only the more active and critical citizens are likely to take advantage of this feature in a context where this is costly and even dangerous. Thus, the expectation is that the higher the democratic quality of the context, the more likely that more people will experience an increase in their levels of personal autonomy as a result of digital media use.

A specific element of democratic standards that deserves special attention is the media system (Gunther and Mughan 2000; Bennet 2001; Hallin and Mancini 2004). Here, the expectations are not clear. On the one hand, if we extend the previous argument, a free media system would enhance the influence of digital media on attitudes. This would be the case if political digital media use concentrates on information consumption through traditional media online, as happened before the recent boom in social networking sites. However, not all aspects of democratic practice must necessarily condition the relationship between digital media use and political attitudes in the same direction. Digital media use may have a stronger effect on attitudes in those countries where information in traditional media is concentrated and limited. In these cases, alternative digital media provide a backdoor for information and dissent. As we have no way of differentiating which online media or applications people are exposed to, I will stick to the initial argument, that the more free the media system in a country, the more likely that internet use will enhance personal autonomy among its citizenry.

To sum up, the following hypotheses will be explored:

H1. Digital media use enhances personal autonomy.

H2. The effect of digital media on political attitudes is different across countries.

H3. The effect of digital media on personal autonomy depends on contextual features related to democracy and development. More precisely:

    a.   The effect of digital media on personal autonomy depends on the level of economic development (stronger where development is higher).

    b.   The effect of digital media on personal autonomy depends on the critical mass of internet users (stronger where there are more internet users).

    c.   The effect of digital media on personal autonomy depends on the quality of democracy (stronger in context of high democratic quality).

    d.   The effect of digital media on personal autonomy depends on the structure of traditional mass media (stronger where traditional media are more free).

Data and research design

Individual data have been obtained from the fifth wave of the World Value Survey (WVS), conducted between 2005 and 2008. This survey includes a large number of countries and measures personal autonomy as a value orientation. Contextual data regarding development, democracy and media characteristics have been obtained from the April 2011 version of the Quality of Government database (at the University of Gothenburg). This database includes for each country, the percentage of internet users (obtained from the World Telecommunication/ICT Development Report of the International Telecommunication Union), Polity VI democratic quality indicators and World Bank economic indicators (Teorell *et al.* 2011). In the merged database, contextual data for each country refer to the year when the WVS was conducted. There are forty countries for which we have complete individual and contextual data values. The following analyses are limited to this set of countries (names and sample sizes can be seen in Appendix Table 8.A.4).[3]

My focus is the relationship between digital media use and personal autonomy. Digital media use is measured as a dummy variable, scoring 1 when the individual used the internet and email to search for information in the last week and 0

---

3.   Descriptive statistics for individual and contextual variables are available in Appendices 8.2 and 8.3. All data at the individual level have been weighted by the weights provided by the WVS that account for age and gender in order to adjust the samples to the distribution of these variables in each country's population.

otherwise. Respondents were asked: 'People use different sources to learn what is going on in their country and the world. For each of the following sources, please indicate whether you used it last week or did not use it last week to obtain information: internet/email'. The possible answers were 'not used last week' and 'used last week'. All other possible situations (not applicable, no answer, don't know, not asked in survey) were recorded as missing values.

The personal autonomy index is a measure constructed by the WVS research group. Respondents were asked: 'Here is a list of qualities that children can be encouraged to learn at home. Which, if any, do you consider to be especially important? Please choose up to five'. The list included: *(1)* independence; *(2)* hard work; *(3)* feeling of responsibility; *(4)* imagination; *(5)* tolerance and respect for other people; *(6)* thrift, saving money and things; *(7)* determination, perseverance; *(8)* religious faith; *(9)* unselfishness; and *(10)* obedience. Each quality constitutes a dichotomous variable where 1 identifies those respondents that select it as one of their five preferred qualities. The personal autonomy index only takes into account four of these qualities which have been shown to tap the same underlying constructs across different countries. The resulting scale ranges from -2 to +2, where -2 indicates a preference for the two values considered most traditional (obedience and religious faith) and not the two autonomy values (determination and perseverance/ independence). A score of +2 indicates the opposite pattern of preferences.

In order to properly assess how much digital media use matters for personal autonomy, I recoded a number of control variables to range from 0 to 1 in order to make their effects comparable. These included gender (man=1, woman=0), age (originally comprising values from 15 to 98), educational level (originally ranging from 1='no formal education' to 9='university degree'), income (a ten-category item provided by the WVS), television and press exposure. These last two variables scored 1 if people had read daily newspapers or listened to news broadcasted on radio or television in the previous week to learn about what was going on in their country and the world. They have the same question format as that on digital media use. Missing values for age and sex were treated as random missing values and cases were thus excluded. Missing values for frequency of media use were coded as 0. Missing values for education and income were imputed based on a procedure taking into account more than twenty variables, including all the controls and independent variables considered in the subsequent analyses.[4]

Contextual explanatory factors refer to the year in which the survey was

---

4. Since Stata 10 was used for these analyses, no multiple imputation option was available. Instead, I followed a single imputation procedure using the Stata command 'impute', which follows a strategy based on a regression estimate. What the software does is regress non-missing values of X on a series of variables, it then uses the resulting regression equation to compute X when X is missing. This is a suboptimal strategy in the sense that it can reduce variability and standard errors, leading to an inflated R^2. Nevertheless, it may be useful when missing data are not too numerous and it is commonly considered better than deleting cases or ignoring the problem. There were 463 missing values for education and 6424 values for income among more than 55,000 cases. None of my hypotheses rely on these two variables and I do not think this introduces serious biases.

conducted in each country and have been measured as follows. *Development* is measured as the mortality rate for under fives (recorded as the number of deaths per 1,000 live births each year). *Internet users* refers to the number of citizens using digital media per 100 people. *Democracy* is an index of institutionalised democracy borrowed from the Polity IV project.[5] It ranges from 0 (low) to 10 (high) and takes into account the presence of institutions and procedures through which citizens can express effective preferences about alternative policies and leaders; the existence of institutionalised constraints on the exercise of power by the executive; and the guarantee of civil liberties to all citizens. It derives from coding the competitiveness of political participation, the openness and competitiveness of executive recruitment and the constraints on the chief executive. *Freedom of press* is a subcategory of the *freedom in the world* measure, computed by summing the following component items: laws and regulations; political pressures and controls; economic influences; and repressive actions. The scale ranges from 0 (most free) to 100 (least free).

The data structure and the mixing of variables at the individual and at the contextual level require a multilevel approach to test the stated hypotheses. When handling pooled cross-sectional surveys, the structure of the errors will probably reproduce similarities within countries, underestimating the standard errors of the macro-level variables. This can only be fixed by clustering errors by country or applying multilevel analysis. Thus, hierarchical linear modelling is recommended for solving this equation, which was done using HLM for Windows (version 6.8) developed by Raudenbush and Bryk (2002). This technique and software allows country-level variables to be used as moderators of individual-level factors; which enables testing of the hypothesis related to contextual variables (H3a, b and c above).

A number of limitations must be acknowledged here with regards to the measurement of our main independent variable and endogeneity concerns. First, our measure of internet use is limited: we do not know what citizens used it for, nor their frequency of use, nor whether they are regular internet users. Nevertheless, it is employed here because it is the only comparable measure available. Second, cross-sectional survey evidence has limited capacity to assess causal relationships, such as that claimed to exist between digital media use and personal autonomy. It can be argued that those with high levels of previously existing political attitudes choose to use digital media more than people with lower levels of these attitudes precisely because these digital media potentialities fit better with their individual attitudes than traditional media. In that case, the role of digital media would range from none to limited, merely reinforcing effects. This potential problem of endogeneity could only be solved by using an experimental design, which is difficult enough in itself, let alone in a comparative perspective. Even if there is evidently room for reverse causality, we can probably assume that providing there is a relatively robust association between digital media use, political attitudes and values, at least part of it will be in the hypothesised direction.

---

5. *See* www.systemicpeace.org for further details.

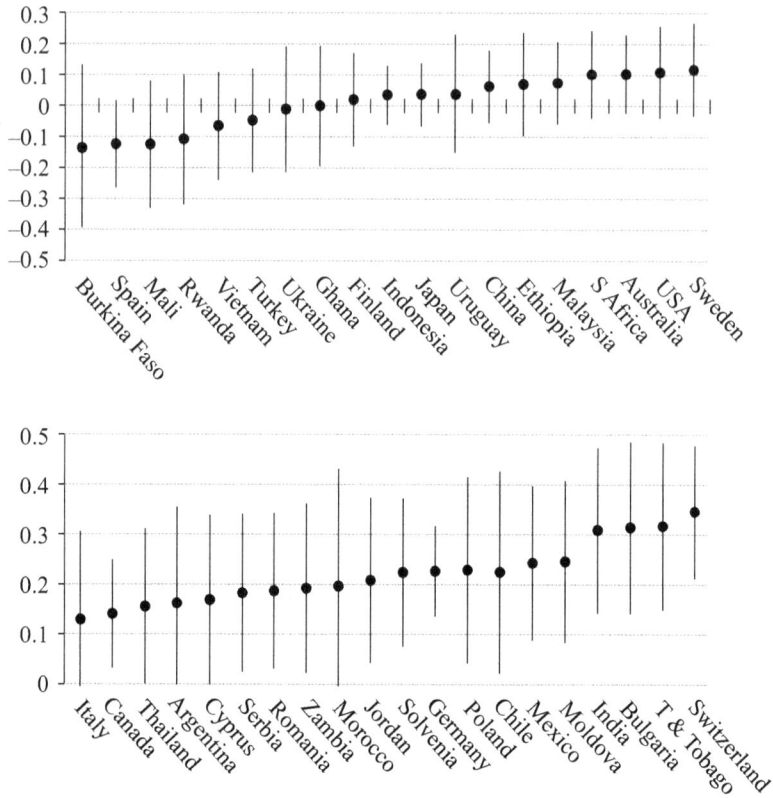

Figure 8.1: Effect of internet use on the personal autonomy index

Notes: Points represent Beta coefficients; lines represent 95% confidence intervals;
Source: data from the fifth wave of the WVS; charts designed by author.

Empirical evidence

A simple comparative test was conducted first by running a separate regression
for each country. The results are shown in Figure 8.1. The points in the graph
reflect the magnitude of the Beta coefficients resulting from OLS regressions
where internet use is the main independent variable and personal autonomy the
dependent variable, controlling for age, sex, education, income and the use of
newspaper, television or radio to get political information. Countries have been
sorted by the magnitude of this coefficient. The lines reflect confidence intervals
and thus when they cross the zero point, the effects cannot be considered to be
different from zero in the population.

The effect for personal autonomy is not significantly different from zero in
many cases, but it is clearly positive in at least seventeen of them and most evident
for Switzerland, Bulgaria, Trinidad and Tobago and India. It therefore seems that
internet use has overall a positive effect and an effect that changes from country to
country, as H1 and H2 predicted.

We turn now to a more sophisticated multilevel approach. Table 8.1 presents the results of seven hierarchical linear multilevel models estimated using maximum likelihood estimation. The first model is a null or baseline model that only takes into account the grouping of the observations in second-level units and that tries to answer how much variance of the dependent variable is located in this second level. The next model introduces predictors at the individual level (coefficients for controls are not reported) and assesses to what extent digital media use affects attitudes, taking into account the multilevel structure of the data. Models 3 to 7 attempt to predict the varying effects of internet use across countries by means of the aforementioned contextual variables. Each model includes one contextual explanatory model at a time, except for model 6 that includes *economic development* and *democratic quality* entered simultaneously.

Model 1 confirms what we already intuitively saw in the figures: the amount of variance to be explained at the second level is large enough to engage in multilevel analysis. A common rule of thumb states that the intra-class correlation value should be larger than 0.05 to justify multilevel modelling (Micceri 2007). As the intraclass correlation value shows, about 21 per cent of the variance in personal autonomy is due to context. As seen in Figure 8.1, there is a fair amount of cross-national variation in the extent to which internet use is related to personal autonomy, confirming H2 and justifying the inclusion of second-level explanatory factors in further models.

Model 2 shows that internet use has a significant effect on personal autonomy, even after controlling for the relevant individual variables. Contextual factors were therefore added to test H3a, b, c and d. Some independent variables that vary widely between countries (such as education and income) have been group-centred to ensure they are only capturing differences between individuals and not the differences in the level of development between countries. Because the number of second-level units is limited (N=40), one contextual explanatory variable is entered at a time, with the exception of model 6, where the effects of *economic development* and *democracy* were entered simultaneously.

Model 3 shows that socio-economic development positively affects the relationship between internet use and personal autonomy. Model 5 shows that the democracy index enhances the positive effect of internet use on personal autonomy. As these two contextual variables are closely related, they need to be included in the same model to estimate their independent effects. This is the aim of model 6, which depicts that the effect of the democracy index on personal autonomy is independent of the level of socio-economic development. The effect of democracy on autonomy holds. The percentage of internet users (model 4) and the degree of media freedom (model 7) also significantly affect the relationship between internet use and personal autonomy.

The main hypothesis concerning the conditioning effect of contextual variables is thus confirmed by these analyses. The potential for internet use to enhance values of personal autonomy is enhanced by certain socio-economic and political features: high economic development, high quality of democracy, high proportion of internet users and high levels of press freedom.

Table 8.1: Hierarchical linear models of civic political attitudes with internet use and contextual factors

Model	1[a]	2[b]	3[c]	4[d]	5[e]	6[f]	7[g]
H1: Internet use ($\beta1$)	—	0.13** (0.02)	0.23** (0.03)	0.05 (0.04)	-0.07 (0.05)	0.07 (0.05)	0.24** (0.05)
H3a: Infant mortality > $\beta1$			-0.00** (0.00)				
H3b: Internet users > $\beta1$				0.00* (0.00)			
H3c: Democracy > $\beta1$					0.03** (0.01)		
H3a/c: Democracy > $\beta1$ (control: development)						0.02** (0.01)	
H3a/c: Infant mortality > $\beta1$ (control: democracy)						-0.00** (0.00)	
H3d: Freedom of press > $\beta1$							-0.00* (0.00)
Random effects							
Variance (intercept) U^0	0.32**	0.29**	0.29**	0.29**	0.29**	0.29**	0.29**

(Cont'd.)

Table 8.1: (Cont'd.)

Model	1[a]	2[b]	3[c]	4[d]	5[e]	6[f]	7[g]
Variance (slope) U^2	–	0.03**	0.03**	0.03**	0.02**	0.01**	0.02**
Variance (residual) r	1.01	1.05	1.05	1.05	1.05	1.05	1.05
Intraclass correlation 1 $(U^0 / U^0 + r)$	22.5%	17.9%	21.5%	21.3%	21.4%	21.5%	20.9%
Intraclass correlation 2 $(U^2 / U^0 + r)$	–	2.1%	1.1%	1.6%	1.5%	0.9%	1.7
Parameters	3	12	13	13	13	14	13
Deviance	160924	159025	159006	159022	159013	158999	159031
AIC	26821	6626	6116	6116	6116	5679	6117

Notes: a. Null model; b. Individual variables; c. Economic development; d. Per cent of internet users; e. Democratic quality; f. Economic development and democratic quality; g. Freedon of press; AIC = Akaike Information Criterion; *p<0.05, **p<0.01; Controls at individual level (not shown) are: sex (1=male), education (country-centred), income (country-centred), newspapers used to retrieve information, television and radio used to retrieve information, age. All variables have been normalised to rank from 0 to 1. Full maximum likelihood estimation applied, weighted at the individual level. Level 1 N=40, Level 2 N= 55.05.

Conclusions and discussion

In this chapter I have claimed that the internet has the potential to change individual predispositions and value orientations, acting as a socialisation milieu that enhances individual autonomy. I have focused on this particular value, since it is related to many attitudes and behaviours that are relevant for democracy. I have found that digital media use is indeed empirically related to what people think of the importance of personal autonomy, more precisely, that its use increases the perceived importance of values such as independence and perseverance with regards to child education.

According to these exploratory results, it would make sense to look at digital media as an environment that has the capacity to trigger non-traditional values consonant with democracy. Those changes may be transmitted to the next generation within the family and crystallise in wider cultural change. Nevertheless, the effects of internet use on personal values are far from universal: there are important cross-national differences in the extent to which internet use matters for personal autonomy. These differences can in turn be explained by differences in socio-economic and political variables such as the level of socio-economic development, the proportion of internet users, the level of democratic quality and the level of press freedom. The effect of internet use on personal autonomy is stronger where the level of socio-economic development is higher, the proportion of internet users is greater, the quality of democracy is better and the press is higher.

Although digital media have the potential, albeit modest, to enhance personal autonomy in most countries analysed, this effect will be larger in contexts of economic development and high democratic quality, that is, in contexts that promote civic attitudes. Though digital media may have significant impacts on other political outcomes which can be more relevant for non-democratic systems, their ability to foster personal autonomy increases as contexts become more developed and democratic. This implies that most current research on the democratisation effects of the internet might be too optimistic. Since they handle cases and data from established Western democracies where institutional conditions interact with the internet's positive effect on personal autonomy, their conclusions about the ability of digital media to trigger a cultural change may be exaggerated.

Further research regarding this question should address different pending tasks. Comparative measures of digital media use, which are definitely too blunt, should be improved. Survey data need to incorporate accurate and comparable indicators of digital media use both across countries and through time. Indeed, a major challenge for comparative research in this field is the inclusion of a temporal dimension that would provide us with some clues about the consequences of digital media diffusion and evolution for modernity and democratic values, as well as for civic attitudes.

Beyond measurement questions, theoretical models regarding the conditioning effect of contextual variables should also be refined. Non-linear relationships or potential interactions between economic circumstances and democratic quality should be explored. It could be, for instance, that the effect of digital media use is higher in highly developed countries with some democratic deficits. It makes sense since there is an increasing number of countries where economic and technologic development is not followed by similar achievements with regards to human rights (e.g. Qatar, Russia, Brunei). This situation may give rise to an elite of disaffected and technologically savvy citizens who may use their skills to draw attention to public issues and lead demands for a deeper democracy. Testing the extent to which this is plausible may require the specification of interactions within country level variables and, in turn, with individual level factors, which clearly exceeds the purpose of this chapter. Finally, we must reinforce the internal validity of research designs that address questions of causality such as the effect of digital media on political attitudes. This would mean engaging in methodological designs that have not been common in comparative research, such as panel surveys or experiments, but that constitute a necessary complement.

Appendix

Table 8.A.1: Descriptive statistics (dependent variable)

	Autonomy Index
N	55045
Mean	0.15
Standard deviation	1.18
Minimum	-2.00
Maximum	2.00

Table 8.A.2: Descriptive statistics (independent variables at the individual level)

	Sex (male)	Age	Education	Income	Newspapers	TV	Internet
N	55045	55045	55045	55045	55045	55045	55045
Mean	0.49	0.27	0.51	0.41	0.53	0.82	0.25
Standard deviation	0.49	0.17	0.31	0.24	0.49	0.39	0.43
Minimum	0.00	0.00	0.00	0.00	0.00	0.00	0.00
Maximum	1.00	0.86	1.00	1.00	1.00	1.00	1.00

Table 8.A.3: Descriptive statistics (independent variables at the aggregated level)

	Freedom of the press	Institutionalised democracy	Infant mortality rate (per 1,000 live births)	Internet users (per 100 people)
N	40	40	40	40
Mean	40.28	7.30	24.68	29.85
Median	35.00	9.00	14.22	21.16
Standard deviation	21.72	3.44	28.05	24.98
Minimum	9	0	2.70	0.37
Maximum	84	10	104.50	86.56

Table 8.A.4: Descriptive statistics for country surveys

	N	%	Year WVS
Argentina	1002	1.8	2006
Australia	1410	2.6	2005
Bulgaria	1001	1.8	2006
Burkina Faso	1478	2.7	2007
Canada	2143	3.9	2006
Chile	1000	1.8	2005
China	2015	3.7	2007
Cyprus	1047	1.9	2006
Ethiopia	1500	2.7	2007
Finland	1014	1.8	2005
Germany	2064	3.7	2006
Ghana	1534	2.8	2007
Guatemala	1000	1.8	2005
India	1999	3.6	2006
Indonesia	2013	3.7	2006
Italy	1012	1.8	2005
Japan	1096	2.0	2005
Jordan	1200	2.2	2007
Malaysia	1200	2.2	2006
Mali	1427	2.6	2007
Mexico	1560	2.8	2005
Moldova	1046	1.9	2006
Morocco	1198	2.2	2007
Poland	1000	1.8	2005
Romania	1776	3.2	2005
Rwanda	1507	2.7	2007
S Africa	2987	5.4	2007
Serbia	1220	2.2	2006
Slovenia	1037	1.9	2005
Spain	1200	2.2	2007
Sweden	1003	1.8	2006
Switzerland	1241	2.3	2007
Thailand	1523	2.8	2007
Trinidad and Tobago	1002	1.8	2006
Turkey	1346	2.4	2007
Ukraine	1000	1.8	2006
Uruguay	1000	1.8	2006
USA	1249	2.3	2006
Vietnam	1495	2.7	2006
Zambia	1500	2.7	2007

References

Abbott, J. P. (2001) 'Democracy@Internet.asia? The challenges to the emancipatory potential of the net: lessons from China and Malaysia', *Third World Quarterly*, 22(1): 99–114.

Abdulla, R. A. (2005) 'Taking the e-train: The development of the Internet in Egypt', *Global Media and Communication*, 1(2): 149–165.

Anduiza, E. (2002) 'Individual characteristics, institutional incentives and electoral abstention in Western Europe', *European Journal of Political Research,* 41(5): 643–673.

Anduiza, E., Jensen, M. J. and Jorba, L. (2012) *Digital Media and Political Engagement Worldwide: A comparative study*, Cambridge: Cambridge University Press.

Bell, D. (1999) *The Coming of Post-industrial Society: A venture in social forecasting*, New York: Basic Books.

Bennet, L. (2001) *Mediated Politics,* Cambridge: Cambridge University Press.

Cantijoch, M., Jorba, L. and San Martin, J. (2008) 'Exposure to Political Information in New and Old Media: Which Impact on Political Participation?' paper presented at 104th APSA Annual Meeting, Boston, August 2008.

Castells, M., Tubella, I., Sancho, T., Díaz de Isla, M. I. and Wellman, B. (2004) 'Social structure, cultural identity, and personal autonomy in the practice of the Internet: The network society in Catalonia', in M. Castells (ed.) *The Network Society: A cross-cultural perspective*, Cheltenham: Edward Elgar.

Coleman, S., Taylor, J. and van den Donk, W. (1999) *Parliament in the Age of the Internet,* Oxford, New York: Oxford University Press.

Colombo, C., Galais, C. and Gallego, A. (2012) 'Internet use and political attitudes in Europe', in E. Anduiza, M. J. Jensen and L. Jorba (eds) *Digital Media and Political Engagement Worldwide: A comparative study*, Cambridge: Cambridge University Press.

Dahlgren, P. (2000) 'The Internet and the democratization of civic culture', *Political Communication*, 17(4): 335–340.

D'Costa, A. P. (2003) 'Catching up and falling behind: Inequality, IT, and the Asian diaspora', in K. C. Ho, R. Kluver and K. C.C. Yang (eds) *Asia.com. Asia encounters the Internet*, London: Routledge: 44–66.

Deutsch, K. W. (1964) 'Social mobilization and political development', *American Political Science Review,* 55: 493–514.

Dutton, W. H. (2005) 'The Internet and social transformation: Reconfiguring Access', in W. H. Dutton, B. Kahin, R. O'Callaghan and A. W. Wyckoff (eds) *Transforming Enterprise: The economic and social implications of information technology,* Cambridge: Massachusetts Institute of Technology Press: 375–398.

Ferdinand, P. (ed.) (2000) *The Internet, Democracy and Democratization*, London: Routledge.

Foa, R. (2007) *Socioeconomic Development, Parenting Values and Multiple Modernities.* Online. Available: http://www.roberto.foa.name/Parenting_Attitudes_Foa (accessed 22 May 2007).

Gallego, A. (2007) 'Unequal political participation in Europe', *International Journal of Sociology,* 37(4): 10–25.

Guillén, M. F. and Suárez, S. L. (2005) 'Explaining the global digital divide: Economic, political and sociological drivers of cross-national Internet use', *Social Forces,* 84(2): 681–708.

Gunther, R. and Mughan, A. (2000) *Democracy and the Media: A comparative perspective,* Cambridge: Cambridge University Press.

Hague, B. N. and Loader, B. D. (1999) *Digital Democracy: Discourse and decision-making in the digital age,* London: Routledge.

Hallin, D. C. and Mancini, P. (2004) *Comparing Media Systems: Three models of media and politics,* Cambridge: Cambridge University Press.

Harwit, E. and Clark, D. (2001) 'Shaping the Internet in China: Evolution of political control over network infrastructure and content', *Asian Survey,* 413: 377–408.

Ho, K. C., Kluver, R. and Yang, C. C. (eds) (2003) *Asia encounters the Internet,* New York: Routledge.

Hoff, J., Horrocks, I. and Tops, P. (eds) (2000) *Democratic Governance and New Technology: Technologically medicated innovations in political practice in Western Europe,* London: Routledge.

Howard, P. N. (2010) *The Digital Origins of Dictatorship and Democracy: Information technology and political Islam,* Oxford: Oxford University Press.

Inglehart, R. (1977) *The Silent Revolution: Changing values and political styles among Western publics,* Princeton: Princeton University Press.

— (1990) *Culture Shift in Advanced Industrial Society,* Princeton: Princeton University Press.

— (1997) *Modernization and Postmodernization: Cultural, economic, and political change in 43 societies,* Princeton: Princeton University Press.

Inglehart, R. and Welzel, C. (2005) *Modernization, Cultural Change, and Democracy: The human development sequence,* Cambridge: Cambridge University Press.

Kalathil, S. and Boas, T. C. (2003) *Open Networks, Closed Regimes: The impact of the Internet on authoritarian rule,* Washington DC: Carnegie Endowment for International Peace/Brookings Institution.

Keen, A. (2007) *The Cult of the Amateur,* London: Nicholas Brealey.

Kenski, K. and Stroud, N. J. (2006) 'Connections between Internet use and political efficacy, knowledge, and participation', *Journal of Broadcasting and Electronic Media,* 502: 173–192.

Kohn, M. (1976) 'Social class and parental values: another confirmation of the relationship', *American Sociological Review,* 41: 538–545.

Lei, Y.-W. (2011) 'The political consequences of the rise of the Internet: Political beliefs and practices of Chinese netizens', *Political Communication,* 28(3): 291–322.

Lipset, S. M., Martin, S., Seong, K. -R. and Torres, J. C. (1993) 'A comparative analysis of the social requisites of democracy', *International Social Science Journal,* 45(2): 154–175.

Lyon, D. (2003) 'Cyberspace, surveillance, and social control: the hidden face of the Internet in Asia', in K. C. Ho, R. Kluver and K. C. C. Yang (eds) *Asia. com. Asia encounters the Internet,* London: Routledge: 67–82.

Margolis, M. and Resnick, D. (2000) *Politics as Usual: The cyberspace 'revolution',* London: Sage.

Micceri, T. (2007) 'The advantages of using multilevel modeling to address institutional research questions', paper presented at Florida Association for Institutional Research Annual Forum, Cocoa Beach, Florida, February 2007. Online. Available: http://www.florida-air.org/ted07.pdf (accessed 14 August 2012).

Niemi, R. G., Craig, S. C. and Mattei, F. (1991) 'Measuring internal political efficacy in the 1988 National Election Study', *American Political Science Review,* 85(4):1407–1413.

Park, N., Kee, K. F. and Valenzuela, S. (2009) 'Being immersed in social networking environment: Facebook groups, uses and gratifications, and social outcomes', *CyberPsychology & Behavior,* 12(6): 729–733.

Pasek, J., More E. and Romer, D. (2009) 'Realizing the social Internet? Online social networking meets offline social capital', *Journal of Information Technology and Politics,* 6(3–4): 197–215.

Penfold, C. (2003) 'Global technology meets local environment: State attempts to control Internet content', in K. C. Ho, R. Kluver and K. C. C. Yang (eds) *Asia.com. Asia encounters the Internet,* London: Routledge: 83–96.

Prensky, M. (2001) 'Digital natives, Digital immigrants Part 1', *On the Horizon,* 9(5): 1–6.

—— (2008) 'Young minds, fast times: The 21st-Century Digital Learner', *Edutopia.* Online. Available: http://www.edutopia.org/ikid-digital-learner-technology-2008 (accessed 3 April 2012).

Prior, M. (2007) *Post-Broadcast Democracy: How media choice increases inequality in political involvement and polarizes elections,* Cambridge: Cambridge University Press.

Przeworski, A. (1991) *Democracy and the Market: Political and economic reforms in Eastern Europe and Latin America,* Cambridge: Cambridge University Press.

Raudenbush, S. W. and Bryk, A. S. (2002) *Hierarchical linear models,* Thousand Oaks: Sage.

Römmele, A. (2003) 'Political parties, party communication and new information and communication technologies', *Party Politics,* 9(1): 7–20.

Rosen, J. (2005) 'Bloggers vs. journalists is over'. Online. Available: http://archive.pressthink.org/2005/01/21/berk_essy.html (accessed 24 May 2013).

Steuer, J. (1992), 'Defining Virtual Reality: Dimensions determining telepresence', *Journal of Communication,* 42: 73–93.

Tapscott, D. and Williams, A. (2008) *Wikinomics: How Mass Collaboration Changes Everything*, London: Atlantic Books.

Tedesco, J. C. (2007) 'Examining Internet interactivity effects on young adult political information efficacy', *American Behavioral Scientist,* 50(9): 1183–1194.

Tekwani, S. (2003) 'The Tamil diaspora: Tamil militancy, and the Internet', in K. C. Ho, R. Kluver and K.C.C. Yang (eds) *Asia.com. Asia encounters the Internet*, London: Routledge: 175–92.

Teorell, J., Samanni, M., Charron, N. Holmberg, S. and Rothstein, B. (2011) *The Quality of Government Dataset, version 6th April 2011*, University of Gothenburg: The Quality of Government Institute.

Verba, S., Schlozman, K. L. and Brady, H. E. (1995) *Voice and Equality: Civic Voluntarism in American Politics,* Cambridge: Harvard University Press.

Visser, K. (n.d). 'Digital immigrants abroad: learning the language of e-learning'. Online. Available: http://www.caudit.edu.au/educauseaustralasia/2005/PDF/A12.pdf (accessed 29 July 2012).

Wallis, C. (2006) 'The multitasking generation', *Time,* 167(13): 48–55.

Ward, S. and Vedel, T. (2006) 'Introduction: The potential of the Internet revisited', *Parliamentary Affairs,* 59(2): 210–225.

Welzel, C. (2010) 'How selfish are self-expression values? A civicness test', *Journal of Cross-Cultural Psychology,* 41(2): 152–174.

Westling, M. (2007) 'Expanding the public sphere: The impact of Facebook on political communication'. Online. Available: http://www.thenewvernacular. com /projects/facebook_and_political_communication.pdf. (accessed 21 July 2012).

Xenos, M. A. and Moy, P. (2007) 'Direct and differential effects of the Internet on political participation and civic engagement', *Journal of Communication,* 57: 704–718.

Yildiz, H. (2002) 'Internet: un nouvel outil de communication multidimensionnel', in V. Serfaty (ed.) *L'Internet en politique des Etats-Unis à l'Europe,* Strasbourg : Presses Universitaires de Strasbourg : 275–290.

Yang, G. (2003) 'The co-evolution of the Internet and civil society in China', *Asian Survey,* 433: 405–422.

Zheng, Y. and Wu, G. (2005) 'Information technology, public space, and collective action in China', *Comparative Political Studies*, 38(5): 507–536.

Chapter Nine

Space, the Final Frontier of Political Socialisation Research: Geopolitical Contexts, Migrant Resocialisation and Political Remittances

Ruxandra Paul[1]

> To the extent that beliefs do affect regimes, we shall want to know what factors determine beliefs (Dahl 1971: 125).

> One's destination is never a place, but rather a new way of looking at things (Miller 1957: 25).

What do migrants learn about politics while abroad? Do mobile citizens become more cosmopolitan or more nationalistic as a result of leaving their homeland? Do ideas that migrants import from abroad or communicate to family and friends transform political life in systematic and predictable ways?

This chapter develops a theory of 'political remittances' based on the geopolitical contexts in which migrants undergo partial resocialisation. In the current globalisation era, people travel to foreign countries more rapidly, easily and cheaply than ever before. Thanks to increasingly fluid boundaries, crossing borders does not mean permanent exit; indeed, returning home after shorter or longer stays abroad constitutes the norm. International temporary migration has complemented or replaced domestic flows, such as rural-urban commuting to work or study. Contextual changes trigger resocialisation, as part of attitudinal and behavioural adaptation mechanisms. Migratory experiences affect migrants' world-views and horizons on a wide range of dimensions. This chapter focuses on interconnected political, socio-economic and cultural transformations. Does learning happen through migration as people move between sending and receiving states? What kind of political resocialisation does international mobility determine in people who live, work or study outside their homeland? Do migrants undergo peripatetic political socialisation?

---

1. I would like to thank Grzegorz Ekiert, Peter Hall, Daniel Ziblatt, Simone Abendschön, Harris Mylonas, Mary Waters, Peggy Levitt, Susan Pharr, Colin Brown, Amanda Garrett, Didi Kuo, Albert Wang, participants of the workshop New Directions in Political Socialisation Research (ECPR Joint Sessions of Workshops, Münster, Germany 2010), as well as colleagues in the Comparative Politics Research Workshop at Harvard University for the useful feedback they provided in the revision process.

Despite the ever-growing literatures on globalisation and migration studies, we still know very little about the migrants' political ties with their homelands.

The once taken-for-granted correspondence between citizenship, nation and state has been called into question as new forms of grassroots citizenship have taken on an increasingly transterritorial character. Resident non-citizens now routinely live and work [...] throughout the world, while maintaining social and political networks that link them to people and places in their countries and communities of origin (Smith and Bakker 2008: 3).

Such major transformations call for a close assessment. Adopting a political socialisation lens allows researchers to study these phenomena rigorously by shifting focus from observing correlations to analysing the causal mechanisms that link migration to attitudinal and behavioural changes. This chapter advances a new research agenda focused on political socialisation dynamics that transcend nation-state borders. It recommends examining how non-permanent international mobilities (circular migration, commuting, seasonal flows, academic or professional exchanges) influence politics and policy making in their interaction with domestic forces, on multiple levels. Recent works in anthropology, sociology and political science include previously omitted spatial variables in analysing migrations, development and remittances (Careja and Emmenegger 2012; Faist 2009; Glick Schiller and Faist 2009; Glick Schiller and Fouron 2001; Kapur 2010; Mügge 2010; Østergaard-Nielsen 2003; Roniger 2011), without drawing insights from the rich socialisation literature. This chapter makes a theoretical contribution, introducing a new typology of socialisation experiences predicated on space and sequence (i.e. socialisation contexts and order of exposure). On the spatial dimension, the framework situates socialisation with respect to a contextual triad: homeland, host country and migratory system. On the chronological-sequential dimension, the typology connects migrant learning and adaptation with a multi-phasic migrant socialisation cycle that includes exit (i.e. culture shedding); secondary socialisation (i.e. culture learning or resocialisation in the receiving country); transnational reincorporation (i.e. reestablishing the connection with the country of origin); and tertiary socialisation (or updating). Migrants go through the cycle after leaving the home country where they underwent formative socialisation along with non-migrants. Transnational migrants experience the cycle repeatedly, while classical migrants stop at the stage of resocialisation in the receiving country. Different migratory experiences produce different attitudinal and behavioural outcomes, ultimately influencing politics in the migrants' homeland.

In a nutshell, migration leads to economic, political and societal transformations. However, the processes behind these shifts have not been systematically examined. I argue that political socialisation constitutes the mechanism through which these bottom-up changes occur. To support this claim, I present original data on the intra-European migrations of Romanian citizens showing how mobility reconfigures citizenship, loyalties and everyday politics in post-communist East-Central Europe. After reviewing the literature on the hypothesised political effects of citizen mobility, I introduce political socialisation as a fruitful strategy for studying migrant learning and its effects on domestic political arenas. I advance a theory of political socialisation as a palimpsest, with political remittances emerging from the synthesis of learning experiences in three contexts: homeland, host country and migratory system. I argue that, for mobile populations, political socialisation adopts a layered structure, a cycle which includes learning occurring within nation states and liminal phases happening in transnational spaces. Finally, I summarise the results of qualitative fieldwork I conducted in Romania (one of the main post-communist migrant-sending countries in Europe) and two destination countries of Romanian migrants (Italy and France). As much as possible, I disaggregate political socialisation from other learning, although migration constitutes an inherently political experience.

Migration as political socialisation: what is learned and unlearned abroad?

Travel broadens the mind. Around the world, ancient and modern rites of passage involve sojourns in foreign environments. Mobility and personal development are seen as inextricably connected. From medieval coming-of-age travels and apprenticeships away from home, to contemporary residence requirements that many US universities impose,[2] separation from what is known expands horizons. Acquiring the knowledge, skills, open-mindedness and maturity needed to navigate life elsewhere constitutes a *sine qua non* condition of personal growth. Anthropologist Arnold van Gennep's general theory of socialisation noted that rites of passage have three phases: *(1)* separation, in which people disconnect from their status, severing links to the familiar; *(2)* transition, a liminal phase in which the individual stands on the 'threshold' between statuses; and *(3)* reincorporation, in which one re-enters society with a new status (van Gennep 1960). By exposing the traveller to conflicting world-views, formative journeys create cognitive dissonance. The migrant then has to reconcile conflicting cognitions to reach a consistent system of beliefs.

Is there socialisation-via-migration? Spatial mobility does trigger status changes for most migrants. Separation, transition and reincorporation aptly capture the stages of migratory experience. Migration may transform world-views, political and apolitical, but this is something to be established. When, where and how do people form and revise their ideas, identities, orientations and behaviours? Of the many contexts in which life unfolds, which ones determine citizens' political views and self-perceptions? How do major context shifts, such as repeated exposures to foreign environments, affect individual values or actions?

2.　To foster community spirit and facilitate transition to adulthood, some colleges require enrolled students to live on campus for six semesters, even when their family happens to live in the town where the university is located. The two semesters of non-mandatory on-campus residence allow students to study abroad for one year, if they want.

In high mobility contexts, one can hypothesise that *(1)* experiences determining individual world-views and behaviours come from several socialisation contexts and political systems; *(2)* migrants' constellation of relevant socialisation agents (individual and institutional) is not circumscribed to a nation-state territory, but rather spreads across multinational migratory systems; and *(3)* citizens' ideas about identity, national loyalty and other attachments or allegiances to domestic and foreign entities may change as a result of migratory experiences. Basically, learning happens through interaction and communication with others, in a household, group, collective, community, formal or informal institution. Socialising interactions happen in time and space. In fact, they happen in multiple spaces and places, each embedded in specific socio-political and cultural contexts. Socialisation agents (individual, institutional, collective, generational) constitute an established focus of political socialisation studies. Research designs explore age groups and life phases to identify corresponding political learning, so time is also a traditionally respectable variable in the field.

Not the same is true, however, of geopolitical space, which, together with spatial mobility, remains the blind spot of socialisation research. If transnationalism is defined as 'those human activities, social networks and movements that extend across national boundaries' (Østergaard-Nielsen 2003; Roniger 2011: 7) or as 'the extent to which individuals are involved in cross-border interactions and mobility' (Mau *et al.* 2008: 5), it becomes obvious that we live in an increasingly transnational world. Analysts note 'a growing awareness that collective identities and personal commitments as well as public spheres and political projects are reformulated as a result of the changing experience of human beings in space and time' (Roniger 2011: 10). Socialisation scholars examine shifts of life experience in time, but not in space or movement. While political socialisation is commonly explored at the national level, where spatial mobility plays a somewhat limited role, there has been little progress in analysing how migration influences world-views, values, behaviours and party preferences. Also unexplored are questions about restructured socio-economic status hierarchies; political cleavages between migrants and the sedentary; and political-cultural change in the migrants' sending communities and countries. For manageability, scholars often focus on domestic factors. Good quality empirical data remain scarce for non-Western countries. Free-movement areas like the Schengen space do not collect information about people crossing internal borders. Yet, since ideas and behavioural patterns travel across state boundaries with ease, considering only national and subnational factors produces a truncated picture of contemporary socialisation.

Researchers hesitate before the transnational political question, but speculate about the effects of border-crossing social relations and experiential spaces on politics, policy and political regimes. Echoing arguments about the virtues of travelling, enthusiasts claim that transnational lives foster cosmopolitanism by positively changing people's cognitive and attitudinal stances (Mau *et al.* 2008). The assumption is that transnationalism generates world-views that accept diversity and facilitate engagement with 'the other' in the spirit of intellectual, socio-cultural and aesthetic openness. 'Cosmopolitanism arises through the interrelated processes of increased connectivity and cultural contact' (Kwok-Bun 2002: 191). Analysts note that migratory flows and social networks have expanded and proliferated, producing 'more cosmopolitans now than there have been at any other time' (Hannerz 1990: 241). Politically, as immigrants grow distant from their homelands over time, many may develop attachments to host societies or the supranational institutions that facilitate mobility. In terms of political behaviours, this may translate into votes for parties that support migration and openness. Exit may result in either loyalty transfers from homeland to other geopolitical entities or the emergence of a postnational perspective based on the international human rights regime (Soysal 1994).

Sceptics fear that citizen-outsiders are prone to nostalgia, vulnerable to manipulation by opportunistic politicians and, thus, likely to develop long-distance nationalism (Anderson 1998, 1992). Cross-border networks and interventions may be subversive because they loosen ascriptive ties without providing stable and strong new references (Habermas 2001). Trying to recreate the 'imagined community' from a dispersed nation, political parties and states may resort to nationalist discourses to gain migrant loyalties and money. The associated risks are high, since a distorted perception of homeland realities impedes communication and politicises cleavages between migrant and sedentary citizens.

To adjudicate between these camps, one needs to study migration through a political socialisation lens. The phenomena in question require an evaluation bridging the gap between migration and political socialisation research. Until now, political socialisation scholars have avoided analysing migration, and migration scholars have relied on anecdotes about changing attitudes in transnational communities. There have been few developments on the theory front, not to mention the persistent dearth of data. Immigration studies examine the socialisation effects of permanent resettlement in another country.[3] Immigration creates high incentives for migrants to replace prior learning with new attitudes and behaviours to fit in and gain acceptance in the receiving country. Diasporic socialisation dynamics cannot be generalised to all migratory experiences, especially temporary ones that do not entail migrants' *de facto* and *de jure* exit from the homeland. Since work on immigration leaves out, by definition, questions about non-permanent flows (circular, temporary, seasonal), the transnational political question remains neglected. The conversation about geopolitical space, migratory movements and learning is long overdue. Political socialisation experts can provide decisive conceptual and methodological insights to advance research in the field.

Increasingly, people include circular migration in their problem-solving and living-making repertoires. They do so to such an extent that scholars mention populations whose existence transcends the nation state; communities where most working-age citizens 'settle in mobility'; transnationalism (Basch *et al.*, 1994;

---

3. Most studies cited above define transnationalism as connections sustained by immigrants (first, 1.5 and second generations), a definition which excludes citizens living abroad temporarily for work, training or study purposes.

Itzigsohn *et al.* 1999); or the 'bifocality' of those who live and plan their life simultaneously in both sending and receiving countries (Vertovec 2004). Some announce the start of a new era of 'de-territorialised' or 'de-nationalised' nation states (Appadurai 1996; Basch *et al.* 1994; Sassen 1998), since 'immigrants forge and sustain multi-stranded social relations that link together their societies of origin and settlement'. Living abroad does not mean leaving one's country: 'the nation's people may live anywhere in the world and still not live outside the state' (Basch *et al.* 1994: 269).[4]

Migrants transport and transmit more than money and *savoir-faire*. Social scientists have acknowledged migration-triggered multidimensional transformations not only in migrant individuals or households (micro level), but also locally or regionally (meso level) and nationally (macro level). Research on the transnational ties that Dominican migrants in Boston maintain with their sending community illustrates how migration causes non-economic change via 'social remittances', the 'ideas, behaviors, identities and social capital that flow from receiving- to sending-country communities' (Levitt 1998). Experts agree that 'migrations can change demographic, economic and social structures, and bring a new cultural diversity'; new political forms may emerge without necessarily replacing states (Castles and Miller 2009: 3–4).

The missing link in the literature becomes striking: one cannot discuss how migration changes ideas, behaviours, identities, priorities and lifestyles without analysing the learning mechanisms underlying these transformations. Learning occurs through interactions between migrants and receiving societies; between migrants and diasporic organisations; between migrants and their non-migrant friends and family back home; between more and less experienced migrants in the receiving country etc. Politicians and government authorities enter the picture when they adapt to appeal to migrants. Demonstration effects and communication play a key role. Learning does not happen in a vacuum: one needs to analyse what attitudes and behaviours acquired in primary socialisation are unlearned and partially replaced with values and action repertoires from the host country.

Crossing borders constitutes a transformative life event with deep psychological, social, cultural and political implications. It broadens the experiential and informational space of individuals and communities, influencing values, restructuring hierarchies and reshaping behaviours. The evidence presented in this chapter suggests that migration changes socialisation landmarks and landscapes. When the experiential space of the individual no longer coincides with national space (Beck 2002), learning occurs abroad in national or supranational environments. One can think systematically about these mechanisms in terms of exposure to socialisation contexts at home and abroad that produces cultural, social and political remittances.

---

4. Elsewhere I examine the sending countries' transnational state-building strategies that accommodate migratory projects and mobile citizens. Since policy proposals vary a lot (some include migrants as political subjects, while others do not), I analyse how political parties situate themselves *vis-à-vis* transnational constituencies (Paul 2013).

Conceptually, the term 'political remittances' captures the elusive aspects of transnational political socialisation, including the side effects of mobility, the cognitive shifts and demonstration effects that migrants trigger when they import ideas, values and behaviours. Political remittances constitute the ensemble of all direct and indirect migration-dependent political influences. Direct influences manifest themselves through migrants and returnees, whose opinions and actions reflect what they learned abroad. In other words, migrants think and act differently. Indirect influences result from migrants' sharing of information with their home community, enabling the sedentary to vicariously experience migration. Migrants become the agents of a new socialisation at home. As Tarrow noted, 'it is through people's relations to significant others that cosmopolitan attitudes are shaped. What is new in our era is the increased number of people and groups whose relations place them beyond their local and national settings without detaching them from locality' (Tarrow 2005: 41).

A focus on political remittances includes and complements the study of transnational political activities, defined as 'direct cross-border participation in the politics of their country of origin by both migrants and refugees [...] as well as their indirect participation via the political institutions of the host country' (Østergaard-Nielsen 2003: 762). Political remittances include, but are not limited to, cross-border political activities: the concept highlights how life abroad changes attitudes and behaviours in those directly or indirectly exposed to foreign socialisation contexts. The term reflects the interpersonal, communicative nature of the process and the important role the host country plays.

Claims about what is learned and unlearned abroad remain in the unstructured realm of intuitions. Most emerge as secondary findings from political science, economics, anthropology or history. The research agenda presented here argues that understanding the bottom-up effects of globalisation and international mobility requires taking socialisation seriously. The observation comes from a political scientist. Socialisation experts must join the conversation to make theoretical, methodological and empirical contributions.

Political socialisation as a palimpsest: political remittances and the contextual triad

How can political socialisation research help scholars tackle transnational political questions? Classic socialisation scholarship focused on individual characteristics as causes of attitudes and behaviours (Campbell *et al.* 1960; Miller and Shanks 1996; Nie *et al.* 1999). Recent work emphasises the importance of context. Gimpel *et al.* (2003) urge scholars to adopt social context as the backbone of socialisation research because contexts ('civic environments') organise and filter the quantity and flow of information. Individuals are 'embedded within a particular context' that structures social interaction patterns. These 'communicate political information on which the individual bases an attitudinal response' (Gimpel *et al.* 2003: 9).

How can migrant learning experiences be decoded in terms of context? Exit removes citizens from the familiar environment of the homeland. Classical research on US immigration described such people as 'uprooted'; alienated from family, community and tradition; on their way to becoming homogenised in another nation's melting pot (Handlin 1979). Others saw immigrants as 'transplanted' citizens, whose diversity defies generalisation: 'even while acquiescing in a changing economic order', migrants carry with them and preserve parts of an inheritance, remnants of traditions and lifestyles from home; the drive to preserve these is so powerful that it 'can sometimes influence the larger economic system itself' (Bodnar 1987: xv). Thus, migrant experiences produce layered socialisation, since migration results in superimposed sets of learning experiences that occurred in particular spaces (contexts) and sequences (chronological orders). As the evidence provided below suggests, socialisation can be defined as the totality of individual learning experiences occurring in different places, at various times, in specific orders.

For sedentary citizens and migrants alike, socialisation resembles a palimpsest, a scroll or tablet used in ancient times to write texts that could subsequently be scraped off to reuse the scroll as a support for another text. Exiting a homeland causes some attitudes and behaviours to be unlearned or erased from the socialisation palimpsest. However, just as erasing texts left traces of the prior writing, partial resocialisation does not eliminate past learning. People can never restart life *tabula rasa*. In fact, socialising experiences from different contexts can interact with one another to create new meanings as learning is synthesised across time and space. Some events leave stronger imprints than others, some spaces have a more lasting impact, but the end result is a combination of all influences through the prism of experience. Conjuncture also matters: what happens in the present activates layers of ideas, attitudes and behaviours from the past, while leaving other socialisation layers dormant.

'People are politically socialised by the information they receive. This information certainly varies over time, but it varies more regularly across space, as communities structure the content and flow of politically relevant messages in distinctive ways.' (Gimpel *et al.* 2003: 7; *see also* Huckfeldt and Sprague 1995) Certain individual characteristics play a decisive role: 'Within a particular age cohort, socialising messages will be received differently, with greater impact on some than on others depending on the attributes of the individuals themselves and characteristics of the places where they live' (Gimpel *et al.* 2003: 7; Huckfeldt and Sprague 1995). While many locations where migrant socialisation takes place are self-selected, many factors constrain the selection process itself (availability of work contracts, transnational networks, etc.). The choice leads to non-self-selected exposure to information. In Central and Eastern Europe, for instance, lack of employment opportunities and the deteriorating quality of education and professional training determine people to resort to European mobility. Penury, urgent family needs and lack of opportunity push the migrants I interviewed – from ophthalmologists to construction workers, from retirees to students, from unemployed high school graduates to the town mayor – toward the exit option. Those who cross boundaries do not have the luxury of choosing between migration and other alternatives. Only those who are either too young or too old to work can afford to stay put. 'Work settings often are sources of cross-cutting, non-self-selected information exposure as most people rarely have complete power to determine the views of those around whom they work' (Gimpel *et al.* 2003: 8). This is especially true for transnational migrants.

While socialisation research traditionally examines the first formative period (Abendschön 2010), interest for 'emerging adulthood' (Arnett 2007), old age socialisation (Fingerman and Pitzer 2007) and learning during maturity have been increasing. Since most migrants are of working age, adult and workplace socialisation research provide valuable guidance for analysing migrant adjustment and learning. Cultural perspectives cast light on socialisation in social, cultural and political spaces abroad. Also relevant are findings from research on acculturation of immigrants in the destination country; cultural transmission of information between sending and receiving countries; and political resocialisation past the formative stage (Berry 2007; White *et al.* 2008).

Acculturation is defined as the 'cultural and psychological change brought about by contact with other peoples belonging to different cultures and exhibiting different behaviours'. Like any rite of passage, it involves separation from one's homeland and primary socialisation content, followed by a transition to the host environment. Scholars talk about culture shedding - 'the gradual process of losing some features of one's culture (such as attitudes, beliefs, and values), as well as some behavioural competencies (such as language knowledge and use)' – and culture learning – the process of acquiring 'features of the new culture, sometimes as replacements for the attitudes and behaviours that have been lost, but often in addition to them' (Berry 2007: 647; 1992). Migrant acculturation happens through oblique cultural transmission, as individuals learn from other adults and social institutions (organisations, schools, workplaces) in a foreign culture. As migration enters the repertoire of living-making strategies, it becomes an everyday reality in high-migration communities, affecting young generations through vertical or horizontal transmission (from migrant parents to children, or from peers in childhood or adolescence) and communicated to the sedentary via oblique transmission (Cavalli-Sforza and Feldman 1981).

Integrating research on spatial mobility (migration) and socio-political mobility (socialisation) makes sense. There are many geopolitical contexts in which it can be done. This chapter explores socialisation patterns resulting from the free movement of people in the EU. Member-state citizens enjoy this right by virtue of being European citizens. In post-communist Central and Eastern Europe, negotiations and EU accession rendered borders more porous. In countries like Poland and Romania, dismantling hard frontiers opened up the exit option. Ever freer varieties of transnational mobility evolved from classical bilateral agreements (illegal migration) to no-visa touristic travel (irregular overstays for work purposes) and, finally, to legal stays for working and studying. EU policy shifts and the ensuing forms of migration create a laboratory where socialisation, political culture, migration and public opinion scholars can test a wide range of claims.

The main claim this chapter makes is that migratory experiences shape individual and collective political culture, where 'political culture' is understood as the 'attitudes toward the political system and its various parts, as well as attitudes toward the role of the self in the system' (Almond and Verba 1965: 12) or, in a more recent definition, 'those points of concern about social and political relations, containing both system-supporting and oppositional elements' (Tarrow 1992: 177). The theoretical framework presented below allows for a systematic evaluation of socialisation abroad: it categorises socialising influences according to the spaces where they emerge and includes information about exposure sequences. The empirical evidence provided suggests that socialisation happens not only at home, but also abroad, in host societies and transnational migratory systems.

All migrants undergo varieties of triadic political socialisation. They learn about the political world and the self as part of it, simultaneously and alternately, in three spaces (socialisation contexts): the homeland, the country of destination and the transnational migratory system. In high-migration communities, all socialisation is triadic, as the sedentary constantly receive information from and about migrant co-nationals, and mobility changes economic, societal and political realities. The triad covers relevant learning spaces and overcomes limitations resulting from methodological nationalism (Wimmer and Glick Schiller 2002) without denying the continued resilience of states. Triadic socialisation entails exposure to and learning experiences in two national and one transnational geopolitical context. National spaces involve exposure to politics and realities within countries. The transnational level depends on the politics and policies of migration: international agreements between sending and receiving countries; interactions with home and host state authorities; transnational institutions and organisations; mass media; and political parties that reach across country borders, thus establishing a systemic presence. Tracking the number and order of exposures helps to classify and understand in basic terms even the most fluid migratory projects.

The framework can be applied to all citizens, migrants and sedentary citizens, as long as their degree of socialisation is explored on all three levels. It synthesises classical research on immigrant acculturation and socialisation, capturing transnational influences, directly or indirectly experienced. To use the palimpsest analogy, the degree of exposure and type of migrant experience result from status overlays in the triad home-host-system. For a summary, *see* Table 9.1. Variations result from associated political opportunity structures at national and systemic level.

Migrant socialisation emerges from exposure to other socio-political contexts which occurs when people cross national boundaries. For clarity, the classification lists migration-related factors, without insisting on structures that shape sedentary socialisations. The first column identifies the spatial context in the triad. The second lists the individual status in that socialisation context (how authorities label the migrant and perceive migrant presence). The third column mentions some issues shaping socialisation that emerged from the literature (Bloemraad 2004; Castles and Davidson 2000; Castles and Miller 2009; Faist 2009; Givens *et al.* 2008) and from the interviews I conducted in Romania, Italy and France with government officials, local authorities, civil society leaders, diplomats and migrants.

Table 9.1 offers a static perspective on migrant socialisation that is obviously incomplete, given the unpredictable, fluid and precarious nature of most migrant trajectories. For a more accurate summary, one needs to integrate the temporal

Table 9.1: Triadic political socialisation – the spatial dimension

Triadic socialisation context	Migrant status	Context features (policies) affecting socialisation
1. Home (country of origin)	Emigrant (former citizen) Legal resident Temporary migrant (citizen) Dual citizen Returnee	Political regime and culture; social security; education; nation-building; taxation; development; political participation (voting); representation; identity etc.
2. Host (country of destination)	Visitor/tourist Temporary migrant Political refugee Legal resident Illegal/overstayer Dual citizen Immigrant/naturalised	Political regime and culture; discrimination; migrant rights; state-building; asylum policy; inclusion/exclusion; multiculturalism; repatriation etc.
3. Migratory system	Legal Illegal/irregular Intra-systemic (*communautaire*) Extra-systemic (*extra-communautaire*)	Security and control; migrant rights; political asylum; policy harmonisation; common standards; democratic deficit; systemic identity; repatriation etc.

and spatial perspectives, while retaining the landmarks of triadic political socialisation. How does the process of migrant socialisation unfold over time? Each crossing of a border constitutes a learning experience, so it becomes useful to identify the elements and sequences that migrant socialisation shares, to specify the mechanisms of the learning-through-mobility phenomenon in its ensemble, before discussing variations and special cases. Table 9.2 addresses this issue; it situates people in space and time, providing a dynamic model of migrant learning.

Migrant socialisation can be disaggregated into five phases: three sedentary phases that occur in national contexts and two liminal phases (postnational and transnational), determined by migratory systems. Using the typology of socialisation in space-time, one can trace the socialisation path of any citizen, sedentary or migrant. The pre-migratory phase marks the first formative period and happens only once, while the other four phases (two systemic – postnational separation and transnational reincorporation – and two national – secondary and tertiary socialisation) form a migration-determined socialisation cycle. Individuals going through the sequence can stop or resume at any point. The framework's flexibility accommodates even the most fluid trajectories. Some may never go through all the phases (e.g. migrants who decide to permanently settle in the destination country). Others may go through the four-stage cycle several times (e.g. transnational migrants who regularly visit home). Immigrants stop at the level of a secondary socialisation in the country of destination; some may preserve limited long-distance loyalty towards the homeland as members of diaspora

Table 9.2: The socialisation palimpsest – the space-time synthesis

The sequence: socialisation phases in chronological order	Migratory stages	Socialisation context (space where it occurs)	Socialisation scope
Primary socialisation	Pre-migratory	Home (country of origin)	National
Separation / exit (culture shedding)	Liminal-migratory	Migratory system	Postnational; emancipation from the nation-state
Secondary socialisation (culture learning; acculturation)	Migratory (living abroad)	Host (country of destination)	National
Transnational reincorporation / long-distance loyalty and voice	Liminal-diasporic	Migratory system (home-oriented)	Transnational; cross-border recreation of the state-citizen link
Tertiary socialisation	Post-migratory	Home	National

(second transnational phase). Return migrants complete at least one socialisation cycle (primary socialisation – exit – secondary socialisation – transnational reincorporation – tertiary socialisation). Circular migrants go through the four phases of the migratory sequence regularly. Seasonal migrants may experience low levels of secondary socialisation, if they have limited interactions with host societies. Each iteration of the cycle affects the substance of socialisation. Transnational migrants do not start *tabula rasa* each time they are back on the road; they rely on previously accumulated knowledge. Second- or third-time migrants differ in terms of learning experiences from those travelling abroad for the first time.

Primary socialisation is the phase that all citizens, migrant and sedentary, experience in the homeland. It precedes exposure to foreign environments and represents the first source of ideas about politics and the self as a political subject. In high migration communities, primary socialisation may include imported elements after a large proportion of the population has migrated and returned.

For migrants, the exit phase marks a transition away from sedentary status.[5] In this threshold phase, citizens leave their country, which frees them from homeland-associated constraints and traditional ties. The length of separation matters: long exits have stronger effects than short visits abroad. Emancipation

---

5. The terms 'exit', 'voice' and 'loyalty' are inspired by Hirschman's work on recuperation mechanisms for firms, organisations and states (Hirschman 1970). Simply put, exit means leaving the state and moving to another country where conditions are better. Voice refers to participation and communication with the state (expressing one's opinion in order to influence circumstances). Loyalty refers to a special attachment that is independent from performance; it reflects allegiance even when conditions are suboptimal.

from state monopoly gives room to subsequent availability for learning new attitudes, attachments and repertoires of action. Migrants may experience a sense of detachment from home and shedding of the familiar. The migratory system becomes a key socialisation space because its features determine what is learned.

Secondary socialisation is a relatively static phase in which migrants adjust to the receiving country. As in the exit phase, during secondary socialisation, the migrant's profile (legal status, socio-professional status, etc.) influences the level of exposure to realities and political culture. The migratory system continues to matter: the more free the cross-border movement, the more ample the opportunities migrants have to learn from and interact with the receiving society. An illegal immigrant who fears deportation avoids interactions with people outside the support network. By contrast, legal migrants can talk to others, participate in civil society and even political life without jeopardising their presence abroad. At the same time, free movement enables migrants to preserve connections transnationally; when borders are rigid, separation becomes more drastic and imposes a higher degree of culture shedding.

Exit is seldom complete and permanent, even for immigrants. Reincorporation is the transnational socialisation phase in which the connection between homeland and citizens living abroad is re-established. This can happen bottom-up, when diaspora members and migrants living abroad initiate the rapprochement, or top-down, when the homeland reaches out across boundaries to its citizens. In many cases, and especially for migrants who do not plan to naturalise in the host state, secondary socialisation and transnational reincorporation happen simultaneously. While abroad, migrants approach official representatives from their homeland (at embassies and consulates, etc.). These interactions give them a different perspective on their place as citizens in the state. Migrants follow mass media from the homeland, especially television stations, online news sites and discussion forums. They communicate regularly with their families and friends, thus updating their views about life at home. The migratory system is once again decisive: more porous borders and free movement facilitate transnational communication and travel.

Returning to the homeland entails an updating of information and perspective, even when migrants remain connected with the homeland while working abroad. Tertiary socialisation represents a readjustment to life in the country of origin and a synthesis of lessons learned elsewhere.

Since every migratory experience has effects, the starting and end positions are different. The socialisation spiral oscillates in the contextual triad, leading to layered learning experiences that accumulate over space and time for both individuals and communities. The palimpsest framework enables us to locate as precisely as possible migrants' positions in the multiphasic political socialisation process and identify the types of influences and environments that they have experienced. The rest of this chapter applies the theoretical framework above to empirical evidence from the EU. A study of Romanian transnational migrants from several locations in Maramures (a county in western Romania, in the Transylvania region) and Neamt (a county in eastern Romania, in the Moldova region) shows the mechanisms of triadic political socialisation at work: at home, in the host country (France and Italy) and in the transnational system (the EU). The chapter compares migrants and non-migrants and analyses variation in attitudes, loyalties, self-perceptions and political choices, categorising individuals relative to three major orientations (traditional, transnational or postnational). The conclusion initiates an interdisciplinary conversation, outlining the directions in which political socialisation research could advance to address the issue of migration as an engine of political change.

A space odyssey: political socialisation within and across national borders

Contexts and country borders matter for political socialisation. As frontiers become porous, the political learning spaces they determine also change. Countries' participation in regional integration projects that 'soften' their borders boosts cross-border information exchange and population mobility. Political socialisation is defined as 'the process by which new generations are inducted into political culture, learning the knowledge, values and attitudes that contribute to support of the political system. Through exposure to various socialisation agents, citizens develop a relationship with their government and political leaders' (Gimpel *et al.* 2003: 13; Almond and Coleman 1960; Almond and Verba 1965; Jennings and Niemi 1974). Many countries derive advantages and legitimacy from participation in supranational integration projects, as was the case for post-communist Central and Eastern European (CEE) governments, who linked transitions to democracy and market economy with the goal of EU accession. European integration opened up the political learning space to socialisation agents from abroad. Migrants with exposure to realities elsewhere became agents of change themselves. Socialisation scholarship states that, over their lifetime, people internalise rules, norms, habits and institutions from their socio-political contexts (Berger and Luckmann 1989). Political socialisation continues in adulthood as a function of socio-political context, which amounts to a partial political resocialisation (White *et al.* 2008). When people are exposed to new contexts, they internalise their specific rules, norms, habits and institutions. At the micro level of the *Lebenswelt* (life-world), fundamental changes occur as a result of international forces and migration. Many researchers interpret this as a paradigm shift, marked by the extension of 'governance and citizenship beyond the nation-state' (Leggewie 2001: 15858). Not only do migrants become accustomed to the rules and institutions in another country, but they also live in a supranational socio-political context, under the aegis of EU citizenship. Mobile citizens internalise the transnational political environment as they travel and work in the EU, in accordance with their rights and responsibilities as European citizens.

For CEE migrants, intra-EU mobility leads to the establishment of new relationships with various governance levels and, hence, to the redefinition of self-understandings as political subjects. As the EU's internal borders are progressively dismantled, in many post-communist states an increasing part of the destitute and backwards countryside is now replaced by lavish neighbourhoods.

Villas substitute dilapidated family houses. Construction sites are mushrooming everywhere. On the streets, grandparents and grandchildren breathe the new air of affluence, waiting for migratory parents and older siblings to return from foreign lands. Necessity and luxury; emergency and whim; free movement on EU territory provides a quick fix for all. Increasingly, Romanians, Poles and others turn their eyes to Europe when it comes to solving problems at home. As prosperity flows down the recently opened migration routes to the South, West and North, so does knowledge about life, democratic politics and the rule of law.

The *nouvelle vague* of European mobility appears to have shaped post-1989 democratic consolidation, influencing citizens' attitudes and behaviours, reshaping hierarchies, opening new avenues for social mobility and challenging the legacies of a non-democratic past. Some claim that European integration 'redistributes power and resources', 'reorganises knowledge and information' and 'reshapes collective identities' (Trenz 2001: 201). The intra-EU geopolitical configuration constitutes a good laboratory for examining how values and political orientations travel from one society to another as political remittances.

This chapter addresses the question of changing world-views, socialisation landmarks and political horizons. The key contention is that transnational migration recalibrates the state-citizen relationship. An exhaustive analysis of triadic socialisation and a full exploration of the socialisation palimpsest are beyond the scope of the chapter. The empirics illustrate how the theoretical framework can reveal the layers of learning in national and supranational contexts. As soon as one formulates research questions, the value of studying processes becomes evident. For instance, let's say we want to find out if migrants remain attached to the homeland. The question itself does not say anything about the mechanisms through which national loyalty is eroded or sustained. In triadic socialisation terms, however, one can ask whether transnational reintegration plays a role or if separation during the first transnational phase is so superficial that migrants are never disconnected from the homeland. Do migrants drift away from the traditional (national) form of citizenship, developing attachments to the transnational system or to the postnational human rights regime? In terms of political orientations, the chapter discusses whether transnationalism turns migrants into nationalists or cosmopolitans; if it creates radical political views, establishes a de-territorialised nation state or emancipates mobile individuals completely from state monopoly, leading them to embrace their status as global citizens.

Migrant in action: traditional, transnational or postnational?

What are the consequences of layered, triadic socialisations on political attitudes and behaviours? Does transnational mobility make migrants more likely to embrace cosmopolitan, democratic and/or liberal values? Or, on the contrary, does it undermine democratic stability by fostering long-distance nationalism? Since increasing numbers of people engage in transnational migration (Mau *et al.* 2008), the answer to the above questions sheds light on a factor that may consolidate or destabilise new democracies.

Among political elites and scholars, opinions are divided among those who believe that cross-border ties improve the quality of democracy and those who think that diasporic or migrant interference through financial, informational and organisational channels radicalises homeland politics. The former argue that migration benefits sending communities and countries by fostering development, instilling openness in places otherwise cut off from new ideas, technologies and realities (Appadurai 1996; Johnson *et al.* 2011; Mau *et al.* 2008) and establishing 'globalisation from below', a way to oppose marginalisation in the existing order (Evans 2000). The latter argue that distance prevents migrants from clearly understanding events and realities at home. Disconnecting from political developments may enhance distorted views and discourses, triggering a re-nationalisation with radical accents (Anderson 1998; Beck 2002; Habermas 2001). When disinformation overlaps with allegiance to a far-off homeland, migrants lacking access to formal participation channels may try to intervene informally in national affairs, which does more harm than good (Ong 2006). Migrants remain connected to the 'imagined community' of the nation, but this connection can be manipulated by opportunistic actors to boost support for nationalistic politicians. According to this view, nostalgic migrants are vulnerable to manipulative discourses, precisely because they see themselves as objective outsiders with better knowledge, willing to pursue the nation's 'greater good'.

Benedict Anderson coined the term 'long-distance nationalism' to describe this sentiment. It applies to people who identify with a state despite living abroad and can allegedly affect anyone: economic migrants, war refugees, political asylum seekers etc. These people cannot participate in formal homeland politics, but want to make their voice heard. Hence, they seek informal avenues of political engagement to serve a 'just' cause. Diaspora nationalists are insulated from the consequences of their actions and unaccountable, which allegedly results in enhanced radicalism:

> While technically a citizen of the state in which he comfortably lives, but to which he may feel little attachment, [the nationalist] finds it tempting to play identity politics by participating (via propaganda, money, weapons, any way but voting) in the conflicts of his imagined Heimat – now only fax-time away. But this citizenshipless participation is inevitably non-responsible – our hero will not have to answer for, or pay the price of, the long-distance politics he undertakes. He is also easy prey for shrewd political manipulators in his Heimat (Anderson 1992: 13).

Anderson's critics note that migrants can now participate through formal channels. They have the right to vote from abroad in national elections. The hypothesised 'disconnect' from the country of origin never really takes place, as migrants maintain close ties with families and friends. Homelands are not 'imagined', but real and accessible.

> 'The *Heimat* becomes *real* when migrants travel back and forth between home and host countries and engage in numerous daily activities related to homeland politics – discussions with relatives over the telephone, cultural immigrant organisation inviting their hometown mayor for special occasions [...]' (Mügge 2010: 23).

Beyond homeland and host-country socialisation, migrants learn about the homeland and interact with it from abroad. The liminal socialisation stages (separation and reincorporation) contribute to migrant learning. The migratory system's fluidity facilitates cross-border interaction, giving citizens abroad an accurate, realistic angle on homeland politics. The implication is clear: the more fluid the transnational system, the less room for nationalism there is. A task for the future is developing methods that disentangle the effects of each socialisation phase. The tentative results below are a modest first step.

We want to know more about migrant orientations towards the three spatial contexts of triadic political socialisation. In particular, we want to determine if migrants develop an exacerbated attachment to the nation-state or if migration emancipates them from state monopoly, fostering a cosmopolitan world-view. If the latter is true, we want to find out if, in the space opened by emancipation from the homeland, new allegiances towards the receiving country or migratory system emerge. Basically, we ask if postnational socialisation (separation) of Romanian migrants trumps national allegiances towards either homeland (transnational reincorporation) or receiving country (secondary socialisation). The chapter follows Bloemraad, who examined dual citizenship claims in Canada and evaluated immigrant orientations in the receiving country (Bloemraad 2004). She proposed three possible citizenship models: traditional, de-territorialised/ transnational and postnational. While superficially apolitical, these orientations reveal the ways in which mobile citizens revise their connection with political entities, actors and institutions. The adapted typology developed here captures potential shifts in loyalty, perceptions and trust. It reflects how people feel about the homeland, host country and the migratory system. This chapter expands the categories to all migrants, temporary and permanent, and reorients the analysis towards broad socio-political world-views, self-identification, political attitudes and party preferences.

The 'Traditional Model' links citizenship to the international system of sovereign states. During the nineteenth century the notion emerged that the apparatus of government – the state – should overlap with a community of identity – the nation (Hobsbawm 1992). Migrants complicate the state-citizen link. Traditional approaches posit that migrants gradually lose loyalty to the homeland and naturalise in the receiving country. This suggests that people feel the need for one primary identity; hence, they transfer subjective and objective attachments to their new home. This should result in high rates of migrant naturalisation in the country of destination and decreases in dual citizenship claims over time.

For socialisation, this model predicts strong separation (shedding of primary socialisation content), coupled with secondary socialisation in the host country. The traditional model does not differentiate between intra-EU migrations and immigration. All migrants are expected to develop an attachment towards host countries and loyalties should gradually transfer, culminating in naturalisation. Migrants would become members of diaspora with weak ties to homelands. Host countries constitute the dominant socialisation context.

The 'Transnational Model' expects forms of de-territorialised citizenship to emerge. In classic migration, dual citizenship is the associated legal status, since it recognises that immigrants' lives transcend borders. Geopolitically, the structure that corresponds to and results from transnationalism is a 'de-territorialised' state, since 'the nation's people may live anywhere in the world and still not live outside the state' (Basch *et al.* 1994: 269). World capitalism is the engine of change: migrants seek employment in developed countries. At destination, black markets develop on the periphery of receiving labour markets. Marginalised in their temporary host society, migrants maintain their homeland orientation and activity (remittances, entrepreneurial activities, etc.). Dual identities reflect attachment to both home and host countries, but, partially in response to exclusion and discrimination in the host country, homeland loyalty remains dominant. Individuals adopt the status reflecting multiple identities. Cross-border activity and belonging change over time and vary from one person to another.

For migrants, the model predicts some culture shedding, limited secondary socialisation (due to marginalisation or irregular status that does not allow any form of political participation) and pronounced transnational reincorporation, possibly with episodes of tertiary socialisation when visiting home is possible. The migratory system is decisive: in rigid systems that block migrants' ability to travel or communicate across borders, one can expect long-distance nationalism to emerge.

The 'Postnational Citizenship Model' moves beyond the nation-state paradigm, challenging the idea that citizenship remains linked with state membership, territorialised or not. Citizenship privileges, such as civil rights and social welfare, are vested in individuals through 'personhood' (Bauböck 1994), independently from the nation state. After World War Two, the West created a human rights regime whose moral and legal norms are now the accepted normative framework. This changed migrants' rights discourse. It has become harder to deny social and civil rights to incoming groups of people based on their citizenship (Soysal 1994).

When international norms are institutionalised in supranational organisations like the EU, they gain further power, as Soysal argues. If this theory is correct, migrants would not seek the receiving country's citizenship because they know that their rights are based on personhood and 'their identities transcend the trappings of citizenship'. Bloemraad calls this 'strict postnationalism' (2004: 397). Most scholars expect a less radical 'weak postnationalism', which postulates that globalisation boosts dual citizenship claims in the short run, but, when residence becomes the universal basis for rights, state-bound citizenship withers away, rendering dual citizenship unnecessary. In the EU case, a postnational mentality would mean that migrants believe their rights not to derive from countries, but rather the migratory system (the EU). Discursively, a postnational migrant would show detachment from national institutions and an orientation towards supranational institutions and the global system, in which rights abroad come from personhood (rights of the individual in a multinational system) rather than from national citizenship (rights of a nation-state citizen). Socialisation-wise, the model predicts that migrants are uninterested in secondary socialisation but are oriented towards the migratory system they navigate. The migratory system is dominant, with the possibility of tertiary socialisation in the homeland.

The next section summarises the results of fieldwork I conducted between 2009 and 2011 in Italy (Venice, Treviso and Rome), France (Paris and Strasbourg) and Romania (Targu Neamt, Piatra Neamt – judetul Neamt; Viseul de Sus, Viseul de Jos, Moisei, Dragomiresti, Salistea de Sus – judetul Maramures; and Bucharest). I interviewed migrants, returnees, people planning to start working abroad, migrant family members and sedentary citizens. I conducted over twenty-five semi-structured interviews in each of the four transnational communities of origin and an average of six informant interviews per sending and receiving community. All interviews included an in-depth component, in which respondents had the opportunity to share their stories in full detail. For migrants, the battery of questions contained items assessing the nature of the migratory experience in terms of exposure to new political contexts and political impact on migrants and their networks.[6] Respondents included migrants from different backgrounds to capture a wide range of experiences: some were highly trained and educated, others were high-school graduates; some studied abroad, others worked as housekeepers to send their children to college; some owned businesses abroad, others were homemakers; some were curators, others were waiters. Their stories are set against the background provided by informants: political party leaders, authorities, embassy high-ranking officials, teachers, priests and journalists.

Enter the wandering EUropeans: between homeland and workland

An 80-year-old former schoolteacher from Targu Neamt reflected on the labour force exodus towards Italy: 'How things have changed! When I was young, people did not leave the place where they were born. They wouldn't even marry in another village'. In Maramures and Neamt, officials reported that many inhabitants work abroad. In Maramures, the primary destination was France, with Italy growing in popularity. In Neamt, most worked in Italy and Spain. Initial migratory waves from Neamt headed to Germany, while recent ones target Britain. In villages like Dragomiresti and Salistea de Sus (Maramures), one in three and, respectively, one in five inhabitants works abroad.[7] In cities and towns, official numbers are lower (approximately 16.5 per cent of the voting-age population of Targu Neamt works abroad).[8] According to Razvan Rusu, the Romanian Ambassador in Rome, 1.2 to

---

6. Other questions concerned occupation, education, marital status; destination, number, length and purpose of trips abroad; economic remittances (and use of earnings upon return); visits home; relationships with family and friends at home; frequency of communication; experiences abroad, including relationships with co-nationals, people in the receiving country, co-workers, homeland and host country authorities; lessons learned as a result of migration; self-reported socio-economic, attitudinal and behavioural changes after living abroad; plans for the future; self-identification; attachment to the country of origin; attachment to and assessment of the EU; political engagement in electoral and non-electoral forms of participation; preferences in terms of government and political parties, etc.

7. Interviews with the mayor of Dragomiresti, Mr. Vasile Iusco, and the mayor of Salistea de Sus, Mr. Stefan Iuga – 29 July 2009.

8. Interview with the mayor of Targu Neamt, Mr. Decebal Arnautu – 20 July 2009.

1.3 million Romanians work in Italy.[9] Recent estimates suggest that 2.8 million Romanians work in the EU, Italy and Spain being the main destinations (Abraham and Stufaru 2009).

With growing numbers of mobile citizens, migration-related economic and socio-political changes are more noticeable. Following the insights from political socialisation scholarship, the enlargement of individual and collective experiential space should be analysed as a change in learning context. One can hypothesise that people with migratory experiences (direct and vicarious) differ from the sedentary and that people engaged in migration differ from those who never left, but learn about other countries through migrant relatives and friends. Political cleavages should be noticeable at the self-identification, attitudinal and behavioural levels. How do migrants position themselves *vis-à-vis* the socialisation triad: their homeland (Romania), their host countries (Italy and France) and the EU (the migratory system enabling free movement of persons)? How does partial resocialisation occur abroad and which facets of political life does it affect? Do migrants relate in the same way to government and politics in the homeland after experiencing life elsewhere? Does their view of the state change when they cease to depend on it for every aspect of their existence? Do loyalties transfer from home to host countries or to the migratory system (the EU)? Any of these changes would mark a profoundly political recalibration of the state-citizen relationship. When citizens emancipate themselves from the homeland, this presumably manifests itself in general views about the government's role toward citizens (e.g. state interventions, taxation, rule of law, relationship with the diaspora, etc.). Mobility may also spawn new political views and political party preferences.

Among Romanian migrants I found evidence of culture shedding and political unlearning in the separation phase, but not amounting to a complete break away from the homeland. Migrants became more self-reliant, not de-nationalised. Many became more critical of politics and politicians at home. They did not exhibit an 'emerging global consciousness', but instead a pragmatic understanding of the migratory system (the EU), coupled with positive evaluations and high levels of trust in European supranational institutions. No respondent relied solely on individual rights derived from personhood. Since national citizenship grants access to European mobility, the homeland and transnational contexts are closely connected in the eyes of the migrant. The better the government's performance when it comes to enacting reforms and implementing the European *acquis communautaire*, the better access migrants get to the integrated market and its opportunities.

For those working abroad, migration is a tough and frustrating experience. Migrant and sedentary respondents see it as a result and a proof of government ineffectiveness. However, while the sedentary typically ask for more effective

---

9.   Interview with H. E. Razvan Rusu, Romania's Ambassador to Italy – Rome, Italy; 20 August 2009.

state involvement in improving their lot, migrants evolve toward a different set of attitudes. The early stages of migration tend to alienate individuals from politics: many first-time migrants simply did not have the time to vote or otherwise participate. Once migrants adjust to life abroad, their political landscape becomes more nuanced. Many vote, no matter how difficult and time consuming it may be. Others participate in Romanian associations, attend social events and even go to church to hang out with co-nationals, as well as to create better professional networks. Migration is far from ideal, but it is better than being stuck at home, deprived of access to lucrative jobs. Of the migrants who tried to return, most resumed their transnational lifestyle after seeing the continuing lack of opportunity and meagre wages at home. Since mobile citizens prefer an environment where they can cross borders easily without excessive bureaucracy and humiliation, they usually support parties with strong pro-European agendas and records of good EU relations. Unsurprisingly, they see Romania's accession to the EU as a good thing. This preference contributed to the stark drop in support for nationalist, Eurosceptic political parties, and partially accounts for the radicals' persistent inability to attract popular support. Migrants think realistically in terms of countries and migratory systems connecting them. In analysing opportunity structures, they discuss citizenship (national and European); forms of residence; and inclusion policies at home and abroad. During the afternoon breaks of Romanian and Moldovan housekeepers in Venice, conversations revolve around residency and legal issues: work contracts; benefits; visas and passports for Moldovans; regularisations; etc.[10] Respondents prefer a minimalistic state that does not interfere in their lives. Across the board, the migrants I interviewed wanted corruption-free states that effectively protect the rule of law and function smoothly, with responsive authorities at home and abroad.

Culture shedding happens pragmatically, as migrants attempt to blend in, protect themselves against discrimination and avoid trouble with authorities. Romanian migrants in both Italy and France reported occasionally speaking the language of their host country among themselves instead of their mother tongue to avoid national or ethnic profiling. Highly educated migrants and professionals did not report encountering systematic discrimination. Many had no difficulty fitting in and interacting with citizens of the host country. Barriers to partial resocialisation (political culture learning) from foreign peers and institutions were relatively low for educated migrants and highly trained professionals, especially those who could speak the language of their receiving country. For those in lower rank occupations, however, discrimination and poor language competency led to exclusion and isolation. Drivers, construction workers and some housekeepers reported socialising only with co-nationals outside the workplace.

Migrants reported learning very much at work. Construction workers operate in teams, so migrants from Targu Neamt had colleagues from Albania, Morocco, Ukraine and China. They were comfortable with this diversity, although some

---

10. Observation notes – Venice, Italy (August 2009).

echoed newly acquired prejudices against North African migrants (attitudes learned from Italian bosses and locals). On construction sites, migrants interacted with French or Italian team leaders. After work, migrants socialised with co-nationals or communicated with family and friends at home via mobile phones or through Skype video-chat at internet cafés. Conversation topics ranged from everyday life and family updates to current affairs and politics, both in the sending and receiving countries.

Women working as housekeepers in Italy live in the employer's family house, witnessing interactions between family members and participating in the household's life. At work, there are no interactions with co-nationals. Housekeepers use their two-hour lunch break to socialise with other Romanians, gathering in nearby *piazzas*. Given the high exposure to everyday life in the host society, housekeepers notice how much conditions for women in Italy differ from the traditional, patriarchal ties that dominate women's lives in Romania's rural environment. The women I interviewed all talked about these contrasts in great detail; clearly, this made a strong impression on them. Many reported being surprised at the privacy that parents gave their children, the independence married Italian women enjoy, the differences in diet (Italian cuisine is lighter and requires less preparation), etc. Upon return, many introduced elements of Italian lifestyle in their home. In a Romanian accent spiced with drawn out Italian vowels, Mariana (who worked as a housekeeper in Alessandria for over six years) said, 'We eat more healthily. I give my daughter more space'. She underwent four cycles of exit-work-return and anticipates restarting work soon. Another *badante* (housekeeper) who worked in Bari exclaimed several times:

> Lucky and lazy, that's what they are! In the morning, women wake up and, if they don't drink coffee at home, they go out to have coffee and a pastry at a bar before heading to work. At noon, they make pasta with some boiled greens; it's simple and ready in no time, nothing like the half-a-day cooking we do.

Positive and negative evaluations of life abroad often appear in the same account: migrants do not idealise the 'workland'. A majority of female migrants see their Italian employers as pampered and somewhat helpless. 'The *signora* wondered at everything I was doing. "Where have you learned all this?" She didn't know how to fix anything around the house. She didn't know how to cook', laughed Viorica, forty-seven years old, from Viseul de Sus, who had worked in Italy three times.

Some migrants and family members talked about learning experiences abroad and the obvious ways in which secondary socialisation – in conjunction with separation from the homeland – changed the mobile person's attitudes and behaviours. Many noted differences in consumption patterns, lifestyle choices, priorities and family values, but the most significant changes that were uniformly reported concerned work ethic, self-reliance and dedication. Sedentary respondents and local authorities in the homeland occasionally mentioned that the returnees' behaviours appeared ostentatious and full of foreign mannerisms, how returnee lifestyle resembled a 'performance' for the rest of the community, a 'show' aimed at demonstrating socio-economic success and the higher degree of civilisation of a self 're-engineered' abroad.

Separation and secondary socialisation emancipated migrants from traditional ties (patriarchy and intergenerational orders), facilitating upward socio-economic mobility. This was especially true for women who became bread-winners through migration, shaking the traditional order at home. Not only did they make more money than the men in the house, but they could also observe how women live and work in less traditional environments. Several informants (authorities, non-governmental organisation workers, priests), as well as migrant and sedentary respondents mentioned the high rates of divorce as a negative consequence of working abroad. However, several migrants talked about women who managed to escape abusive marriages, alcoholic husbands and poverty. Regardless of gender, migrants gained resources that allowed them to invest in a business, buy land and send children to college. Not only did migrants move up the socio-economic status hierarchy, but they also gained confidence and experience in dealing with government officials. Many migrants interacted with high-level representatives of the Romanian state when abroad. They learned to petition, write official letters and navigate a complicated consulate and embassy system.

Family members reported that migrants and returnees watched the news and discussed current affairs more frequently. They worked harder, with exemplary discipline and motivation. Many relatives reported that, upon return, migrants worked 'like robots' (this was a recurrent comparison in the interviews I conducted).

Does European integration erode connections between citizens and nation states? The empirical findings suggest that national identifications are alive and kicking, but perceived government corruption and poor performance cause frustration. Without exception, transnationals reported having strong ties with their homeland. The nostalgia of 'exile' consolidates identifications for temporary labour migrants. 'Bad as the bread may taste, it still tastes better when you are in your country'[11] – the old Romanian adage reappeared in my conversations with homesick migrants and the sedentary justifying their decision not to stay home. Intra-EU migratory work experiences involve many hardships. It is a self-imposed temporary exile that people assume to acquire economic and educational resources. Qualitative evidence confirms the transnational model and the strength of loyalty towards the homeland. Free movement allows migrants to visit Romania as often as they want. Most go home in August for the summer vacation and in December for Christmas. Migrants never grow out of touch with political evolutions in the homeland; in fact, they are more informed abroad than they used to be at home: they follow the news online, read Romanian newspapers, watch Romanian channels, exchange opinions on internet forums.

For students and highly educated professionals, the migratory experience crystallises along other coordinates. In Venice, a young curator in Romania's pavilion at the Biennale exhibition enthusiastically remembered his travels: 'I

---

11. 'Fie pâinea cât de rea, tot mai bună-n țara ta.'

enjoyed these trips a lot. They were all connected to my goals. I never had any difficulties and I did not experience homesickness since I was never away for very extended periods of time.' About his attachment to Romania, he added: 'Romania is OK for me. My nature is such that I make light of things that do not work well. I have never considered leaving for good'. A college graduate working at the Romanian Cultural Institute in Venice echoes this view:

> That's how it happened to be: I was born in Romania, I grew up there, my development as an individual occurred in Romania. It's fine. Romania hasn't repulsed me so much that I want to leave; nor has it enchanted me so much that I really want to stay.

The migratory experiences of highly educated individuals are less frustrating, since the migratory system provides advantages in crossing national boundaries. Highly educated migrants are more cosmopolitan pre-migration and remain so. They learn about resource-rich and efficient work environments that they later try to replicate at home: 'Whenever I go back, I experience a kind of shock. I suddenly find myself in an "under-civilized" environment. I start thinking about how I can change things to imitate at home what I saw abroad', says a young artist and art historian who has studied in the UK on an Erasmus grant, bartended in a British pub and travelled around Europe. Very often, educated respondents and students declared themselves committed to becoming agents of positive change in Romania, by importing ideas and professional models from abroad.

Partial resocialisation at the workplace reveals itself in professional standards of excellence and other work ethic changes. Labour migrants 'work like robots'. They acquire new skills and adopt the higher professional standards of French and Italian businesses. High-ranking Romanian government officials discussed the phenomenon, pointing out that financial prosperity and savings transform mentalities and lifestyles. They also mentioned how migrants imitate what they see abroad in terms of consumerism, values and behaviours. Most officials assessed these as positive changes. Some informants complained about the migrants' emulation of foreign lifestyles, especially conspicuous consumption.

Several respondents insisted that migration has positive effects because they put Romanians in contact with a 'new reality of political life', a situation in which the Romanian state is absent. These voices argue the Romanian authorities abroad are not doing enough to facilitate transnationals' political reincorporation, but that this ends up being a good thing. Many migrants felt abandoned by their homeland. Most complained that Romanian officials treat them poorly: each contact with homeland authorities abroad meant full days wasted queuing, high fees and inefficient service. Some migrants reported being treated with disrespect.

Among migrants arrested abroad, many claim to be innocent and accuse foreign authorities of discrimination. Arrested migrants ask Romanian consulate officials to come and meet them in prison and to intervene in their trial. At the other end, embassy and consulate officials claim migrants have unreasonably high expectations about what the state can do for them abroad. Mr. Ion Calciu, the

Romanian Consul in Rome,[12] said consulates help Romanians with documents; translations; information about rights and duties related to integration after acquiring residency; and provide details about pay rights. The consulate network does assist Romanians who get arrested, but Calciu underscored that it cannot intervene in criminal law cases, which causes disappointment when Romanians contact the consulate to ask for help. Many migrants imprisoned abroad go on hunger strikes to draw attention to their case and request either Romanian consulate intervention or release from arrest. A couple of migrants died in prison after hunger strikes (the most recent case occurred in May 2012). Romanian officials said arrested migrants routinely claim their innocence and accuse Italian authorities of encroaching upon their rights. According to consulate officials, 'I don't have a fair trial' has become a formula that migrants repeat without being able to explain in what way their rights were violated.

Discrepancies and frustrations emerge because the state has not yet adjusted to a situation in which a large proportion of its workforce seeks employment abroad without planning to permanently resettle there. While consulates have been expanding, citizens still feel ignored and many officials perceive migrants as individuals who have exited the state and, therefore, do not have the right to demand protection or support. Interactions with such officials reinforce migrants' beliefs that they need to be self-reliant and that the state does more harm than good. In terms of political values and preferences, this generates inclinations towards a small and effective state ideal that protects the rule of law; that intervenes in favour of its citizens only when needed; and that pursues an ambitious EU policy to enhance integration and acceptance into the Schengen space (the ultimate marker of full European citizenship).

How do the realities of migratory life influence political socialisation? Elements of the traditional and transnational models appear with a twist: unlike in classical migration, intra-EU migrants do not transfer loyalty from their homeland to the receiving country. The incentives for allegiance shift are small. The interviews revealed that migrants assess the host society as external observers and learn from it without an 'emotional rapprochement'. According to *Caritas Migrantes*, Romanians have low naturalisation rates in Italy. The desire to return is so great that in the Romanian community of about 10,000 people that are affiliated to the Christian Orthodox Romanian parish of Treviso, there have been only four or five funerals since 1998 when Father Marius Kociorva started his activity. 'The rest wanted to be buried back home. Romanians feel connected to their country. They keep the traditions. The church provides a focal point. It helps them identify with Romania and stimulates their solidarity as a community.'

Migrants are disillusioned with the performance of Romanian authorities. Time spent abroad reinforces the mistrust and frustration that migrants developed in Romania during the decades of communism and the uncertain post-1989 transitional times. There is demand for reincorporation on the migrant side, but

---

12. Interview with Mr. Ion Calciu, Consul of Romania – Romanian Consulate, Rome, August 2009.

supply has only recently picked up. The discrepancy has led, in the past, to further separation from homeland and deepening adaptation to life in a migratory system, the space that provides solutions to migrants' problems. There are two versions of the story: one coming from Romanian migrants and migrant civil society leaders, another coming from Romanian authorities (consulate and embassy officials).

Labour migrants often felt abandoned by the Romanian state while abroad. Romanian political parties reaching out to migrant constituencies were perceived as opportunistic. Diaspora representatives complained that consulates failed to provide help. Respondents referred to bureaucratic inefficiencies that force people to stand for several hours queuing for consulates to translate documents like birth certificates or driving licenses. Some civil society leaders mentioned a certain animosity and mistrust that Romanian migrants feel towards the Romanian institutions abroad. These complaints concern the Romanian migrant presence in Italy more than in France, where immigration from Romania has a longer tradition and a highly educated professional diaspora is established. Politically, wherever present, the sense of abandonment triggered by the lack of insufficient top-down channels for reincorporation becomes an engine for political engagement. In Italy and Spain, Romanian migrants have formed political parties and fight for their rights. After EU accession, migrants supported the centre-right, pro-European Liberal Democratic Party (PDL), who has advocated for the inclusion of transnational migrants in political processes at home.

Some officials interpret the migrants' attempts to reconnect or rely on the Romanian state for protection as evidence that migrants are needy. Romania's Ambassador to Italy remarked that the presence of three million Romanian citizens abroad is an 'unprecedented experience for the Romanian state'.[13] In the last years, the number of Romanian associations skyrocketed from eighteen registered associations on the embassy website to over eighty associations in 2009. Inevitably, available resources are spread thin. To respond to exponentially increasing demands, the state has developed a system of assistance connecting migrants to their homeland (summer camps for the migrants' children; Romanian book donations; programmes that send Romanian teachers to schools that have over ten Romanian students to teach the Romanian language; literature; culture and civilisation; geography). Politically, migrants can vote in presidential elections and can elect diaspora representatives to the Romanian Parliament. Despite government efforts, Mr. Rusu remarks, Romanian migrants are still dissatisfied. 'Paternalism persists as an attitude despite the intervening detachment [...] Romanians in Italy still ask "what does the state do for me?" even though it is they who initiated the detachment in the first place.'

Do Romanian migrants feel European? Migrants' discourses invoke European citizenship rather than national belonging when asking for protection of their rights against abuse. Many business owners have noticed the post-EU accession change in employees' behaviour. Signora L., a Romanian migrant herself who now owns her own *pizzeria* in Venice, complained about the attitude of Romanian waitresses:

---

13. Interview with H. E. Mr. Razvan Rusu, Romania's Ambassador to Italy – Rome, August 2009.

Things have changed since Romania entered the EU. Once our Romanians didn't need the *soggiorno* permit anymore, they became impertinent and started acting up. Since Romania joined the Community, Romanian employees treat you differently: they talk in a different tone, they try to control you. They forget they have debts, they demand only rights.

Pragmatic deployment of EU citizenship increases without a parallel loyalty transfer. Migratory systems lack the capacity and the political will to foster massive migrant allegiance through institutions and policies. As a result, between the two liminal socialisation phases, postnational and transnational, the latter still dominates, even though the former is clearly on the rise. Migrants welcome the economic advantages and new opportunities that EU citizenship offers, but assess them realistically. 'It is good that we can now move freely without being humiliated at the border, without having to bribe guards,' concludes a 35-year-old man from Targu Neamt who worked in Italy and Spain in construction and agriculture. 'I do not feel more European than before, but for us it is a great thing to be able to go to work without visas. This makes our lives so much easier, since we have to work abroad anyway. We cannot make a living here,' says a 47-year-old woman from Viseu, Maramures. Free movement makes it easier for people to connect with families back home. 'Before Romania entered the EU, I was not able to return and see my family. I spent one year and six months indoors; the only people I saw were the family that hired me. I was afraid to go out,' confessed a mother of two from Targu Neamt, a former chemistry lab technician who quit her job at a local high school to work in Milan. 'After I was in order, "legal" as they say, I could visit my family and they could visit me,' she added. Since their presence abroad has been placed under the aegis of European citizenship, migrants have mobilised to form a vibrant civil society in their receiving countries. These associations and businesses help transnational migrants protect their mobile lifestyle, their rights abroad and connection with those at home.

Politically, migrants and returnees are frustrated with unresponsive local authorities and corrupt officials. After seeing interactions between citizens and authorities abroad, migrants evaluate the performance of Romanian politicians and bureaucrats using upgraded standards. Migrants deplore the state's inability to defend the rule of law and implement reforms. Political candidates' attempts to reach out to migrants are positively evaluated, in principle, but often judged insufficient and opportunistic. Still, the centre-right PDL is increasingly popular among migrants after promoting policies to reintegrate mobile voters in homeland politics (correspondence voting, increased migrant representation in parliament, the creation of a ministry for the Romanian diaspora). Strikingly, migrants in both Italy and France were willing to travel long distances or queue for hours in order to cast their vote for elections in the homeland.

Overall, intra-EU socialisation-through-migration generates postnational orientations coupled with pronounced transnational attachments to the homeland, reinforced by episodes of cross-border reincorporation and tertiary socialisation for temporary returnees. Migrants are self-reliant, individualistic and pro-European in the separation, system-oriented phase of migration. As temporary outsiders, migrants develop a non-idealised view of the homeland while abroad. Secondary socialisation leads Romanian migrants to change some attitudes, world-views and behaviours, but has limited political implications, since labour migrants face discrimination and exclusion. Liminal socialisation phases help maintain a delicate balance: separation helps migrants gain a more realistic outsider's view of the homeland, while transnational reincorporation and communication with friends and family prevent nostalgic drifts into long-distance nationalism.

Conclusion

Until recently, political socialisation scholarship and migration studies have neglected each other and both have ignored transnational forces. One can blame theoretical obstacles, data scarcity and interdisciplinary methodological incompatibilities for this. However, as people gain daily exposure to international media, foreign education, professional partnerships, everyday life and political realities abroad, ignoring the impact such experiences have on socialisation becomes unsustainable. Not taking action results in further deterioration of research horizons: data remain riddled with severe issues and disciplines drift apart, eliminating opportunities for mutually enriching dialogue. The communication breakdown between migration studies and political science has deepened: the disciplines have advanced on distinct paths, developing different languages and relying on different methodologies.

On the theory front, this chapter synthesizes insights from three relevant bodies of literature: political socialisation, transnationalism and immigrant resocialisation. First, it proposes a new, spatial understanding of political socialisation (one that complements previous interpretations developed almost exclusively with respect to the time dimension). This approach allows studies of a wider range of cases, including transnational groups with high international mobility, moving beyond the classic one-time movers (immigrants who leave their country permanently to resettle elsewhere and, naturally, undergo political resocialisation to integrate at destination). Second, the chapter suggests a possible general typology of migrant socialisation. In doing so, it expands and improves on existing resocialisation frameworks used to assess immigrant adjustment to new political environments.

On the empirical front, the chapter summarises original qualitative data the author collected over the course of several years of fieldwork. The chapter illustrates how the theory can be adapted and applied to track current trends in political socialisation, in a way that acknowledges the importance of local, national and supranational contexts.

Findings suggest that, for temporary migrants, political socialisation abroad – systemic and, to a lesser extent, secondary in the host country – can overwrite world-views and behaviours acquired in the primary socialisation phase. World-views, as well as individual material and cognitive circumstances, shift as a result of exposure to new environments. Migration breaks previous traditional ties, rendering individuals available for new attachments. For those who experienced their first political socialisation in the context of a 'flattened' post-totalitarian polity (Linz and

Stepan 1996), working abroad constitutes the first opportunity to experience living in a democratic society. Migration provides a fresh perspective on the homeland itself. It leads citizens to deal with bureaucrats and government officials at a higher level (embassy, consulate) than typical contacts in the local community. It offers grounds for a comparative assessment of government performance. This recalibration of the state-citizen relationship does not generate long-distance nationalism but rather a pronounced pragmatic orientation towards EU citizenship and decreased dependence on the homeland for economic and educational opportunities, as well as advancement in socio-economic status hierarchies.

References

Abendschön, S. (2010) 'The beginnings of democratic citizenship: Value orientations of young children', *Politics, Culture and Socialisation,* 1:59–82.

Abraham, A. and Stufaru, I. (2009) '3 milioane de romani, la munca in strainatate', *Jurnalul National.* Online. Available: http://jurnalul.ro/special-jurnalul/3-milioane-de-romani-la-munca-in-strainatate-528860.html

Almond, G. and Coleman, J. S. (eds) (1960) *The Politics of the Developing Areas,* Princeton, New Jersey: Princeton University Press.

Almond, G. and Verba, S. (1965) *The Civic Culture: Political attitudes and democracy in five nations,* Boston and Toronto: Little, Brown and Company.

Anderson, B. (1992) 'Long-distance nationalism: World capitalism and the rise of identity politics', Amsterdam: Center for Asian Studies Amsterdam.

— (1998) *The Spectre of Comparisons: Nationalism, Southeast Asia and the world,* New York: Verso.

Appadurai, A. (1996) *Modernity at Large: Cultural dimensions of globalization,* Minneapolis: University of Minnesota Press.

Arnett, J. J. (2007) 'Socialisation in emerging adulthood: From the family to the wider world, from socialisation to self-socialisation', in J. E. Grusec and P. D. Hastings (eds) *Handbook of Socialisation: Theory and Research,* New York and London: The Guilford Press: 208–231.

Basch, L., Glick Schiller, N. and Szanton Blanc, C. (1994) *Nations Unbound: Transnational projects, postcolonial predicaments, and deterritorialized nation-states,* Longhorne, Massachusetts: Gordon and Breach.

Bauböck, R. (1994) *Transnational Citizenship: Membership and rights in international migration,* Aldershot, UK: Edward Elgar Publishing.

Beck, U. (2002) 'The cosmopolitan society and its enemies', *Theory, Culture & Society,* 19:17–44.

Berger, P. and Luckmann, T. (1989) *The Social Construction of Reality,* Garden City, New York: Anchor Books.

Berry, J. W. (1992) 'Acculturation and adaptation in a new society', *International Migration,* 30:69–85.

— (2007) 'Acculturation', in J. E. Grusec and P. D. Hastings (eds) *Handbook of Socialisation: Theory and research,* New York and London: The Guilford Press: 543–558.

Bloemraad, I. (2004) 'Who claims dual citizenship? The limits of postnationalism, the possibilities of transnationalism, and the persistence of traditional citizenship', *International Migration Review,* 38:389–426.

Bodnar, J. (1987) *The Transplanted: A history of immigrants in urban America,* Bloomington: Indiana University Press.

Campbell, A., Converse, P. E., Miller, W. E. and Stokes, D. E. (1960) *The American Voter,* New York: John Wiley & Sons, Inc.

Careja, R. and Emmenegger, P. (2012) 'Making democratic citizens: The effects of migration experience on political attitudes in Central and Eastern Europe', *Comparative Political Studies,* 45:871–898.

Castles, S. and Davidson, A. (2000) *Citizenship and Migration: Globalization and the politics of belonging,* New York: Routledge.

Castles, S. and Miller, M. (2009) *The Age of Migration: International Population Movements in the Modern World, 4th edn,* London, New York: The Guilford Press.

Cavalli-Sforza, L. L. and Feldman, M. (1981) *Cultural Transmission and Evolution,* Princeton, New Jersey: Princeton University Press.

Dahl, R. A. (1971) *Polyarchy: Participation and opposition,* New Haven: Yale University Press.

Evans, P. (2000) 'Fighting marginalization with transnational networks: Counter-hegemonic globalization', *Contemporary Sociology,* 29: 230–241.

Faist, T. (2009) 'The transnational social question: Social rights and citizenship in a global context', *International Sociology,* 24:7–35.

Fingerman, K. L. and Pitzer, L. (2007) 'Socialisation in old age', in J. E. Grusec and P. D. Hastings (eds) *Handbook of Socialisation: Theory and research,* New York and London: The Guilford Press: 232–255.

Gimpel, J. G., Lay, J. C. and Schuknecht, J. E. (2003) *Cultivating Democracy: Civic environments and political socialisation in America,* Washington DC: Brookings Institution Press.

Givens, T., Freeman, G. P. and Leal, D. L. (eds) (2008) *Immigration Policy and Security: U.S., European, and Commonwealth perspectives,* New York: Routledge.

Glick Schiller, N. and Faist, T. (eds) (2009) *Migration, Development, and Transnationalization: A critical stance,* Oxford: Berghahn Books.

Glick Schiller, N. and Fouron, G. (2001) 'Terrains of blood and nation: Haitian transnational social fields', *Ethnic & Racial Studies,* 22: 340–366.

Habermas, J. (2001) *The Postnational Constellation: Political essays,* Cambridge: Polity Press.

Handlin, O. (1979) *The Uprooted. The epic story of the great migrations that made the American people, second edition.* Boston, Toronto, London: Little, Brown and Company.

Hannerz, U. (1990) 'Cosmopolitans and locals in world culture.' *Theory, Culture & Society,* 7:237–251.

Hirschman, A. O. (1970) *Exit, Voice, and Loyalty: Responses to the decline of firms, organizations, and states,* Cambridge, Massachusetts: Harvard University Press.

Hobsbawm, E. J. (1992) *Nations and Nationalism since 1780: Programme, myth, reality,* Cambridge: Cambridge University Press.

Huckfeldt, R. and Sprague, J. (1995) *Citizens, Politics, and Social Communication: Information and influence in an election campaign,* New York: Cambridge University Press.

Itzigsohn, J., Cabral, C. D., Hernandez Medina, E. and Vazquez, O. (1999) 'Mapping Dominican transnationalism: Narrow and broad transnational practices', *Ethnic and Racial Studies,* 22:316–339.

Jennings, M. K. and Niemi, R. G. (1974) *The Political Character of Adolescence: The influence of families and schools,* Princeton, New Jersey: Princeton University Press.

Johnson, C. H., Sabean, D. W. and Teuscher, S. (eds) (2011) *Transregional and Transnational Families in Europe and Beyond: Experiences since the Middle Ages,* New York and Oxford: Berghahn Books.

Kapur, D. (2010) *Diaspora, Development, and Democracy: The domestic impact of international migration from India,* Princeton and Oxford: Princeton University Press.

Kwok-Bun, C. (2002) 'Both sides, now: Culture contact, hybridization and cosmopolitanism', in S. Vertovec and R. Cohen (eds) *Conceiving Cosmopolitanism: Theory, context and practice,* Oxford: Oxford University Press: 191–208.

Leggewie, C. (2001) 'Transnational citizenship: Cultural concerns', in *International Encyclopedia of Social and Behavioral Sciences,* Oxford: Elsevier Ltd.: 15857–15862.

Levitt, P. (1998) 'Social remittances: Migration driven local-level forms of cultural diffusion', *International Migration Review,* 32: 926–948.

Linz, J. and Stepan, A. (1996) *Problems of Democratic Transitions and Consolidation,* Baltimore: John Hopkins University Press.

Mau, S., Mewes, J. and Zimmermann, A. (2008) 'Cosmopolitan attitudes through transnational social practices?', *Global Networks,* 8: 1–24.

Miller, H. (1957) *Big Sur and the Oranges of Hieronymus Bosch,* New York: New Direction Publishing Corporation.

Miller, W. E. and Shanks, J. M. (1996) *The New American Voter,* Cambridge, Massachusetts: Harvard University Press.

Mügge, L. (2010) *Beyond Dutch Borders: Transnational politics among colonial migrants, guest workers and the second generation,* Amsterdam: Amsterdam University Press.

Nie, N. H., Verba, S. and Petrocik, J. R. (1999) *The Changing American Voter,* Bridgewater, New Jersey: Replica Books.

Ong, A. (2006) *Neoliberalism as Exception: Mutations in citizenship and sovereignty,* Durham, North Carolina, and London: Duke University Press Books.

Østergaard-Nielsen, E. (2003) 'The politics of migrants' transnational political practices', *International Migration Review,* 37: 760–786.

Paul, R. (2013) *Citizens of the Market: New forms of international migration and their consequences for people, parties and political systems,* Cambridge, Massachusetts: Harvard University, Dissertation manuscript.

Pérez-Armendáriz, C. and Crow, D. (2010) 'Do migrants remit democracy? International migration, political beliefs, and behavior in Mexico', *Comparative Political Studies,* 43:119–148.

Roniger, L. (2011) *Transnational Politics in Central America,* Gainesville: University Press of Florida.

Rother, S. (2009) 'Changed in migration? Philippine return migrants and (un) democratic remittances', *European Journal of East Asian Studies,* 8: 245–274.

Sassen, S. (1998) *Globalization and its Discontents: Essays on the new mobility of people and money,* New York: New Press.

Smith, M. P. and Bakker, M. (2008) *Citizenship across Borders: The political transnationalism of El Migrante,* Ithaca, New York: Cornell University Press.

Soysal, Y. N. (1994) *Limits of Citizenship: Migrants and postnational membership in Europe*, Chicago: University of Chicago Press.

Tarrow, S. (1992) 'Mentalities, political cultures and collective action frames', in A. D. Morris and C. McClurg Mueller (eds) *Frontiers of Social Movements Theory,* New Haven, Connecticut: Yale University Press.

—— (2005) *The New Transnational Activism*, Cambridge: Cambridge University Press.

Trenz, H. -J. (2001) 'Global Denken-Lokal Handeln. Zur Mobilisierungslogik von Migranteninteressen in Europa', in A. Klein, R. Koopmans and R. Roth (eds) *Globalisierung, Partizipation, Protest,* Opladen: Leske & Budrich: 179–205.

Van Gennep, A. (1960) *The Rites of Passage*, Chicago: The University of Chicago Press.

Vertovec, S. (2004) 'Migrant transnationalism and modes of transformation', *International Migration Review,* 38: 970–1001.

White, S., Nevitte, N., Blais, A., Gidengil, E. and Fournier, P. (2008) 'The political resocialisation of immigrants. Resistance or lifelong learning?', *Political Research Quarterly,* 61: 268–281.

Wimmer, A. and Glick Schiller, N. (2002) 'Methodological nationalism and beyond: Nation–state building, migration and the social sciences', *Global Networks,* 2: 301–334.

Chapter Ten

'Who is Ready to Vote at Sixteen?': New Perspectives in the Study of Political Reasoning

Bernard Fournier

For several years, probably under the dominant influence of the rational choice theory in political science, political socialisation was only studied in restricted specialised circles. However, this research field seems to have gained more attention recently, particularly among those working on civic participation and democracy (Jennings 2007). In parallel, while only a minority of young people were interested in traditional politics in the last few decades (Dorzée 2009), a new picture has recently emerged: young people are at the centre of 'revolutions' in several countries, or openly contesting government policies. Is a new political generation rising? More research is certainly needed before reaching such a conclusion, but careful thought on the political socialisation process is more important than ever (Fournier forthcoming).

Certainly the most recent data still shows contrasting attitudes in young people regarding politics. This should not surprise us. Like any other major sociological category, this concept does not represent the reality of a group that is homogeneous by nature. The notion of 'young people' encompasses very different experiences that depend on the circumstances of the individual concerned (Muxel 2010). A single image cannot show the complex web of relationships in the various levels of participation and interest among today's youth (Fournier 2009). Youth calls for heterogeneity.

According to Percheron (1993), we are not born with an interest in politics, we become interested in politics. Political interest results from various processes that are not only based on the deterministic impact of the environment (the family, the peers or school), as Renshon convincingly explained (1977: 27). Modernity offers a web of various opportunities during individuals' lives (Martuccelli and de Singly 2009) and even if it seems contradictory, personal experience should be at the centre of the social analysis as it is always unique (Berman 1982). In his research among children, Jean Piaget, among others (*see* Percheron 1974, 1982, 1985, 1993), suggested that each individual, beyond their concrete membership of groups, also creates their own vision of the world and shapes a frame of reference in a dialectical process with their environment.

Those dialectical processes can be operationalised in part with the notion of 'structures of thought' developed by Rosenberg (1988a) to mean the 'medium of exchange between the individual and the political environment' (Rosenberg *et al.* 1988: 12). Recently, we have been interested in Rosenberg's approach for a study on lowering the age of majority to sixteen. Even though an important public debate took place in Austria not so long ago – where the 16-year-old threshold was finally adopted (*Le Monde* 2007) – this question has not really been debated in most Western democracies (Hudon and Fournier 2003). The majority of young people even appears to be against lowering the age to vote.[1] However, we think that this absence of debate is appropriate for a reflection on the 'patterns of political reasoning' among young people. Among the tiny minority that supports the idea, are there differences? Are the opponents of this idea homogeneous? Do they change their minds if we present all the arguments for and against lowering the voting age? Can we better understand political interest among the young with the concept of political reasoning? These are the questions we will try to answer in this chapter.

Data and Methods

Several research designs can be applied to study structures of thought (Rosenberg 1988b). For the present research, around 200 young French-speaking Belgians gathered in Liège on 28th October 2009[2] for a whole day of debate and discussion inspired by the method of 'citizen conferences'. Participants completed a survey at the beginning and end of the day to measure the evolution of opinions. In the morning, a panel of four experts presented the issues for and against lowering the age of majority; in the afternoon there were a series of 90-minute discussions in small groups (there were twenty-seven groups with eight to ten young people per group).[3] Originally, the sample had been designed to be representative of all 16- to 22-year-olds in Wallonia and Brussels. Unfortunately, several logistical problems beyond our control prevented this. The final sample completing both questionnaires was made up of 182 young people: 62 per cent were female; 44 per cent were under eighteen; 92 per cent were Belgian (out of whom 77 per cent had fathers born in Belgium); 60 per cent were in the regular high school programme.

The study was not originally designed to measure structures of thought. 'Deliberative Polling®' methods – under one name or another – are popular in various contexts these days (Fishkin 1995;[4] Mutz 2006; Elliott 2005). However,

---

1. For example, in a previous survey conducted in Liège in 2007 among 16- to 18-year-olds, only 25 per cent of respondents were in favour of voting at sixteen (Rocour 2007).

2. Raphaël Darquenne was responsible for the collection of the data and we would like to thank him, as well as Élodie Flaba who assisted us in this research. We would also like to thank the head teachers and the teaching staff of the schools for their enthusiastic involvement in this project; the 200 students who spent a whole day discussing politics; as well as the Athénée Maurice Destenay of Liège, particularly its deputy head teacher. About sixty trained moderators also helped to make our project come to fruition. The University of Liège funded this research.

3. The groups were constituted to ensure diversity in social background and school membership and to encourage confidentiality in the discussions. The trained moderators were instructed to appear neutral and to encourage the young people to discuss the various arguments for and against the right to vote at sixteen.

4. Online. Available: http://www.cdd.stanford.edu

in addition to the questionnaire survey, we recorded and analysed the small group discussions in order to study the evolution of discourse when confronted with conflicting opinions.

It is interesting to note that analysing discourse in this way is in a sense analogous to the live discussions among political scientists about democratic deliberation. Indeed, Rosenberg (2007), rather than focusing on the individual or collective outcomes of deliberations, as scholars usually do, has focused on the deliberative processes themselves, or, 'how individuals actually engage one another when they are asked to deliberate' (Rosenberg 2007: 2). There are certainly several fruitful connections between structures of thought and citizen deliberation processes. We do not develop this link extensively in this chapter, but it arguably justifies the use of this method to study structures of thought.

Opinions before and after the discussions

Before analysing the patterns of political thinking in our sample of young French-speaking Belgians, it is necessary to compare opinions before and after the discussions on the issue of lowering the age of majority to sixteen. Only a fraction of young people wanted to change the threshold, even after the discussions. However, it is interesting to note that the discussions changed the view of some young people. At the beginning of the day, only 6 per cent thought young people should vote at sixteen (although 11 per cent said they would have been ready to do so). By the end of the day, 22 per cent of the participants thought young people should vote at sixteen. Of course, the success of the experiment is not in this increase; indeed, on an individual level, a change of mind indicated in the second questionnaire is as important as a strengthening of a previous opinion. We are inevitably confronted with a better-informed opinion by the end of the day and therefore, information that is more relevant to the study of opinions (Luskin *et al.* 2002).

The increase in support for voting at sixteen is supported by participants' responses to other questions which asked about their reasons for advocating or opposing the right of 16-year-olds to vote. As Table 10.1 shows, several variables related to maturity, interest in politics at sixteen and so on increased (or decreased) in accordance with their overall view at the end of the day. There were two exceptions to this: it seems that most of the respondents at the start and end of the day considered 16-year-olds to have little knowledge of politics and did not believe that voting at sixteen would make young people more responsible.

Experts' arguments for and against voting at sixteen

The purpose of the discussion process is to challenge individual opinions with a larger range of arguments or opinions on a specific topic, in this instance, the right to vote at sixteen. During small group discussions, young people could have taken onboard new arguments and rejected others but at the very least, they were made aware of these other points of view such that a better-informed reasoning could occur in the discussion process. Can we measure any structures of thought during this process?

Table 10.1: Opinions on voting at age sixteen, time 1 and time 2

	Agree or strongly agree (%)		
	Time 1	Time 2	Difference
Young people are mature enough to vote at 16	8	26	+18
At 16, young people would vote like their parents	66	49	-17
Maturity of a person does not depend on his/her age	72	91	+19
Young people would be more interested in politics if they could vote at 16	27	47	+20
At 16, young people do not know enough about politics to vote	90	86	-4
A lot of adults do not have more interest in politics than a 16-year-old	72	8	+10
Voting at 16 would make young people more responsible	44	49	+5
At 16, we are less responsible than at 18	69	57	-12
Political parties would give more consideration to youth interests if they could vote earlier	48	59	+11

Source: Research on the right to vote at 16, day of discussions, Liege, October 2009; N = ±180.

As explained earlier, the discussion process involved an initial phase in which four panellists presented the issues, two putting the arguments in favour and two putting the arguments against. This session took the format of a two-hour debate including contributions from the study participants; the debate was very active. Next, after lunch, participants continued the discussion in small groups with a group moderator (as well as an observer who took notes but did not interrupt the discussion). Discussions were recorded and transcribed.

Generally speaking, three main arguments were put forward by the panellists against the idea of lowering the voting age to sixteen and these were particularly well received by the young people. First, many participants appeared very concerned by the possibility that lowering the voting age could mean (or even will mean) the lowering of penal majority for crime; second, it was noted that the only European country so far that had lowered the voting age to sixteen is Austria, a country associated with strong right-wing extremists; third, the panellists (and the participants) emphasised the dearth of political knowledge and even political maturity at the age of sixteen. The latter point was not, however, generally accepted as a reason for not lowering the voting age. Some of the participants felt that more information was needed and suggested that a course on politics during the final years in high school should be introduced (these is no such course in the present curriculum). These three arguments were reiterated during the morning session and tended to reinforce opinions opposed to the right to vote at sixteen.

Among the arguments put forward by the panellists in favour of lowering the age of majority, the first was related to the place of young people in society: with an ageing population, allowing 16-year-olds the right to vote could be a way of addressing the age pyramid. The second argument was based on several examples showing that young people have the right to participate in the public debate because laws and political decisions concern them. One of the panellists was particularly enthusiastic about lowering the voting age and his charismatic contributions impressed a lot of participants, although did not always win them over.

With this range of opinions in mind, participants gathered in small groups to discuss the issues further. On the whole, discussions appeared to be dominated by opposition to voting at sixteen: 'I don't know; I am not mature enough to take such decisions on political issues,' was an opinion often relayed.

Interpretation and discussion of findings

Close analysis of three of the twenty-seven discussion groups will be presented here. Five young people took part in the first group, three girls and two boys. They came from three different schools.[5] Nine young people took part in the second group (all girls coming from the same three schools). Finally, eleven young people were in the last group (seven girls and four boys). At the beginning of the day, all of them were against lowering the right to vote from eighteen to sixteen; by the end of the day, three of them were in favour (all from the second group).

Initial analyses of the transcripts show at a glance that students reacted differently during small group discussions. Of course, their arguments were influenced by their own opinions and by what they heard in the morning, but it was obvious from the way in which they interacted during the small group discussions that their global attitudes were not the same. The identification of various key words in those attitudes are associated with different forms of political reasoning.

Broadly speaking, the individuals we studied can be divided into three categories: at one end, there are the young people who put forward almost no arguments during the discussion or who tended to reject the whole process. These were relatively few. At the other extreme, there are the young people who were very interested in the process and put forward long and structured argumentation, using many examples. Between these two extremes was a 'middle of the road' group who had some level of interest, put forward some arguments, but there was nothing unique in their contributions.

This typology of attitudes towards the idea of lowering the voting age accords with Rosenberg's typology of individual structures of reasoning, which, as we have noted, reveal 'the interplay between social environments and subjectivity in the development of cognition' (Rosenberg 1988a: 2). According to Rosenberg (1988b), there are three structures of reasoning: sequential thought (when people track the world only as it appears before them), linear thought (when people

---

5. We attempted to make sure that the schools respected the socio-cultural diversity of the French Community of Belgium. Students came from private and public schools in Liège, Namur and Brussels; and from general, professional and technical programmes of study.

analyse the activity they observe by placing one action in relation to another) and systematic thought (when people juxtapose the relationships that exist between actions, considering each of them in its context). Rosenberg provides examples to support this typology which are helpful for determining whether the typology can be applied to the present analysis.

Sequential political reasoning is described as follows: 'the sequential thinker reasons by tracking the world which appears before him' (Rosenberg 1988a: 102). He asks himself, 'What do I see in front of me?' and then describes this reality. This reality is not conceptualised nor generalised to new circumstances: this type of thought is characterised by the description of the present. Rosenberg uses a metaphor of the stars in the sky to describe it:

> In sequential thought, the night sky is comprehended as it appears. It is a blackness punctuated by a host of stars. The stars themselves are simply there and do nothing. Occasionally, there may be a shooting star. This will be noticed and the trajectory of this unusual event may be remembered. Whatever happens up there, however, is never really a part of the immediate events of daily life. The night sky is thus a remote world, one that is rarely a matter of any particular consideration (Rosenberg 2002: 242–43).

Linear political reasoning is described as follows: 'linear thinkers analyse the sequence of activity they observe. They do so by focusing on specific actions and then placing one in relation to another' (Rosenberg 1988a: 116). For Rosenberg, this type of thought is the most common. The individual asks himself: 'What causes this observation?' Rosenberg uses the example of a theatre play to explain it:

> As reconstructed in linear terms, politics is something of a play, one already written by gods, fate, or nature herself. [...] The action unfolds in several rooms simultaneously, but a member of the audience can observe only what is in one room at a time. From the perspective of linear reasoning, the action occurring in the different rooms is not integrated. Rather the play is a collage of fragments; each room has its own space and time. The events in a given room are understood relative to one another. They are related to events in other rooms only when the observer can actually watch how action in one room leads to or from action occurring in another (Rosenberg 2002: 117).

Systematic political reasoning is described as follows: 'systematic thinkers juxtapose relationships among actions and beliefs' (Rosenberg 1988a: 137). In political terms, an individual who analyses a political event with systematic reasoning will have a very sophisticated conception of politics. In this case, the individual will ask her/himself: 'What are the conditions under which the relation I observe takes place? Which function does an activity or an interaction play in a system?' This type of thought exists without any temporal dimension. It is important to note that, according to Rosenberg, there is no hierarchy between these three types of thought and that the same individual could develop all of them with respect to different issues.

The three small group discussions were analysed using this framework. All sections of text were coded according to Rosenberg's definition of sequential, linear and systematic political reasoning. Four researchers analysed the three groups independently using the same criteria.[6]

The variations in discourse of each individual could have been analysed in terms of whether they were sequential in the beginning, then systematic or linear later on. However, this analysis, although interesting, quickly revealed its limits: even though the discussions lasted ninety minutes, not enough participants spoke for long enough for individual variance or deliberation to be measured. Therefore, the analysis turned to focus on how constant individuals were during the 90-minute discussion. When a person was characterised as sequential, it was clear that they treated each topic of discussion only as if they were noticing something. They would note, for example, that their friends were against the right to vote at sixteen, or that the majority were against and that was all:

> For me, personally, politics and me are two different things. I was against the right to vote at sixteen in the beginning and I think I will still be against at the end. That's all.

When a person was characterised as linear, he often proposed two concepts (sometimes a clear chain of events) in the discussion. One of the most frequent, for example, was the relationship between the lack of information, interest in politics and the vote. A close analysis of those discourses is particularly interesting: the non-involvement of young people is clearly evident, but neither the social consequences of the actions nor the reasons why young people might act this way are considered:

> Frankly, I think it is more a question [...] not a question of interest, but a question of information. This is really the basis of everything. We cannot be interested in politics if we do not have good information. It is as if we had done nothing.

Finally, a young person was characterised as systematic when their thought was highly developed, when several examples were mentioned, when those examples did not concern the individual directly and when those examples showed a lot of knowledge. This was not always easy to detect and we did not necessarily expect a lot of systematic thinking in the rigid scheme we adopted.[7] In addition, politics is

---

6. For this analysis, sincere thanks are due to Stéphanie Meuleman, Quentin Genard and Geoffrey Grandjean.

7. As twenty-seven groups were held at the same time, this activity needed to be structured and a framework of discussion was accordingly given to the moderator of the group. The discussion was divided into four main topics. First, we asked the students their first impressions following the general discussion with the 'experts'; second, we asked them how they see their place in society as young people today (the idea was to open up a broader discussion on politics issues, political involvement, and so on); third, we discussed their vision of politics and how the idea of voting at sixteen fits into this; and finally, in a fourth section, we asked them if their opinion about the right to vote had changed and why. After the event, we realised this organisation of the discussion

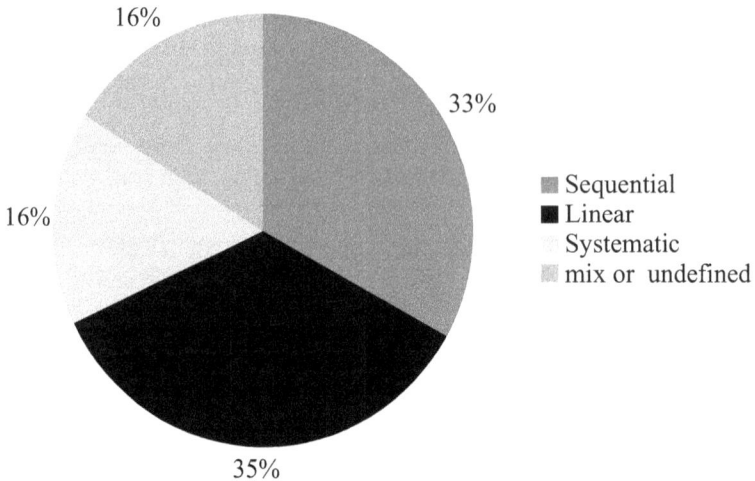

Figure 10.1: Distribution of structures of thought observed in small group discussions

not a very popular topic and a lot of young people do not have a lot to say. However, some discourses were clearly systematic: 'Yes, for example, when we listen to some teachers who speak very well. Last year, I preferred to attend the ethics class instead of religious studies. The teacher argued very well'. This participant then explained that the class had asked her why she did not want to be involved in politics. She explained her reasons and talked about the role of movements and associations as alternatives. She also talked about the politics of Nicolas Sarkozy (who was the French President at the time of the study): 'If Sarkozy runs again in the next elections, look out for different aspects of his personality, the different ways he exerts his power [...]'. This kind of discourse was not common in the group discussions.

The distribution of the structures of thought we identified among the discourses can be seen in Figure 10.1. There is a risk in giving a quantitative impression of this analysis here and the figure should be interpreted with caution; moreover, the presence of a 'mixed or undefined' segment shows that it is not always easy to categorise young people's discourses as discrete structures.

In the small sample used in the present analysis, one third of the young people can be identified by their sequential discourses, another third by their linear discourses, and 16 per cent by their systematic discourses. This is an interesting result that allows us to better understand young people's thoughts about lowering

---

prevented more interaction between young people and also prevented opening their discourses to reveal more 'structures of thought', but we concluded it was difficult to do otherwise. For the analysis in this chapter, we used only the discussions of the second and third topics.

of the voting age to sixteen after a discussion on the issue.

Interestingly, not all of the three young people who changed their minds during the discussion employed systematic thought. On the contrary, and perhaps surprisingly, one was a sequential thinker, one was a linear thinker and the last one a systematic thinker. This is an interesting finding: one's mind does not change just because of a tendency to compare ideas and analyse systematically the pros and cons. Let us resume the analysis of participants' discourses by examining their accounts of changing their minds:

- Sequential thinker: 'Yes, as for myself, I also found the debate interesting and as number 089[8] [said], I was against when I arrived here, but with the arguments I heard, people were convincing, so I think I am changing into being for [lowering the voting age][...] It was interesting.'
- Linear thinker: 'When I arrived here I was against and the arguments but changed my mind. I am in favour now, but only if it is not an obligation.[9] When that is the case, young people will have a stronger voice and decisions will be taken for a longer term, for the future and I will gain more maturity somewhat with regards to politics and our future.'
- Systematic thinker: 'Being mature is an individual issue because some people can be mature at sixteen and feel that they are citizens when others are not like that at all. It is a question of information, of education for the development of different tools, and [...] having a critical mind [...] [that is] able to compare the information we receive, otherwise, it is useless. We are not able to judge this information.'

These three structures of thought, though only a temporary construct, show an interesting coherence when the results of the questionnaires are compared. In the second questionnaire, seven questions attempted to measure the impact of the day on the young participants. Obviously, it is a limited self-measurement, but it is indicative. According to their responses, nearly a third believed that 'today's discussion changed their opinion about the right to vote at the age of sixteen'; 80 per cent thought that a day like this was useful; 51 per cent thought that the arguments in favour of lowering the voting age were more convincing than those against it (but they did not necessarily change their opinion accordingly). Probably more interesting for the present study, a quarter thought that some people had expressed opinions too strongly during the afternoon discussions. However, although 93 per cent thought that they were able to express their own opinion during the discussion, this differed according to how involved individuals were: only 60 per cent of the participants who were not very involved in the debate felt this way. Does this reflect their position in their group? Another interesting finding was that among the expert panellists, the one who was very enthusiastically in favour of lowering

---

8. A random number was given to each participant.
9. Voting is mandatory in Belgium.

the voting age was most popular among the participants who were also in favour of lowering the voting age (91 per cent of these participants considered him the most convincing), even if only 53 per cent ultimately agreed with him. It seems that enthusiasm is not always enough to convince people to change their opinions.

Conclusion

Can we find different patterns of reasoning on a topic such as lowering the voting age to sixteen? Does the concept of political reasoning developed by Rosenberg give us a better understanding of political interest among young people? We tried to structure an experiment for answering those questions – an experiment, we realised afterwards, that had its limits but also its strengths. We think that four conclusions can be drawn, but they are not definitive.

Firstly, it is obvious that a full day of discussions played a part in the construction of an informed opinion and therefore contributed to the construction of a better-informed opinion on the topic. The analysis of the answers to the questionnaires before and after the debate with experts and the small group discussions, brought to light several reinforcements (of already existing opinions) as well as changes (to those opinions). These two dynamics have to be stressed: the success of the experiment was not predicated on finding huge discrepancies between the answers in the first and second questionnaires. Such a result would in fact have been worrying for the value of traditional surveys! The process obviously also brings about a reinforcement of opinions. Is this reinforcement more frequent for certain types of individuals? The homogeneity of our population does not give us an answer to this question, which is why we did not pursue this aspect any further in this chapter, but it would be something to consider in further research.

Secondly, can we say anything about the idea of lowering the voting age? Let us say first that in a previous research study, we compiled a list of the different (and numerous) arguments used in France dating from the French Revolution until the voting age was lowered to eighteen (Fournier and Pépratx 1991). We were amazed by so many changes in legislation during this period, which shows that the determination of the electoral and eligibility thresholds is indeed arbitrary. Nineteen, eighteen, seventeen? No social or electoral necessity calls for a change of this threshold today in Belgium, but it could happen in the future. In fact, when we analyse the data collected on the issue of lowering the voting age to sixteen, one option seems to emerge: 82 per cent would accept the idea of lowering the voting age to sixteen if it was not mandatory. This option covers a variety of opinions, but represents well the ambiguity of the participants. Clearly, it represents the position of our first category of young people (sequential thinkers). All of them were in favour of this option. People who have a more developed forms of argumentation, on the other hand, only had a 68 per cent agreement rate.

Thirdly, we are convinced that study of the various forms of political reasoning is a fruitful way for understanding the relationship between the individuals and their environment. However, no deterministic conclusions can be drawn. In our sample, three students changed their opinion and agreed with lowering the voting age. But as we have seen, not all of their discourses can be classified as systematic. Why should that have been the case anyway? A very coherent, structured, systematic political reasoning could also disapprove of the lowering of the voting age, could it not? In our opinion, this result shows that a particular 'world of reference' (a vision of the world each of us develops) is not linked to a particular structure of thought. Do all young people need systematic reasoning to defend the right to vote at sixteen? No. Sequential reasoning, where someone is only influenced by the opinion of their peers for example, might also be conducive to the same opinion. In fact, this is also the way it works in politics in general: an interest in politics is not always the result of a juxtaposition of 'relationships among actions and beliefs' (Rosenberg 1988a: 137). It could be, but is not always the case. This is why this diversity should be kept in mind when promoting citizen participation among the youth (Fournier and Hudon 2012).

Fourthly, we have to recognise that the analysis of discourse has limitations. It certainly opens up a different field of research for political socialisation, but its success may also depend on new measurement tools. Rosenberg's structures of thought constitute an interesting framework, but we are aware that it was not easy to identify them during the discussions in our research. The researcher is strongly implicated in the data construction – which is the case for a lot of analysis in social sciences, of course, but it was more obvious to us in this case. Some exceptions have to be chosen, others eliminated. Is it always relevant to measure how many arguments were used by a participant? What if they only reacted, or defended their own perspective?

Certainly, the final challenge will be to transpose those patterns of arguments, those patterns of 'political reasoning', onto the issue of political interest in general and, more importantly, onto the understanding of a political socialisation perspective based on the exchanges between the individual and their particular and contemporary environment. Nevertheless, it would be a fruitful challenge for the development of new directions in the study of political socialisation.

References

Berman, M. (1982) *All That's Solid Melts into Air*, New York: Simon and Schuster.

Dorzée, H. (2009) 'Le jeune vote, sans passion', *Le Soir*, 19 May: 4.

Elliott, J. (2005) 'Méthodes participatives: Un guide pour l'utilisateur. Deliberative Polling®', in B. Duvieusart, H. Lisoir, G. Rauws and A. van Campenhout (eds) Brussels: Fondation Roi Baudouin and Vlaams Instituut voor Wetenschappelijk en Technologisch Aspectenonderzoek (viWTA).

Fishkin, J. S. (1995) *The Voice of the People: Public opinion and democracy*, New Haven: Yale University Press.

Fournier, B. (2009) 'Socialisation politique et mosaïque des possibles: l'apport de Jean Piaget', in D. Vrancken, F. Schoenaers and C. Dubois (eds) *Penser la négociation. Hommages à Olgierd Kuty*, Brussels: De Boeck Université: 83–91.

— (forthcoming) *Socialisation politique. Concepts et méthodes*, Brussels: De Boeck Université.

Fournier, B. and Hudon, R. (eds) (2012) *Engagements citoyens et politiques de jeunes. Bilans et expériences au Canada et en Europe,* Québec: Presses de l'université Laval.

Fournier, B. and Pépratx, F. (1991) 'La majorité politique: étude des débats parlementaires sur la fixation d'un seuil', in A. Percheron and R. Rémond (eds) *Âge et politique*, Paris, Economica: 85–110.

Hudon, R. and Fournier, B. (2003) 'How old is old enough to vote: Youth participation in society', *Perspectives électorales/Electoral Insight*, 5(2): 38–43.

Jennings, M. K. (2007) 'Political socialization', in R. J. Dalton and H.-D. Klingemann (eds) *The Oxford Handbook of Political Behaviour*, Oxford: Oxford University Press: 29–44.

Le Monde (2007) 'L'Autriche instaure le vote à 16 ans', 20 March.

Luskin, R. C., Fishkin, J. S. and Jowell, R. (2002) 'Considered opinions: Deliberative polling in Britain', *British Journal of Political Science,* 32: 445–487.

Martuccelli, D. and de Singly, F. (2009) *Les sociologies de l'individu*, Paris: Armand Colin.

Mutz, D. C. (2006) *Hearing the Other Side: Deliberative versus participatory democracy*, Cambridge, New York: Cambridge University Press.

Muxel, A. (2010) *Avoir 20 ans en politique. Les enfants du désenchantement*, Paris: Éditions du Seuil.

Percheron, A. (1974) *L'univers politique des enfants*, Paris: Fondation nationale des sciences politiques/Armand Colin.

— (1982) 'The influence of the socio-political context on political socialization', *European Journal of Political Research*, 10: 53–59.

— (1985) 'La socialisation politique, défense et illustration', in M. Grawitz and J. Leca (eds), *Traité de science politique*, Paris: Presses universitaires de France: 165–235.

—   (1993) *La socialisation politique* (textes réunis par Nonna Mayer et Anne Muxel), Paris: Armand Colin.

Renshon, S. A. (1977) 'Assumptive Frameworks in Political Socialization Theory', in S. A. Renshon (ed.) *Handbook of Political Socialization*, New York: The Free Press.

Rocour, V. (2007) 'Les jeunes ne veulent pas voter à 16 ans', *La Libre Belgique*, 3 November: 8.

Rosenberg, S. W. (1988a) *Reason, Ideology and Politics*, Princeton, New Jersey: Princeton University Press.

—   (1988b) 'The structure of political thinking', *American Journal of Political Science,* 32(3): 539–566.

—   (2002) *The Not so Common Sense: Differences in how people judge social and political life*, New Haven: Yale University Press.

—   (2007) 'Types of democratic deliberation: The limits of citizen participation?', paper presented at Center for the Study of Democratic Politics, Princeton University. Online. Available: http://www.princeton. edu/csdp/events/Rosenberg011807/Rosenberg011807.pdf

Rosenberg, S. W., Ward, D. and Chilton, S. (1988) *Political Reasoning and Cognition: A Piagetian view*, Durham: Duke University Press.

Chapter Eleven

A Picture Paints a Thousand Words: Children's Drawings as a Medium to Study Early Political Socialisation

Lena Haug[1]

The research project: children's interest in politics

In political science the premise that children are not untouched by politics has been established since the late 1960s. During that initial period, socialisation studies conducted on the political and societal understanding of children were the first to show that political socialisation begins in early childhood (cf. Easton and Dennis 1969; Greenstein 1960, 1965; Hess and Easton 1960; Hess and Torney 1967). These studies primarily examined topics commonly investigated in research on political education involving adults (e.g. elections, government, political symbols and party preference). Although some of these topics have only a remote connection to children's environment, it was shown that children have their own knowledge and opinions about politics; they also show concern about political themes – mostly loaded with emotion (e.g. Connell 1971: 169). Although research on children's political socialisation continued throughout the 1980s and 1990s (e.g. Moore *et al.* 1985), 'the initial enthusiasm [...] was replaced by disillusionment and frustration' (van Deth *et al.* 2011: 149), because attempts to present statistical evidence on the persistence of early acquired political orientations failed (ibid.) However, a lot of time has passed since Conover and Searing (1994: 24) stated that political socialisation research has 'lost its children'. Meanwhile, at least some recent research projects have rediscovered these 'lost' children. They all agree with the findings of former studies, namely, that children's political worlds begin to take shape early on. In contrast to the bulk of former studies, however, more recent research dissociates from stage theory in favour of other approaches such as domain-specific approaches (e.g. Berti and Vanni 2000; Berti and Andriolo 2001; Moll 2001; Hafner 2006; Dondl 2010; Kalcsics and Raths 2011; van Deth *et al.* 2011).

Research on political socialisation, however, is still primarily concerned with adolescence (*see* Abendschön, Chapter One in this volume). Undoubtedly, one of the reasons lies in the complex process of data collection in young children.

---

1.   I would like to thank Susanne Meisel, PhD student at University College London, for her correction of this chapter.

Conducting research using standardised surveys is challenging, because reading and writing skills are lacking and children have difficulties in self-expression (concerning active and passive vocabulary). However, excluding children from political socialisation research cannot be the solution; instead, it is essential to develop research methods that are appropriate for children's abilities and conceptions without compromising scientific standards. Following the main research questions 'Are children interested in politics?' and 'What are the objects of concern?' the study presented in this chapter aims to examine the proportion of children showing interest in political issues and to identify the political issues that attract children's attention. Furthermore, potential connections between individual factors (i.e. gender, age, socio-economic residence area, migration background) and political interest should be tested.[2] These research questions are examined by using a relatively uncommon research method, namely children's drawings. This chapter suggests that the use of children's drawings can open up new possibilities for political socialisation research, because it is a child-typical, age-appropriate and language-independent data collection method. After having discussed the relevance of children's political interest, I focus on the advantages and disadvantages of using children's drawings and introduce special characteristics of children's drawings. This will provide a better understanding of the method used in the empirical research project on political interest in young children, which is presented in the second part of the chapter. In this study 230 children from different schools and preschool groups between the ages of four and ten illustrated their visions of the future. Drawings were analysed focusing on those containing political aspects, i.e. political symbols and issues.

Why children's political interest matters

Political interest 'is typically the single most important determinant of political knowledge and overall political participation' (Shani 2009: 3, citing Luskin [1990] and Verba *et al.* [1995]), as research with adults has shown. A good democratic system cannot exist without a minimum level of engagement of its citizens. Prerequisite for political engagement is, among other things such as time and knowledge, at least some political interest. Therefore, the basis of a functioning democratic system ought to be a minimum level of political interest (cf. van Deth and Elff 2004: 478). Political science has shown that, for adults, 'politically interested individuals are far more likely to seek and acquire political information, to have an opinion on a wide range of issues, to vote, and to participate in a variety of other ways compared to disinterested citizens' (Shani 2009: 3, citing Lazarsfeld *et al.* 1948; Milbrath and Goel 1977; Luskin 1990; Verba *et al.* 1995; Delli Carpini and Keeter 1996). In the majority of cases, political science research focuses on the level of political interest in adolescents and adults (which is, undeniably, also an important task), instead of researching the barely known origins of political

---

2.   For a detailed description of the research project and its findings *see* Haug (2011).

interest. However, it is very unlikely that political interest manifests suddenly when reaching adolescence. Research on political interest should therefore be extended to (early) childhood.

Another individual rather than societal reason for extending research on political interest needs to be emphasised: if children are considered to be able citizens with their own rights, research on children's political interest and opinions is obligatory because children's political behaviour constitutes an independent aspect of democratic society (van Deth 2005: 6). The United Nations' *Convention on the Rights of the Child* emphasises the necessity to take children's interests and participation into consideration, in every matter that concerns them (OHCHR 1989: § 3 par.1, §12 par.1).

To conclude thus far, a child's interest in politics is as important as an adult's. Therefore, the point of departure for the present study is to explore if children are interested in politics and, if so, what precisely it is that they are interested in. It is assumed that political interest is, at least in part, a product of political socialisation, which is considerably reflected in gender differences within the political sphere. Therefore potential explanatory factors (i.e. gender, age, socio-economic residence area and migration background) for the development of political interest in children are examined for the purpose of generating hypotheses about the socialisation of political interest, thereby providing a starting point for further research.

Measurement of political interest in children

It is already challenging to measure political interest in adults because of the construct's complexity. In research with young children, the lack of reading and writing skills as well as a limited active and passive vocabulary further aggravate the problem. Hence the decision to use drawings as a research method, which alleviates the problem of limited literacy skills. Nevertheless, the problem of measuring political interest in children remains.

First it is necessary to define the term 'political interest' more precisely. Political interest is not clearly defined; different concepts of political interest are used in different contexts, e.g. political awareness, political involvement, political saliency and political sophistication (cf. Neller 2002: 489). In the present study, children's attention to political events (political awareness) and their concern about politics (political saliency) is, I argue, classifiable as political interest, based on the premise that these concepts correspond best with children's particular potential to be involved in politics. Accordingly, political interest is defined for the present study as a state of curiosity, concern about or attention to politics.[3] In adults, political interest is usually measured by self-reported interest in politics (e.g. 'How interested would you say you are in politics? Very interested, fairly interested, not very interested, or not at all interested' [Shani 2009: 60]). In political socialisation

---

3.   This definition is based on the definition of political interest by van Deth (1990: 278) who defines political interest as the 'degree to which politics arouses a citizen's curiosity'.

research involving children, political interest is rarely investigated. Schneekloth and Leven (2007) as well as Hafner (2006) attempted to adapt items developed for adults for research with children. Here, the children reported little interest (cf. Schneekloth and Leven 2007: 208; Hafner 2006: 93), although it remains unclear whether the children understood the term 'politics' or what they associated with politics (cf. Hafner 2006: 80). There is some evidence that children often either do not know the term 'politics' or believe this term only refers to the concept's structural, formal or procedural dimension (polity and politics). This is illustrated by comparing children's responses in questionnaires and interviews: although denying political interest in the questionnaire, children report clear interest in political issues when interviewed (*see* Picot and Schroeder 2007: 349; Burdewick 2003: 104–8). From this it follows that the use of the term 'politics' should be avoided as long as we do not know what children associate with this term.[4]

Other popular approaches of measuring political interest are to question political saliency, i.e. the importance of the political sphere in comparison with other areas of life, or political communication, i.e. the frequency of discussions or conversations about politics with others. Concerning the latter, it is assumed that talking about politics or initiating conversations about politics is an expression of political interest, which is easily comprehensible.

Given that children should not be questioned using specialist terms (such as politics), a more indirect approach of measuring political interest was developed for the present study. If children themselves raise and discuss political matters, they express political interest. Therefore, the expression of political issues[5] in response to an open question (in this case a drawing task) can work as an indicator of political interest as well. Furthermore, it can be assumed that the depiction of political elements in response to an open question may function additionally as an indicator of political saliency because the presentation of a particular topic must be seen as the result of a selective process, which means that priority is given to the depicted topic instead of other topics. This selection underlines the importance of the chosen topic for the individual child.

By means of the chosen research design (drawings in response to an open question) it was possible to investigate a large group of children who do not yet possess (advanced) reading and writing skills. Moreover, it was possible to abstain from specialised political language, thereby reducing the risk of misunderstandings and circumventing the researcher's 'communicative advantage' (Clark 1999: 40). At the same time, the approach should help to develop new possibilities for measuring political interest. Because scientific evidence on political interest of children (or political socialisation generally) is rare, as noted earlier, the study was set up to be exploratory.

Before the study is described in more detail, deliberations on the method are presented below, due to the fact that the use of children's drawings as a research

---

4. Besides, the prevailing lack of precision concerning the term 'politics' could also be problematic in adults (*see* Westle and Schoen 2002; van Deth 1990).

5. As per the definition of 'political' given below (*see* 'Definition of the political dimension').

method is relatively novel in political socialisation research. The following description is therefore intended to introduce the approach, as well as its advantages and disadvantages.

Children's drawings as research method

Although the use of children's drawings for research is a new and rarely used approach, some studies have in fact successfully made use of drawings. The following list is incomplete but provides an overview of the various possible applications. Psychological (i.e. for measuring personality or therapeutic devices) and developmental approaches (for measuring cognitive development or maturity) are not considered here because the meaning-making approach with its focus on the message of the drawing (perceptions, thoughts, experiences) is more useful for political socialisation research (for a short description of the different approaches *see* Holliday *et al.* [2009: 247–52].) Studies using the meaning-making approach are, as mentioned earlier, deployed in different research domains. Martin (1994) used drawings of adults to explore how they understand their immune system; Herth (1998) examined children's representations of themselves and their social world; Williams *et al.* (1989) focused on health beliefs of children; Victora and Knauth (2001) surveyed adults beliefs about their reproductive system; Bowker (2007) as well as MacPhail and Kinchin (2004) evaluated learning experiences; Dockett and Perry (2005) explored children's views on starting school; Bosacki *et al.* (2006) examined the topic of bullying; Driessnack (2006) did some research on children and their experience of fear; Coates (2002) examined free drawings; Holliday *et al.* (2009) used drawings as a possibility to listen to children with communication impairment; Punch (1998, 2002) investigated children's everyday lives; Brown *et al.* (1987) used children's drawings to reveal their changing perceptions of nuclear power stations; Götz (2004) and Neuß (1998, 2000) explored media reception; and Wasmund (1976) examined children's perception of an election campaign. There are also several studies that used drawings for international comparative research (Barraza 1999; Kaiser 2003; Götz *et al.* 2005; Lemish and Götz 2007). This list already illustrates the broad range of applications for drawing analyses. The following will clarify the reasons for using drawings as a research method instead of (or in addition to) other methods.

Advantages of using children's drawings as research method

Four specific benefits underlie the use of drawings as a research method: *(1)* the opportunity for non-verbal expression; *(2)* the opportunity to address not only cognition but also emotion; *(3)* the opportunity to gain an immediate insight into children's mindscape; and finally, *(4)* their expressive power. However, the use of children's drawings or of drawings in general is tied to difficulties of interpretation. Therefore, a communicative and context-orientated approach for analysis and interpretation is advisable.

Children's drawings as a non-verbal communication system

Commonly, children's drawings are used as a form of communication. Simply put, children address someone and want to say something with their drawing (cf. Richter 1987: 131; Neuß 2000: 133). The use of colour and the composition of picture elements (e.g. size, scaling, position and detailing) all offer opportunities for communication that exceed verbal means of expression (cf. Nguyen-Clausen 1987: 32). Moreover, the viewer of a painting is able to experience the impact of a drawing immediately; allowing for the transmission of information that is not constrained by verbal skills of sender or recipient (cf. Neuß 2000: 132). Further, Mitchell (2006: 62) points out that because 'visual methods do not give a "communicative advantage" [Clark 1999: 40] to the adult researcher', they 'offer a means of redressing or minimising the power imbalances' (Mitchell 2006: 61) between the adult researchers and the children participating in research.

Drawings tell emotions

Children's drawings provide an intensified inclusion of emotions in data-driven surveys through various means of expression. Emotions are not only conveyed by picture content, but also by colouring and pictorial design. Thus, children's drawings are not purely cognitive products but a combination of cognitive and emotional aspects. The latter can slip into the drawing through conscious and unconscious intent (cf. Neuß 2000: 136; Schoppe 1991: 174). Research on children's beliefs based on verbal skills (especially the questionnaire) addresses children mainly at a cognitive level, but if we want to get an idea of children's mindscape, we have to consider emotion as well as cognition.

Immediate insights

Through their conscious, unconscious and affective components, children's drawings give us a chance to gain an insight into children's minds 'in ways that language cannot' (Malchiodi 1998: 1). What children know often exceeds what is suggested by their oral or written responses (*see* Driessnack 2006; Holliday *et al.* 2009). Through images children (as well as adults) can 'articulate thoughts and experiences that cannot be put into words' (Holliday *et al.* 2009: 247). Furthermore, children can paint their view of the world, how they perceive reality and how they cope with it (Guillemin 2004: 275).

Expressive power

Drawings, like other visual media, have enormous expressive power. This expressivity has different advantages, two of which were noted earlier: a means to express things that are not (or not easily) conveyed by words and the potential to express emotions better than words can. Another considerable advantage is that drawings can not only display the topic but also give an overview of the perceptions and attributions connected to it.

I would like to illustrate the latter with two examples: imagine the question 'What are you scared of?' The verbal response (written or spoken) of a child might

Figure 11.1: 'I am afraid of war', boy aged eight

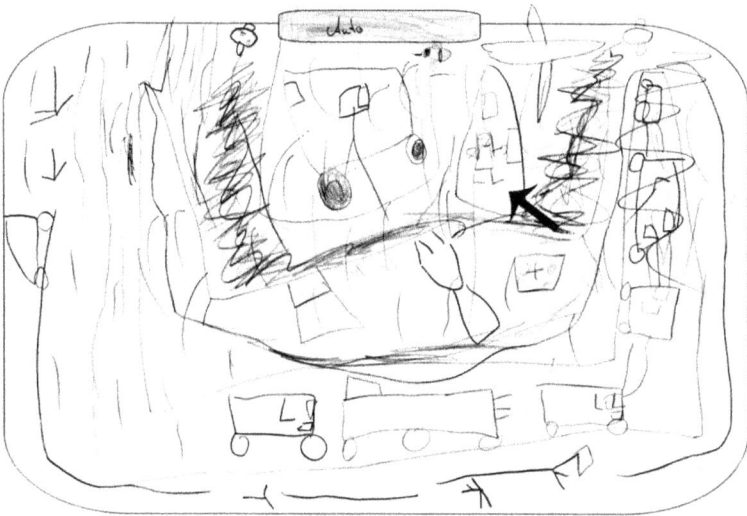

Figure 11.2: 'Car', girl aged six

Note: the girl painted herself inside the secure environment of her own home (*see* arrow) whereas the remainder of the drawing is crowded with traffic chaos.

be: 'I'm scared of war'. The visual response might be similar to Figure 11.1.[6] This drawing not only reveals the information that the child is scared of war, but also conveys an impression of the beliefs the child attaches to war.

The second example (*see* Figure 11.2) shows the futuristic vision of a girl who believes that in the future, streets will be crowded by cars. Her picture illustrates what that means for her life and thereby conveys an emotional component, which will not for instance be evident in the statement: 'There will be a lot of traffic'.

To summarise, children's drawings are a meaningful and informative data resource and extremely useful for research, especially with young and/or illiterate children, although critical reflection on the method must be considered. This is outlined in the following section.

Using drawings – critical aspects and difficulties

Interpretation difficulties – understanding children and subjective distortion

The interpretation of children's drawings is accompanied by several difficulties. A general problem in research involving children is the limited ability of adult researchers to understand the world from a child's point of view (Punch 2002: 6). Another general problem linked to the latter is the risk of subjective distortion. This general problem is exacerbated by the specific characteristics of children's drawings (i.e. iconography conventions and hidden or invisible elements and persons). Knowledge about the interpretation of drawings is essential to avoid misinterpretations but a detailed description of all particularities would go beyond the scope of this chapter. For further information, reference is made to the numerous sources of information in the relevant literature (*see* Cox 1992; Matthews 2003; Anning and Ring 2004; Golomb 2004; Willats 2005).

Trusting children's accounts? – Validity and reliability

The question of whether children's statements are trustworthy is frequently discussed. Do children tell the truth or do they perhaps invent things for different reasons? Certainly, we can assume that children as well as adults sometimes tell lies (or not the entire truth) to researchers. Punch (2002) states different possible reasons for this behaviour. According to her, children lie 'to avoid talking about a painful subject; to say what they think the researcher wants to hear; or through fear, shame or a desire to create favourable impressions' (Punch 2002: 8).

However, it is unclear why statements made by children are believed less than statements made by adults. Potentially, the issue is an adult construction: 'The nature of childhood in adult society means that children are used to having to try to please adults, and they may fear adults' reactions to what they say' (Punch 2002: 8). However, the likelihood of children lying can be reduced by researchers' behaviour (cf. Ennew 1994: 57). The researcher's task is to build a trustful relationship with the researched. This includes ensuring the anonymity of all personal data, treating the children in a respectful manner and ensuring the voluntary participation of the children. Unfortunately, children's rights of voluntary participation, informed

---

6. The images presented here were created by children participating in the study described in this chapter.

consent and anonymity are often not taken as seriously as those of adults.

In addition to the validity of children's answers, their reliability is often also critically questioned. Do children give consistent answers? Can research with children be reproduced with equal results? These are, again, questions that are also valid for research with adults. In contrast to the natural sciences, social science research produces data that pertain to perceptions and opinions. These are (fortunately) malleable – otherwise all educational efforts would be futile. As a consequence, the researcher has to keep in mind that 'valid data can tell a different story in different contexts or at different times' (Dockett and Perry 2007: 49). Therefore, thorough logging and description of research design; research implementation; and consideration of cultural, historical and individual context are vital.

Just a copy of neighbour's work?

One of the important drawbacks of using children's drawings as a research tool is that 'responses' cannot be easily hidden. Their visibility to neighbours, researchers and teachers endangers the anonymity of the data. This presents two problems: first, the lack of anonymity and second, the possibility that some responses are mere copies of a neighbour's work. Copying works 'may illustrate socially constructed rather than individual ideas' (Leonard 2006: 61) and therefore they might distort the results. Both problems can be reduced by an appropriate research setting. Research settings can be designed to prevent others (including researchers) from seeing responses. However, the construction of a 'private setting' entails the risk of being perceived as a test situation in school, which may have an impact on validity because responses may be designed to please adults. As long as the option of drawing in anonymity exists, the question of which approach (hidden or open drawing) is best depends on research topic and aims.

Is drawing for everyone?

Although drawing is perceived as being fun for children, different authors point out that drawing is a method that may not suit every child for a variety of reasons (Fargas-Malet *et al.* 2010: 183). Children may be inhibited about their drawing capabilities; they could perceive drawing as babyish (ibid.); or may have difficulties with drawing because practice is lacking – especially in less developed countries (Punch 2002: 331). Once again, the individual research design dictates whether the use of drawings is appropriate. For example, if high quality drawings are required for analysis, very young children or children without drawing experience should not be in the target group. One could argue, however, that drawings are at least as appropriate for children as questionnaires or interviews. A questionnaire or interview is also not suitable for every child and is not enjoyed by everyone (i.e. neither are useful for questioning children with communication impairment, *see* Holliday *et al.* [2009]). However, the voluntary participation[7] of the children in any particular research project is crucial.

---

7. This means voluntary participation and informed consent of the children (not just their parents). Furthermore, children must be provided with the option of withdrawing from the study if they want to do so.

The context tells the whole story

Researchers experienced in interpreting children's drawings perceive context information to be obligatory for 'correct' interpretation of the drawings (*see* Dockett and Perry 2007: 49; Panofsky 1974: 26–7). 'Meanings are produced through a complex social relationship that involves at least two elements besides the image itself and its producer: *(1)* how viewers interpret or experience the image and *(2)* the context in which the image is seen' (Sturken and Cartwright 2001: 45). Contextual information includes the child's thoughts about the drawing and their interpretation of it; the environment in which the drawing is produced (setting, communications, available material, etc.); the school context (content of lessons); individual background and personality; and last but not least, historical and cultural background. Not all contextual information is required (or available) every time; however, contextual information should be considered for explanation and clarification, especially if a drawing is difficult to interpret or erratic in composition.

Considering contextual information means among other things (*see* above) that children's explanations are needed to understand the meaning of the drawings. The particularities of children's drawings (or drawings in general) – such as simultaneity of all picture elements, individual symbolic language and non-visible (only imagined) picture elements – require verbal or written validation of the picture in detail and as a whole. The child's subjective meaning can only be revealed through the communication process (cf. Neuß 1998, 2000: 134; Richter 1987: 130).

To summarise this section I should like to emphasise that many of the critical aspects mentioned not only apply to research with children or research with drawings, but also to research in general. However, the above-mentioned points warrant reflection upon the chosen approach, as well as exact research documentation and the use of a variety of methods. Therefore, I concur with Guillemin (2004: 274) who recommends 'the use of an integrated approach that involves the use of both visual and word-based research methods', because it 'offers a way of exploring both the multiplicity and complexity that is the base of much social research interest in human experience'.

Avoidance of misinterpretations – the importance of knowing the characteristics of children's drawings

> Once, when I was six years old, I saw a beautiful picture in a book about the primeval forest called *True Stories*. It showed a boa constrictor swallowing an animal [...] I then reflected deeply upon the adventures in the jungle and in turn succeeded in making my first drawing with a colour pencil. My drawing number 1 was like this:

I showed my masterpiece to the grown-ups and asked them if my drawing frightened them. They answered: 'Why should anyone be frightened by a hat?' My drawing did not represent a hat. It was supposed to be a boa constrictor digesting an elephant (de Saint-Exupéry 1995: 9–10).

As mentioned earlier, there are certain characteristics of children's drawings that need to be considered for a valid interpretation. I would like to explain some of these characteristics (such as perspective), that allow conclusions to be drawn about what the child intended to represent in the picture and the relative importance of particular picture elements.[8] Characteristics should be explored that help avoiding misinterpretations while identifying the drawings' key features.

View-specific and object-centred representation

As Matthews (2003: 91) points out, children often draw more information than is necessary for the simple recognition of a picture element. They try to involve information that is linked to the object. Classical developmental theory of children's drawings named this characteristic 'intellectual realism' (*see* Piaget and Inhelder 1956: 49–52), which means that children try to draw all they know about an object regardless of perspective (Matthews 2003: 91). Matthews contradicts the assumption that children are unable to draw impressions of objects prior to reaching a certain age. Instead, he stresses that the intention of the illustrator when analysing pictures is crucial. He states that the rationale for depicting an object can be to show 'view-specific' information or 'object-centred' information (Matthews 2003: 100). View-specific drawings contain a particular perspective, while object-centred drawings contain the main features of an object without including the perspective (ibid., *see also* Marr 1982; Willats 1997). The combination of view-specific and object-specific drawing intentions may lead to confusing and 'unrealistic' drawings. In these drawings, children try to solve the problem of showing the main characteristics of an object as well as a correct representation of perspective (Matthews 2003: 100).

Therefore, Matthews considers the so-called errors in children's drawings to be 'very sensible decisions about which information should be encoded in a drawing' (Matthews 2003: 162). In conclusion, this means that children not only draw the way they do because they are unable to draw a different way (for developmental reasons), but instead draw objects in a particular way because they make decisions about visual structure and about 'which information to keep and which to sacrifice' (Matthews 2003: 162). The awareness of children's tendency

---

8. However, I have to stress that this description does not claim to be complete. Some characteristics (e.g. x-ray drawings and tadpole men) are not discussed here, because their relevance for socialisation research is low. Psychological and developmental approaches to interpretation are excluded for the same reason. Furthermore, I believe that psychological interpretation of drawings should be handled with care and is to be made only by experts in connection with therapeutic interventions. A drawing itself may only give a hint toward a particular interpretation and is useless for psychological purposes without further contextual information.

to depict different perspectives in the same picture as drawing intentions change is important because it may reveal to the researcher which information about an object should be conferred; or, which characteristics of an object or person are, from the child's point of view, important and distinctive.

Representation purposes – concentrating on the essentials

When drawing, children have representational intentions, whether or not they are drawing for another viewer or they are drawing just for themselves. The picture aims to express something in particular. Through painting, children want to tell stories, reflect events, dive into fantastic worlds, and express emotions and fears. In their paintings they present objects by showing the objects' typical characteristics (Reiß 1996: 15). However, children are thinking about how to present an object to best express what is from their point of view the most important information. A painted object does not need to be represented particularly realistically in order to be identifiable. It is sufficient to draw an object that is (in detail or structure) merely similar enough to be recognised. Minimal similarity or use of well-known symbols suffices to confer meaning.

But why is knowledge about the drawing technique of children important for research? On the one hand, it helps to avoid misinterpretations and on the other it is important for identifying picture elements and recognising their references. When interpreting the drawings, it is therefore essential to reflect on the representational intentions of each child. The manner of presentation may be chosen to facilitate identification of objects and persons; to symbolise something; and/or to confer information about special and important features of the element; but it can also be influenced by other factors i.e. drawing abilities.

In conclusion, children develop their own 'drawing language', which aims to confer the meaning of the depicted object clearly to the viewer and to display the most important characteristics of an object or person. In doing so, children reveal their powers of accurate observation. The final drawing is to be seen as a productive synthesis of skillful illustration and intentions for narration (Richter 1987: 101). Therefore, researchers should focus on the essentials and reflect on their interpretation by also incorporating the possible representational intentions of the child.

Size, colour and richness of details – indicators of importance

As mentioned above, I prefer to treat psychological interpretations of drawings cautiously. Therefore, I want to stress at first that size, colour and detail should not be the main focus of interpretation. However, these attributes may give valuable hints about the importance of individual picture elements and thus, may help to identify central picture contents and messages. In the following paragraph, I specify how several image characteristics may function as indicators for detecting the importance of individual elements in the picture. For this purpose, the richness of detail and size of an object may be investigated. Children apparently draw more important elements or persons bigger and in greater detail (Schuster 2010: 108–

22). This assumption was confirmed in studies that examined drawings of Santa Claus prior to, on and after Christmas-day. The analysis showed that size and detail of Santa Claus increased the closer it was to Christmas-day. After Christmas-day, Santa shrank again as he became less important (cf. Solley and Haigh 1957; Craddick 1961; Sechrest and Wallace 1964).

The choice of colour can also allow us to draw conclusions on the importance of topics and elements. If some elements are striking in colour they are likely to be of particular importance. Striking colouring can point out the important themes or elements of the drawing. Therefore, colouring can be used in combination with size and position as an indicator of the relative importance of picture elements. However, as I have said previously, the features mentioned may work as indicators, but need not necessarily do so. For instance, elements may be drawn in a certain colour because it was the only colour available; or elements may be drawn bigger or smaller for perspective or space reasons (Matthews 2003: 168). Again, knowing the circumstances in which the picture was drawn (i.e. the drawing situation, available colours) will help to reduce the risk of misinterpretation.

Development of an interpretative framework

Despite their special requirements for interpretation, children's drawings provide various opportunities for research and have, in fact, been used in various research areas in the past. However, in political socialisation research, children's drawings have hitherto been referred to only rarely. One reason for this is, *inter alia*, the lack of appropriate approaches to the interpretation of children's drawings. Unfortunately, methodological approaches for a non-psychological content analysis of children's drawings are extremely rare. Hence, a new interpretative approach was developed for the research project. This is presented below and follows the interpretative framework proposed by Niesyto (2006: 280–6). However, Niesyto's framework had to be adapted for use with drawings, because it was originally developed for interpreting photos. Niesyto's framework supports the life-world approach and prioritises the analysis of content but is not orientated towards classical developmental or psychological methods of interpretation that are usually used to analyse drawings. In the following section, a step-by-step description of his framework is given and the modifications made for this study will be briefly explained.

Niesyto's interpretative framework

- Documentation and selection of images: images are archived and, depending on the research context, selected for further examination.
- Initial understanding: initial understanding contains subjective and intuitive attempts at understanding. Interactions between seeing and feeling ought to enable the researcher to access the image. The main aim of this stage is to get a first (emotional) impression of the image.

– Image description and formal analysis: a description of all persons, objects, formal presentations and structures is carried out in as detailed a manner as possible.

– Understanding of symbols: building on the previous stages, possible meanings and readings are generated. These have to be proved on the individual image. In other words, the content of the image is explored in this step.

– Involving the context: only after generating readings and hypotheses of meaning is context information used to ensure plausibility.

– Summarisation: the findings of each stage are summarised in relation to the particular research questions.

– Inter-subjective validation: findings ought to be made accessible to others in order to critically examine the generated meanings (Niesyto 2006: 280–6).

Even though the research project's analysis was based on the foundation above, the exact transference of all stages was not possible for the analysis of children's drawings due to their special characteristics as noted earlier. In addition to the drawings, the children's self-descriptions were logged, in accordance with my previous remarks on communicative validation. Further, in contrast to Niesyto's approach, image descriptions and formal analyses were mainly made orally because the logged self-descriptions offered sufficient information to identify picture content or particular picture elements. Children's oral responses were also taken into account – even though they had no equivalent in the drawings – in order to include hidden and imagined elements as well as context information into the analysis. Furthermore, formal aspects of the children's drawings (e.g. size, detail, position, and colour of picture elements) were respected only in the case of difficulties with the identification of central and important picture elements. A more detailed explanation of the research design and method is given in the following section.

Children's interest in politics

Exploration – are children actually politically interested?

Because scientific evidence on political interest of children (or political socialisation generally) is rare, as noted earlier, the study described below was set up to be exploratory. The study aimed to explore whether children are politically interested. Further, the thematic orientation as well as potential influencing factors (e.g. gender) for the socialisation of political interest should be explored. The research project was designed as an explorative study in order to generate hypotheses that should provide a basis for further investigation.

As described above, it was decided to use free drawings produced in response to an open question for data collection. The drawing of political issues was considered as being linked to corresponding interest, knowledge and affective connections, while also taking into consideration that the child's choice of a particular topic is the result of a well-considered selection process and that this decision therefore matters.

The children were tasked with drawing their vision of the future. Using the future as a topic of interest meets two requirements: on the one hand it can be assumed that visions of the future also reflect current wishes, fears and attitudes as well as their importance for each child; and on the other hand, children develop their visions of the future on the basis of previous experiences, taking into account their knowledge of the world. Visions of the future present a new combination of subjective experiences of the present and the past (Lersch 1956: 373–4). A further reason for choosing future visions as a topic was that it is children especially who have to bear the consequences of today's political decisions. Some of these are, for example, decisions on climate change and high government debt. It is thus interesting to find out if children derive consequences for their adult future from the political events they perceive today and if they express fears or make demands – towards politics, adults or society – in this context. Thus, the question about the future is suitable for identifying political topics that are particularly important for children and for finding out about associated fears and wishes.

In addition to the drawings, gender, migration background and age were recorded. Furthermore, the paintings were supplemented by the children's self-descriptions and titles to facilitate accurate interpretations of the drawings. During the drawing process additional context information was logged, i.e. conversations and discussions between the children about the content of the drawings; additional observations such as copying neighbours' work; seating arrangements (boys and girls mixed or separated); and further information from the children about their topic selection and other considerations associated with the drawing. This provided additional information that should help to avoid data misinterpretation. Moreover, this information is used during interpretation of the results.[9]

Participants

Data was collected at four primary schools and two preschool institutions in Oldenburg, Germany. At each primary school, children from first to fourth grade took part. A total of sixteen school classes were involved. In the preschools, the sample only included children in the last year before starting school. In total, 230 children, aged between four and ten, took part in the study: forty-one preschool children and 189 school children. The primary schools and preschools were selected from contrasting urban areas to discern possible relations between socio-economic home environment and political interest. Areas were identified by using statistical data of the city (e.g. proportion of foreigners, rental prices, subsidised housing); it was found that the differences between inner and outer city were the starkest.

---

9. For instance, in the first data collection session a seating arrangement separated by gender was striking. Therefore, the seating arrangements were logged in subsequent sessions. Later these data could be used to re-examine gender-specific results in combination with a mixed or separated seating arrangement to test for a possible connection between gender-specific responses and type of seating arrangement.

The willingness of individual teachers to take part determined which classes took part in the research project at each selected school. In preschool, every child in the year prior to starting school was invited to participate and nearly all eligible children joined the study. In contrast, in primary school, the willingness to participate differed from class to class. The proportion of children participating in the city centre and in the outer district was relatively balanced but differed between individual schools. The proportion of girls and boys participating was balanced as well.

Among the 230 children participating, fifty-two had an immigrant background (22.6 per cent), and of these, sixteen had personal migration experience.[10] The gender ratio was balanced within this group – although girls were on average older than boys (*see* 'Immigrant children's choice of topics' below) – while in the group of children without migration background, mean age did not differ remarkably. Furthermore, the proportion of children with an immigrant background was higher in the outer city areas.

Data collection

Prior to data collection the instructions were pretested in two preschool groups to prove its comprehensibility. It was found that the instructions initially formulated were too long and complicated for children this age. This was further aggravated by problems with the meaning of 'future' for the children. When talking to them it became clear that they could manage at best the instruction already used by Kaiser (2003): 'Draw yourself as a grown-up'. However, this instruction established a personal, rather than societal association; therefore it was decided that the older children should receive a less directional instruction.[11] All children beyond preschool age drew their pictures in response to the instruction: 'Imagine you were grown-up. How will you or other people live? What are you looking forward to or what are you afraid of?'[12] This exercise was well understood by all children participating in the study. Predominantly, they decided to draw one part of the question (i.e. how I will live) or they chose to draw opposing aspects (i.e. joy and fear). Selecting only parts of the instruction as the basis for their pictures did not constitute a problem because this was seen as part of the individual's selection process and therefore another indicator of specific interest.

Data collection took place between September and November 2009. In the primary schools, two lessons (one lesson is forty-five minutes) were made available for the project in each participating class. This time frame was sufficient, although some children would have liked to spend more time on their drawings. In preschool,

10. A migration background was assumed if the child or one of his parents moved from another country to Germany.

11. Except for the shortened task, the procedure was the same for all children. The results showed no major differences in topics according to the instruction. The differences found are most likely explained by age differences.

12. The text of the instruction was developed with help of Sarah J. (eight years old).

no time limit was given but the children commonly finished their drawings within half an hour. After the completion of the drawing task, the self-description of the child was noted on the back page, either by the children themselves and/or by the researcher. This gave the children an additional opportunity to give further information about their drawing. Names were not recorded and the children knew about the anonymity of their responses. Usually, the drawing activity took place in their respective classrooms. Only a few drawing sessions were carried out outside of the classroom when the participants were too few. In preschool, all drawings were made in small groups in a separate room (usually in the presence of preschool teachers).

The same procedure was chosen for all groups in order to ensure good comparability of the results: first the researcher and the research project were introduced. At the same time, central terms such as research were explained and children had the opportunity to ask questions about the research context. Some classes showed a lot of interest and a high capacity for critical thinking. Subsequently, the drawing instruction and drawing paper were presented to the children. First, the children determined how old they would be in the year 2030. Calculations and comparisons were made on this basis (i.e. in 2030 I would be as old as my teacher is now) to help the children to grasp the progression of time and to imagine themselves in the future. Thereafter, children collected potential topics as a group, in order to reduce the influence of interjections, which can in the worst case shape the drawings of all members of a class (cf. Schoppe 1991: 221). A choice of topics should be available in every class in order to stimulate ideas. No specific topics were mentioned by the researcher and so the issue of politics was purposefully avoided. Instead, the children were questioned if they believed that in the future everything would remain as it is today, i.e. if nothing would change or whether changes were to be expected.

On this basis, the researcher asked about potential changes, if they were not spontaneously expressed. A variety of topic suggestions was collected in all classes until no new ideas were produced. After brainstorming, the children could begin drawing and painting. They could use all coloured and uncoloured pencils available (with the exception of slow drying colours). Most children elaborated their drawings with concentration and great perseverance. After handing in their drawings, the researcher had a conversation about the picture content with each child; this was recorded on the back of the drawing. Attention was paid so that no leading questions were asked.[13] Most children selected an individual title for their drawing. The children's explanations and titles were meant to aid interpretation, to make it possible to identify picture elements, to find out about the importance of elements, and to make the unseen seen – thereby avoiding the risk of misinterpretation. This procedure turned out to be extremely useful for interpretation because the titles conveyed the key messages of the drawings. Additionally, the researcher listened to the children's conversations about their

---

13. Usually, the conversation started with the question: 'Would you please tell me about your picture?'

pictures during the drawing process. Context information about political issues revealed through these conversations and discussions was logged by the researcher following data collection to facilitate the subsequent image categorisation.

All children received a research assistant certificate in return for their effort. After evaluating the data, posters presenting the most important findings were provided to every (pre-) school in order to give feedback to the children, parents and teachers involved.

Data analysis

Raw data were qualitatively examined for the content of the drawings. This was followed by a quantitative analysis of group differences. The latter should help to identify the potential impact of individual characteristics (such as gender, age, socio-economic residence area and migration background) on the socialisation of political interest. Qualitative examination included the identification of chosen topics and their categorisation by the researcher. The categorisation was subsequently evaluated by a group of external interpreters to ensure inter-rater reliability. The method of analysis followed the interpretation framework as described previously.

Development of the categorical framework and coding technique

In the first instance, all drawings were analysed with regard to their content;[14] no selection of drawings was made. This provided an overview of the topics in general. For this purpose, all drawings and the accompanying self-descriptions were inductively coded following grounded theory (Strauss and Corbin 1990). In other words, individual codes for content description were developed for each drawing (e.g. career aspiration policeman; me and my children; I am afraid of war; war in Afghanistan; air pollution; electric cars; etc.) This was supplemented by a systematic and rule-guided approach for qualitative content analysis (Mayring 2008).[15] Therefore, pictures were coded by means of predefined selection criteria: before data analysis, it was determined what image material should be the basis for the coding. It was decided to concentrate on the key message of the drawings. Self-descriptions of the children should be included and any unimportant details (e.g. sun, birds and trees) should be excluded from analysis. More than 300 inductive codes were generated and subsequently reviewed to check which ones could be summarised in a meaningful way. By structuring and combining the single codes, nine core categories with several subcategories were developed (*see* Table 11.1).

---

14. All drawings were scanned and transferred to the qualitative data analysis software MAXQDA. Additionally, the children's descriptions and the drawings' titles were entered.

15. For a short English description of his approach *see* Mayring (2000).

Table 11.1: Core categories and their contents

Category	Subcategories/contents
Career aspirations	All kinds of career aspirations/professions (e.g. footballer, teacher)
Architecture	My home/how I want to live; buildings (e.g. Eiffel Tower); cities
Politics	National symbols; wealth and poverty; war and peace; institutional politics; destruction of the environment/pollution; protection of the environment; natural disasters
Me and my family	Family situation (e.g. single parents); desire to have children; self-portraits; pets; family events (e.g. weddings, funerals); family of origin
Leisure time activities	All kinds of leisure time activities (e.g. swimming); adult activities (e.g. taking a driving test, buying a car)
Fantastic/fairy tales	Fantasy characters and worlds (e.g. mummies, unicorns)
Technology	Robots; (flying) vehicles; space travel and space stations; inventions (e.g. teleport)
Landscape	Islands and flowery meadows
Abstract	Abstract paintings that could not be allocated

Thereafter, all drawings were, on the basis of these criteria, assigned to the previously developed categories. Drawings could be assigned to more than one category; due to the multitude of topics in some drawings this was even necessary. After categorisation by the first interpreter had been completed, the drawings were re-examined by a group of interpreters who also categorised the drawings without prior knowledge of previous category assignments, in order to assure the validity of the first categorisation. Where opinions differed on the correct assignment, the group members discussed their reasoning until they achieved a consensus. Formal aspects of picture presentation (e.g. colour, size, position) and other characteristics of children's drawings (as described above) were considered especially in the case of difficulties with categorisation. The assignments of the interpreter group were subsequently taken as the final result. Ten per cent of randomly chosen drawings were again re-examined by another person, using the same procedure as the interpreter group, in order to measure inter-rater agreement. In the following, the level of consistency between the interpreters group and the last examiner was measured with Cohen's *kappa*, which demonstrated a high correlation between both interpretations (k=0.91; *see* Bortz and Döring 2006: 276–7).

Definition of the political dimension

A definition of the term 'political' was required to detect the percentage of political features in the drawings. In the present study, the term political was therefore restricted to the content-related dimension of politics ('policy'). As van Deth *et al.* (2011: 154) state, 'social and political problems are probably the most concrete topic [*sic*] to deal with politics'. The concrete social and political problems characterise, in the majority of cases, the term politics and everyday political life, rather than the abstract ideas and theories behind them (van Deth 2007: 83). It can be assumed that children are closer to specific political questions that are related to the worlds they inhabit than to the formal or procedural aspects of politics, which are less relevant to their lives and moreover, are complex and difficult to understand. In addition to the concentration on policy, a second limitation was needed in order to know which issues and problems could be interpreted as political in contrast to topics and problems of private life. *The American Heritage Dictionary of the English Language* (2006) defines 'political issues' as 'a point or matter of discussion, debate, or dispute' within the political arena. The term 'political problem' differs from the more neutral term 'political issue' in so far as 'the concept "political problem" refers to a specific situation, which is considered to be undesirable' (van Deth *et al.* 2011: 154) and therefore needs to be changed. This definition is broadened by Claußen (1996), Hurrelmann (1994) and Mansel (1995), who take into account not only the undesirability of problems, but also their stress- and anxiety-evoking potential. Destruction of the environment and environmental risk; nuclear disasters and nuclear threat; impoverishment and economic crisis are exemplary political topics mentioned by Mansel (1995: 9) and Claußen (1996: 379–80), which entail the risk of provoking fear. Due to the definition of the term 'political' described above, drawings that contained political topics or displayed political problems were coded as political.

Children's political issues and topics – previous studies' findings

Research on the relevance of and interest in political topics in children is rare. Nevertheless, it is possible to extract some information from other studies involving children, even though politics usually represents only a small part of the study. The LBS-Kinderbarometer, for instance, asked children what they would change if they were politicians. Five core areas of interest emerged: environment protection, children's rights, unemployment and peace (Eichholz and Schröder 2002: 94). Other research, such as the study by Burdewick (2003) or Gemmeke (1998), asked about interest in political issues using interviews. In the study by Burdewick (2003: 104), the topics of environment, nuclear energy, finances and feminist politics were introduced by the children. In her study, Gemmeke combined the topics mentioned by the children (aged six to thirteen years) into the categories equal treatment, war, unemployment, immigration, environment, economies, Europe and starvation (reported by van Deth 2007: 88). All studies mention the topics of war in relation to peace and destruction in relation to protection of the environment. Also, the subject of social inequality, in the form of unequally distributed resources and capabilities, is repeatedly referred to. Thus, in the present study, drawings with illustrations of the topics war and peace; destruction of environment; protection of environment; and poverty and wealth were attached to the category *politics*. Drawings showing natural disasters were – following the risk-related approach of Claußen (1996), Hurrelmann (1994) and Mansel (1995) described above – also interpreted as political and were subordinated to the category *environment*. Additionally, it was assumed that drawings of national flags and the conscious use of national colours show knowledge of political symbols and were therefore also coded as *political* (cf. Vollmar 2007: 133).

Quantitative analysis

During the next phase of analysis, the qualitatively derived categories were quantitatively evaluated using the Statistical Package for Social Sciences (SPSS; version 18) with regard to individual characteristics (e.g. gender) and correlations between several (sub-) categories (e.g. *destruction of environment* and *eco-friendly technology*). Dichotomous variables were generated for each category and subcategory, since each drawing could be coded with multiple categories as noted above. These were combined into sets of variables for further analysis. Additionally, variables for school, class, age, gender, migration background and seating arrangement (separated by gender or not) were created. First, the relationships between several variables (e.g. gender and choice of topic) were explored using cross-tabulations. Differences in frequency distribution were checked for their statistical significance using Pearson's *Chi*-squared test or Fisher's exact test. The strength of association between two variables was measured using Cramer's V.

Results

According to the predefined framework of *politics*, many of the children included political aspects in their drawings. In total, sixty of 230 drawings contained representations of political reference (26 per cent of the sample), which made the category *politics* one of the three most important topics in the children's drawings (*see* Figure 11.3).

    War and peace as well as *environmental problems* were the most frequently drawn political topics (70 per cent of the category *politics*). Drawings of *flags and national colours* came third. The topic *poverty and wealth* was noticeably less painted and *political institutions* were found only in one drawing, which, interestingly, was drawn one day after general elections in Germany (*see* Table 11.2). The following section gives a short overview of the picture contents within the subcategories of *politics*.

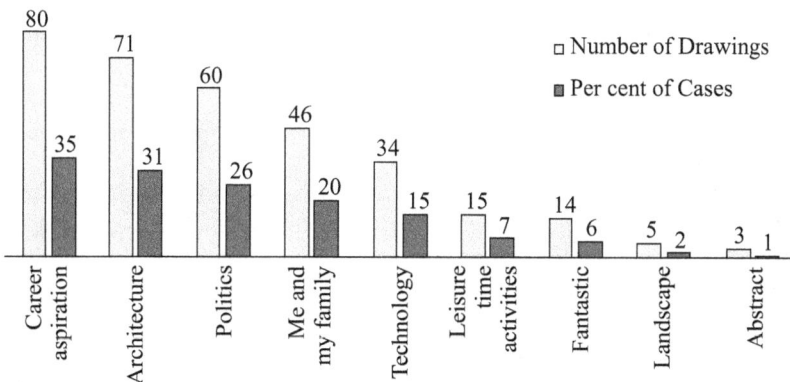

Figure 11.3: Frequency of topics in children's drawings

Notes: N=230; includes drawings coded in multiple categories.

Table 11.2: Subcategories of 'politics': frequencies

		Responses[a]		Per cent of cases
		Number	Per cent	(N=60)
Subcategories of *politics*	Wealth and poverty	6	8.7	10.0
	National symbols	12	17.4	20.0
	Institutions	1	1.4	1.7
	War and peace	21	30.4	35.0
	Environmental destruction/protection	6	8.7	10.0
	Pollution	7	10.1	11.7
	Environmental protection	8	11.6	13.3
	Natural disasters	8	11.6	13.3
Total		69	100.0	115.0[b]

Notes: a. Dichotomous group tabulated at value 1; b. Multiple subcategories included

Subcategories of politics

War and peace

Twenty-one drawings were assigned to the category *war and peace*. These varied greatly and included paintings of acts of war (e.g. fighting between humans; persons and buildings threatened by military equipment), aftermath of war (e.g. building walls such as the Berlin Wall), armament (tanks, warplanes, etc.) and written statements (e.g. 'I am afraid of war'). Some of the images were influenced by films such as *Star Wars* and were usually painted in great detail. However, others were presented only briefly and schematically, which could have reflected either the complexity of the topic or difficulties in drawing. Some pictures in this category also displayed connections to current events, e.g. the war in Afghanistan (*see* Figure 11.4).

Environment

Twenty-nine drawings dealt with environmental issues. Seven images broached the issue of extent and consequences of environmental degradation and pollution. These images displayed the deforestation of rainforests; pollution from garbage; personal burdens or distress caused by traffic and air pollution; and effects of climate change. In contrast to the problems, however, were the drawings that dealt with protection of the environment. In eight drawings, children concentrated on environmentally-friendly technologies and renewable energies. The subcategory *environmental protection* contained, among other things, depictions of electric cars, solar cells and improved wind power plants. Some drawings showed environmental destruction as well as protection. This was often constructed in the form of a problem-solution-confrontation, making distinctions between good and bad. An example is the depiction of climate change effects (e.g. melting of the polar ice caps) on the one hand and the approval of environmentally-friendly technologies (e.g. hybrid drive) on the other (*see* Figure 11.5). At the same time, depictions of natural disasters, such as flooding, volcanic eruptions and forest fires shaped the rest of this category.

Figure 11.4: 'War is mine', girl aged seven

Figure 11.5: 'Good and Bad', boy aged ten

National symbols

All drawings containing flags and national colours were coded as *national symbols*. In these cases, children drew mainly the German flag and German national colours. In addition, some paintings contained depictions of French, British, or Italian flags. Illustrations of flags and national colours normally occurred in typical everyday situations (e.g. sporting competitions, ships and buildings).

Wealth and poverty

Altogether, only six drawings displayed this topic. These either demonstrated the desire for wealth or for less poverty. Individual images contrasted wealth and poverty by splitting the drawing into two sections.

Group differences

Girls and politics – the gender gap in early childhood

Empirical research has shown that women have a more reserved attitude towards politics than men and are assumed to have less political knowledge and interest (cf. Conway 1985; Delli Carpini and Keeter 1991; Jamieson and Kenski 2000). This could be explained in part by gender-specific socialisation processes. Assuming that gender identity is socially constructed, girls are socialised with regard to the private life (e.g. family), whereas boys are more likely socialised with regard to public life (e.g. profession), which leads to the 'gender gap' in political subjects (cf. Bennet and Bennet 1989). Therefore, data evaluation focused on differences in choice of topics between boys and girls to examine if a gender gap already exists in early childhood. If so, then girls would focus more on the home and less on public and political life.

Between-group comparisons revealed a big difference in terms of the frequency with which some topics were drawn by boys and girls (*see* Figure 11.6). In addition to the categories *family* and *technology*, this difference also occurred in

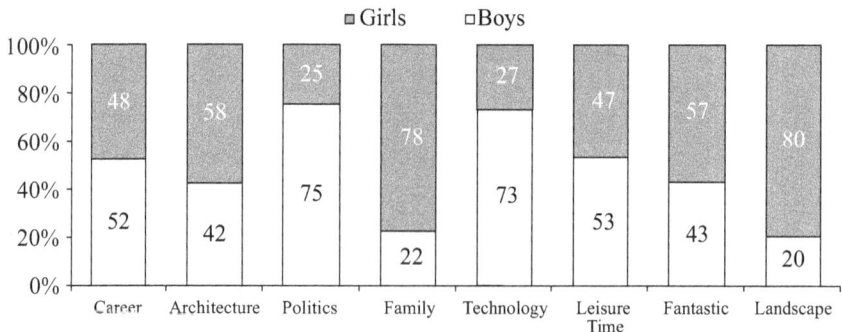

Figure 11.6: Topics in children's drawings by gender (within topic)

Note: girls N=113; boys N=117.

the category of *politics*. Only one quarter of all drawings coded as 'political' was made by girls (25 per cent; fifteen drawings) whereas 38 per cent of all boys (forty-five drawings) made reference to political aspects (x^2=18.91; df=1; p<0.001).

As can be seen in Table 11.3 the main concerns in boys' drawings were politics (coming first) and career aspirations – both of which are associated with public life. The girls' main concerns, however, were architecture, career aspirations and family. Most of the girls' drawings within the category *architecture* referred to their homes in the future and could therefore be considered as related to private life (whereas the boys more often drew futuristic buildings and cities). The same applies for the category *family* (which mainly concerns the desire to have children). Although the category *career aspiration* is associated with public life, it was striking that the majority of girls chose traditional female professions (such as teacher, dancer and nurse).[16] Interestingly, 24 per cent of the girls, depicting their career aspiration, also drew themselves having children, whereas none of the boys chose this combination.

Table 11.3: Topics in children's drawings by gender (within gender)

			Gender	
			Female	**Male**
Category[a]	Career aspirations	Count	38	42
		% within gender	33.6	35.9
	Architecture	Count	41	30
		% within gender	36.3	25.6
	Politics	Count	15	45
		% within gender	13.3	38.5
	Me and my family	Count	36	10
		% within gender	31.9	8.5
	Leisure time activities	Count	7	8
		% within gender	6.2	6.8
	Fantastic/fairy tales	Count	8	6
		% within gender	7.1	5.1
	Technology	Count	9	25
		% within gender	8.0	21.4
	Landscape	Count	4	1
		% within gender	3.5	0.9
	Abstract	Count	3	0
		% within gender	2.7	0.0
Total N			113	117

Notes: Percentages are of total respondents; a. Dichotomous group tabulated at value 1

---

16. Traditional male professions (e.g. policeman) were predominant in the boy's drawings too, but overall their drawings were distinguished by a broader range of professions.

A matter of age?

Political socialisation research assumes that awareness of political issues and interest in politics increase with age (e.g. Niemi and Hepburn 1995: 9; cf. van Deth *et al.* 2011: 149). This is illustrated by several studies on political interest and children's understanding of society (e.g. Connell 1971; Schneekloth and Leven 2007). This effect is explained on the one hand by increasing possibilities of coming into contact with political matters, and on the other hand by increased cognitive and social development (cf. Furth 1980; Kohlberg 1981). Therefore, choice of topic was examined in connection with age. Examination of the statistical associations between topics and age indicated that the everyday world of children may differ by age (e.g. older children are more likely to be unsettled by changing schools) and therefore the topics of concern may also differ by age.

Average age varied in the different categories. Political aspects were mainly drawn by older children. Children aged eight, nine and ten drew more than 60 per cent of the pictures assigned to the category *politics*. After the category *technology* (average age=8.26), the category *politics* achieved the highest average age (7.72). Younger children preferred drawing family and leisure time activities, as well as fantastic representations. The proportion of drawings containing political aspects noticeably increased at the age of eight (*see* Figure 11.7).[17] In addition to age, gender was taken into account as a control variable. It is important to note that the increase in political drawings by age was only significant among boys. The proportion of girls that drew political aspects remained constant for all age groups (11–16 per cent), whereas 63 per cent of the boys at age eight drew something political. The *Chi*-square test correspondingly confirmed the association between male gender and choice of politics (x^2=13.56; df=4; p<0.01). Additionally, Cramer's V showed a weak relationship between age and politics for the girls (V=0.063) and a considerably stronger connection for the boys (V=0.341). These findings imply that the gender gap in political interest between boys and girls

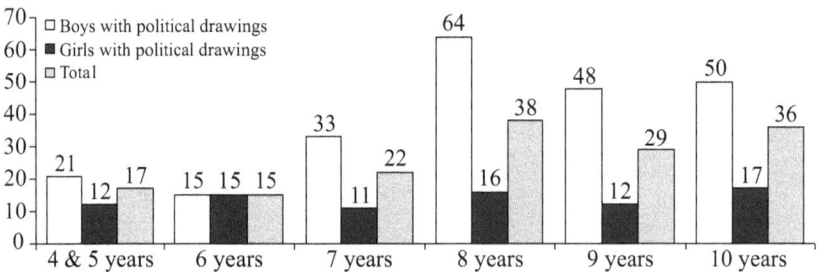

Figure 11.7: Political drawings by age and gender (per cent within age group)

17. The current study's purpose was exploration; generalisation was not the intention and is, as noted before, from my point of view always limited. All of the reported results are considered to be valid only for this particular sample; even though it is assumed, on the basis of previous research, that most of the results are transferrable to children in general.

already exists in early childhood and increases even more with age, although further research is required (*see* Figure 11.7).

Although the majority of political aspects were drawn by older children, the drawings of younger children also displayed political issues. However, the content of the drawings changed the older the children were. Younger children preferred to draw natural disasters, whereas the topic of war and most of the other environmental issues were more frequently evoked by the older children.

Immigrant children's choice of topics

In the current research project, it was assumed that children with an immigrant background may be interested in different topics compared to children of German descent, due to 'different experiences with politically relevant phenomena such as unemployment or migration' (van Deth *et al.* 2011: 158; *see also* Hess and Torney 1967: 126).

Overall, no difference in choice of topic was observed between children with and without an immigrant background. Furthermore, no differences between the groups were found concerning the frequency of political elements in the drawings. Political elements were drawn by 25 per cent of the children with an immigrant background and by 26 per cent of the children of German descent. In both groups, topics with reference to politics were drawn less often by girls. However, girls with an immigrant background depicted political issues more often than girls of German descent (19 per cent compared to 12 per cent). In contrast, boys with an immigrant background depicted political issues less often than boys of German descent. However, this effect may be affected by age, because boys with an immigrant background constituted the youngest age group (average age=7.04) whereas the average age of the girls with an immigrant background was highest (7.93). The examination of the subcategories of *politics* showed that children of German descent most commonly drew images of environmental issues, while the main topic of children with an immigrant background was war. A particularly interesting aspect was the almost complete absence of flags and national colours in the drawings of children with migration backgrounds. With only one exception, all depictions of national symbols were made by boys with German backgrounds.

Socio-economic residence area

In the recent study by van Deth *et al.* (2011: 13–4), correlations between the socio-economic residence area and awareness of political issues were found. Therefore, data in the current study were examined in terms of topic differences between schools.[18] As noted earlier, the participating schools were selected by city area in order to contrast the residence areas (city centre and outlying districts). The

---

18. In Germany, children normally have to attend the primary school closest to their home. Therefore, it can be assumed that the children live in the same area where they go to school.

analysis found more topic differences between individual schools than between city districts. However, differences between the individual schools were not significant (x^2=7.78; df=5; p>0.169).

Drawings with reference to politics were made by 29 per cent of children attending schools in the city centre and from 23 per cent of children in schools outside the city centre. However, more than 60 per cent of the drawings related to politics were produced in just two schools – one in the city centre and one in the outer district. These results show the necessity of collecting further socio-economic data as a basis for reliable analyses. Contrasting the schools by city areas proved insufficient to draw conclusions on the association between political awareness and socio-economic background.

Seating arrangement and choice of topics

During data collection, it was noticed that boys and girls were sitting separately in many classes. It was decided to log the seating arrangement and to include it in statistical analyses because children were allowed to talk to each other and to look at each other's drawings, which could have led to contamination of the results. As a result, an analysis of topic choice by gender was conducted, with seating arrangement as a control variable. The findings of this analysis have to be treated cautiously because the age differences between the groups with a separated seating arrangement and the groups with a mixed arrangement may have influenced results. The average age of separated children was higher (8.36; SD=0.90) than the average age of the mixed-seating children (7.33; SD=1.18). The analysis showed fewer differences between boys and girls in mixed seating arrangements: in separated seating arrangements, 8.4 per cent of girls depicted political aspects in their drawings, whereas the proportion of drawings with reference to politics in mixed seating arrangements is 18.4 per cent (despite the low average age of this group). The *Chi*-square test indicated a highly significant difference between girls and boys for separated seating arrangements (x^2=21.99; df=1; p<0.001) and no significant difference between girls and boys for mixed seating arrangements (x^2=2.55; df= 1; p>0.110) which indicates that differences between boys and girls were reduced in mixed seating arrangements.[19] These findings were replicated in other categories with gender-specific choice of topics (e.g. family).

Political issues and emotions

Previous studies as well as the current study revealed that children appear to prefer certain topics, such as environment and war. Moreover, it has become apparent in different studies that when the topics tend to induce fear, concern or anger, girls express fear more often than boys (e.g. *see* Petri *et al.* 1987; Petri 1992:

---

19. The preschool groups were excluded in this calculation to avoid distortion, because they always painted in a mixed seating arrangement.

84; Schneekloth and Leven 2007: 204; Unterbruner 1991: 22–9; Walper and Schröder 2002: 111). This finding was replicated in the current study; the children expressed feelings of fear especially in connection with war. As regards the environmental topics, fear was expressed less often; instead, the children voiced criticism, made requirements and expressed their concern about environmental destruction. In contrast to the drawings of war, the drawings of environmental issues also contained positive aspects; environmental situations perceived as negative were diffused by contrasting them with positive situations and offering solutions. Nevertheless, politics was mostly linked to negative emotions and this was particularly true for girls; the positively connoted categories *national symbols* and *environment protection* showed up only in two drawings by girls.

Discussion

Results from the present study support the notion that even young children are interested in political issues, further supporting previous research. In fact, the proportion of drawings referring to political issues is relatively high, despite the deliberate avoidance of such topics in the instructions. It becomes clear that children not only have knowledge about political issues and societal problems but are also particularly interested in certain political topics. Furthermore, the drawings often reveal children's emotional relationships with politics, which are in many cases tainted by fear.

Topic limitations

Nevertheless, the topics chosen by the children are limited to only a few areas that appear to be of interest to them. Other research focusing on visions about the future and anxieties supports this preference for certain topics (e.g. Petri *et al.* 1987; Schneekloth and Leven 2007; Unterbruner 1991; Walper and Schröder 2002). However, over time preferences appear to have changed to correspond to topics currently discussed in the media. In the 1980s and 1990s, for example, the ozone hole and death of forests by acid rain were some of the most frequently mentioned environmental topics (*see* Munker 1985; Petri 1992; Rusch 1989). The children's environmental drawings in the current study addressed the topics deforestation, environmental pollution from waste, air pollution and climate change. Like environmental topics, political topics have changed. In the 1980s, the topic nuclear power and nuclear threat were frequently mentioned by children. This would have been due to the political context at that time (e.g. the Chernobyl disaster, the Cold War). More recently, nuclear issues no longer seem to be important because they are rarely referred to by children in recent studies (cf. Schneekloth and Leven 2007; Walper and Schröder 2002),[20] although it can be assumed that the Fukushima

---

20. In my research I only received two drawings that addressed nuclear issues. One drawing criticised the use of nuclear power; the other drawing depicted a war plane equipped with a nuclear bomb.

disaster brought the topic back to the fore (*see* IZI 2011). This change of topics demonstrates how current political and societal debates influence children's perceptions. Children apparently have preferences for certain topics, although the question remains why they have these preferences.[21] Further, the change of topics linked to current public debates suggests that children pay attention to daily political activities and appear to be affected by them, which is supported by the studies of Kaiser (2003), Walper and Schröder (2002). Interestingly, these studies did not intentionally focus on political interest of children; Kaiser (2003), for instance, was actually researching career aspirations but received a lot of drawings of the Kosovo War and the terrorist attacks on 11 September 2001.

In short, children do not only take note of political events but are also mentally and emotionally involved. This is unsurprising, given the fact that they are not protected from exposure to mass media, which often discuss political issues and societal problems. The depiction of climate change in the children's drawings is a good example of how children pick up the common mass media representation of certain topics: some of the children decided to draw a picture of the 'last polar bear' to indicate climate change – a symbol frequently used by mass media when reporting climate change issues.

Comparisons between the findings of the current study and previous research reveal that the interest in particular topics does not seem to differ much between younger and older children.[22] This brings us back to the question of the origins of children's interests. Future research should therefore focus less on the topics and more on the reasons and causes of interests. The research question has to be modified from 'what are children interested in?' to 'why are children interested in a certain topic and how do children come into contact with these topics?' The topics environment and war provide a good starting point for future political socialisation research with children, due to the fact that these topics are mentioned in nearly every research study (including the current study) – independent of the research context (e.g. visions of the future, anxieties, career aspirations and politics).

Is there a gender gap?

In the current study, boys and girls often displayed stereotyped role models in their drawings. Girls drew more images concerning home and family, whereas boys addressed politics and public life more often. This role orientation was also identified in other studies with children and studies investigating contents of children's drawings (*see* Aissen-Crewett 1989; Kaiser 2003; Lark-Horovitz *et al.* 1967; Reiß 1996; Walper and Schröder 2002). The phenomenon of a gender gap with regard to political knowledge and interest is well-known from research

---

21. I hypothesise that children's awareness of certain topics is determined by their anxiety-provoking potential and by the limited range of topics presented in children's media.

22. Most previous research studies have included children aged ten or above, whereas the study presented here involved children aged four and above.

with adults. Surprisingly, the current research indicates that the gender gap already exists in early childhood. A lack of political interest in women is usually explained by means of structural, situational and political factors as well as by gender-specific socialisation processes. Following the socialisation explanatory approach, girls are educated and socialised into emphasising home life. The situational explanatory approach, however, supports the hypothesis that a low level of political interest in women is the result of their current living conditions; women remain more strongly attached to the home and thus are less likely to develop political involvement (Westle and Schoen 2002: 216). However, when applied to children, the latter approach lacks explanatory power. This is also true for the structural explanatory approach which assumes structural discrimination toward women, providing a barrier to accessing the political sphere. Lastly, the political explanatory approach refers to a gender-specific dissatisfaction with the established political actors and the political system (Westle and Schoen 2002: 217). The political approach is based on the assumption that women's interests are less respected in political decisions which in turn generates political dissatisfaction and apathy among women. The absence of women in the political arena and thus the absence of role models might further enhance women's political apathy (ibid.) I believe the political approach has high explanatory power for the lack of political interest in children in general, because children's interests (except for protection and care) are rarely taken into account by politics; however, as with the other approaches, the political explanatory approach may apply to men and women but not boys and girls, because decisions are made in respect to children and seldom take boys and girls into account separately. For all the reasons mentioned above, it is argued here that gender-specific socialisation provides the best explanation for the gender gap in political interest.

However, we might also take into consideration the possibility that the gender gap may be a misconception. There are two lines of argument that support this assumption: the first states that women are not less interested in politics, but that they are interested in another way. A male understanding of politics is thus assumed to conceal women's real interest (Jacobi 1991: 99). The second argument anticipates that the threat of being stereotyped leads to responses that fit the stereotypes (a self-fulfilling prophecy). Some research supports this theory (e.g. on political knowledge: Davis and Silver 2003; McGlone et al. 2006; on women's performance in maths: Spencer et al. 1999; Inzlicht and Ben-Zeev 2000). Following this argument, the gender gap is socially or scientifically constructed by stereotypical perceptions of groups and the group's knowledge about this 'stereotype threat' (Spencer et al. 1999).

Westle and Schoen (2002: 236) also identified subjective political competence as a crucial factor in explaining the gender gap in political interest among adults. It is possible that the stereotype threat is already present in childhood because children are faced with stereotypes just as adults are. Unfortunately, the effects of the stereotype threat have hitherto not been investigated in children. The findings of the current study taking seating arrangements into account may point in this direction.

Nevertheless, in compliance with previous remarks it is assumed that gender-specific socialisation processes have the greatest influence on the emergence of the gender gap in early childhood. This is not contradicted by stereotype threat theory because the gender-specific stereotype threat is understood as a consequence of gender-specific socialisation. Future research should focus more on the gender gap in early childhood and factors influencing its development because if the gender gap emerges in early childhood then the means to forestall it are best initiated at this time.

In any case, girls preferred to draw traditional women's issues instead of political or technical issues. Naturally, this does not imply that girls actually know less about politics than boys; however, it seems that the girls attach less importance to politics. Despite having the opportunity to choose from a number of topics, girls did not choose to present political themes in their drawings. In contrast, boys sometimes drew images relating to politics among other topics, e.g. career aspirations. Considering that the distance in political interest between boys and girls increases with age – partially as a result of an increase in boys' political interests – this finding gives special cause for concern. The closer relationship between boys and public life was also reflected in their use of national symbols. The low number of national symbols in the girl's drawings may indicate that girls experience less national sentiment. Possibly, boys identify, for instance through sport, more closely with the nation. However, in this case it is surprising that boys with an immigration background did not draw national symbols either – neither German nor foreign. This finding may also indicate a lack of national sentiment or, so to speak, a loss of nation, considering that national symbols in general are missing in their drawings. Further research is required in this area as well.

Conclusion

It has been shown that children are interested in particular political issues. Their interest is linked to cognition (issue knowledge, political demands and proposals for solutions) and to emotion (desires, anxiety and sadness). Of note is that politics is predominantly addressed in negative contexts (fear of threats) and only rarely in positive contexts (e.g. national pride). Moreover, differences according to interest in political issues were dependent on gender and age of the children. The gender-specific differences especially merit further consideration. The explorative approach of the current study showed that some children are actually interested in politics and have political pet-subjects, but new questions emerged and remained unanswered (e.g. why only boys without migration backgrounds drew national symbols; why children favour certain topics and how children come into contact with political information). For this reason the current study should be taken as a starting point for future research, because the findings have shown once more that political socialisation is of particular relevance long before adolescence. However, the remaining questions about gender differences and origins of interest demonstrate that knowledge about political socialisation processes and especially about the socialisation of political interest in early childhood is still scarce. A conscious shift of political socialisation research towards socialisation processes in early childhood therefore appears necessary not only for scientific and democratic reasons but also as a way of respecting children's rights of expression and participation.

Concluding remarks on children's drawings as a research tool

This study has shown that children's drawings provide a research method that is suitable for children. As specified above, there are a number of reasons why children's drawings should be established as a research tool. The main reason (besides the fact that children enjoy drawing) is that drawing already constitutes a means of expression for children long before they are able to read or write. This enables the questioning of even very young children, which is often excluded from investigation due to methodological complexities. It would be unfortunate if the opportunities for research provided by using children's drawings remain unused, although certain aspects need to be considered when using drawings as research method.

First there is the risk of subjective distortion. As shown by the current project this risk can be reduced by using a clear categorical framework and clear criteria of allocation. Further, independent monitoring of categories and allocations is indispensable. Of course, the risk of subjectivity cannot be completely abolished. Therefore, a complete and comprehensible description of the research project including details on implementation and data analysis is necessary to enable readers to draw their own conclusions about the research project and its findings.

Supplementary explanations given by the children regarding their drawings as well as all context information available should always be taken into account in order to avoid misinterpretations. Sometimes it is impossible for third parties to comprehend the drawings in the spirit in which they were produced without additional information. In short, children should be the first interpreters and/or co-interpreters of their drawings. This means that children should have the possibility to talk (or write) about their drawings, to explain their drawings, to evaluate the importance of elements and to mention things that can't be seen in their drawings (like a person in a house or other not drawn but imagined picture elements).

To enhance validity and reliability, research projects should not restrict themselves to children's drawings as a research method. Drawings should be used in combination with other methods; for example, drawings could serve as a conversational stimulus, they could provide additional information and could represent issues and emotions which are difficult to express with words alone.

There is always the danger that children will copy their neighbour's work when answering questions together in the same room (regardless of whether they are asked in interviews, questionnaires or drawings). In the present research project, this was not a problem because the conversations during data collection clearly demonstrated that even if children copied others' work, they expressed their own interest, knowledge and opinion about the depicted issues (and didn't copy because they lacked their own ideas).

Not every research topic is suitable for investigation by means of drawings. Therefore, the enthusiasm for the method should not determine the approach. The extent to which the use of drawings enhances knowledge should be carefully considered because the analysis of drawings is complicated and time-consuming and, of course, not always the best way to gain the desired information.

Overall, however, I believe that the range of established research methods should be extended to using children's drawings as a common method, although they are in need of a better scientific foundation. In order to satisfy scientific standards, children's drawings, as well as other research methods, must not be used without first gaining expertise in and a deeper understanding of the method.

If we manage to ensure the development and maintenance of scientific standards for the application of children's drawings as a research method, we would gain a new method which could enrich childhood research.

References

Aissen-Crewett, M. (1989) 'Geschlechtsspezifische inhaltliche Unterschiede in Zeichnungen von Schulkindern', *BDK-Mitteilungen,* 1: 26–33.

The American Heritage Dictionary of the English Language, 4th edn (2006) Boston, MA: Houghton Miflin.

Anning, A. and Ring, K. (2004) *Making Sense of Children's Drawings,* New York, NY: McGraw-Hill.

Barazza, L. (1999) 'Children's drawings about the environment', *Environmental Education Research,* 5(1): 49–66.

Bennett, L. M. and Bennett, S. E. (1989) 'Enduring gender differences in political interest: The impact of socialisation and political dispositions', *American Politics Quarterly,* 17: 105–122.

Berti, A. E. and Andriolo, A. (2001) 'Third grader's understanding of core political concepts (law, nation-state, government) before and after teaching', *Genetic, Social and General Psychology Monographs,* 127: 346–377.

Berti, A. E. and Vanni, E. (2000) 'Italian children's understanding of war: A domain-specific approach', *Social Development,* 9(4): 478–496.

Bortz, J. and Döring, N. (2006) *Forschungsmethoden und Evaluation für Human- und Sozialwissenschaftler,* Heidelberg: Springer.

Bosacki, S., Marini, Z. and Dane, A. (2006) 'Voices from the classroom: Pictorial and narrative representations of children's bullying experiences', *Journal of Moral Education,* 35(2): 231–245.

Bowker, R. (2007) 'Children's perceptions and learning about tropical rainforests: An analysis of their drawings', *Environmental Education Research,* 13(1): 75–96.

Brown, J., Henderson, J. and Armstrong, M. (1987) 'Children's perceptions of nuclear power stations as revealed through their drawings', *Environmental Psychology,* 7: 189–99.

Burdewick, I. (2003) *Jugend – Politik – Anerkennung. Eine qualitative empirische Studie zur politischen Partizipation 11- bis 18-Jähriger,* Bonn: Bundeszentrale für politische Bildung.

Clark, C. D. (1999) 'The autodriven interview: A photographic viewfinder into children's experiences', *Visual Sociology,* 14: 39–50.

Claußen, B. (1996) 'Politisches Lernen in der Risikogesellschaft: Krisen, Gefährdungen und Katastrophen als Sozialisationsfaktoren', in B. Claußen and R. Geißler (eds) *Die Politisierung des Menschen. Instanzen der politischen Sozialisation,* Opladen: Leske + Budrich, 375–398.

Coates, E. (2002) '"I forgot the sky!" Children's stories contained within their drawings', *International Journal of Early Years Education,* 10(1): 21–35.

Connell, R. (1971) *The Child's Construction of Politics,* Melbourne: Melbourne University Press.

Conover, P. J. and Searing, D. D. (1994) 'Democracy, citizenship and the study of political socialisation', in I. Budge and D. McKay (eds) *Developing Democracy: Comparative research in honour of J.F.B. Blondel,* London: Sage, 24–55.

Conway, M. (1985) *Political Participation in the United States*, Washington, DC: Congressional Quarterly Press.

Cox, M. V. (1992) *Children's Drawings,* London: Penguin Books.

Craddick, R. (1961) 'Size of Santa Claus drawings as a function of time before and after Christmas', *Journal of Psychological Studies,* 12: 121–125.

Davis, D. W. and Silver, B. D. (2003) 'Stereotype threat and race of interviewer effects in a survey on political knowledge', *American Journal of Political Science,* 47(1): 33–45.

de Saint-Exupéry, A. (1995) *The Little Prince*, Hertfordshire, UK: Wordsworth.

Delli Carpini, M. X. and Keeter, S. (1991) 'Stability and change in the U.S. public's knowledge of politics', *Public Opinion Quarterly*, 55: 583–612.

— (1996) *What Americans Know about Politics and Why it Matters*, New Haven: Yale University Press.

Dockett, S. and Perry, B. (2005) 'Researching with children: Insights from the Starting School Research Project', *Early Child Development and Care,* 175(6): 507–521.

— (2007) 'Trusting children's account in research', *Journal of Early Childhood Research,* 5(1): 47–63.

Dondl, J. (2010) 'Die Kompetenzen der Kinder und Inhalte politischen Lernens in der Grundschule – Überlegungen anhand einer Studie zu den Vorstellungen von Viertklässlern zum Thema "Macht"', *Zeitschrift für Grundschulforschung,* 3(2): 60–71.

Driessnack, M. (2006) 'Draw-and-tell conversations with children about fear', *Qualitative Health Research*, 16(10): 1414–1435.

Easton, D. and Dennis, J. (1969) *Children in the Political System: Origins of political legitimacy*, New York: McGraw-Hill.

Eichholz, R. and Schröder, R. (2002) 'Kinder und Politik', in LBS-Initiative Junge Familie (ed.) *Kindheit 2001 – Das LBS-Kinderbarometer. Was Kinder wünschen, hoffen und befürchten*, Opladen: Leske + Budrich: 71–98.

Ennew, J. (1994) *Street and Working Children: A guide to planning, Development Manual 4*, London: Save the children.

Fargas-Malet, M., McSherry, D., Larkin, E. and Robinson, C. (2010) 'Research with children: Methodological issues and innovative techniques', *Journal of Early Childhood Research*, 8(2): 175–92.

Furth, H. G. (1980) *The World of Grown-Ups: Children's conceptions of society*, New York: Elsevier.

Gemmeke, M. (1998) *Politieke betrokkenheid van kinderen op de basisschool*, PhD Thesis, Amsterdam: Thesis Publishers.

Golomb, C. (2004) *The Child's Creation of a Pictorial World*, Mahwah, New Jersey: Lawrence Erlbaum.

Götz, M. (2004) '*We're Against it!' Children in Germany and their Perception of the War in Iraq*. Online. Available: http://www.br-online.de/jugend/izi/english/ publication/televizion/17_2004_E/17_2004_E.htm (accessed 5 January 2012).

Götz, M., Lemish, D., Aidman, A. and Moon, H. (2005) *Media and the Make-Believe Worlds of Children: When Harry Potter meets Pokémon in Disneyland*, Mahwah, New Jersey: Lawrence Erlbaum.

Greenstein, F. (1960) 'The benevolent leader: Children's images of political authority', *The American Political Science Review*, 54: 934–945.

— (1965) *Children and Politics*, New Haven: Yale University Press.

Guillemin, M. (2004) 'Understanding illness: Using drawings as a research method', *Qualitative Health Research*, 14(2): 272–289.

Hafner, V. (2006) *Politik aus Kindersicht. Eine Studie über Interesse, Wissen und Einstellungen von Kindern*, Stuttgart: ibidem.

Haug, L. (2011) *Junge StaatsbürgerInnen? Politik in Zukunftsvorstellungen von Kindern*, Wiesbaden: VS Verlag für Sozialwissenschaften.

Herth, K. (1998) 'Hope as seen through the eyes of homeless children', *Journal of Advanced Nursing*, 28(5): 1053–1062.

Hess, R. D. and Easton, D. (1960) 'The child's changing image of the president', *Public Opinion Quarterly*, 24(4): 632–644.

Hess, R. D. and Torney, J. V. (1967) *The Development of Political Attitudes in Children*, Chicago: Aldine.

Holliday, E. L., Harrison, L. J. and McLeod, S. (2009) 'Listening to children with communication impairment talking through their drawings', *Journal of Early Childhood Research*, 7(3): 244–63.

Hurrelmann, K. (1994) 'Orientierungskrisen und politische Ängste bei Kindern und Jugendlichen: Sozialisationstheoretische Perspektiven', in J. Mansel (ed.) *Reaktionen Jugendlicher auf gesellschaftliche Bedrohung: Untersuchungen zu ökologischen Krisen, internationalen Konflikten und politischen Umbrüchen als Stressoren*, Weinheim: Juventa: 59–78.

Inzlicht, M. and Ben-Zeev, T. (2000) 'A threatening intellectual environment: Why females are susceptible to experiencing problem-solving deficits in the presence of males', *Psychological Science*, 11(5): 365–71.

IZI [Internationales Zentralinstitut für das Jugend- und Bildungsfernsehen] (2011) *TelevIZIon*. Online. Available: http://www.br-online.de/jugend/izi/ deutsch /publikation/televizion/24_2011_2.htm (accessed 29 February 2012).

Jacobi, J. (1991) 'Sind Mädchen unpolitischer als Jungen?', in W. Heitmeyer and J. Jacobi (eds) *Politische Sozialisation und Individualisierung. Perspektiven und Chancen politischer Bildung*, Weinheim: Juventa: 99–118.

Jamieson, K. and Kenski, K. (2000) 'The gender gap in political knowledge: Are women less knowledgeable than men about politics?' in K. Jamieson (ed.) *Everything you Think you Know about Politics and why you're Wrong*, New York: Basic Books: 83–92.

Kaiser, A. (2003) *Zukunftsbilder von Kindern der Welt. Vergleich der Zukunftsvorstellungen von Kindern aus Japan, Deutschland, Chile*, Baltmannsweiler: Schneider Verlag Hohengehren.

Kalcsics, K. and Raths, K. (2011) 'Macht mit Legitimation: Vorstellungen von Kindern über Herrschaft im demokratischen System', *Zeitschrift für Didaktik der Gesellschaftswissenschaften*, 2(2): 58–81.

Kohlberg, L. (1981) *The Meaning and Measurement of Moral Development*, Worcester: Clark University Press.

Lark-Horovitz, B., Lewis, H. and Luca, M. (1967) *Understanding Children's Art for Better Teaching*, Columbus, Ohio: Charles E. Merill Books.

Lazarsfeld, P. F., Berelson, B. R. and Gaudet, H. (1948) *The People's Choice: How the voter makes up his mind in a presidential campaign, 2nd edn*, New York: Columbia University Press.

Lemish, D. and Götz, M. (2007) *Children and Media in Times of Conflict and War*, Cresskill, New Jersey: Hampton Press.

Leonard, M. (2006) 'Children's drawings as a methodological tool: Reflections on the eleven plus system in Northern Ireland', *Irish Journal of Sociology*, 15(2): 52–66.

Lersch, P. (1956) *Aufbau der Person*, München: Barth.

Luskin, R. C. (1990) 'Explaining political sophistication', *Political Behaviour*, 12(4): 331–361.

MacPhail, A. and Kinchin, G. (2004) 'The use of drawings as an evaluative tool: Students' experiences of sport education', *Physical Education and Sport Pedagogy*, 9(1): 87–108.

Malchiodi, C. A. (1998) *Understanding Children's Drawings*, New York: The Guilford Press.

Mansel, J. (1995) *Sozialisation in der Risikogesellschaft: Eine Untersuchung zu pyschosozialen Belastungen Jugendlicher als Folge ihrer Bewertung gesellschaftlicher Bedrohungspotentiale*, Neuwied: Luchterhand.

Marr, D. (1982) *Vision: A computational investigation into human representation and processing of visual information*, San Francisco: Freeman.

Martin, E. (1994) *Flexible Bodies: Tracking immunity in American culture – from the days of polio to the age of AIDS*, Boston: Beacon.

Matthews, J. (2003) *Drawing and Painting: Children and visual representation*, London: Sage.

Mayring, P. (2000) 'Qualitative content analysis', *Forum: Qualitative Social Research*, 1(2): Article 20.

— (2008) *Qualitative Inhaltsanalyse. Grundlagen und Techniken*, Weinheim: Beltz.

McGlone, M. S., Aronson, J. and Kobrynowicz, D. (2006) 'Stereotype threat and the gender gap in political knowledge', *Psychology of Women Quarterly*, 30: 392–398.

Milbrath, L. W. and Goel, M. L. (1977) *Political Participation: How and why do people get involved in politics?* Washington DC: University Press of America.

Mitchell, L. M. (2006) 'Child-centred? Thinking critically about children's drawings as a visual research method', *Visual Anthropology Review*,

22(1): 60–73.

Moll, A. (2001) *Was Kinder denken: Zum Gesellschaftsverständnis von Schulkindern*, Schwalbach am Taunus: Wochenschau.

Moore, S. W., Lare, J. and Wagner, K. (1985) *The Child's Political World*, New York: Praeger.

Munker, J. (1985) *Die Welt in 100 Jahren. Wie Kinder die Zukunft sehen – Ein Bilderbuch für Erwachsene*, Düsseldorf: Richard Fuchs.

Neuß, N. (1998) 'Bilder des Verstehens: Zeichnungen als Erhebungsinstrument der qualitativen Rezeptionsforschung', *Medien praktisch*, 3: 19–22.

— (2000) 'Medienbezogene Kinderzeichnungen als Instrument der qualitativen Rezeptionsforschung', in I. Paus-Haase and B. Schorb (eds) *Qualitative Kinder- und Jugendmedienforschung. Theorie und Methoden. Ein Arbeitsbuch*, München: Kopäd: 131–154.

Nguyen-Clausen, A. (1987) 'Das Bild im Spiel', in W. Zacharias (ed.) *Spielraum für Spielräume. Zur Ökologie des Spiels 2*, München: Internationale Vereinigung für das Recht des Kindes zu spielen (IPA) und Pädagogische Aktion e.V. (PA): 31–33.

Neller, K. (2002) 'Politisches Interesse', in M. Greiffenhagen and S. Greiffenhagen (eds) *Handwörterbuch zur politischen Kultur der Bundesrepublik Deutschland, second edition*, Wiesbaden: Westdeutscher Verlag: 363–369.

Niemi, R. G. and Hepburn, M. A. (1995) 'The rebirth of political socialisation', *Perspectives on Political Science*, 24(1): 7–17.

Niesyto, H. (2006) 'Bildverstehen als mehrdimensionaler Prozess. Vergleichende Auswertung von Bildinterpretationen und methodische Reflexion', in W. Marotzki and H. Niesyto (eds) *Bildinterpretation und Bildverstehen. Methodische Ansätze aus sozialwissenschaftlicher, kunst- und medienpädagogischer Perspektive*, Wiesbaden: VS Verlag: 253–286.

OHCR [Office of the United Nations High Commissioner for Human Rights] (1989) *Convention on the rights of the Child.* Online. Available: http://www2.ohchr.org/english/law/crc.htm (accessed 24 January 2012).

Panofsky, E. (1974) *Meaning in the Visual Arts,* Woodstock, NY: The Overlook Press.

Petri, H. (1992) *Umweltzerstörung und die seelische Entwicklung unserer Kinder*, Zürich: Kreuz.

Petri, H., Boehnke, K., Macpherson, M. and Meador, M. (1987) 'Zukunftshoffnungen und Ängste von Kindern und Jugendlichen unter der nuklearen Bedrohung. Analyse einer bundesweiten Pilotstudie', *Psychologie & Gesellschaftskritik,* 11(2/3): 81–105.

Picot, S. and Schroeder, D. (2007) 'Kinderpersönlichkeiten. Porträts von 12 Mädchen und Jungen', in World Vision Deutschland e.V. (ed.) *Kinder in Deutschland 2007. 1. World Vision Kinderstudie*, Frankfurt: Fischer: 227–360.

Piaget, J. and Inhelder, B. (1956) *The Child's Conception of Space*, London: Routledge and Kegan Paul.

Punch, S. (1998) *Negotiating Independence: Children and young people growing up in rural Bolivia*, unpublished thesis, University of Leeds.

— (2002) 'Research with children: The same or different from research with adults?' *Childhood*, 9(3): 321–341.

Reiß, W. (1996) *Kinderzeichnungen: Wege zum Kind durch seine Zeichnung*, Neuwied: Luchterhand.

Richter, H.-G. (1987) *Die Kinderzeichnung. Entwicklung – Interpretation – Ästhetik*, Düsseldorf: Schwann.

Rusch, R. (ed.) (1989) *So soll die Welt nicht werden. Kinder schreiben über ihre Zukunft*, Kevelaer: Anrich.

Schneekloth, U. and Leven, I. (2007) 'Wünsche, Ängste und erste politische Interessen', in World Vision Deutschland e.V. (ed.) *Kinder in Deutschland 2007. 1. World Vision Kinderstudie*, Frankfurt: Fischer: 201–225.

Schoppe, A. (1991) *Kinderzeichnung und Lebenswelt. Neue Wege zum Verständnis des kindlichen Gestaltens*, Herne: Wissenschaft und Kunst.

Schuster, M. (2010) *Kinderzeichnungen: Wie sie entstehen, was sie bedeuten, 3rd edn*, München: Reinhardt.

Sechrest, L. and Wallace, J. (1964) 'Figure drawings and naturally occurring events', *Journal of Educational Psychology*, 55(1): 42–4.

Shani, D. (2009) *On the Origins of Political Interest*, unpublished thesis, Princeton University.

Solley, C. and Haigh, G. (1957) 'A note to Santa Claus', *Topeka Research Papers, The Menninger Foundation*, 18: 4–5.

Spencer, S., Steele, C. and Quinn, D. (1999) 'Stereotype threat and women's math performance', *Journal of Experimental Social Psychology*, 35(1): 4–28.

Strauss, A. and Corbin, J. (1990) *Basics of Qualitative Research: Grounded theory procedures and techniques*, London: Sage.

Sturken, M. and Cartwright, L. (2001) *Practices of Looking: An introduction to visual culture*, Oxford: Oxford University Press.

Unterbruner, U. (1991) *Umweltangst – Umwelterziehung. Vorschläge zur Bewältigung der Ängste Jugendlicher vor Umweltzerstörung*, Linz: Veritas.

van Deth, J. W. (1990) 'Interest in politics', in M. K. Jennings, J. van Deth, S. Barnes, D. Fuchs, F. Heunks, R. Inglehart, M. Kaase, H.-D. Klingemann and J. J. A. Thomassen (1990) *Continuities in Political Action: A longitudinal study of political orientations in three western democracies*, Berlin and New York: De Gruyter: 275–312.

— (2005) 'Kinder und Politik', *Aus Politik und Zeitgeschichte*, 41: 3–6.

— (2007) 'Politische Themen und Probleme', in J. W. van Deth, S. Abendschön, J. Rathke and M. Vollmar, *Kinder und Politik. Politische Einstellungen von jungen Kindern im ersten Grundschuljahr*, Wiesbaden: VS Verlag für Sozialwissenschaften: 83–118.

van Deth, J. W. and Elff, M. (2004) 'Politicisation, economic development and political interest in Europe', *European Journal of Political Research*, 43: 477–508.

van Deth, J. W., Abendschön, S. and Vollmar, M. (2011) 'Children and politics: An empirical reassessment of early political socialisation', *Political Psychology*, 32(1): 147–174.

Verba, S., Schlozman, K. L. and Brady, H. E. (1995) *Voice and Equality: Civic voluntarism in American politics*, Cambridge, Massachussetts: Harvard University Press.

Victora, G. and Knauth, D. (2001) 'Images of the body and the reproductive system among men and women living in shantytowns in Porto Alegre, Brazil', *Reproductive Health Matters*, 9: 2–33.

Vollmar, M. (2007) 'Politisches Wissen bei Kindern – nicht einfach nur ja oder nein', in J. van Deth, S. Abendschön, J. Rathke and M. Vollmar, *Kinder und Politik. Politische Einstellungen von jungen Kindern im ersten Grundschuljahr*, Wiesbaden.: VS Verlag: 161–203.

Walper, S. and Schröder, R. (2002) 'Kinder und ihre Zukunft', in LBS-Initiative Junge Familie (ed.) *Kindheit 2001 – Das LBS-Kinderbarometer. Was Kinder wünschen, hoffen und befürchten*, Opladen: Leske + Budrich: 99–126.

Wasmund, K. (1976) 'Kinder und Wahlkampf. Eine empirische Untersuchung zur politischen Sozialisation bei Viertklässlern', in B. Claußen (ed.) *Materialien zur politischen Sozialisation*, München: Ernst Reinhardt, 29–56.

Westle, B. and Schoen, H. (2002) 'Ein neues Argument in einer alten Diskussion: "Politikverdrossenheit" als Ursache des gender gap im politischen Interesse', in F. Brettschneider, J. W. van Deth and E. Roller (eds) *Das Ende der politisierten Sozialstruktur?*, Opladen: Leske + Budrich: 215–244.

Willats, J. (1997) *Art and Representation: New principles in the analysis of pictures*, Princeton, New Jersey: Princeton University Press.

— (2005) *Making Sense of Children's Drawings*, Mahwah, New Jersey: Lawrence Erlbaum.

Williams, D., Wetton, N. and Moon, A. (1989) *A Picture of Health: What do you do that makes you healthy and keeps you healthy?* London: Health Education Authority.

Index